Yale Law Library Series in Legal History and Reference

An Empire of Laws

LEGAL PLURALISM IN
BRITISH COLONIAL POLICY

Christian R. Burset

Yale UNIVERSITY PRESS

New Haven & London

Published with support from the Lillian Goldman Law Library, Yale Law School.

Published with assistance from the Annie Burr Lewis Fund.

Copyright © 2023 by Christian R. Burset. All rights reserved. This book may not be reproduced, in whole or in part, including illustrations, in any form (beyond that copying permitted by Sections 107 and 108 of the U.S. Copyright Law and except by reviewers for the public press), without written permission from the publishers.

Yale University Press books may be purchased in quantity for educational, business, or promotional use. For information, please e-mail sales.press@yale.edu (U.S. office) or sales@yaleup.co.uk (U.K. office).

Set in Adobe Garamond type by Integrated Publishing Solutions.
Printed in the United States of America.

Library of Congress Control Number: 2022949568
ISBN 978-0-300-25323-8 (hardcover : alk. paper)

A catalogue record for this book is available from the British Library.

This paper meets the requirements of ANSI/NISO Z39.48-1992 (Permanence of Paper).

10 9 8 7 6 5 4 3 2 1

For my family

Contents

Introduction, 1
1 Forging a Common-Law Empire, 15
2 Experimenting with Law and Development, 39
3 The Quebec Act and Its Alternatives, 64
4 Varieties of Pluralism in Bengal, 90
5 Despotic Humanitarianism and the New Imperial Common Law, 119
Conclusion, 149

Acknowledgments, 169
Notes, 171
Index, 253

Introduction

In 1782, Jeremy Bentham asked whether it would be possible to craft a body of laws that was fit for every society. His test case was Bengal, a place "as different as can be" from England, although Britain's East India Company (EIC) had controlled it for a quarter century. Britons had debated for decades whether English law belonged in India, and Bentham knew the consensus that most of his contemporaries had reached. For them, English law stood near "the summit of perfection." But although they considered English law to be the best in the world, they thought it was unsuitable for export. "Laws which are fit for a free country," they reasoned, were "for that very reason, incompetent for a country where the government is arbitrary and despotical"—a description that matched a growing share of Britain's empire.[1]

Bentham disagreed on both counts. On the one hand, he denied the goodness of English law: "a great part of" it was not only unfit for Bengal but "of such a nature as to be bad every where," including England. On the other hand, he challenged the assumption that Bengal and England needed radically different legal systems. Of course, the two places were dissimilar in many ways—including climate, culture, resources, and religion—and their institutions had to reflect that. Nor was uniformity desirable for its own sake: "No law should be changed," he warned, without "some specific assignable benefit." But the existing laws in both countries left room for improvement; and in both England and Bengal, a reforming legislator would need to proceed from

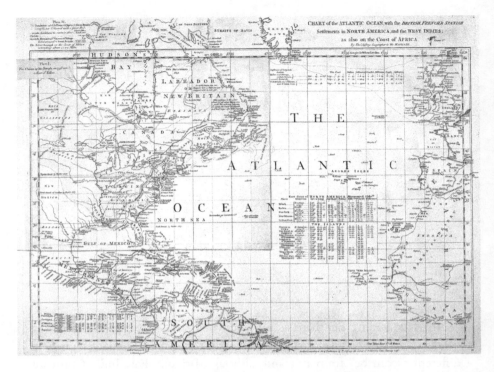

The Atlantic world, 1763. Thomas Jefferys, *A General Topography of North America and the West Indies* (London: R. Sayer, 1768). Courtesy of the Library of Congress, Geography and Map Division.

the same utilitarian principles. As a result, "a system might be devised which, while it were better for Bengal, would also be better even for England at the same time."[2] Bentham had no love for *the* common law; but he suggested that Britain might still pursue *a* common law for its empire.

Although Bentham's tone was proudly contrarian, he knew that the dogma he attacked was young. In the seventeenth and early eighteenth centuries, Britain had usually tried to impose its own laws on the peoples it conquered.[3] The laws of Britain's colonies were never identical to those of England (or to each other); nobody thought that *every* part of English law made sense everywhere. Nonetheless, some version of English law generally followed the Union Jack. But that commitment to a common imperial law changed in the 1760s. Britain emerged from the Seven Years' War (1754–63) with a greatly expanded empire. It had gained Quebec, the Illinois Country, several West Indian islands, and Senegal from France. Spanish Florida had become British West

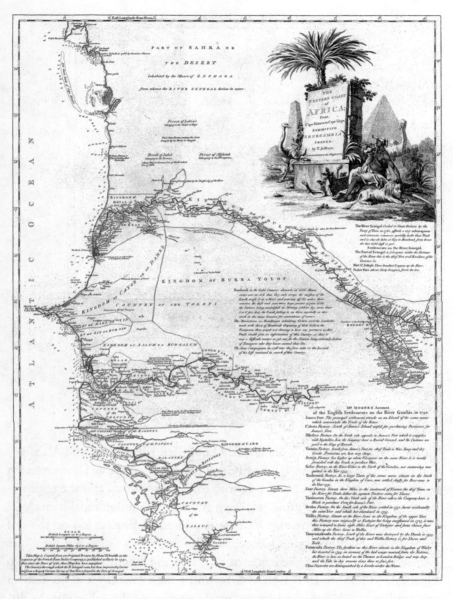

Senegambia. Thomas Jefferys, *The Western Coast of Africa, from Cape Blanco to Cape Virga, Exhibiting Senegambia Proper* (London: R. Sayer, 1771). Courtesy of the Beinecke Rare Book and Manuscript Library, Yale University.

India. From Richard Owen Cambridge, *An Account of the War in India* (Dublin: George and Alexander Ewing, 1761). © The Trustees of the British Museum.

Florida (including parts of present-day Louisiana, Mississippi, and Alabama) and East Florida. Meanwhile, the EIC was making itself the de facto sovereign of Bengal. In 1765, it gained the right to collect taxes from, and the responsibility to administer civil justice to, the region's thirty million inhabitants.[4]

In keeping with its past practice, Britain imposed English law on most of these places. But in Bengal, Quebec, and Illinois, it took a different path. The Quebec Act of 1774 applied French civil law and English criminal law to Quebec and Illinois. In Bengal, courts run by the Company and the Crown applied English, Hindu, or Islamic law, depending on the subject of the dispute and the status of the parties.[5] In short, between the 1760s and the 1780s, the British Empire abandoned its old aspiration of a global common law in favor of a new policy of legal pluralism, in which the empire chose to administer different laws for different groups. This book explains why.

The implications of this history go well beyond the eighteenth century. As the conclusion will show, it matters for how we think about law's effect on economic development; whether we should view law's history as contingent or path-dependent; and how we define empire itself. But despite the significance of the topic, this book is the first to explain Britain's new approach to colonial legal policy. To be sure, many scholars have written about colonial law. But their scope has typically been broader or narrower than mine: either investigating legal pluralism as a global phenomenon (as with Lauren Benton's path-breaking work) or addressing particular colonies or regions, rather than taking the British Empire as the unit of analysis. There have been important books about Britain's imperial constitution and how particular institutions or doctrines functioned within the empire. But nobody has made a sustained attempt to explain why the common law became less common in the crucial century between the Glorious and American Revolutions.[6]

BRINGING THE MIND BACK IN

One reason that historians haven't examined Britain's imperial legal policy is that they've neglected imperial policymaking more generally. The Victorian historian J. R. Seeley famously quipped that Britain had acquired its empire "in a fit of absence of mind." Few historians today would let it off the hook so easily (and Seeley himself was only half-serious).[7] But the field has continued to follow his lead when it comes to law. State-of-the-art scholarship gives the impression that colonial legal systems emerged principally from the activities of litigants and local officials, not the grand designs of imperial policymakers. There's some truth to that; and it would be silly to depict colonial institutions as emerging fully armored from the head of some undersecretary in Whitehall. But it's worth reexamining the place of deliberate policymaking for colonial law—to insist on Britain's presence of mind not only when it "conquered and peopled half the world" (to quote Seeley again), but also in governing it.[8]

Several factors have discouraged historians from focusing on the policies that shaped imperial legal history. The first was the influential work of Sir Lewis Namier (1888–1960), who gave plausibility to Seeley's quip by describing eighteenth-century politics as devoid of ideology. Hanoverian politicians, Namier wrote, "no more dreamt of a seat in the House [of Commons] in order to benefit humanity than a child dreams of a birthday cake that others may eat it." In his telling, politics was a matter of interests and appetites, not ideas.[9] With metropolitan politics evacuated of meaning, many historians of empire turned their attention to events in the colonies.[10] Their pivot to the periphery was complemented by trends in legal history, which was paying more attention to the social contexts in which law operated.[11] This, too, tended to draw attention to local rather than imperial arrangements; at most, empire was the stage on which the story unfolded. And *story* is the right word: the emphasis was on narrative and thick description, more than causal explanation.[12]

Those approaches have been fruitful. Paying attention to local contexts has yielded richer and more realistic accounts of how people experience and construct legal authority. Concentrating on the colonies has revealed the limits of imperial power while highlighting the agency of colonial subjects. And a relaxed focus on causation has freed historians to spot patterns that span centuries and cross continents.[13] But there have also been costs. Privileging local stories can make it hard to see what was distinctive about the British Empire as a whole or to evaluate the role of the imperial state (rather than assuming its irrelevance). In response to such concerns, a growing number of British historians have emphasized the need to write truly *imperial* histories.[14]

Building on that insight, this book reasserts the importance of the imperial state for colonial legal history. That doesn't mean ignoring local factors or focusing only on elites. The story told here features a wide variety of actors: not only ministers and members of Parliament, but also merchants, mid-level bureaucrats, and litigants from across the empire. But because this book seeks to explain why Britain pursued a particular set of policies, it will necessarily focus on the perspective of those policies' authors. Like every approach to writing history, this one also has its costs. The list of dramatis personae will sometimes look lopsided, and subalterns will speak more often through the pens of imperial politicians than in their own voices. (Indeed, one of the themes of this book will be how British officials misinterpreted or misrepresented the laws and desires of the people they were trying to rule.) The goal is to supplement, not replace, other ways of approaching colonial legal history.

THE LAW-DESTROYING STATE?

There's another reason historians have neglected Britain's embrace of colonial legal pluralism: they've forgotten to be surprised by it. Contemporaries like Bentham appreciated the novelty of Britain's decision to administer many kinds of law. But by the early twentieth century, when legal history first emerged as a modern field of study, Britain's policy had come to seem natural. "As to the laws in force in the colonies, *of course* they vary greatly," F. W. Maitland, the father of English legal history, wrote in 1908. It was too obvious to dwell on.[15]

Part of the problem is that *legal pluralism* is a slippery notion. If the phrase describes any situation in which the law varies from place to place (or from group to group), then it seems both ubiquitous and unremarkable. New York and New Jersey have different laws; why not England and India? To complicate things further, writers have invoked "legal pluralism" to describe very different phenomena: internal variation within state law, on the one hand, and the interplay between state and non-state sources of authority, on the other.[16] To avoid confusion, a definition is in order. This book explores *strategic legal pluralism*—a polity's deliberate application of different legal systems to different groups of people. Two features mark strategic legal pluralism. First, the pluralism is "manifest," to borrow a term from Brian Tamanaha. Participants view the legal systems in question as strikingly different from each other. Minor variations aren't enough; the laws must seem like different languages rather than dialects of a common tongue.[17] One way to think about this is by asking whether a lawyer could easily practice across the legal divide. From that perspective, we can sense that Islamic and English law differ in a way that the laws of New York and New Jersey don't. Second, strategic legal pluralism reflects an official decision to administer multiple kinds of law. In other words, the concept isn't concerned with the competition between "official" and "unofficial" sources of authority. Instead, it focuses on situations in which the state itself deploys legal difference.[18]

With this definition in mind, legal pluralism starts to seem less natural. In fact, it's hard to square with some common assumptions about how states usually behave. For example, this is how Charles Tilly begins his classic study of state formation: "[T]he ruler of a small Mesopotamian city-state conquered all the region's other city-states, and made them subject to Marduk, his own city's god. Hammurabi, ruler of Babylon, became the supreme king of Mesopotamia. By conquering, *he gained the right and obligation to establish laws for all the people.*"[19] On Tilly's account, to rule is to make everyone follow *your* rules. Max Weber lists the development of uniform law as one of modernity's defining attributes, while Robert Cover describes "jurispathic" states as pruning "too much law" into "'a uniform rule of civil justice.'"[20] According to many historians, the British Empire shared this instinct for sameness. Mary Sarah Bilder presents the British Empire as trying to extend "a uniform body of law" across its colonies.[21] "When the British governed a country," Niall Ferguson tells us, "there were certain distinctive features of their own society that they tended to disseminate," including "The Common Law" and "English forms of land tenure."[22] And yet, as these same authors acknowledge, colonial laws were rarely uniform in practice. If states lust after legal uniformity, why have they so rarely attained it? Scholars have offered three kinds of answers.

1. *Some states are weak.* A state might want uniformity but lack the capacity to achieve it. Jean-Laurent Rosenthal and Roy Bin Wong, for example, argue that rulers in early modern Europe feared legal pluralism but accepted it "to reduce the likelihood of revolt and because it was often the only way to secure prompt tax revenue."[23] Brian Tamanaha writes that "[i]n most situations of manifest legal pluralism," the state "had no real choice in the matter because state law was *too weak* to trump indigenous legal forms or to replace the functions they fulfilled."[24] Legal pluralism is an offer the state can't refuse.

2. *Some states are tolerant.* Alternatively, a state might feel it has a moral or legal duty to administer multiple kinds of law. Scholars of law and religion, for instance, have sometimes described the accommodation of religious law in liberal democracies as an example of this.[25]

3. *Empires are a special case.* Or perhaps empires are different from other kinds of states. As Jane Burbank and Frederick Cooper tell us, the very concept of empire "presumes that different peoples within the polity will be governed differently."[26] That might be because empires lack the strength to project uniform laws onto faraway places.[27] Alternatively, legal pluralism might be a technique of domination—an aspect of what Partha Chatterjee has termed the "rule of colonial difference," in which imperial rule depends on a distinction between colonizer and colonized.[28] Whatever the cause, pluralism is simply a fact of imperial law.[29]

These three explanations are not mutually exclusive. In fact, historians of the British Empire have sometimes explained its acceptance of legal pluralism as the product of limited state capacity reinforced by a growing commitment to toleration.[30] That's partly true. But it leaves out the most important part of the story.

THIS BOOK'S ARGUMENT

The eighteenth-century British Empire didn't stumble into legal pluralism because it was too weak to avoid it, because of a reflexive commitment to colonial difference, or because it felt obliged to administer the laws of the people it conquered. Instead, Britain's selective denial of English law to its colonies reflected a conscious effort to shape their political and economic development. Eighteenth-century Britons believed that English law could turn any territory into an anglicized, commercial colony like Britain's earlier American settlements. Just as English law had transmuted Dutch New Amsterdam into English New York, the common law could work the same alchemy on the former subjects of Bourbon and Mughal empires. Legal pluralism, in contrast, would keep colonies culturally distinct, politically dependent, and economically subordinate. Thus, by deciding how much English law each colony received, British officials could determine what kind of colony it would become. Britain's selective turn toward legal pluralism after 1763 reflected the triumph of a particular vision of the British Empire—politically hierarchical, economically extractive, and culturally tolerant.

It wasn't inevitable that Britain would take this path. From the middle of the seventeenth century until the 1760s—what historians sometimes call the "first" British Empire—England, and then Britain, preferred that its colonies conform to English law.[31] What that meant in practice was contested. Depending on the occasion, "English law" could be identified with a body of doctrines, a set of institutions and procedures, or even a certain way of thinking—what J. G. A. Pocock has labeled "the common-law mind." There were ambiguities about whether "the laws of England" included statutes or only the common law, and whether "common law" should be defined broadly to encompass equity, admiralty, and ecclesiastical law.[32] But despite disagreements about the definition of English law, English commentators generally agreed that it ought to rule the empire. Other legal systems sometimes survived (most prominently in Scotland), but not as the favored outcome of London's legal and political elite. As Chapter 1 explains, that remained true even after Montesquieu and other Enlightenment philosophers started to insist that law was intertwined with local climatic, geographic, and cultural conditions. In fact, some of Montesquieu's earliest British readers saw no conflict between his writings and their own efforts to forge a common law for Britain and its empire. To the contrary, they believed that his *Spirit of the Laws* (1748) was consistent with an aggressive campaign to anglicize the laws of Scotland in the wake of the 1745 Jacobite uprising.

Britain's commitment to a common-law empire began to waiver after the Seven Years' War, as Chapter 2 explains. Although Britain had defeated its chief European and Asian rivals, its victory struck many observers as precarious. The war had been hugely expensive, and the scale of Britain's new possessions amplified longstanding anxieties about the empire's stability. These concerns sparked an aggressive effort to remake imperial governance and a backlash that culminated in the American Revolution.[33] They also generated a new debate about whether Britain could survive as a common-law empire.

In the 1760s, there were three basic visions for the empire's future, each of which had different implications for colonial legal policy. This book will refer to supporters of these visions as *populists, paternalists,* and *moderates,* respectively. Those terms are deliberately anachronistic, and they're meant to evoke ideological tendencies rather than organized parties. There were political parties at the time, but their memberships were unstable, and even experienced politicians struggled to define them. Traditional partisan labels like "Whig" and "Tory" had lost much of their meaning, and they were more often used as rhetorical cudgels than as neutral descriptors.[34] Indeed, what it meant to belong to a party was itself a contested question.[35] Accordingly, this book will focus on ideologies rather than party allegiances (although there was substantial overlap between them).

Populists wanted to create a relatively "inclusive" empire, in which the residents of Britain and its colonies enjoyed similar political status and economic opportunity. "Inclusive" here has the sense suggested by Daron Acemoglu and James Robinson, who use that term for institutions that "allow and encourage participation by the great mass of people" in economic and political life, rather than funneling wealth and power to a narrow elite.[36] Inclusivity is relative. Populists could be remarkably intolerant of religious and cultural minorities, even by eighteenth-century standards. But compared to their opponents, populists envisioned greater parity between Britain and its colonies, and to some extent between Britons and their conquered subjects. In Parliament, populists were led by William Pitt (later first Earl of Chatham) and William Petty, second Earl of Shelburne. Populist ideas also attracted many future leaders of the American Revolution. On both sides of the Atlantic, populists were sometimes called "patriots."[37]

Paternalists focused on maintaining a stable empire and on extracting wealth from the colonies to solve Britain's fiscal woes. In many respects, their priorities reversed those of the populists: paternalists were less economically and politically egalitarian but more culturally and religiously tolerant. Their leaders included William Murray, first Earl of Mansfield (the influential lord chief justice), as well as politicians linked to George Grenville and John Russell, fourth Duke of Bedford. Their enemies sometimes called them Tories, although paternalists mostly thought of themselves as Whigs.[38] Moderates, as the name suggests, pursued a middle path. Presenting themselves as the true heirs of the Whig tradition, they criticized both paternalists' eagerness to subordinate the colonies and populists' lack of concern for colonial minorities. Edmund Burke was the moderates' intellectual heavyweight, Lord Rockingham their parliamentary leader.[39]

Each of these groups tried to use colonial law to effect its vision of empire. The idea that different kinds of law might produce different kinds of colonies had a long history. Since the early seventeenth century, colonial governments had used the promise of English law to lure settlers.[40] But starting in the 1760s, paternalists explored new ways of manipulating colonies' legal systems for developmental purposes. Their first project was an attempt to resurrect feudalism in North America. Most readers today are more likely to associate feudalism with the age of chivalry than the age of enlightenment. But for some imperial policymakers—including Thomas Gage, the commander in chief of British forces in North America, and John Perceval, second Earl of Egmont—the future lay in a legal system that linked political power to land ownership. The second paternalist project was to use state-sponsored arbitration as a substitute for courts in certain colonies. Paternalists worried that litigiousness was tearing the empire apart, and they hoped that more informal modes of dispute resolution might restore harmony to Britain's increasingly diverse empire. At the same time, paternalists hoped that the absence of courts might deter immigration to places that it was in Britain's interest to keep underdeveloped, such as the American interior. The failure of these initiatives led paternalists to the more radical project of using foreign laws to tame the empire.

Chapter 3 tells that story for the colonies that Britain had taken from France and Spain: Quebec, Illinois, Senegambia, Florida, and the Ceded Islands in the West Indies. For most of these new acquisitions, there was a broad consensus that Britain should continue its old policy of introducing English law in order to facilitate the development of anglicized settlements. But when it came to Illinois and Quebec, politicians divided sharply about what kind of colonies they wanted. As a result, they disagreed about whether to introduce English law or to retain the laws that had been in place under France.

Paternalists wanted to make Quebec and Illinois easy to govern and economically dependent on the rest of the empire, and they thought that retaining French law would advance that goal in three ways. First, paternalists worried that English law had become excessively libertarian, and they hoped that French law would promote a sense of obedience. Legal pluralism would also make colonists easier to control by cutting off those colonies from the rest of North America. Divide and rule is a common imperial strategy, but paternalists gave it a particular economic twist. Withholding English law would discourage the immigration and investment Quebec needed to develop advanced commercial economies, because British settlers and merchants would refuse to entrust their bodies or their property to jurisdictions that lacked English law. Populists and moderates, in contrast, wanted to transplant English law in order to create an integrated empire in which colonial subjects enjoyed the same political status and economic opportunities as people in England. A global common law, populists argued, would encourage Anglophone immigration. These new arrivals would stimulate economic development and hasten the assimilation of Britain's newest subjects. The Quebec Act of 1774, which restored French civil law to Quebec and Illinois, marked the triumph of the paternalist vision of empire over populist and moderate alternatives.

Chapter 4 takes the story to India. In many ways, the debate about what law to apply to Bengal mirrored the debate over Quebec and Illinois. Once again, a group of populists wanted to install English law to create an anglicized settler colony; and their opponents fought to withhold English law in order to create a more extractive, hierarchical, and culturally distinctive colony. But there were also important differences between the North American and Indian debates. In Bengal, the most intense disagreement after the mid-1760s was about what kind of legal pluralism to administer, not whether to accept legal pluralism at all. One group of EIC officials, led by Robert Clive, saw legal pluralism primarily as a way to facilitate the collection of taxes while avoiding the fiscal and moral costs of governance. Another group, led by Warren Hastings, took a more interventionist approach that sought simultaneously to preserve Indian laws and to reconstruct them in order to facilitate the Company's extractive project. This tension—between preserving Indian laws and reforming them—would remain an organizing feature of debates about India into the nineteenth century (and beyond).

Chapter 5 explains why paternalists won the debates over colonial law. To some extent, their victory reflected the contingencies of parliamentary politics. But two ideological changes also contributed. First, although paternalists initially embraced legal pluralism because of its effect on colonial development, they came to reframe their position as a moral issue. Building on older vocabularies of humanitarian intervention and religious toleration, paternalists successfully persuaded many Britons that they had a humanitarian duty to preserve the laws of their conquered subjects. Over time, this humanitarian defense of legal pluralism persuaded even the common law's staunchest advocates that legal pluralism was sometimes an imperial obligation. Second, even as paternalists were withdrawing the common law from the colonies, courts in England became increasingly willing to adjudicate disputes arising overseas. As a result, politicians could comfort themselves with the hope that the courts of Westminster Hall would prevent the colonies from diverging entirely from British notions of justice.

Understanding colonial legal pluralism as a contested choice has broader implications for how we think about both law and empire. The conclusion will explore those ideas in greater detail, but it might be helpful to preview them here.

Broadly speaking, scholars tend to describe empire using one of two paradigms: elimination or difference.[41] The former focuses on so-called settler colonies, such as Australia and the United States, where the colonial project sought to erase indigenous inhabitants (whether literally through genocide or displacement, or fictively through forced assimilation). The latter paradigm is used to describe "colonies of exploitation," such as those in Africa and South Asia, where Europeans sought not to exterminate natives but to control their labor. These two forms of colonialism had very different implications for how empires managed difference. Settler colonialism aims for a homogenous (settler) society. Extractive colonialism, in contrast, required natives to remain—and to remain different—both to ensure that there is someone to exploit and as an excuse for imperial rule. Recent work has challenged the settlement/exploitation dichotomy, but it remains central to how many scholars write about empire.[42]

What determined whether settlement or extraction predominated in any given colony? Scholars have tended to focus on the conditions that Europeans encountered when they first arrived. Where the climate and disease environment allowed large-scale settlement, we are told, Europeans sought to eliminate natives in order to build "neo-Europes" in an empty land. But where an unhealthy environment forced Europeans to remain scarce, they sought to exploit natives instead.[43] The mode of empire, in turn, determined the nature of colonial institutions. In neo-Europes, settlers reproduced the institutions they had known at home, including European law. In extractive colonies, however, Europeans designed uniquely colonial institutions to facilitate exploitation. As we'll see, this deterministic model of colonial institutions has been attractive to social scientists, who have relied on it in treating the postcolonial world as a natural experiment about institutions and economic development.[44]

The following chapters will question this deterministic model. At least in the British Empire, the institutions that each colony received reflected a conscious imperial strategy, not just the conditions that Europeans happened to find. British conquerors met similar environments in New Netherland in 1664 and Quebec in 1759, but they chose to rule each place differently. In the 1760s, the climates of Senegambia and Bengal were both deadly for Europeans; differences in settler mortality can't explain why Britain tried to turn the former but not the latter into an American-style plantation colony. Moreover, proposals for European migration didn't always assume the elimination of prior inhabitants. It was possible for commentators and politicians to imagine an empire that was united in law but diverse in color and creed. The point of saying this is not to obscure the forms of exploitation and elimination that did in fact emerge in the British Empire. It is instead to reveal what they were: a choice.

CHAPTER I

Forging a Common-Law Empire

Utopia had just one set of laws. When Sir Thomas More designed his imaginary republic, he endowed it with a firm commitment to forging a legally uniform empire. Whenever Utopia's population became too large, explained More's narrator, its inhabitants would "found a colony under their own laws." The colonizers would willingly intermingle with the local population, but only if the natives would "absorb the same way of life and the same customs" as the Utopians. Anyone who refused to accept Utopian law was expelled.[1]

It's unclear whether More himself would have endorsed this approach.[2] But his book gave a pretty good forecast of England's legal policy in the first phase of its imperial expansion. In the seventeenth and early eighteenth centuries, England (after 1707, Britain) generally sought to extend English law throughout its empire. This pursuit of a common-law empire was never seamless. The laws of Scotland and of England's overseas possessions all differed to varying degrees, and the common law itself made room for local customs. But although each jurisdiction was different, lawyers and policymakers generally saw legal diversity as something to be managed, not encouraged.

This chapter provides an overview of Britain's approach to legal pluralism in the early modern era, especially between the Restoration (1660) and the Seven Years' War (1754–63). It begins with a broad overview of the competing impulses toward uniformity and diversity within English legal and political thought, describing how the law varied in practice and the extent to which policymakers extended English law to new territories and populations. The chapter then zooms in to take a closer look at the 1740s, which marked the zenith of Britain's commitment to legal uniformity. Focusing on Whig responses to the 1745 Jacobite uprising, this chapter shows that many politicians and legal theorists believed that the security and prosperity of Britain depended on more closely harmonizing English and Scottish law. Importantly, writers who reached that conclusion did so despite their engagement with Montesquieu's analysis of legal diversity in *The Spirit of the Laws* (1748). Although that treatise is sometimes treated as a turning point in European approaches to colonial law, it initially did little to check Britain's commitment to building a common-law empire.

THE EXPANSION OF ENGLISH LAW

Lawyers today usually presume that the same law should govern everyone. Specialized laws are exceptional and often cause for suspicion (at least in a liberal democracy).[3] But the ideal of one law for all took centuries to develop, and in England it was never a reality. Medieval and early modern justice was administered not by a single hierarchy of courts but by a kaleidoscope of specialized tribunals, whose jurisdictions depended on geography, subject matter, and party status. The substance of English law was equally lumpy. The "common law" got its name, in the late twelfth century, to distinguish it from the patchwork of local customs that governed most of medieval life.[4] Gradually, the common law of the king's courts gained supremacy over its rivals. But even in the eighteenth century, "English law" was "a very mixed and heterogeneous mass," as Edmund Burke put it, encompassing the law of nations, Roman law, ecclesiastical law, statute law, and equity, among other things. And even the label of "common law" could be misleading. That law was administered by three courts—King's Bench, Common Pleas, and Exchequer—that lacked a formal mechanism for reviewing each other's decisions. As a result, the common law wasn't even common to every corner of Westminster Hall, where those courts sat.[5]

The diversity of English law was a fact. But by the sixteenth century, English elites saw it as something to tame. As the seventeenth-century judge Sir Matthew Hale put it, the common law was an effort to replace "all those Provincial Laws" with "one Law to be observed through the whole Kingdom."[6]

Officially, that one law had always made room for local customs; but royal courts gradually made it harder to prove that such customs existed. This destruction of local law wasn't necessarily an unwanted imposition from above. In Kent, landowners petitioned Parliament to replace their custom of gavelkind, a form of land tenure and inheritance, with ordinary common-law rules. Parliament declined—there was some concern that eliminating gavelkind might reduce tax revenues—but offered Kentish landowners other ways to bring their estates into conformity with the common law.[7]

By the end of the seventeenth century, England still had many kinds of law, but the common law had achieved ideological preeminence. The history of martial law provides an example. Under Henry VIII, the Crown had used martial law to prosecute treasons and felonies committed by civilians. Although it did so to circumvent the common law's protections, common lawyers didn't always object. Thomas More, for example, thought it appropriate to employ non–common law systems to protect public order. Under the Stuarts, however, martial law came to seem more problematic. Parliament sought both to restrict its scope and to make courts-martial more closely resemble common-law trials. By the late seventeenth century, Hale could deny that martial law should even be numbered among the laws of England, and eighteenth-century politicians generally viewed it as dangerous to English liberty. Even the Duke of Bedford, who was generally enthusiastic about military discipline, warned in the 1750s that soldiers weren't really Englishmen "because they live under a quite different sort of laws, and are very uncertain of its being ever in their power to restore themselves to . . . the laws of their country."[8]

Martial law wasn't quite as anomalous as Bedford suggested. Many English subjects had to deal with specialized or summary forms of adjudication, such as excise tribunals. Parliament created a special court to process claims arising from the Great Fire of London (1666), and it continued to create "fire courts" to deal with urban conflagrations throughout the eighteenth century. But contemporary writers tended to describe such tribunals as targeted responses to specific problems, rather than an ordinary feature of English law.[9] By contemporary standards, England was building a remarkably uniform legal system. When Voltaire complained in 1751 that a traveler in France must "change laws every time you change horses," he was contrasting it with England—"a nation, who live under the same laws" but "have a score of different religions."[10]

Meanwhile, English law was also expanding its geographic reach. When Henry VIII and his ministers sought to tighten their grip on Wales, they drew it within the circle of English law. Just as courts had been a crucial instrument of state formation within England, they would be a primary means of projecting the state beyond England's borders.[11] A similar rationale guided England's approach to Ireland. The English Crown had started transplanting the common law to Ireland in the thirteenth century, but the work was still in progress during the reign of Elizabeth I. Her officials had little doubt that they ought to smash what remained of Irish law; the only question was what would replace it. Some writers, including the poet Edmund Spenser, argued that the Irish were too barbarous to receive English law, and that the only way to govern the island was by force. Elizabethan and early Stuart officials took a slightly different path, electing to pacify Ireland using the common law—both for reasons of state, and because they thought it their duty "to teach them our English lawes and civilitie."[12] This became the conventional wisdom. In 1628, the great judge and parliamentarian Sir Edward Coke declared, with Ireland in mind, that the "union of lawes is the best meanes for the unity of countries."[13] That maxim remained current well into the eighteenth century. William Blackstone, the first professor of English law at Oxford, wrote that the imposition of English law on Wales "gave the utmost advancement to [Welsh] civil prosperity, by admitting them to a thorough communication of laws with the subjects of England." Sir Robert Chambers, who succeeded Blackstone at Oxford before becoming a judge in Bengal, told his students the same thing.[14] (Scots law followed a different path, as this chapter will discuss.)

English law also predominated in England's transatlantic expansion. As a technical matter, it wasn't clear that the common law could travel overseas. Seventeenth-century lawyers didn't think of the common law primarily as a portable body of substantive rules. Rather, they saw it as a system of writs administered by a particular set of English courts, which had geographically limited jurisdictions. For that reason, even Coke, perhaps the common law's most tenacious defender, thought that it "meddles with nothing that is done beyond the seas."[15] But even if the common law stopped at the water's edge, colonial courts could still imitate it. There were precedents in England for that kind of copycat common law. The County Palatine of Durham, for example, was outside the original jurisdiction of the Westminster courts—and therefore outside the common law as Coke conceived of it. Nonetheless, the palatinate's judiciary administered a law that closely tracked the law in the rest of England. This was a frequent pattern in England's local jurisdictions, which by the sixteenth century generally followed the example set by the central common-law courts. In part, this was because even "independent" courts like those of Durham were subject to Parliament and the royal prerogative, and (via writs of error) to the supervision of King's Bench. More importantly, perhaps, local courts were often staffed by officials trained at the Inns of Court—the same institutions that trained common lawyers. In what would become a frequent imperial pattern, the circulation of personnel generated convergence even among institutions that were formally independent from each other.[16]

Imitating the common law in the colonies had practical advantages. Colonial proprietors learned that it was easier to attract English settlers to new places if they promised a familiar legal system. And imperial administrators found it easier to make sense of colonies whose courts took their cue from Westminster Hall.[17] Nonetheless, lawyers throughout the British Empire understood that each colony would have slightly different laws. But how much difference was acceptable? The answer developed by the Privy Council (which heard appeals from colonial courts) was that colonial laws could not be "repugnant" to the laws of England. Of course, that standard left plenty of room for debate about particular cases. But the debates themselves reinforced the idea that English law was the benchmark, to be matched as nearly as colonial conditions would permit. Over the course of the eighteenth century, colonists increasingly took pains to give their deviations from metropolitan law as English an appearance as possible.[18]

This was true even with respect to slavery. Historians have described slavery as exemplifying legal pluralism in two respects. First, many colonies excluded enslaved people from ordinary law. For example, in many colonies, slaves' alleged crimes were adjudicated not according to the common law but by the summary procedures of "slave courts." Second, slavery itself survived only because metropolitan elites could pretend that it was a uniquely colonial phenomenon—one whose brutality lay "beyond the line" of European civilization and English justice.[19] There is some truth to those claims, but they risk obscuring the extent to which the institution of slavery was a product of English law, not an exception to it.

Although many of slavery's elements were first developed in the colonies, slavery itself depended on the protection of English law. The transatlantic slave trade required an abundant supply of credit, which was facilitated by a shared legal framework between American planters and metropolitan lenders. The judges of Westminster Hall developed many of the common-law doctrines that allowed persons to be treated as property; Caribbean and American enslavers eagerly imported them. (Perhaps not coincidentally, it was colonies in the Caribbean and southern mainland that sent aspiring lawyers to train at the Inns of Court in London in the greatest numbers.) When Lord Mansfield suggested in *Somerset's Case* (1772) that colonial slavery might be inconsistent with metropolitan law, planters were shocked.[20]

The assumption that colonial law shouldn't be repugnant to metropolitan law pertained both to "settled" and "conquered" colonies. Coke was skeptical about the common law's portability, but not because he believed that foreign legal systems deserved any special respect. To the contrary, in *Calvin's Case* (1608), he made it clear that a conqueror had the right—and sometimes the duty—to abrogate the laws of any people he conquered. If the conqueror took over "a kingdom of a Christian king," Coke explained, existing laws would remain in place by default, but the conqueror could alter them "at his pleasure." If the conquest was of "a kingdom of an infidel," the conquest automatically abrogated any laws contrary to Christianity, divine law, or natural law. But in neither situation could the conquered assert a right to the continued administration of their own laws.[21] Later writers abandoned Coke's distinction between infidel and Christian territories, but they reaffirmed Britain's right to replace the laws of conquered (or ceded) colonies.[22]

This understanding of conquest informed England's legal policy whenever it acquired territory from European rivals. Jamaica, taken from Spain in 1655, was a relatively easy case: Spanish settlers evacuated or were expelled within a few years, leaving English officials with little reason to preserve Spanish law.[23] One of the first English governors issued a proclamation "promising that justice should be administered according to the 'known laws of England,' or laws made by the freeholders themselves."[24] New York, conquered from the Netherlands in 1664, was trickier. A substantial Dutch population remained, and the articles of capitulation provided that Dutch law would continue to control key areas of private law, particularly testation and preconquest contracts. But England's invasion fleet had included three lawyers for a reason. Almost immediately, New York's new rulers began to suppress Dutch influence on the legal system, especially after the colony's inhabitants welcomed the brief Dutch reconquest in 1673. Limited state capacity and local resistance sometimes made for slow progress; but even in the upper Hudson Valley, where Dutch influence lasted longest, England quickly introduced trials by jury.[25] Finally, in 1691, in the aftermath of Leisler's Rebellion, New York's English rulers declared the common law fully in force. Although some Dutch settlers resisted this change, the introduction of English law was not just an alien imposition. It also reflected the priorities of Anglo-Dutch merchants, who were less invested in preserving their traditional laws than in accessing the trading networks of the English Atlantic world.[26]

That English law should govern English colonies was a political principle, not a legal one. Seventeenth-century lawyers interpreted *Calvin's Case* to mean that the king "may give to any Countryes conquered by him, what Lawes he pleaseth which are not contrary to the Lawes of Nature, or to natural reason."[27] But even if the Crown was legally free to depart from English law, it was risky for it to do so. During the 1670s, critics of Charles II accused him of governing Tangier—which he had personally acquired from Portugal in 1661 as a part of his queen's dowry—outside of English law. In some ways, that was true. He had instructed his governors to permit a degree of religious toleration that was foreclosed by statutes at home.[28] But other deviations from metropolitan law were just the product of poor governance. (When one governor declared that he administered "the law of Tangier" and not "the law of England," he was searching for a rule that would maximize his intake of bribes, not announcing a principle of legal pluralism.)[29] Charles himself thought that anglicizing Tangier's law would be crucial for building the colony into a thriving commercial center. Only by permitting English merchants to trade under familiar laws, he and his advisers believed, could Tangier outcompete more established Mediterranean ports like Cadiz.[30]

English law also guided the East India Company's ventures. When the Company first arrived in South Asia, its territorial possessions were limited to a network of trading posts, or "factories," centered on the towns of Bombay, Madras, and Calcutta. Although the Company's early operations focused on commerce rather than territorial conquest, it was responsible for administering justice to the inhabitants of its settlements. Each of the presidency towns administered justice independently of the others, but the general trend in all three was toward an anglicized legal system.

Charles II had acquired Bombay from Portugal as part of the same marriage arrangement that brought him Tangier. He decided that the distant island wasn't worth keeping for himself, and he transferred it to the East India Company. As it turned out, Bombay had the best harbor in South Asia, and within three decades its population had swelled to 60,000.[31] As the settlement grew, the Company replaced Portuguese law with rules of its own creation. As Philip Stern has emphasized, it was Company law, not English law, that governed Bombay. But as in other colonies, English law was the lodestar. The royal patents for Bombay included the same principle of non-repugnancy that the

Privy Council had developed for North America, and local officials sought to draw Bombay's legal practices "as neare as possible . . . to the Custome and constitution of England."[32] As with the American colonies, "repugnancy" and "nearness" were contestable terms. But that was the point: to provide a framework that kept the settlement tethered, but not nailed, to English law. The same framework guided legal developments in Madras (Fort St. George) and Calcutta (Fort William), which looked to Bombay as a model.[33]

Like Charles II in Tangier, the Company tended to view English law not as a burdensome constraint but as a useful resource. When it obtained a new charter in 1726, it used the occasion to intensify its efforts to anglicize Indian law. As Mitch Fraas has observed, that charter sought "to bring legal practice in India firmly into communion with that of metropolitan England and the rest of the empire."[34] It created mayor's courts at Bombay, Madras, and Calcutta, which would administer local varieties of English law. Appeals from those courts would go to the Privy Council, just like in the American colonies. At the same time, the new courts continued to allow for variation and experimentation. For example, the mayor's courts fused equity and common-law procedure, which wouldn't happen in England for another century and a half. The mayor's courts also relied heavily on arbitration, which gave continued vitality to local customs without formally incorporating them into the courts' jurisprudence. But despite these departures from metropolitan practice, the courts' procedures remained legible to lawyers in England, and the Company's courts in India remained part of the same legal world as England and North America.[35]

Indian litigants, like the Dutch inhabitants of New York, had mixed reactions to the Company's anglicized legal regime. Some merchants found it useful; indeed, some seem to have settled in the presidency towns precisely to take advantage of their courts. Accordingly, when Company courts departed from English law, they faced objections not only from London-educated lawyers but also from native litigants who had elected to rely on that law. Other litigants preferred other forums.[36] And some local elites viewed English law as a threat to their social and political status, and they asked the Company to limit the jurisdiction of its courts. Meanwhile, some Company officials had started to chafe at the limits that English law placed on their freedom in governing. These two movements came together in the 1740s and culminated in 1753, when they persuaded the Company to obtain a new charter that made it harder for Indian litigants to sue in the mayor's courts.[37]

In retrospect, it's tempting to see the 1753 charter as a big step toward legal pluralism. The charter erected a double separation: first, between Indian and European litigants; and second, between India, with its dual judicial system, and the rest of the British Empire. Some of the arguments used to obtain the 1753 charter also seemed to anticipate later rhetoric about the unsuitability of English law for India or for Indians.[38] On closer inspection, however, the 1753 charter looks less significant. As an initial matter, its text was ambiguous. One provision barred the mayor's courts from hearing suits between Indian litigants unless both parties consented to its jurisdiction. Some Company officials hoped that provision would signal that the mayor's courts were strictly English—in law and in clientele.[39] But other parts of the charter sent a different message. Its preamble praised the 1726 regime as a success, and it recited that Company courts "had, by a strict and equal Distribution of Justice . . . very much encouraged, not only Our own Subjects, *but likewise the Subjects of other Princes, and the Natives of the adjacent Countries,* to resort to and settle in the" Company's settlements. In other words, it recognized that one of the purposes of the Company's courts had been to attract Indian residents by offering a superior dispute-resolution service.[40] Later commentators assumed the 1753 charter had the same goal—namely, "the acquiring of Inhabitants, and carrying on the Trade of the Country" by offering impartial justice to European and non-European litigants alike.[41] The lawyers who reviewed the 1753 charter—including Charles Yorke (later the attorney general and lord chancellor), Attorney General Sir Dudley Ryder (later chief justice of King's Bench), and Solicitor General William Murray (the future Lord Mansfield)—didn't treat it as a major departure from earlier policy. Yorke, in particular, seems to have assumed that Company courts would continue to administer English law to Indian litigants. The charter even created a new small-claims court (the court of requests) whose jurisdiction extended to Indian and European litigants alike.[42]

After the new charter came into effect, residents of the Company's settlements continued to contest its meaning. Although the exclusion of Indian litigants had ostensibly been at their own request, it soon became apparent that this supposed favor was "by some thought a Grievance."[43] Indians continued to seek justice in the mayor's courts; and in 1755, the court at Calcutta petitioned the Company's directors to restore its jurisdiction over Indian litigants. The directors declined to do so—not because they objected on the merits, but because revising the charter would have been expensive.[44] In many respects, then, the post-1753 regime looked a lot like its predecessor, even if the politics of English law had grown more fraught. As a result, it was easy for local officials to keep thinking that English law belonged in India, even as some of their colleagues challenged that idea.

METROPOLITAN COURTS AND COLONIAL LAW

Building an imperial common law wasn't just a matter of erecting new courts abroad. It also required the common law itself to accommodate Britain's expanding and increasingly diverse empire. Historians have long emphasized the crucial role played in this process by the Privy Council as the final court of appeal for British colonies.[45] But some of the most important work was done by the ordinary courts of Westminster Hall.

In theory, those courts should have been irrelevant. As explained above, they had no extraterritorial jurisdiction. This reflected the medieval origins of the remedies they administered. But lawyers and judges deployed a series of legal fictions that gutted that territorial limitation. The most famous of these was the "Bill of Middlesex," which emerged in the fifteenth century. The procedure depended on plaintiffs' alleging a fictitious trespass in the county of Middlesex—even though everyone involved, including the judges, understood that no such trespass had occurred—in order to invoke the jurisdiction of King's Bench.[46] Similar geographic fictions allowed plaintiffs to plead that they were suing for a debt incurred at "Fort St. George, in the East Indies, to wit, at London, in the ward of Cheap."[47] For jurisdictional purposes, Madras was just a neighborhood in London.

To be sure, colonial cases were uncommon in Westminster Hall. Even legal fictions couldn't evade the cost of litigating so far from home. The relatively few colonial lawsuits that did make it to England mostly landed before the Privy Council, which was the ordinary destination for appeals from colonial courts. But it nonetheless remained possible for a dispute in Virginia or Calcutta to end up in Chancery or King's Bench.[48] When that happened, judges were sometimes able to decide according to established precedents. But in some cases, they had to adapt common-law rules to the needs of non-English litigants. In doing so, they crafted a capacious common law that was suited to Britain's expanding empire.

Omichund v. Barker provides a prominent example. In 1736, a Sikh merchant named Omichund, who was the East India Company's leading trading partner in Bengal, sued Hugh Barker, a Company official, in the Calcutta mayor's court to recover a debt of £7,600. Omichund won, but Barker fled India before the court could issue its judgment. He died on the voyage home, and Omichund sought to recover his judgment from Barker's estate in England. Acting through an associate in London, he hired the barrister Philip Carteret Webb to sue Barker's heir and executor in Chancery. The chancellor—Philip Yorke, first Earl of Hardwicke—delegated fact-finding to a chancery master, who issued commissions to take depositions from witnesses in India. When Omichund's lawyers tried to introduce those depositions as evidence, the defendant objected that they were inadmissible because the deponents were not Christians—and, therefore, hadn't sworn the "oath upon the Evangelists" prescribed by English law.[49]

This objection forced Hardwicke to confront an issue that had been percolating for years. As the Company's lawyers had long insisted, the charters of the mayor's courts required them to receive evidence according to English law. That meant requiring witnesses to take a "corporal oath," which involved touching and kissing a copy of the Gospels.[50] That requirement created an obvious problem for courts that depended on the testimony of witnesses who weren't Christian. There were some precedents for such situations. Parliament had already made a partial exception for Quakers, who were permitted to affirm rather than swear; and earlier cases had held that Jewish witnesses could be sworn on the Hebrew Bible. But it wasn't clear whether those precedents could be extended to "Gentoos," as Sikhs, Hindus, and other non-Muslim natives of India were called at the time.[51]

The problem wasn't just that non-Christian witnesses might balk at taking a Christian oath. English lawyers also struggled with the trustworthiness of their testimony. Traditionally, English courts had relied on what John Langbein calls an "oath-based" theory of perjury, which "presupposed the witness's fear that God would damn a perjurer."[52] Under that theory, witnesses who didn't profess a Christian fear of damnation were inherently unreliable. There was lingering anxiety, for instance, about whether Quaker affirmations were really substitutes for oaths when it came to preventing perjury.[53]

This put the Company's courts in an impossible position: the law didn't authorize sworn testimony by non-Christians, but courts in India couldn't function without it. When the Company asked its attorneys to clear things up, the best that they could do was avoid giving any definite opinion at all—probably because they feared that a forthright analysis would have called into question the legality of the courts' proceedings. One of the lawyers, John Browne, looked for a way out by proposing a distinction between voluntary and compelled testimony. Although Company courts could not *force* a witness to undergo "any Pagan Cerimony in the nature of an Oath," they might *allow* non-Christian witnesses to take such oaths voluntarily. In such cases, the "oath" would lack legal effect, but judges might still consider it when weighing a witness's credibility. As Browne explained, "all that you can do is to afford a Greater or less share of Credit to his Evidence, according to the Solemnity and the nature of the Oath taken, and the degree of Reverence in which it is held by the Indians."[54] This was at best a partial solution, since it offered no way to compel testimony from unwilling non-Christian witnesses.[55] And Browne seems to have had doubts even about this partial measure. Three years later—while the *Omichund* litigation was pending—he cosigned a memorandum stating that "the Laws of England . . . take no notice of the Oaths of Heathens."[56] Remarkably, one of the memo's coauthors was Sir Dudley Ryder, who was simultaneously engaged in defending Omichund's right to present the depositions of non-Christians in his Chancery litigation.

Hardwicke understood the question's importance and difficulty. He had empowered the commissioners to swear deponents in India "in the most solemn manner, as in [the commissioners'] discretions shall seem meet." His instructions had deliberately failed to prescribe the form for such an oath, "because I may possibly direct a form that is contrary to the notions of religion entertained by the *Gentoo* people." At the same time, he reserved judgment as to the validity of whatever oath was ultimately administered.[57] When the case returned to his court several years later, he asked three senior judges—Sir William Lee, the chief justice of King's Bench; Sir John Willes, the chief justice of Common Pleas; and Sir Thomas Parker, the chief baron of the Exchequer—for assistance in resolving it.

After hearing argument (in which Omichund was represented by Ryder and Murray), all four judges found that the testimony of "Gentoo" witnesses ought to be admitted. Although their opinions offered varying rationales, they agreed about the importance of a witness's belief in a "Supreme Being" who was "the rewarder of truth, and avenger of falsehood."[58] This belief mattered because of its functional importance: only a witness who feared divine punishment could be trusted. On the one hand, this meant that English law didn't need to draw a bright line between Christian and non-Christian testimony; it could recognize the oath of anyone who believed that his lies would merit divine punishment. On the other hand, a witness's religion had evidentiary significance. Even though a court could accept the testimony of "infidels," it didn't have to treat their evidence as equivalent to the testimony of a witness who professed a Christian fear of hell.[59]

Omichund was primarily about the law to be applied in English courts, and it left an enduring impression on the common law.[60] But it also had implications for the administration of English law in India. Although the decision removed any doubt about the competence of Hindu and Sikh witnesses, it left unresolved the precise weight their testimony should receive, as well as the form that their oaths should take. As British officials worked out the answers to these questions, they followed *Omichund*'s example by searching for answers within the common law, rather than trying to craft exceptions to it.

Two years after *Omichund*, a crisis erupted over oaths in Bombay. Hindu witnesses there had customarily sworn an oath on a copy of the Bhagavad Gita. (This had also been the form of oath at issue in *Omichund*.) The practice had an intuitive appeal: just as Christians swore on their "books of Law & Religion," so, too, would adherents of other religions.[61] In 1746, however, the judges of the mayor's court alleged that the oath on the Gita was insufficiently solemn and insisted that Hindu witnesses instead swear upon a cow. Many of Bombay's merchants refused to take the new oath. Swearing on a cow, they explained, was a sacrilegious act that "would cause them to 'lose their Cast and consequently Credit and Reputation throughout all Parts of India.'"[62] They also argued that the cow oath was contrary to English law. The Company's own courts, the merchants pointed out, had long recognized the Gita oath as valid. By reversing course, the members of the mayor's court had not only offended Hindus' faith but also "substitut[ed] their own will and pleasure" for "the Laws of their own Country."[63] From the perspective of this group of Indian merchants, their right to take the "Gita oath" was the product of English law, not an exception to it.

They reinforced their legal argument with an economic threat. Requiring the cow oath effectively excluded Hindu merchants from English courts; accordingly, it was "no small impediment to their credit and commerce." Access to English justice had "allured [Indian merchants] to settle" in Bombay in the first place; without that access, they had little reason to stay.[64] Governor William Wake and his allies on the Bombay council took that threat seriously. They had been unable to persuade the members of the mayor's court to change their position, and they now sought help from the Company's directors in London. Continuing to administer the cow oath, the council warned, "in all probability will cause many of the principal Inhabitants to remove as well as discourage others from coming to reside amongst us." Accordingly, the council urged the directors to tell the mayor's court to jettison the cow oath—which, they added, would do nothing to enhance the reliability of evidence. Because "reputable people" would never swear on a cow, only the least trustworthy Hindus would be willing to testify. Only a reversion to the "Gita oath" would secure Bombay's economic future and the smooth operation of its courts.[65]

The Company's directors, in turn, referred the matter to their lawyers, including three of the usual suspects: Attorney General Ryder, Solicitor General Murray, and John Browne. They advised that the mayor's court "ought to administer to Indians such an Oath, as is held to be sacred, & in such a manner as is esteemed the most solemn & binding by their respective sects or casts of Religion." That sounds like a dodge; but their memorandum was meant less to answer the question than to provide a framework for doing so. Instead of dictating an answer from London, the lawyers encouraged Company officials to answer it themselves in the context of litigation. If the mayor's court ordered someone to take an oath to which he objected, the witness should appeal the issue to Bombay's governor and council, which was to consider record evidence as to what kind of oath was customary for that witness.[66]

In *Omichund*, Chief Justice Willes had suggested that the form of an oath in India should reflect information that the court learned through litigation, rather than generalized speculations or secondary literature about South Asian religions.[67] The Company's lawyers followed that advice: rather than making their own determination about which oath to use, they allowed the legal system itself to develop the answer. As Solicitor General Murray had explained when he argued *Omichund,* one of the common law's virtues was its capacity to adapt to new situations. "All occasions do not arise at once; now a particular species of *Indians* appears; hereafter another species of *Indians* may arise," Murray told the judges. No statute—and, for that matter, no rule crafted for the Company by its London lawyers—could anticipate every new situation. Therefore, "the common law, *that works itself pure* by rules drawn from the fountain of justice, is . . . superior to an act of parliament."[68] Murray's statement would become famous as a paean to the common law. What he was praising, above all, was the common law's capacity to adapt to Britain's expanding empire.[69]

EXCEPTIONS: MINORCA, GIBRALTAR, AND NEWFOUNDLAND

By the middle of the eighteenth century, English law reached nearly every part of Britain's empire. But there were exceptions: Newfoundland, Gibraltar, and Minorca. (The next section will take another look at Scotland.) Some historians have seen in those territories a preview of Britain's later turn toward a more deliberate policy of legal pluralism. In the 1770s, some commentators made similar arguments, citing those places as precedents for policies like the Quebec Act.[70]

But that seeming continuity is an illusion. At least until the Seven Years' War, none of those places reflected a deliberate policy of colonial legal pluralism. As an initial matter, none was a "colony" in the usual sense. Newfoundland was a seasonal fishing station; it didn't even have a governor until 1729. Even in that lightly governed jurisdiction, officials were committed to administering laws as close as possible to those of England. As in England itself, that sometimes meant incorporating local custom. But as legal institutions became more settled—especially after the arrival in 1749 of Governor George Brydges Rodney—it became clear that Newfoundland was being incorporated into the common-law framework that governed the rest of the empire.[71]

Gibraltar was, in the words of one judge, "a mere fortress and garrison," which was legally and politically distinct from ordinary colonies.[72] It had fewer than two thousand civilian inhabitants in the 1750s. In the early years after Britain acquired Gibraltar via the Treaty of Utrecht (1713), the most prominent characteristic of Gibraltarian law was confusion. It took until 1739 for the Crown to establish Gibraltar's first civil court, which was instructed to follow English law.[73] Implementing that instruction proved difficult: a decade later, the garrison's governor still had occasion to lament the poor quality of civil justice, and in 1768 the secretary at war wrote that Gibraltar had "no species of Civil Government whatever."[74] Throughout the 1740s and 1750s, Crown lawyers and military officials kept asking how they might apply "the Laws of England" while also "considering and allowing for the circumstances and situation of the Place and the Inhabitants."[75] That was the same problem that confronted officials in North America. But solving it was harder in a place that barely had a civil government at all.

Many contemporaries saw Minorca, like Gibraltar, as "nothing more than a garrison-town."[76] Unlike Gibraltar, however, Minorca had a large and permanent civilian population, which was used to living under the laws of Spain (which had governed the island until Britain captured it during the War of the Spanish Succession). British observers treated Minorca's distinctive law as the regrettable consequence of the island's terms of cession.[77] Policymakers repeatedly proposed ways to craft a "new modell" of Minorcan law that would "Corrispond with the Constitution of England."[78] One suggestion, made in about 1753, was to expel all Spanish lawyers who weren't natives of the island.

A less disruptive alternative, offered by Lieutenant Governor Richard Kane, sought to make English courts more welcoming for Minorcan litigants. In a proposal that paralleled *Omichund*, he suggested that "the Subjects of all Nations" should be able to "take Oaths in the Manner used in theyr owne Country and that all such oaths be allow'd as valid & authentick in the Courts of Minorca."[79]

Until Spain reconquered Minorca during the American Revolutionary War, commentators continued to hope that Britain might establish common-law courts that would wean litigants from their attachment to Spain and its legal tradition. But officials doubted that Britain's commitments under the Treaty of Utrecht would allow them to abolish Spanish law on the island.[80] Bureaucratic neglect was perhaps an even more powerful obstacle. In 1764, a group of merchants complained that "there have been no regulations or Ordonances established here" for three decades. The lack of new legislation had led magistrates "to revive old Spanish Customs, some of which are so foreign from the present practised Method in all other parts of the World" that merchants found them impossible to follow.[81] There was legal pluralism in Minorca, but it could hardly be described as strategic.

ENLIGHTENED UNIFORMITY: MONTESQUIEU AND SCOTLAND

Scotland was the most obvious exception to Britain's common-law empire. When James VI of Scotland became James I of England in 1603, his person joined two kingdoms with distinctive laws and legal systems. James thought that was a problem, and he often voiced his desire to "reduce the whole Iland" to "one Law." Although he recognized that some local particularities would remain—as was true within England itself—he urged a "Vnion of Lawes" that would bring English and Scots law into general harmony.[82] Especially in the early years of his reign, commentators suggested a number of ways to bring that about, including the imposition of English law on Scotland, the creation of a new "British" legal system, or a hybrid, in which the two kingdoms would retain distinct private-law traditions within a common public-law framework. But none of those proposals came to anything. Scots lawyers worried that the destruction of Scots law would also destroy Scottish sovereignty, much as the anglicization of Welsh law had facilitated the subordination of Wales to England. English lawyers feared that James would use the union of laws as an opportunity to augment his own authority and to curtail common-law liberties. And so, much to the king's disappointment, the project of legal union stalled. It was briefly revived after James's son lost his throne and his head. Following Oliver Cromwell's successful invasion of Scotland in 1650, the English Commonwealth suspended Scottish courts, installed English judges, and generally tried to anglicize the legal system. That project enjoyed at best partial success before the Restoration of 1660 cut it short; and although Charles II continued to tinker with Scots law on the margins, he showed little interest in reprising the Cromwellian experiment.[83]

The historical memory of occupation during the 1650s seems to have hardened the resolve of Scottish elites to resist the imposition of English law; and when Scottish commissioners negotiated a legislative union with England in the early eighteenth century, they insisted that Scotland's legal system remain largely intact. Their English counterparts agreed. (Among other things, they worried about the political consequences of putting the entire Scottish legal profession out of work.)[84] The Acts of Union in 1707, which united Scotland and England into a single kingdom of Great Britain, mostly left Scots law alone—with some important exceptions. "Laws concerning public Right, Polity, and Civil Government" were to be made the same throughout Britain; Parliament gained the right to alter even Scots private law "for evident Utility of the Subjects within Scotland"; and the House of Lords gained ultimate jurisdiction over Scottish appeals. Scots law survived, but was subject to the legislative and judicial oversight of a mostly English Parliament.[85]

The Union of 1707 made it clear that Scotland's law was not going to receive the same treatment as that of Wales or Ireland, but it didn't end concerns about splitting a kingdom between two legal systems. Reformers on both sides of the border continued to complain about the divergence between progressive England, which had abolished feudal land tenures during the Interregnum, and backward Scotland, where feudal forms of property survived. Even more troubling to many writers was the persistence in Scotland of heritable jurisdictions—local courts run by feudal lords. According to their critics, these institutions had stunted Scotland's economic development and denied Scots the full range of British political rights.[86] After the failed Jacobite rebellion of 1745, these critiques took on new importance. That uprising had enjoyed disproportionate support in Scotland, and the British ministry concluded that the surest way to prevent a repetition was to integrate Scotland more fully with England. In part, that meant anglicizing Scots law.[87]

The abolition of heritable jurisdictions was the most prominent example of the resulting program, which was largely designed by Lord Hardwicke. Although heritable jurisdictions had long been criticized, the acts of union had expressly preserved them, and they were valuable to their owners. They not only allowed local magnates to run their own criminal courts, but also bestowed prestige and (thanks to fines and fees) income. Their abolition thus amounted to an attack both on the terms of the 1707 Union and on the property rights of elite landowners. Nonetheless, Parliament agreed to eliminate the feudal courts and to compensate their owners. Other elements of Hardwicke's program included introducing English-style grand juries, circuit courts that would give "a more exact and useful uniformity" to British justice, and anglicized evidentiary rules (specifically, abolishing the requirement that evidence in capital cases be reduced to writing).[88]

On their face, these were minor adjustments, but proponents described the stakes in lofty terms. The Duke of Newcastle called it a "Battle for our Constitution"; for Hardwicke, it was nothing less than a "Scotch Reformation."[89] Some Scottish elites objected to such an intrusive course. "[A]n Attempt to introduce a Conformity betwixt our Circuit Courts . . . and the Assizes or Commissions of nisi prius in England, is vain, and against our Constitution," one anonymous pamphlet warned.[90] Even some Scottish politicians who supported Hardwicke's efforts, such as the Duke of Argyll, did so grudgingly. The abolition of heritable jurisdictions struck them as punitive, an intrusive attack on private property, and a foretaste of more general interference in Scots law.[91] But other Scottish writers, especially those with political ties to the ministry in London, embraced Hardwicke's program enthusiastically. "I think it impossible for England and Scotland to be on a Right Foot," Lord Grange told Hardwicke, until they are on the "same foot" with respect to "Law and Courts and the Administration of Justice."[92] An unnamed memorialist found it "unlucky" for Scots "that so many Reservations were made in favour of some of their antient Laws, Customs, & Jurisdictions." The persistence of Scots law, the memorialist continued, had "excluded [them] from participation in any of the Priviledges or Immunities designed by the Union."[93]

Some of the fullest defenses of anglicized institutions came from writers linked to the Scottish Enlightenment, many of whom had been inspired by the recent publication of Montesquieu's *Spirit of the Laws* (1748). Today, that text is usually seen as inaugurating a new appreciation for legal pluralism. Comparative lawyers, in particular, focus on its claim that transplanting laws is rarely possible and always risky.[94] That interpretation of Montesquieu has a long history. Jeremy Bentham identified 1748 as a watershed for colonial legislation. "Before Montesquieu," Bentham wrote, "a man who had a distant country given him to make laws for, would have made short work of it" by imposing the laws of his own country. After Montesquieu, conquerors had become more cautious about slapping their own laws on new possessions.[95]

But Montesquieu's prescriptions aren't as clear-cut as that reading might suggest. He was indeed skeptical of legal transplants; but he also noted that Britain had given "the form of its own government to the people of its colonies" and that it had imposed its law on Ireland.[96] Such tensions between general principles and specific cases allowed early readers to square Montesquieu's theories with Hardwicke's policies. The Scottish lawyer Sir John Dalrymple, for example, initially struggled to reconcile the abolition of heritable jurisdictions with Montesquieu's observation that intermediate powers served as bulwarks against royal tyranny. "[I]t appeared to me," he confessed to his friend Charles Yorke, "that his principles laid down tended to blame that measure." But Yorke had a ready solution. (Yorke, the future attorney general, was Hardwicke's son, and he had explained his father's Scottish legislation to Montesquieu during a visit to France.)[97] He explained that Montesquieu had praised intermediate powers only in absolute monarchies; but he had suggested that the centralization of power could enhance liberty in limited monarchies like Britain. (David Hume said something similar in a letter to Montesquieu himself.)[98] Dalrymple relied on Yorke's advice to claim a Montesquieuean mantle for anglicizing reform. When he wrote his influential history of feudal property, he took the book's epigraph from *The Spirit of the Laws*, called Montesquieu "the greatest genius of our age," and noted that Montesquieu himself had provided feedback on his work.[99] And yet Dalrymple framed his book as an attempt to show "how much greater [the] similarity [between Scots and English law] might yet be made."[100]

Dalrymple wasn't alone in urging a more uniform system of laws in Britain. His work built on Yorke's *Considerations on the Law of Forfeiture* (1745), which had also suggested the further integration of English and Scottish laws. The Scottish judge Lord Kames, who like Dalrymple praised Montesquieu as "the greatest genius of the present age," considered it "an unhappy circumstance, that different parts of the same kingdom should be governed by different laws."[101] By the 1740s, it had become a frequent refrain among Scottish writers that Scots law needed reform, that English law ought to serve as the model, and (less confidently) that convergence was likely.

Not everyone accepted this diagnosis. Lord Glenorchy, a Scottish Whig, defended the abolition of heritable jurisdictions but also suggested that "[t]he Commonalty of the Highlands must be dealt with in a different manner from those of England."[102] Even those who agreed that uniformity was the goal disagreed about how to bring it about. One extreme was represented by General Humphrey Bland, commander in chief in Scotland (and former governor of Gibraltar). "I think Oliver Cromwell has set us an Example how to bring this Country under the obedience of England," he told Hardwicke, "and which render'd the People happy, by sending down English Judges to regulate their Courts of Law."[103] As we've seen, Scots who personally experienced Cromwell's ministrations saw things differently; but Bland's assessment was common in the later eighteenth century, and not just among the English. Nonetheless, most writers were wary of such indelicate methods. Dalrymple and Kames both cautioned Parliament against anglicizing Scots law too quickly. Instead, they suggested that British legal pluralism should be permitted to "decay by degrees"—helped along by reform-minded judges like Kames himself.[104]

EMPIRE WITHOUT DIFFERENCE

This interest in anglicizing Scots law reflected the period's prevailing confidence in the transformative power of institutions. Mainstream political thinkers insisted on both the universality and the malleability of human nature. "Mankind are undoubtedly the same in their natural State in every Climate, every Country, and every Age," the politician John Perceval wrote of efforts to abolish feudalism in Scotland. "It is their respective constitutions or different modes of government which create all the difference that can be found between one Nation and another."[105] Duncan Forbes, the most senior judge in Scotland, agreed: the Highlands were poor not because of any defect in the Highlanders themselves, but because they had been left in "possession of their own idle customs and extravagant maxims."[106] If bad laws were the problem, good laws were the cure. "[I]t must appear to every one that travells the Highlands, that the Laws lately made to civilize the People have already done so much that they will with proper Management become His Majesties loyal Subjects," one correspondent reported to Hardwicke in 1755.[107] Not everyone was as optimistic that Hardwicke's program would work.[108] But even skeptics of the "Scotch Reformation" nonetheless believed that English law could turn anyone—even a Highlander—into a reliable British subject.

This point is crucial for understanding Britain's approach to colonial law. One influential paradigm for thinking about empire has been "the rule of colonial difference," in which the power of colonial states depends on preserving "the alienness of the ruling group."[109] That framework can make legal pluralism seem inevitable, since uniform laws would have undermined the very distinctions that made empire possible.[110] But in the middle of the eighteenth century, the British state sought to eradicate difference, not to preserve it—just as earlier generations of officials had tried to do in Ireland, Wales, and New Netherland.[111]

The Hanoverian state's appetite for assimilation depended on the assumption that human nature was universal. In the nineteenth century, racial hierarchy would come to play a crucial, even defining role in structuring the British Empire. But in the eighteenth century, the racial attitudes that characterized the age of "high imperialism" hadn't coalesced. Britons used a variety of categories, including religion, culture, color, and ancestry, to define and evaluate different groups of people. But those classifications remained fluid and contested, and even writers who treated them as meaningful often viewed them as secondary to questions of politics, governance, and institutions. Indeed, as Jennifer Pitts has observed, the eighteenth century "stands out . . . as one of striking openness on the part of Europeans to the possibility of shared legal frameworks and mutual obligations" between different ethnic or religious groups.[112]

A striking example of this openness comes from a proposal for the gradual abolition of slavery, which Maurice Morgann prepared in 1765. Morgann was close to the heart of imperial policymaking. He had advised Lord Shelburne when the latter was president of the Board of Trade, and in 1766 Morgann would become an undersecretary in the Southern Department, with responsibility for its American business. In that capacity, he would play a key role in developing legal policy in Quebec. It's therefore worth taking a close look at his views about institutions and their relationship to human nature.[113]

Morgann began his essay by positing a "corporal distinction" between "whites and blacks." But this was only the product of exposure to different sorts of climates, he argued; and "both experience, and the nature of man, . . . forbid us to suppose that there is any original or essential difference in the mental part." This mix of mental similarity and physical difference presented an opportunity for Britain. Because Africans fared better than Europeans in hot climates, Morgann argued, Britain should turn over its southern colonies to free black subjects, who would occupy the same roles as their white counterparts to the north. This plan hinged on Morgann's assumption that shared institutions could unite the empire and, eventually, pave over racial differences. In the end, he predicted, white and black subjects "will talk the same language, read the same books, profess the same religion, *and be fashioned by the same laws.*" Eventually, the British Empire would become a vast coalition of colonies alike in everything but the appearance of their inhabitants.[114] Like Hardwicke's "Scotch Reformation," Morgann's proposal assumed that English institutions could transform anyone, anywhere, into "assimilated, productive, loyal Britons."[115] Morgann's faith in institutions was far from exceptional. If anything, the tight connection he drew between race and climate suggested a more rigid view of human nature than that held by many of his contemporaries, who were more optimistic about the possibility of acclimatization.[116]

This is not to deny the virulent racial thinking that had already emerged by Morgann's day. Slavery and African ancestry were already linked in many Britons' minds, and Morgann's very need to deny any "original or essential difference" between races indicates the existence of a contrary view. A few prominent writers, such as the Jamaican planter Edward Long and the philosopher David Hume, denied that Europeans and Africans even shared a common creation (*pace* the Book of Genesis). But one shouldn't exaggerate the contemporary importance of such views, which were usually treated as heretical—literally so in the case of polygenists, whose views were at odds with the orthodox Christian teaching that God had created a single human race.[117]

It's also important not to assume that prejudice based on color or non-European ancestry was uniquely powerful in the eighteenth century.[118] Long's outrageously racist depiction of enslaved Africans is shocking—but it also has much in common with Samuel Johnson's contemporary portrait of Scots, which emphasized both their backwardness and their capacity to be civilized by English law. Even in Jamaica, where the economy depended fundamentally on exploiting people of African descent, the legislature acknowledged the malleability of racial categories by selectively "whitening" mixed-race individuals with paternal ties to the planter elite. This frankly positivist approach to race began to fade in the 1780s; but only in the nineteenth century did empire come to be imagined primarily in terms of racial hierarchy. This isn't to say that the earlier racial paradigm was benign. It permitted slavery, among other evils; and it was marked less by a commitment to equality than by the absence of a firm commitment to racial inequality. But that absence was important, because it allowed Britons to imagine that new institutions might enable new political and social arrangements.[119]

Those new arrangements weren't always welcomed by their supposed beneficiaries. As we saw, some Scots protested Hardwicke's attempt to reform their institutions. Religious minorities had their own troubles with Britain's assimilative state. By the middle of the eighteenth century, British elites prided themselves on their broad-minded toleration of non-Anglican faiths.[120] But that meant little more than the absence of violent persecution. The Toleration Act of 1689, often hailed as a landmark of religious liberty, merely guaranteed freedom of worship to dissenting Protestants. Religious minorities of all kinds continued to endure civil disabilities, and the relative freedom that Catholics enjoyed by the late eighteenth century depended on the non-enforcement of harsh penal laws that remained on the books.[121] Although *Omichund* had illustrated the common law's willingness to accommodate non-Christians, that accommodation occurred on the common law's own terms. The British state showed little interest in acknowledging the laws of non-established religions, even for something as anodyne as the validity of a non-Anglican marriage.[122] This was the other side of Britain's confidence in the assimilative power of its institutions. Because anyone could be turned into a good British subject, there was little room for those who wanted something else. Britain did tend to respect the internal laws of Native American tribes—but only to the extent that Britain recognized them as distinct polities that retained at least some degree of sovereignty. Natives who lost control of territory tended to lose control of their law as well.[123]

John Locke's *Second Tract on Government*, written shortly after the Restoration, includes a fable meant to illustrate the power of custom. A Chinese city surrendered after a long siege. Its inhabitants agreed to surrender everything— "their wives, families, liberty, wealth, and in short all things sacred and profane." But when the conquerors ordered the vanquished "to cut off the plait of hair" that they wore "by national custom," they foreswore their surrender "and fought fiercely until, to a man, all were killed."[124]

For the young Locke, the moral of the story was to be skeptical about toleration: because religious and cultural idiosyncrasies were irrational, there was no reason to exempt them from the state's reach. Over time, he came to a somewhat more generous view of religious pluralism (although he still found Catholics intolerable).[125] But he never abandoned his assumption that conquerors would, and perhaps should, insist on uniformity when it came to law. Nearly thirty years later, in his *Two Treatises of Government*, Locke observed that it "seldom happens, that the Conquerors and Conquered never incorporate into one People, under the same Laws and Freedom."[126] Indeed, he seems to have concluded that religious toleration was less important than equality under the law. In a plan for Virginia he drafted in 1698, Locke urged "That a

Law be made, that all Negroes Children be baptized—catechized, and bred Christian." As Holly Brewer has shown, this proposal for religious compulsion was meant to facilitate legal equality between black and white Virginians at a time when English subjecthood was rooted in Christianity. Although Locke professed to favor "Lybertie of Conscience," he thought it more important that "people of all Nations be naturalized, and enjoy equal priviledges."[127]

About seventy years later, Edmund Burke also concluded that legal pluralism was both rare and undesirable. In an unfinished essay, Burke told the story of English legal history as a series of invasions. "The Anglo-Saxons came into England as conquerors," Burke wrote. "They brought their own customs with them; and doubtless did not take Laws from, but imposed theirs upon, the people they had vanquished." Although the conquerors made some alterations "suitable to the circumstances of their new settlement," their customs "were without question the same, for the greater part, they had observed before their migration." In time, Anglo-Saxon law also yielded to conquest—this time by the Normans, who introduced their own courts, land tenures, and legal language. Burke drew a normative lesson from this narrative: that assimilation was the best sequel to conquest.[128]

Locke and Burke reached these conclusions in the context of an empire that tried to extend English law to any territory it conquered. That effort didn't always succeed, but by the 1750s, British lawyers and politicians tended to see their efforts toward a global common law as effective. In those places where non-English law persisted, such as Minorca and Scotland, officials accepted the reality of legal pluralism while still trying to tame it. Yet even as Britain's official commitment to a unified imperial law flourished in practice, the seeds of the later turn to legal pluralism had already been planted.

CHAPTER 2

Experimenting with Law and Development

In 1771, a renegade Jesuit named Pierre Roubaud presented George III with a remarkable document: a letter written by the Marquis de Montcalm three weeks before his death in battle. In the letter, composed while British forces besieged Quebec in 1759, the French general contemplated the implications of his imminent defeat. He predicted that Britain's conquest of Canada would be disastrous for the victor. If Britain allowed Canadiens to keep "their religion, laws and language, their customs and ancient form of government," then it would have no trouble securing their loyalty. "[B]ut this is not the policy of Britain," Montcalm continued. "If the English make a conquest, they are sure to . . . introduce their own laws, customs, [and] modes of thinking." Britain failed to grasp that it was no easier to transplant its own laws abroad than "to transport the trees and fruits" of England to a foreign clime. As a result, Quebec would become useless and rebellious.[1]

As it turned out, the letter had been forged by Roubaud himself. But like other forgeries, it can tell us something about its audience. Roubaud expected his readers to nod along to "Montcalm's" predictions about British policy.[2] The Seven Years' War had increased the size and diversity of Britain's empire, but nobody thought that meant it would stop trying to anglicize its dominions. When the French governor of Canada surrendered to Britain, General Jeffery Amherst rejected his request that New France "continue to be governed according to the custom of Paris, and the Laws and usages established for this country." Amherst found it unthinkable that conquered colonists would retain alien laws. Canadiens were to "become Subjects of the King," Amherst explained, and that meant becoming subject to English law.[3] The Crown ratified Amherst's decision with the Proclamation of 1763, which provided that the colonies Britain had conquered from France would receive laws "as near as may be agreeable to the Laws of England."[4] The first instructions to Quebec's new governor and chief justice confirmed that English civil and criminal law would apply.[5]

The Proclamation also provided for English law in the other colonies Britain had acquired through the Treaty of Paris: the Floridas and Grenada (whose governor also supervised Dominica, St. Vincent, the Grenadines, and Tobago). In Grenada, unlike Quebec, the articles of capitulation had provided that French law would remain in place until Britain settled on a long-term policy. Grenadians—1,225 people of European descent, 455 free people of color, and 13,680 enslaved people on Grenada itself, plus a similar population on the other islands—didn't have to wait long. The colony's first British governor declared French laws void a few days after he arrived. From the start, officials sought "to render the civil Constitution of [the islands], as nearly as possible, similar to that of" other British colonies and "to check in their Infancy, all irregular and unnecessary deviations from the Laws and Constitution of the Mother Country."[6] That was easier said than done, especially because French law proved indispensable for sorting out titles to land.[7] But anglicization was the goal, as it had been a century earlier in New York.

Britain's new colonies received English law as refracted through earlier colonial experiences. Quebec's first laws were patterned on those of Nova Scotia, whose constitution was considered especially friendly to royal authority. The judiciaries of Wales, Ireland, Jersey, and other American colonies also served as models, as did some of the post-1745 reforms in Scotland. Grenada's laws tracked those of Barbados, while West and East Florida received the laws of Georgia. But although these colony-to-colony transplants gave Britain a head start in building new legal systems, important questions remained about how to adapt English law to new circumstances.[8]

This chapter describes two important examples of that project. First, Britain's new subjects were mostly Catholic and therefore subject to various disabilities under English law. Did "the laws of England" necessarily include those discriminatory provisions? The question implicated not only religious toleration but also the relationship between statute and common law. Were acts of Parliament (such as the Test and Corporation Acts) an integral part of English law or merely local regulations that might be discarded overseas? The same question arose for statutes related to credit and bankruptcy. Quebec was poorer than other British colonies, and its merchants debated what that meant for Quebec's laws. One group argued that English statutes governing bankruptcy and debt litigation were unsuited to an underdeveloped economy. Other merchants disagreed, insisting that only a near facsimile of English law would let Quebec catch up to the rest of the British Empire.

Although these disagreements sometimes grew heated, they assumed a shared commitment to a common imperial law. Starting in the 1760s, however, some policymakers started to question that commitment. In Illinois, General Thomas Gage and his allies tried to govern without any civil courts at all, using a program of state-backed arbitration to strengthen the power of local elites while deterring new settlement. Gage and like-minded politicians also explored a revival of feudalism in North America, which they hoped would ensure colonies' security and obedience. Together, these two experiments revealed a new interest in withholding English law to shape the political economies of Britain's wartime acquisitions.

CATHOLICISM AND COMMON LAW

John Pownall, secretary to the Board of Trade, had "no doubt" that Britain's new possessions should receive constitutions like those of other colonies. But he also warned that the former subjects of France and Spain weren't "in a capacity to receive the full Impression of [Britain's] free Constitution to its full Extent."[9] One obstacle was that they were Catholic and thus excluded by English law from office-holding and many other aspects of civic life. Although the Board of Trade assumed that the new colonies would attract Protestant settlers, it also hoped that existing inhabitants would remain. That meant Britain needed some way to accommodate their faith.

As Linda Colley and David Armitage have argued, prewar Britons had imagined their empire as fundamentally Protestant, obvious exceptions like Ireland notwithstanding.[10] By the 1760s, however, that paradigm had lost its purchase with many political elites. Anti-Catholic laws remained on the books, but it was unfashionable to enforce them too rigorously, and it had become easier to imagine Catholics as loyal British subjects. This was partly due to changes within Catholicism itself. During the eighteenth century, many upper-class British Catholics embraced a conciliarist theology that denied the pope's right to intervene in the temporal affairs of other countries. As a result,

British Catholics could more easily present themselves as devoted to their Protestant king. Their professions of loyalty gained credibility in 1766, when the Holy See declined to acknowledge Charles Edward Stuart, the Jacobite "Young Pretender," as Britain's lawful sovereign.[11] In light of these developments, Catholics no longer seemed worth persecuting. "The holy Representative of St. Peter, is no longer formidable in the Christian World; nor are the best Catholics Fools enough to transmit their Money to Rome," one newspaper asserted.[12] There was no need to fear "[t]he errors of a declining church," an anonymous pamphlet agreed.[13]

As Catholics became less frightening to the Protestant elite, some policymakers started to see them as demographic resources. William Knox, a prominent commentator on colonial affairs (and later colonial undersecretary), observed that Pennsylvania and Maryland had flourished because they attracted religious minorities who faced persecution elsewhere—a model that other colonies would do well to follow. The pamphleteer John Shebbeare argued that religious toleration "greatly accelerates [a colony's] improvement," so that "the American plantations . . . are quickly filled, without dispeopling the mother-country." And Malachy Postlethwayt, an influential political economist, argued that liberal naturalization policies promoted economic growth.[14] The connection between toleration and demographic expansion encouraged colonial officials to make their institutions friendly to Catholics in former French colonies. Breaking with practice in England, Grenada permitted Catholics to hold a limited number of official positions. In Quebec, Governor James Murray allowed Catholics to serve on juries.[15] Maurice Morgann, who visited Quebec on behalf of Lord Shelburne, suggested further modifications, like permitting Canadiens to practice as lawyers (Catholics in England and Ireland couldn't appear in court) and permitting "all legal Disputes between Canadian and Canadian" to "be carried on in the French tongue and decided by a French jury."[16] In 1766, the Board of Trade instructed Quebec's government to implement Morgann's suggestions.[17]

One shouldn't exaggerate the generosity of these accommodations. The Board of Trade thought it would be compatible with "a free exercise of the Religion of the Church of Rome," as required by the Treaty of Paris, to abolish or restrict entry to religious orders, to confiscate their property, and to use the proceeds to fund Protestant clergy.[18] And even this cramped and partial toleration produced a backlash. In 1764, the Protestant members of Quebec's grand jury complained that it was illegal to allow Catholics to be empaneled as jurors or to hold any office.[19] In Grenada, the conflict over Catholic toleration became even more intense. In 1766, self-described "British Protestants" petitioned Governor Robert Melvill against Catholics' participation in an upcoming election. Catholics counter-petitioned, asserting their new rights as British subjects. They received support from a group of Anglophones, who "argued that the 'adopted subjects' were entitled to the 'name and immunities of British Subjects' and should be allowed to vote."[20] Although Governor Melvill sided with the ultra-Protestant faction, the Privy Council admonished him for his anti-Catholic stance when news of the dispute reached England.[21]

The status of Grenadian Catholics also came to the Privy Council's attention via the case of *Scott v. Brebner* (1771), which presented the question of whether a Catholic mother could serve as guardian of her own daughter after the father's death. The Grenada court of chancery had denied custody, citing English statutes that disabled Catholics from acting as guardians. When the mother appealed that decision to the Privy Council, she forced it to confront the broader question about the application of penal laws in former French colonies.[22]

The Crown's law officers had already formed a consensus about the answer. In 1765, Attorney General Fletcher Norton and Solicitor General William de Grey gave their opinion that the penal laws didn't extend to colonies recently acquired from France. Two other opinions (given in 1767 and 1768) reached the same answer with respect to Grenada in particular. Another opinion, given by the law officers in 1768, reached the same conclusion for Canada.[23] The opinions of law officers, although less authoritative than judicial decisions, were usually treated with great respect, and it would have been uncontroversial for the Privy Council to follow their lead.[24] Curiously, however, the Privy Council's decision in *Scott* dodged the question of the penal laws' application in the colonies. Instead, it held that even *English* law wouldn't deprive a mother of the guardianship of her child on religious grounds. The opinion was never published, and we only have a one-paragraph summary from a lawyer present at the hearing. But the case apparently ignored the law officers' analysis. Nor did the Privy Council engage with cases such as *Rex v. Vaughan* (1769), in which Lord Mansfield had articulated a presumption against the colonial application of parliamentary statutes.[25]

In short, the Privy Council elected to expound a new rule of English law, rather than to ride the growing consensus that certain statutes didn't apply overseas. That choice has puzzled historians. Joseph H. Smith attributed it to ignorance or incompetence and described the resulting opinion as "untenable and patently nonlegalistic." Mary Sarah Bilder has offered a more charitable reading, suggesting that the opinion "reveals the degree to which the appeals were decided under a constitutional jurisprudence that differed from common law," and in which considerations of "justice" and "sound policy" played a larger role than in domestic cases.[26] Neither interpretation is entirely satisfying. The opinion's probable author, Sir John Eardley Wilmot, was the former chief justice of Common Pleas. His colleagues respected his legal abilities, including on colonial matters. (Blackstone asked him for feedback on his *Commentaries,* and Mansfield asked him to help correct his early opinions).[27] Moreover, the appellant in *Scott* had been represented by two leading barristers, Alexander Wedderburn and John Dunning, who were themselves experts in colonial law. Their brief actually raised both arguments considered here: that English law didn't take children away from their mothers; and that penal laws had limited force in the colonies.[28]

Scott, then, reflected a deliberate choice, not ignorance of earlier authority. Bilder's distinction between "common law jurisprudence" and a more policy-oriented Privy Council is more convincing, but it also seems incomplete. It's true that *Scott* was a politically sensitive case: the dispute had attracted the attention of French diplomats (who complained that Grenadian courts had violated the Treaty of Paris) and the British secretary of state; and the issues it raised had far-reaching implications for imperial governance.[29] But common-law cases often have political implications, and prudential considerations weren't alien to common-law reasoning. At the same time, Privy Counsellors often looked to common-law precedents for guidance.[30] To be sure, the Privy Council wasn't an ordinary court like King's Bench and Common Pleas, and it had to weigh different considerations in making its judgments. But there was no reason why Wilmot couldn't have drawn on common-law principles limiting the extraterritorial application of statutes—particularly when those principles would have led to the same conclusion he ultimately reached.

We might instead explain *Scott* as an attempt to avoid a sensitive constitutional question. By the time the case was decided, the crudest forms of religious discrimination had fallen out of favor with elite lawyers in London.[31] Few of Wilmot's colleagues on the bench or at the bar would have objected to an opinion that narrowed the legal disabilities of Catholics. Nor would his reliance on considerations of "justice and sound policy" have been surprising.[32] The same approach had been apparent in *Omichund v. Barker,* in which the judges had similarly used principles of "natural justice" to make English law more welcoming to non-Protestants.[33] But if Wilmot had elected to focus on the colonial application of parliamentary statutes, he would have waded into an increasingly controversial area. Although there was a growing consensus that anti-Catholic laws didn't extend to the colonies, the application of British legislation to North America had become a politically fraught topic, and Wilmot might have wanted to avoid raising any doubts about Parliament's capacity to legislate overseas.[34]

Whatever Wilmot's motivation, *Scott* did little to quell the political battles over toleration in Grenada. Anti-Catholic activists continued to resist the inclusion of Catholics in the island's political life, and governors twice had to suspend Protestant council members who refused to sit alongside Catholics. Grenada's government essentially shut down between 1768 and 1774, as hard-line Protestants boycotted the legislature and refused to pay taxes. Local judges, who were less enthusiastically tolerant than their English counterparts, supported the dissidents, who framed their resistance to toleration as a battle for the English constitution. (One of those judges was the brother of John Wilkes.)[35]

The dissidents were right insofar as the battle over religious toleration in Grenada was in part a debate about what it meant to apply English law. For ultra-Protestant colonists, English law meant the strict application of English statutes—all of them. Wilmot agreed with colonists that Grenada's law had to be English, but he disagreed about that law's content. Other elite lawyers—including Mansfield, Yorke, and de Grey—took a different approach, depicting statutes as local regulations that need not travel with the more cosmopolitan common law. Importantly, however, none of these perspectives imagined Grenada outside of English law.

DEBT AND BANKRUPTCY

Questions about the nature of English law also emerged in the less obviously divisive field of commercial litigation. Quebec's Francophone inhabitants were mostly willing to accept English commercial law, as Chapter 3 will show. Nonetheless, they had two objections to the English approach to debt litigation. First, they complained that English procedure was too expensive for a relatively poor colony like Quebec. Second, they were stunned by the practice of arresting a debtor on mesne process—at the outset of litigation, before the case had reached judgment—which struck Canadiens as unnecessarily harsh. Officials in Quebec and London responded by crafting a "gentler method of proceeding," which allowed for the distraint of debtors' goods but not their bodies. Francis Maseres, the attorney general of Quebec, defended this concession to local sensibilities by appealing to English legal history. Although arrest for debt was ubiquitous in *contemporary* English practice, he argued, it was "not agreeable to the mildness of the *antient* law of England."[36] Quebec's law could diverge from the law of England—but only in a way that made it even more authentically English than England itself. Maseres also responded to Canadien concerns about the cost of litigation. Together with William Hey, Quebec's chief justice, and Charles Yorke, England's attorney general, Maseres designed a summary procedure for small-debt litigation based on existing practices in Ireland and Barbados. In adapting English law to local concerns, imperial officials tended to draw on their own empire's institutional repertoire, rather than the laws of the people they had conquered.[37]

Quebec's relative poverty also caused problems with another area of law: bankruptcy. Bankruptcy was a particularly contentious area of law in the eighteenth century, even within England. Blackstone praised England's bankruptcy laws as "highly convenient" for "a great commercial people," but Mansfield thought they "had done more harm than good."[38] Although many merchants found bankruptcy law useful, they also criticized its procedures as cumbersome and its substantive provisions as overly harsh. (It was a capital offense, for instance, for a bankrupt to refuse to give information to bankruptcy commissioners.)[39] Unsurprisingly, then, merchants trading in Quebec disagreed about whether English bankruptcy laws would benefit the colony.

That question arose after the collapse of a firm known as Gershon Levy and Company. In 1763, the Montreal-based partnership suffered severe losses as a result of Pontiac's War (1763–65). In November 1767, the partners (joined by Isaac Levi, one of their creditors) petitioned Governor Guy Carleton for relief. Specifically, they asked Carleton and the legislative council "to pass a particular ordinance, in the nature of a private act of Parliament," to appoint commissioners "to execute the laws and statutes of England relating to bankrupts" for the insolvent partnership.[40]

The petition divided Quebec's merchant community. One group of eighteen British merchants—including many of Gershon Levy's creditors—presented a counter-petition against the introduction of an English bankruptcy regime. Their chief argument was that it would hurt the colony's already fragile ability to attract investment from England. "The credit of this Province with the Mother Country is now unhappily upon no very good footing," the counter-petitioners explained; "but [bankruptcy] Acts must make it infinitely worse; for an European merchant will scarcely trust his Goods to Quebec when he knows that his Correspondent can at any time be made a Bankrupt, if he owes to any person on the Spot one Hundred Pounds."[41] On its face, English bankruptcy law seemed friendly to creditors, who were the only parties able to initiate bankruptcy proceedings. But the case of Gershon Levy showed how an insolvent firm might be able to invoke that law if it convinced even a single creditor to cooperate. The possibility of such collusion led some merchants to worry that English bankruptcy laws would be "too indulgent to debtors to be useful in" Quebec.[42]

According to the counter-petitioners, Quebec needed a distinctive credit regime because it lacked England's strong commercial culture. "Business here we are sorry to say is not so punctually carried on as it is in England," those merchants explained. Introducing English bankruptcy laws would only slow the process of Canadiens learning to trade like Britons. This was not simply a case of anti-French chauvinism: as the counter-petitioners stressed, Scotland, Ireland, and most other North American colonies also lacked English-style bankruptcy legislation. A brief attempt to introduce bankruptcy legislation in Boston, the merchants claimed, had ended in disaster, and Bostonians "to this day feel its bad Effects."[43] Indeed, the counter-petitioners seem to have been expressing a point of view that was shared across the empire. A decade earlier, the lord president of the Court of Session had made a similar judgment about Scotland. Although he generally bemoaned the "Diversity of the Laws of England & Scotland," he made an exception when it came to bankruptcy. Extending English bankruptcy laws there, he thought, "would be the occasion of many frauds that no act of Parliament could prevent." Only when Scotland and England had more similar economies would they be able to share the same commercial institutions.[44]

Not everyone accepted this sort of analysis, and a second group of merchants wrote to Carleton in support of introducing English bankruptcy laws. "[T]he introducing and inforcing here the Laws of England relating to Bankrupts will be very beneficial to the Trade of this Province," these twenty-two Montreal merchants argued, because those laws would make it *easier* to get credit from England.[45] This second group had the support of Attorney General Maseres, who had advised Gershon Levy to petition for bankruptcy relief in the first place. In a letter to a London barrister, he expressed surprise at "the opposition made by a great number of the merchants to the introducing the use of the bankrupt laws," which seemed to him "to be very wise and beneficial *as well as to be in force*."[46] In Maseres's view, the bankruptcy act had already been introduced with the Proclamation of 1763, and Quebec's traders ought to have acted accordingly. (He was wrong about that; the Privy Council had held repeatedly that England's bankruptcy statutes didn't bind the colonies.)[47]

In the months that followed, the debate about bankruptcy laws moved into the pages of the *Quebec Gazette,* where the opposing groups of merchants advanced different conceptions of what it meant for English law to apply. The key question was whether Canadian law should mirror all of English law—including its statutes—or only the common law. The group favoring bankruptcy laws believed that Quebec would thrive if its laws differed as little as possible from England's. Their opponents, in contrast, emphasized the primacy of a universal common law, which statutes might modify in response to local needs. While it was "undoubtedly clear law, that Englishmen carry the laws [of England] with them wheresoever they go," the anti-bankruptcy group argued, those laws included only what was necessary to protect "their Lives, Liberty, or Property." In other words, the law that applied throughout the empire was "the common Law of England," which was "the only clear Rule and Direction, for the Protection of our Civil Rights and Properties." Statutes, in contrast, were "a Labyrinth" as likely to destroy common-law protections as to improve them. Legislation was essentially local.[48]

In the end, Governor Carleton and Lord Hillsborough, the colonial secretary, sided with the merchants who opposed bankruptcy laws.[49] As we will see in the next chapter, their decision was motivated partly by doubts about the wisdom of applying *any* English law to Quebec. In the short term, however, it reinforced the notion that Britain's empire ought to share a universal common law, tempered by a statutory regime that acknowledged the different conditions of England and its colonies.

ANOTHER VISION OF EMPIRE

The Quebec bankruptcy debate was about means, not ends. Both sides wanted to commercialize Quebec's society and to connect its merchants to English capital. But by the late 1760s, some policymakers had started to doubt whether commercialization and imperial integration were desirable. In the decade after the Treaty of Paris, a growing number of politicians began to champion an alternative model of colonial development. Instead of assuming that colonial societies would (or should) converge on something resembling England or its older American colonies, proponents of this new model emphasized the need to keep colonies different. The rest of this chapter will describe the origins of that alternative vision of empire, as well as some early attempts to put it into practice.

British politics experienced a profound transformation between the start of the Seven Years' War and the end of the American Revolution. From the Exclusion Crisis of the 1670s to the Hanoverian succession in 1714, politics had revolved primarily around the conflict between Whigs and Tories. But when George I acceded to the throne, he proscribed Tories from office, and Britain became a one-party state. Whigs consolidated their power under the premiership of Robert Walpole. Between 1721 and 1756, Walpole and his successors, Henry Pelham and his brother, Thomas Pelham-Holles, first Duke of Newcastle, managed an oligarchic party establishment that was remarkably durable, especially compared to the civil war and revolution of the previous century.[50]

The Whig oligarchy didn't go unchallenged. A dissident "Patriot" movement emerged almost as soon as Walpole came to power. Patriotism's priorities changed over time (and varied among individual adherents), but it generally sought to cure the corruption that it diagnosed as afflicting the British Empire in general and the Whig oligarchy in particular. The Walpole-Pelham establishment, Patriots argued, had achieved stability in England only by suppressing civil liberties and mistreating the rest of the empire. The Patriots' proposed solution for this imperial malaise included a new focus on the colonies, the reinvigoration of England's ancient legal institutions, and greater opportunities for political participation throughout the empire.[51] During the 1750s, Patriotism gained strength, and by the end of the Seven Years' War, the Whig supremacy had met its end. One crucial blow was the rise of William Pitt, who in 1756 began the first of several stints as joint or sole head of the government. Although Pitt sometimes worked alongside establishment leaders like Newcastle, he was widely seen as a Patriot outsider whose inclusion in government marked a new political era. The accession of George III in 1760 sealed the tomb of the old system. The new monarch abandoned his predecessors' preference for Whigs and presented himself instead as a king "above party" who welcomed Tories into office.[52]

The result was a reshuffling of partisan politics. The Patriot movement fragmented now that it no longer had the Whig establishment as a common enemy. Some of its members evolved into the group that this book calls populists, who continued Patriots' focus on colonial development. Other Patriots joined the group this book calls paternalists. Paternalists endorsed the old Patriot diagnosis that Whig rule had left Britain morally exhausted, economically precarious, and politically unstable. But their proposed cure was quite different. Instead of broadening opportunities for political participation, as Patriots and populists wanted, paternalists sought a restoration of hierarchy, both within English society and between Britain and its colonies. One such figure was George Grenville, who worried that Pitt's style of government had plunged the nation into debt and disarray. Although Grenville and Pitt were allies in the 1740s, Grenville broke away from the Patriots during the Seven Years' War in order to fight the prevailing "spirit of licence and disorder," which "demand[ed] the strictest union in all who wish to put a stop to an evil that threatens equally the King and his people."[53]

Other paternalists were refugees from the old Whig oligarchy. These included William Murray, who became the first Earl of Mansfield. Although Mansfield was born into a prominent Scottish Jacobite family, he pointedly declared his fealty to the Whig establishment while a student at Oxford in the 1720s. Some of his contemporaries suspected that his conversion to Hanoverian orthodoxy was opportunistic, but by the 1740s he was to all appearances a true believer. The regime rewarded him for his loyalty, naming him solicitor general, attorney general, and, in 1756, chief justice of King's Bench. During the 1750s, he remained close to mainstream Whig figures, particularly Newcastle, who depended on Mansfield for political advice. During the Seven Years' War, however, Mansfield became increasingly concerned about imperial and popular disorder, the taming of which became one of his political priorities.[54] Alexander Wedderburn, though younger than Mansfield, was another Whig lawyer who migrated toward paternalism.[55] Still other paternalists were old-school Tories, who brought into the new movement their longstanding concern for loyalty and obedience.[56]

The diversity of the paternalist coalition meant that its members didn't agree about everything. But they were united in their conviction that Britain needed to strengthen its control over its colonies. General Thomas Gage summed up this attitude shortly after he was appointed governor of Massachusetts. "My Reception at Boston . . . was very ceremonious," he wrote to a military colleague, "but I should like less Ceremony, and more Submission, much better."[57] How to achieve that submission was a harder question. Brute force had limited potential. As Sarah Kinkel has shown, the Royal Navy played an important role in projecting the will of the imperial state.[58] But the navy's guns could only reach so far inland, and soldiers were too few (and too expensive) to police the entire American continent. Accordingly, many paternalists came to believe that colonial obedience would require new imperial institutions.

Paternalists' focus on colonial dependence led them to question the longstanding assumption that colonial laws ought to be patterned on the laws of England. Divergence between Britain and its colonies, long accepted as a ne-

"I should like less Ceremony, and more Submission, much better." General Thomas Gage (c. 1768), by John Singleton Copley. Courtesy of the Yale Center for British Art, Paul Mellon Collection. Acc. no. B1977.14.45.

cessity, came to be seen as a positive good. Robert Orme, the East India Company's first official historiographer (and Robert Clive's close friend), reached that conclusion as he reflected on Montesquieu's history of ancient Rome. "[T]he original cause of the Decadence of the Roman Empire," Orme gathered from his reading, was its promiscuous extension of Roman citizenship to its allies in 90 B.C. In the wake of the Stamp Act's repeal, Orme wondered whether Britain was taking a similar path by adopting an overly inclusive attitude to colonial subjecthood. Only "Time and future Events" would tell.[59] But this much was clear: Rome had thrived when its subjects preserved their "ancient usages"; the universalization of Roman law had led to anarchy and decay.[60]

Detail from Anonymous, *The Closet* (January 28, 1778). Courtesy of the Metropolitan Museum of Art. Gift of William H. Huntington, 1883. Acc. no. 83.2.1030. Lord Mansfield holds "A Code of Laws for America" while warning, "Kill them or they will Kill you." The comment paraphrases a remark he made in the House of Lords on December 20, 1775. See *PH*, 18:1100–1103.

Although Orme (and Montesquieu) focused on political institutions, many paternalists thought the fundamental danger to the empire was economic—specifically, colonial economic independence. Starting in the mid-1760s, colonists used boycotts to protest new taxes. Although the boycotts had only a limited impact on Britain's economy, they alerted paternalists to the connection between colonies' economic self-sufficiency and their capacity to resist imperial control. In response, paternalists made it a priority to block Americans' efforts to "manufacture for themselves." "Surely . . . the people in England can never be such dupes to believe that the Americans have traded with them so long out of pure Love, and Brotherly Affection," Gage wrote to Lord Barrington, the secretary at war. "The disposition the Americans have shown, I think shou'd teach . . . one instructive lesson, which is to keep them weak as long as we can, and avoid every thing that can contribute to make them powerfull." Colonial manufacturing, he feared, would aid Americans' "struggle for independency" by enabling them "to lessen their Imports from Britain."[61] The Stamp Act boycotts had failed partly because they proved burdensome to the colonists themselves. The outcome might have been different if Americans had truly been in a position to make their own substitutes for British goods. Lord Mansfield agreed: once colonists began manufacturing, he asked, "what then will become of us?"[62]

This was not simply a case of protecting metropolitan producers from colonial competition. The primary concern was political, not economic.[63] Edmund Burke, a critic of the paternalist approach, summarized it well: "[A]ny Growth of the Colonies, which might make them grow out of the Reach of the authority of this Kingdom, ought to be accounted rather a morbid Fulness than a sound & proper Habit."[64]

Withholding English law was the key to paternalists' plan to constrain colonial economies. Since the early seventeenth century, policymakers had associated English law with colonial growth. The Virginia Company, for example, had learned that it was easier to recruit settlers by promising them English law rather than martial law.[65] In the 1760s, paternalists flipped that insight on its head. By denying English law, or at least certain features of it, paternalists might usefully hinder a colony's development. The Illinois Country was an early proving ground for this approach.

GOVERNING THROUGH ARBITRATION

The Illinois Country—the vaguely defined region south of Quebec, northwest of the Ohio River, and east of the Mississippi River—was an early exception to Britain's policy of transplanting English law. Because the Proclamation of 1763 had forbidden European settlement in the region, imperial officials saw no need to create any legal system at all. But some 1,500 former French subjects remained in Illinois, mostly in villages on the eastern bank of the Mississippi River, and some British traders had moved in despite the Proclamation. At first, imperial officials hoped "the Inhabitants of the Illinois Country" would "remove into the Province of Quebec, that of West Florida, or any other of the settled Colonies."[66] But officials eventually gave up that hope. "I have always thought . . . that the thing most to be wished for in respect to the Illinois District would be the Removal of the Inhabitants," Hillsborough confided to General Gage in 1771; "but I fear there are too many obstacles to such a Measure."[67] If Britain couldn't drive its subjects from Illinois, it would need to govern them.

For Hillsborough and Gage, the challenge was to find a legal system that would keep order without making Illinois too inviting. British colonists had been interested in settling the region for decades, and the eviction of French forces from Canada made it even more attractive. Many proponents of settlement were investors with an obvious financial stake; but they also argued that a new colony in Illinois would have public benefits. It could be a useful buffer against Spanish or indigenous attacks. In its early days, it would provide raw materials, such as fur, flax, and military stores, to the rest of the British Empire.

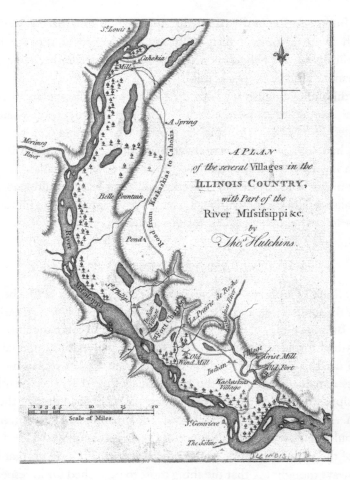

Thomas Hutchins, "A plan of the several villages in the Illinois Country, with part of the River Mississippi &c." (c. 1778). Courtesy of New York Public Library Digital Collections.

Later, as its population grew larger and wealthier, it would provide a valuable market for British exports. The best way to achieve these aims, Illinois's proponents argued, was to establish a civil government "agreeable to the Principles of an English Constitution," which would attract settlers and investment.[68]

Paternalists were skeptical. They acknowledged the security advantages of a frontier colony, as well as the risk that France or Spain might exploit Britain's absence from the region.[69] In 1764, Attorney General Fletcher Norton declared it "a matter of the highest Importance" that former French and Spanish territories be settled, preferably by foreign Protestants recruited for the purpose, in order to prevent a power vacuum.[70] But paternalists also worried that Illinois's geographic isolation would make it ungovernable and economically useless. Because it lacked easy access to the sea, it would be unable to send raw materials cheaply to Britain or to buy many British goods. As a result, it would have to trade with other North American colonies rather than the mother country. The lack of close economic ties with Britain would eventually inspire fantasies of political independence.[71] Thus, even if the speculators were right about Illinois's economic potential, that was "a very strong argument *against* forming settlements in the interior country." Furthermore, a successful colony in the American interior would sap population from the eastern colonies, where they could more usefully participate in the Atlantic economy—and could be more easily controlled.[72] Finally, some officials worried that a new colony in Illinois would unnecessarily risk war with indigenous peoples. Even Britain's limited incursions into the region had been enough to provoke Pontiac's War, a costly stalemate that led officials to appreciate the limits of British military power in the area.[73]

While metropolitan officials debated Illinois's future, its day-to-day governance fell to the army, which happened to be led by two paternalists: General Thomas Gage, the commander in chief of North American forces, and Lord Barrington, the secretary at war. Gage and Barrington agreed that Illinois shouldn't be settled. They also agreed that it wouldn't work simply to forbid Britons from moving there. The Proclamation of 1763 had tried that approach and had managed only to annoy colonists without halting their westward migration.[74] Accordingly, Gage and Barrington decided to make the region unattractive by leaving it undergoverned.

Gage understood that most colonists didn't want to settle a wilderness (contrary to popular stereotypes of the pioneer spirit). Instead, they wanted to enjoy the same institutions that had allowed other colonies to thrive. "[T]he Establishment of a regular Government at the Ilinois, would be the most hurtfull of any, as it would tend to increase a Settlement, that it's more for our Interest to annihilate," Gage wrote.[75] Barrington agreed. Regular courts were necessary for other colonies "because without them Englishmen would not settle in the Country & make it populous & flourishing." But because "the interior parts of America ought to be a Desert, & all British Settlement discouraged," it would be better to have "no species of Civil Government whatever."[76] Gage proceeded accordingly. At first, he not only declined to establish a civilian government in Illinois, but also sabotaged what remained of the old

French system. He ordered Captain Thomas Sterling, Illinois's first British commander, to "allow no French judges to remain" in the country, thus ensuring that colonists wouldn't be able to rely on older forms of justice. But Gage also insisted that Sterling "make no alteration" in the area's form of government, "further than what the King's Service may absolutely require."[77] In other words, Sterling was to do nothing for civil justice except to expel anyone who knew anything about it.

As it became clear that the rest of Illinois's inhabitants weren't going to leave, Gage realized he needed to provide some kind of legal system. He also realized that his initial plan—martial law—was unconstitutional as a long-term solution.[78] He accordingly sought to find a form of civilian government that would allow for Illinois's residents to settle their differences, but not so efficiently as to make the territory attractive to potential settlers. His solution was for the residents of Illinois to govern themselves through state-sponsored arbitration. "When disputes happen between the Inhabitants," he instructed the local commander in 1767, "assemble arbitrators from amongst themselves of the best Characters, and let their differences be decided by Arbitration according to their own Customs."[79]

Arbitration seemed to satisfy all of Gage's requirements. It had a long history in English law, so nobody could accuse him of ruling unconstitutionally. It didn't require lawyers—convenient, since there weren't any—or indeed any paid personnel at all. It would also reinforce the authority of local elites (who would serve as arbitrators) and British military commanders (who would appoint umpires in cases about which the arbitrators couldn't agree).[80] Unlike litigation, which stirred up "Dirt, Invectives, Law and Indecencies," arbitration would reflect and reinforce the hierarchies that Gage wanted to defend.[81]

His enthusiasm for arbitration was rooted in paternalists' more general ambivalence about litigation. During the 1760s, paternalist officials across the British Empire became disgusted with what they perceived as an explosion of lawsuits. This was most evident among military officers, who often faced personal liability for activities they performed in their official capacities. But even some paternalist lawyers complained about "that Litigation . . . which is already a Disgrace to the Country," as Lord Mansfield later put it.[82] In Quebec, Governor Guy Carleton hoped that a reformed legal system might encourage amicable settlements and cease "forcing [Canadians] to litigate, what, if left to themselves, might have been easily accommodated."[83] As Chapter 4 will show, East India Company officials in Bengal made similar comments.

But Gage's arbitration scheme was also directed at Illinois's economy. At least since the seventeenth century, political economists had understood that economic growth required a functional court system. Merchants preferred to settle their differences through arbitration; but at least in the 1760s, arbitration itself often depended on state support.[84] The Stamp Act crisis drove this lesson home. When Parliament decided in 1765 to tax legal documents in the colonies, Americans responded by boycotting courts. The results were disastrous. One Virginia merchant lamented that court closures had left the colonies "entirely without law" and mired in "anarchy and confusion."[85] In Philadelphia, business partners pondered "the many Mischiefs that will attend us" until the courts reopened; meanwhile, they feared, "we know not whose Lot it may be to be ruin'd."[86] Edmund Burke, writing from London in 1768, remembered the recently repealed Stamp Act as causing "an universal stop to the course of justice."[87] The Stamp Act crisis was important for many reasons. But for many observers in the British Atlantic, one of its central lessons was that one couldn't trade on arbitration alone.

Illinois's inhabitants understood as much, and they continued to demand ordinary courts, much to Gage's frustration.[88] Despite his instructions, one local commander, John Wilkins, did try to introduce English law in 1768, or at least as much of it as he thought possible in a colony empty of lawyers. The experiment failed, thanks partly to Gage's lack of support.[89] Eventually, the settlers' persistence persuaded imperial officials that Illinois needed more robust legal institutions.[90] In response, Gage offered various compromises, such as a hybrid civil-military administration, that sought to assuage local concerns without rising to the level of an ordinary civil government. In 1772, he suggested a more formal version of his arbitration scheme, in which the local military commander would appoint a "certain number of the most respectable Inhabitants . . . as Magistrates" and empower them "to determine Disputes and Differences that frequently arise amongst the People according to their own Laws and Customs," with a right of appeal to the commander.[91] When that proved unsatisfactory, Gage asked Illinois's inhabitants to offer a suggestion of their own. They responded by demanding a civil government modeled on that of "les autres Colonies Anglaises"—and, specifically, that of Connecticut, which they deemed to have the most republican constitution in North America.[92]

This led to a stalemate: Gage was unwilling to create a New England–style government, and the inhabitants of Illinois refused to accept anything less. (Of course, Illinois's institutional limbo suited Gage's purposes just fine.)[93] Illinois remained without a formal government until 1774, when the Quebec

Act placed the region under French law—to the dismay of its inhabitants. Their wish for an English-style government was only fulfilled during the Revolutionary War (and then only partially), when George Rogers Clark seized Illinois in the name of the Republic of Virginia. One of his first official acts was to establish a civil judicial system.[94]

NEOGOTHIC COLONIAL LAW

One reason that Gage wanted to govern through arbitration was to confirm the power of local elites. The same impulse motivated another paternalist proposal: introducing feudal tenures to North America. In 1766, just before Gage started to encourage arbitration in Illinois, he suggested that the area might be settled by "establishing a Military Government, and granting Lands on Military Tenure."[95] This plan promised the security advantages of a frontier settlement without the political or economic challenges that might arise if Illinois were to have a government modeled on one of the eastern colonies. It was only after ministers in London rejected this suggestion that he turned to arbitration.

Like his encouragement of arbitration, Gage's "Military Government" reflected broader intellectual trends. In the seventeenth century, English lawyers had discovered (some historians would say invented) the "feudal" roots of England's "ancient constitution." By the 1760s, it had become routine to insist that English law was impossible to understand without looking back to its medieval foundations—a conclusion boosted by the first generation of academic common lawyers, who put feudal law at the center of English legal history.[96] But those same lawyers also insisted that Britain had happily moved beyond feudalism. Starting with the abolition of feudal tenures in the seventeenth century, England had shaken off the outdated elements of medieval law and entered a modern commercial age.[97]

It was no accident, according to this narrative, that the part of Britain that had remained the most feudal—the Scottish Highlands—was also the most backward. Specifically, commentators pointed to the enduring connections in Scotland between land ownership and the administration of justice and between property and personal loyalty, both of which had delayed Scotland's development and endangered Britain as a whole. As Chapter 1 showed, Whigs like Lord Hardwicke presented the abolition of feudal tenures as an essential step for ensuring Scotland's political integration with the rest of Britain. Later commentators agreed. Sir Robert Chambers, Blackstone's successor as Viner-

Lord Egmont's home, Enmore Castle. From W. Watts, *The Seats of the Nobility and Gentry* (Chelsea: W. Watts, 1779–86). Courtesy of Wikimedia Commons.

ian professor at Oxford, praised Scotland's "deliverance from the oppression of old feudal establishments, and of incommodious and vexatious tenures." Through these reforms, he told his students, "Scotland gained an immediate admission" to English commerce, while England had secured a more perfect union with its northern neighbor. Feudalism seemed so obviously backward, and its elimination so obviously progressive, that Granville Sharp invoked it in his campaign to abolish slavery. The *"distinction of Persons"* inherent in slavery, Sharp argued, mirrored "[t]he intolerable Burthen of the Feudal Tenures."[98]

Yet even as many Britons celebrated the demise of feudalism, some paternalists were plotting its revival. Between 1763 and 1765, John Perceval, second Earl of Egmont, wrote a series of memorials urging Britain to create a feudal regime in North America. Historians have tended to dismiss Egmont's interest in feudalism as an inconsequential eccentricity. The instinct is understandable. In the 1750s, he built a moated castle in Somerset, complete with a working drawbridge and defensive "spike holes." Even Horace Walpole, who had built his own Gothic Revival villa, mocked Egmont for preparing to defend his home "with cross-bows and arrows." But when Walpole ridiculed Egmont for being "smitten with the exploded usages of barbarous times," he wasn't laughing because his ideas were irrelevant. Instead, he was trying to marginalize what he feared to be a plausible effort to reintroduce feudal principles into colonial government.[99]

Egmont was First Lord of the Admiralty and a member of the cabinet, not some marginal crank, and his promotion of feudalism reflected a considered policy position. In the 1740s, he had held the orthodox Whig position that feudalism was bad. "The nation growned under grievous oppression, were agitated with Storms of Faction, and crippled in their Trade and Liberty, to the most apparent detriment," he had said of feudal England. "Nor did perfect Freedom and Industry ever flourish here till the Powers of the Great Subjects were destroyed & the feodal Tenures utterly abolished." He made those statements in the course of supporting Hardwicke's efforts to abolish feudal tenures and heritable jurisdictions in Scotland.[100]

By the 1760s, however, Egmont had come to believe that the destruction of feudalism had been a "fatal excess of Reformation," and that that institution might be useful for governing Britain's postwar empire. If Britain settled its new American colonies just a little more densely than England, he calculated, they could "maintain 320 millions of People—probably more than now exist upon the face of the whole habitable Earth." But "if this vast Territory should be settled upon the loose Improvident Principles upon which the other Parts of our American dominions have been settled," it would soon face the same problems as the older American colonies—namely, "Pursuits of Commerce indulged upon Views of Private Gain, Principles of Government totally Neglected . . . Licentiousness, Leveling Notions, Anarchy, & Insolence to all Authority from Hence." Ultimately, the bad example and commercial wealth generated by these new colonies would rebound on the mother country, so that "the popular, mercantile, & moneyed Interests headed by Factious Leaders in Great Britain will render the present monarchical Constitution impossible to be maintain'd." In other words, if Britain failed to settle North America properly, the entire empire would collapse. These concerns led Egmont to conclude that the new colonies needed a system of government that would preserve "constitutional order, subordination & dependence upon the Crown." In keeping with longstanding British tradition, he remained adamant that this government contain "nothing materially repugnant to the Antient or Modern Constitution of England." Accordingly, he proposed reviving the ancient English institution of feudal law.[101]

Egmont began his proposal by arguing that early medieval Europe had looked a lot like eighteenth-century North America: underpopulated and unstable. Feudalism had managed to make medieval Europe thriving and orderly. "Experience has shown its Efficacy," Egmont wrote, "and History can shew no Instance of the like, in any Human Institution for the same Purpose." The success of feudalism had depended on two "fundamental principles": that political power derived from owning land (which was held ultimately from the king); and that landowners were responsible for administering justice in manor courts. Anyone without sufficient land to hold a manor court would have no role in governance. In short, feudal systems linked governance, property, and loyalty.[102]

Although Egmont drew inspiration from the Middle Ages, he tailored his proposal to reflect the concerns of his own day. He proposed that litigants at manor courts have access to trials by jury—a necessary protection for their civil rights, he argued, since they would have no other political power. In addition, he presented feudalism as the ideal way to integrate Britain's newly diverse empire. Feudalism, in his telling, had given medieval rulers a framework for conquering new subjects without oppressing them. He acknowledged that medieval warlords had sometimes made a sharp distinction between the conqueror and the conquered. But these were "abuses . . . of the feodal System," which feudalism itself eventually eliminated. Properly understood, feudalism offered the best chance to assimilate and unify colonial subjects.[103]

Egmont tried to make these speculations a reality on the Island of St. John (now Prince Edward Island). Backed by a syndicate of merchants, politicians, and military officers, he petitioned in 1764 for land grants that would divide the island into manors. Although the Crown rejected his first proposal, Egmont and his allies continued to press for a feudal colony on St. John's until 1767. In part, its eventual failure was the product of politics. Not everyone shared Egmont's enthusiasm for militarized and subordinate colonies; populists, in particular, had very different ideas about colonial development. There were also doubts about whether the king could lawfully grant Egmont's petition. As Attorney General Charles Yorke and Solicitor General William de Grey observed, the king had authority to grant lands only under forms "not repugnant to the Statute and Common Law of this Kingdom." Unfortunately for Egmont, Yorke and de Grey interpreted that restriction as referring to *contemporary* English law; and Parliament had abolished feudal tenures in the seventeenth century. Yorke and de Grey acknowledged that colonial constitutions "have considerably varied from time to time as the Circumstances of this Nation . . . have required." But they stressed that these differences represented "different modes of settlement in Practice and Policy," not differences "*in Law.*"[104] It was one thing for a colony to modify English law to suit local needs; it would be something else entirely to erect a colony on principles that Parliament had expressly rejected.[105]

This legal analysis was accompanied by political discomfort with paternalists' imperial agenda. Populists and moderates agreed with paternalists that there was a potential tradeoff between colonial prosperity and imperial stability. A sufficiently large colonial population would eventually be able to support manufacturing on a scale that competed with British industries; and large, wealthy colonies would be harder for Britain to control. Maurice Morgann, an architect of populist colonial policy, assumed that unfettered colonial growth "will be at last destructive of the Mother Country." But Morgann, like many of his political allies, believed that was a problem so "[d]istant that it is not an object of Policy."[106] The possibility of imperial dissolution was too remote to worry the present generation. And, for populists especially, dissolution itself was not the worst outcome imaginable. In 1777, Charles Pratt, first Baron Camden, found himself unable to wish wholeheartedly for a British victory in rebellious America. "The misfortune is, that the news must be bad, be it what it may," he wrote to his son-in-law. "But of the two extreams, America independent, or America conquered, the first is best for England."[107] Paternalists and their opponents disagreed not only about what it would take to keep the empire together but also about what kind of empire would be worth keeping.

In 1775, Henry Dundas, the recently appointed lord advocate, wrote a long letter to William Eden, the undersecretary of the department responsible for Scotland. British officials had started to worry about the high level of emigration from the Highlands, and Dundas wanted to explain the region's apparent decline. The cause, he argued, was "the destruction of clanship" as a result of the post-1745 reforms. Although efforts to destroy Scottish feudalism had been "necessary at the time," they had outlived their purpose now that Jacobitism was no longer a threat. Dundas suggested that it was time to revive the feudal system, which had generated the "strong cement and bond of union" that had once tied Highlanders to each other and to the region.[108]

Dundas's memorandum revealed a willingness to rethink the legal structures that had long underpinned the British Empire. His pessimistic assessment of Hardwicke's reformation harmonized with the skepticism of other Scottish intellectuals, such as Adam Ferguson and William Robertson, about remaking institutions. Although the Enlightenment is often associated with an appetite for radical reform, its Scottish variety was more conservative, emphasizing the costs of change as much as the prospect of improvement. Maintaining (or reviving) old institutions, Ferguson and Robertson argued, was the surest way to halt the social and political disruptions that afflicted Scotland, England, and the colonies.[109] Not every Scottish intellectual subscribed to such ideas. (Adam Smith, for example, favored a more institutionally uniform empire, as Chapter 4 will discuss.) But they found a ready audience among paternalists looking for an alternative to a common-law empire that struck them as precarious. It helped that many paternalists, including Dundas and Alexander Wedderburn, had social and political ties to the Scottish literati.[110]

Dundas's memorandum is notable not only for its traditionalism but also for its comfort with a certain kind of pluralism. His vision of revitalized clanship applied only to the Highlands, whose development would necessarily diverge from that of England. Unlike earlier generations of imperial reformers, who had assumed that the empire's future lay in a greater standardization of legal systems, Dundas sketched a more institutionally diverse vision. In 1805, Thomas Douglas, fifth Earl of Selkirk, suggested that Highlanders might revive their feudal traditions on St. John's Island—the intellectual child, in a sense, of Egmont and Dundas.[111]

For other writers, however, feudalism remained a badge of backwardness.[112] The most famous critique of feudalism from this period came from Adam Smith's *Wealth of Nations*. A decade earlier, John Adams had published a *Dissertation on the Canon and Feudal Law*, which described the Whig fight for liberty as a battle against the two titular legal systems. "It was this great struggle," in Adams's view, "that peopled America." Contrary to more narrowly sectarian histories of colonization, Adams denied that "religion alone" had driven the early Puritans to New England. Rather, he insisted, they had settled Massachusetts "in *direct opposition* to the *cannon* and the *feudal* systems." Adams periodically repeated his warnings to friends and in the colonial press, where he presented feudalism as the key to understanding a range of pernicious imperial policies, from the Stamp Act to the insecure tenure of colonial judges.[113] His obsession was vindicated in 1774, when the Quebec Act actually did restore feudal tenures to North America. Adams reacted accordingly.

CHAPTER 3

The Quebec Act and Its Alternatives

John Adams was not known to be a calm man. But even by his own standards of irascibility, the Quebec Act of 1774 inspired a strong reaction:

CANADA BILL. . . .
Proof of Depth of Abilities, and Wickedness of Heart. . . .
Romish Religion.
Feudal Government.
Union of feudal Law and Romish Superstition.
Knights of Malta. Orders of military Monks. . . .
Danger to us all. An House on fire.[1]

These notes, made during a debate in the Continental Congress, reveal both the intensity of his aversion to the Quebec Act and why he thought it so dangerous. Like many populists, Adams distrusted its relative lenity toward Catholics. But while his fear of "Romish Religion" gave his reflections their apocalyptic flavor, the force of the Act's threat came from its imposition of "feudal Law" and "Feudal Government." For Adams and like-minded Americans, it was the Quebec Act's legal policy that made its religious policy so menacing.[2]

The Quebec Act ended a decade-long experiment with administering English law in Canada. It had four major provisions. First, it made some accom-

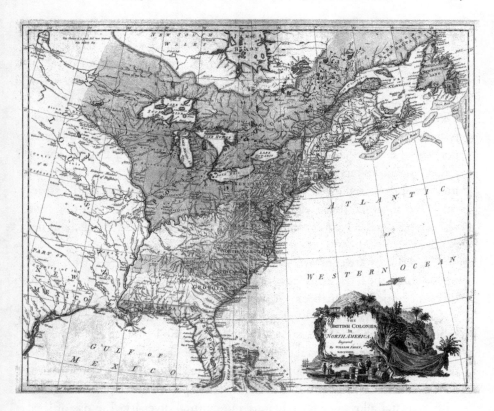

The province of Quebec, as redefined in 1774. *The North American Atlas* (London: Printed for William Faden, successor to the late Thomas Jefferys, 1777). Courtesy of the Library of Congress, Geography and Map Division.

modations for Quebec's religious majority: it guaranteed toleration of Catholicism in the colony; restored the Catholic Church's right to collect tithes; and allowed Canadiens to swear an oath of allegiance without rejecting transubstantiation and other Catholic doctrines, as the oaths of allegiance and supremacy otherwise would have required. Second, the Quebec Act provided for an appointed legislative council—but not an elected assembly, as in other American colonies. Third, it expanded Quebec's boundaries to include the Illinois Country, plus much of what is now Ontario and the midwestern United States. Finally, it restored the use of French private law and civil procedure; English law would continue to govern criminal and administrative matters.[3]

For Adams and like-minded populists, each of these features was cause for suspicion.[4] But the Quebec Act's most provocative provision was its innovative use of legal pluralism to shape colonial development. As Chapter 2 explained, paternalist policymakers had experimented with law and development during the 1760s. General Thomas Gage had tried to use the absence of formal legal institutions to deter immigration to the Illinois Country; and Lord Egmont had argued that feudal land tenures would stabilize colonial politics by strengthening landed elites. The Quebec Act's restoration of French law was the culmination of those projects. By withholding English law, it made Quebec less appealing to Anglophone settlers and investors. By preserving French law, it allowed Britain to take advantage of existing feudal structures. Put together, those features promised to advance paternalists' objective of keeping Quebec economically underdeveloped, politically docile, and dependent on Britain.

These aims were controversial. Moderates and populists agreed with paternalists about the likely consequences of keeping French law, but they had very different hopes for Quebec's future. Populists wanted to turn Canada into another New York or New England, with a thriving commercial economy and robust public sphere. Doing so would require English legal institutions, which would allow Quebec to attract the settlers and capital it needed to grow—and to assimilate culturally and politically to the rest of British North America. Moderates offered a compromise that leavened populists' developmental agenda with a greater allowance for religious and cultural diversity. The rise of legal pluralism in North America reflected the victory of the paternalist vision of empire over these populist and moderate alternatives.

The Quebec Act has been described as a milestone in Britain's turn toward a more tolerant form of empire.[5] That's certainly true of its religious policy; but toleration had little to do with the Quebec Act's option for legal pluralism. That becomes clear if we consider the other colonies Britain had taken from France and Spain. In every other colony acquired in 1763—in North America, the Caribbean, and Africa—Britain continued its old policy of imposing English law. This wasn't because British rule in those places was less tolerant, but because it reflected a different developmental agenda. The Quebec Act's reintroduction of French law was primarily about directing the colony's social, economic, and political future, not a new appreciation for multiculturalism.

Understanding the Quebec Act as developmental policy matters not only for our understanding of the British Empire but also for the history of the common law. Traditionally, common lawyers had imagined their law as a system of writs, in which each form of action had its own procedures, rules, and remedies. Gradually, lawyers reimagined the common law as a body of substantive doctrines—not a law of trespass or assumpsit, but a law of tort or contract administered through a transsubstantive civil procedure. Legal historians usually attribute this transition to the nineteenth century. The Quebec Act debates, however, reveal its earlier roots. When imperial policymakers discussed whether to transplant English law overseas, they had to be specific about what parts of English law they had in mind—whether it would be possible, for example, to combine an English-style jury with a French-style property regime. In the course of those conversations, lawyers moved away from the older vocabulary of writs and toward the modern vocabulary of doctrines. In doing so, they shaped both the laws of Canada and how Britons thought about the common law more generally.

DIVIDE AND RULE

As Chapter 2 explained, paternalist politicians wanted to ensure that North America remained firmly under imperial control. They thought that legal pluralism would advance that goal in three ways.

First, a distinctive legal system would isolate Quebec from the other American colonies—and thus make it less likely that Canadians would join the resistance brewing to the south.[6] Commentators had known for years that law could be used to divide American colonies from each other. When British armies started stacking up victories during the Seven Years' War, some politicians worried that the empire was becoming too big to manage and that overmighty colonies might one day unite to throw off British rule.[7] Benjamin Franklin, an enthusiastic supporter of imperial expansion, tried to allay that concern. He argued that the colonies would never cooperate in rebellion because their "different laws" made union unattainable. For Franklin, this reflected a timeless truth about imperial law. "The *Romans* well understood" the utility of colonial division, he explained; hence their "edict that every state should live under its own laws."[8] Franklin himself was at best ambivalent about colonists' discord. (His famous cartoon of 1754 had warned colonists to "Join, or Die.") His analysis of American legal pluralism was merely descriptive, and he was more focused on getting Britain to keep Canada than on shaping its legal system. A few years later, however, Francis Maseres, Quebec's attorney general, made a normative argument for retaining French law. If

"Join, or Die" (1754). Benjamin Franklin appreciated the danger of divided colonies. Courtesy of the Library of Congress.

Quebec had "laws and customs considerably different from those of the neighbouring Colonies," he explained, its inhabitants would be less inclined to "Join with those Colonies in rejecting the Supremacy of the Mother country."[9]

Both Maseres and Franklin later came to see artificial disunion as troubling, and both men opposed the Quebec Act.[10] But paternalists saw a lot to like in the idea, especially as relations with the American colonies deteriorated during the 1760s. James Marriott, one of the law officers of the Crown, worried that Canada might "form the head" of "a new independent empire, upon a general revolt of all the colonies," unless Britain did something to inhibit their sense of common identity.[11] Guy Carleton, Quebec's governor, urged policies that would prevent Quebec from becoming "united in any common principle, interest, or wish with the other Provinces."[12]

The Quebec Act responded to these calls for separation. Lord Lyttelton noted with approval that the "political separation of Canada from the rest of America might be a means of dividing their interests" from other American colonies.[13] When some members of Parliament accused paternalists of trying to cut off Quebec from the other colonies, Sir William Meredith readily conceded the point. In the "melancholy event" that Britain needed "to *coerce* America," he asked, "do you wish . . . to combine the heart of the Canadian with that of the Bostonian?"[14] A year after the Boston Tea Party, the question was meant to be rhetorical.

Moderates and populists agreed that legal pluralism would isolate Quebec—which is why they insisted that the colony receive English law. One law for all, they argued, would both acknowledge the equality of all British subjects and effect new subjects' assimilation. They cited Wales, Ireland, and New York as precedents of successful anglicization through law.[15] As one pamphleteer argued, introducing English law to Quebec would "make the rising generation [in that colony] look upon themselves as Englishmen."[16] But preserving French law would perpetuate the differences between Britain's new and old subjects. Charles James Fox opposed the Quebec Act, he explained, because it would frustrate his desire to "make Englishmen mix as much as possible with the Canadians."[17]

The opposition's distrust of the Quebec Act reflected its broader anxiety about the fragmentation of empire. A year earlier, Edmund Burke had raised related concerns about a proposed tax on absentee landowners in Ireland. Burke warned that the government led by Lord North (prime minister from 1770 to 1782) had concocted the scheme not merely to raise revenue but to stimulate a "forced separation" among the pieces "of *this too well-united empire.*" By making it more expensive for landowners to spend time in multiple jurisdictions, the tax would frustrate connections between England and Ireland. Burke was particularly worried that the tax would lead to a greater divergence between English and Irish law by discouraging Irish landowners from traveling to England to appeal the decisions of Irish courts. Even if the tax itself failed to deter appeals from Ireland, it would create a precedent for their ultimate elimination: "They who may restrain may prohibit," Burke warned. Ireland, in turn, would serve as a precedent for other parts of the empire. The "next step," he continued, "will be to encourage all the colonies, . . . to keep their people from all intercourse with each other and with the mother country," so that "[a] gentleman of New York, or Barbadoes, will be as much gazed at as a strange animal from Nova Zembla or Otaheite."[18] When Burke opposed the Quebec Act the following year, he did so because he worried that it would contribute to that same project of disunion.[19]

ENCOURAGING SUBORDINATION

Legal pluralism operated partly through the mere fact of difference. But paternalists were also attracted to the content of French law, which they thought would encourage a due sense of obedience—both from the lower orders to their superiors, and from colony to metropole. As Governor Carleton put it,

French law had "established Subordination, from the first to the lowest, which preserved the internal Harmony, [that Canadiens] enjoyed untill our Arrival, and secured Obedience to the Supreme Seat of Government from a very distant Province."[20] Edward Thurlow, the attorney general, agreed: under French law, "all orders of men habitually and perfectly knew their respective places."[21]

Paternalists' enthusiasm for French law reflected their concern about the common law's potential as a tool of resistance. To some extent, they were responding to what we might anachronistically call the rise of impact litigation. Traditionally, common lawyers had conceived of courts primarily as resolving individual disputes between "subject and subject."[22] Criminal cases sometimes took on great importance, as with James II's attack on the seven bishops in 1688 or the prosecution of John Peter Zenger in 1735. But those earlier causes célèbres tended to be defensive responses to politically motivated prosecutions.[23] Starting in the 1760s, however, it became more common for activists to bring affirmative suits against government officials. These suits, sometimes orchestrated and funded by opposition politicians, were meant to change policy, not just to vindicate the rights of individual plaintiffs.[24] Imperial officials knew that such tactics could be used to challenge their policies in North America. In 1761, Governor Francis Bernard of Massachusetts warned the Board of Trade that a member of his own council, John Erving, was trying to use a trespass suit against a customs collector "to destroy the Court of Admiralty & with it the Custom house."[25] General Gage worried that an agitator motivated by "spite and malice" might "support[ ] and buoy[ ] up the People to commence frivolous and vexatious Suits against the Officers, who were carrying on the King's Service."[26] The prophesy was fulfilled, and an officer in Illinois soon complained to Gage about "Schemes that are laid to Engage me in Litigious Suits of Law."[27]

Paternalists didn't object in principle to suits against government officials. Lord Mansfield, who helped draft the Quebec Act, thought that such litigation was crucial for preventing the abuse of authority; and as chief justice of King's Bench, he was notably aggressive in using habeas corpus to safeguard individual liberty.[28] But paternalists worried about vexatious litigation, the use of lawsuits as political props, and the risk that English-style litigation might lead newly acquired subjects to forget their place. As one official in Quebec warned, the introduction of English law would lead "the middling & lower Sort of People" to "daily lose of that Deference and Respect they used formerly upon all Occasions to shew their Superiors."[29]

The leveling tendency of English law came partly from juries, which often claimed a political as well as a judicial role.[30] In Quebec, which lacked an elected legislature, the grand jury became the focus of popular politics. It claimed, as "the only Body representative of the Colony," "a right to be consulted, before any Ordinance . . . be pass'd into a Law," or before taxes were levied. Its presentments sparked debates about the proper constitution of courts, the powers of justices of the peace, and religious toleration.[31] Although the Privy Council disapproved of the grand jurors' "assuming to themselves authority similar to that of a House of Representatives," there was little that metropolitan authorities could do to stop it.[32] In the end, grand juries survived the Quebec Act, thanks to its retention of English criminal procedure. (Not everyone agreed with that decision.)[33] But the Quebec Act did exclude civil juries from the province.

That was a predictably controversial decision, and paternalists tried to downplay its importance. Civil actions, Lord North insisted, were merely matters of "private dispute" in which "government can have no interest, good or bad."[34] As a result, there was little to fear from leaving them in the hands of judges. But opposition lawyers disagreed. "[I]t is not in criminal laws only the right of the Crown can come in question," the barrister John Glynn countered.[35] Tort suits against government agents were the primary means of checking official misconduct, as Glynn knew from his own professional experience. A decade earlier, he had represented plaintiffs in landmark cases such as *Entick v. Carrington*, which had used an ordinary action for trespass to establish new limits on the searches conducted by government agents. Juries had proved crucial to his success.[36]

The government-checking function of juries was especially important in the colonies, where judges lacked the professional status and independence of their English counterparts. Unlike English judges, who enjoyed good-behavior tenure, colonial judges typically served at the pleasure of the governor, and they often had close ties to the imperial establishment. Thomas Hutchinson, for example, served simultaneously as lieutenant governor and chief justice of Massachusetts, despite having no legal training.[37] Moreover, colonial merchants were often local political leaders, whose activism might put them at risk of retribution from the officials who judged their private suits.[38] The salience of civil juries in debates about colonial legal pluralism thus seems to have reflected not only a desire to check the government directly but also the fear that a hostile imperial state might use its leverage over merchants to quash their dissent.

But Glynn wasn't only worried about the power of the state. He also reminded Parliament that juries were bulwarks against "any man who is great enough, or who thinks himself great enough to [undertake] oppression."[39] Quebec's landowners retained many of the powers that Britain had abolished in Scotland in the 1740s. In that kind of hierarchical society, judges couldn't be relied on to dispense equal justice between the parties, and only civil juries could ensure that all litigants came into court on an equal footing. The lawyer James Mansfield, who represented a group of London merchants trading to Quebec, agreed: the "defence of liberty" required "that civil, as well as criminal causes should be decided by juries."[40] Paternalists dismissed these concerns, because their goal was precisely to construct that kind of deferential society.

DEVELOPING A DEPENDENT ECONOMY

Finally, paternalists thought that French law would make Quebec's economy more dependent on Britain and more useful to the rest of the empire. This economic agenda stemmed from their focus on colonial obedience. As Chapter 2 explained, paternalists worried that economic self-sufficiency would make a colony more inclined to resist imperial control. Accordingly, they wanted to stop North Americans from manufacturing their own goods, so that they would remain dependent on British imports. This goal, as James Marriott explained, had to "direct the spirit of any code of laws" for Quebec.[41]

Fears of colonial autarky were strongest for Quebec's richer and more populous southern neighbors. But even in Quebec, imperial officials worried that the economy had started to move in the wrong direction. Lord Hillsborough, the colonial secretary, told Governor Carleton in 1768 that he was "very concerned" about the advanced state of the "Manufacture of Linen & Woollen" in that colony. But the trend was easier to diagnose than to reverse. Hillsborough thought that a simple prohibition on manufacturing would be "equally impracticable and impolitic."[42] Britain's imperial state was powerful by the standards of its time, but it still had a limited ability to enforce its commands overseas. When the Proclamation of 1763 had forbidden settlers from crossing the Appalachian Mountains, many had simply ignored it.[43] In fact, outright prohibitions on manufacturing could be worse than useless, because colonists would resent them as "impertinent badges of slavery" (as Adam Smith would later put it). Regulations that overtly marked the colonists' economic interests as inferior would only alienate colonists further.[44] With brute force off the table, paternalists needed to find subtler "means of diverting the Peoples attention from" unhelpful employments.[45]

The solution was to deprive Quebec of the capital and labor that manufacturing would require.[46] Again, paternalists worried that a direct prohibition on investment or settlement would be counterproductive. (And rightly so: Britain's attempt to restrict immigration to the colonies was among the grievances that pushed Americans toward independence.)[47] So paternalists used legal pluralism as an indirect way to do the same thing. They knew that Anglophone settlers and merchants would be reluctant to entrust themselves or their capital to a colony that lacked the protections of English law.[48] This was the same insight that had inspired Gage's decision not to erect civil courts in the Illinois Country (discussed in Chapter 2). And unlike direct prohibition, legal pluralism allowed for a degree of deniability. Paternalists could stage the preservation of French law as a humanitarian accommodation rather than a coercive restriction on colonists' economic freedom. (More on that in Chapter 5.) Moreover, the policy would be self-enforcing. No soldiers or customs officials would need to search for illicit activity, nor would the Crown need to convince colonial juries to convict offenders. All Britain had to do was to withhold a certain set of English institutions. It was an ideal strategy for an imperial state that had started to worry about its limited power.[49]

Paternalists had ample evidence that French law would limit Quebec's economic prospects. Only a few years after Quebec's conquest, a group of British merchants had warned that English law would be crucial for building their confidence in the new colony. Any laws "contrary to the Establishment of all the other Courts of Law in the British Dominions," they warned, would have "the most ruinous consequence to every Person in Trade."[50] They repeated this warning after Parliament passed the Quebec Act. "[I]f we had supposed the French laws . . . to be still in force there, or to be intended to be revived," the merchants complained, "we would not have had any commercial connections with the inhabitants of the said province, either French or English."[51] British politicians understood these concerns. It was no secret that a merchant preferred to be familiar with "the laws of the country from which he must seek redress," as Adam Smith would write two years later.[52] Merchants would not trade with Quebec, Maseres explained, because they wouldn't regard their property as "equally secure, if the common law of England with respect to civil trials was entirely abolished."[53] "No [English] merchant thinks himself armed to protect his property," Edmund Burke told Parliament, "if he is not armed with English law."[54] For paternalists, that was the point. French law would scare away investment.

It would also scare away people—particularly Britons whose connections to the metropole might have stimulated the Canadian economy. As Solicitor General Alexander Wedderburn put it, the Quebec Act reflected a belief that "[i]t is not the interest of Britain that many of her natives should settle" there.[55] That's also why the Quebec Act redefined "Quebec" to include much of the American interior. French law, like Gage's arbitration-only regime in Illinois, would make the whole region uninviting for Anglophone settlers. As colonial undersecretary William Knox explained, the Quebec Act had "the avowed purpose of excluding all further settlement" west of the Appalachians.[56]

It was one thing to suppress the settlement of the trans-Appalachian west. Although that was unpopular among land speculators and many American colonists, it was at least intelligible as an effort to secure peace in Indian Country.[57] But inhibiting the population of Quebec itself was something else entirely. Britons had long assumed that the point of gaining colonies was to settle them; and this was particularly true of Canada. In 1745, a Harvard-educated merchant named William Vaughan had fantasized about "settl[ing] [Canada] with Protestants," including "great quantities of poor People transported out of Germany, Switzerland, &c."[58] A few months after the Seven Years' War, the Board of Trade declared that "[t]he chief objects of any new Form of Government" in Canada included "increas[ing] the numbers of British & other Protestant Setlers."[59] The Proclamation of 1763, issued shortly thereafter, introduced English law to Quebec for that very reason.[60] Deliberately suppressing the development of Quebec was thus a massive and unprecedented change of policy.

Unsurprisingly, then, some of the Quebec Act's supporters tried to downplay its economic and demographic implications. Governor Carleton equivocated when asked whether "the diminution of the number of British subjects" in Quebec would be "an advantage, or disadvantage to the province." That was a "political question," he told the House of Commons, that went beyond his duties as governor.[61] But even his evasion is revealing: it was astounding for a colony's governor not to commit himself to increasing its population. Wedderburn also hedged. After one moderate MP claimed that the introduction of civil juries had tripled the amount of trade to Canada, Wedderburn "positively den[ied]" any connection between English law and economic growth. But, he added coyly, even if juries *had* augmented Canadian trade, they would still be wrong for Quebec. Trade primarily benefitted merchants, and there was no evidence that Quebec's landed elites shared merchants' affection for English institutions. In Wedderburn's telling, juries amounted to class legislation; and he professed himself unable to imagine that anyone would "form so random an idea as to imagine, that sacrificing one class of the people can in any case be right policy to the remainder."[62]

Despite those evasions, there was no hiding the Quebec Act's purpose. Wedderburn framed his defense of seigneurs as a matter of justice, but it had an unmistakable economic implication: Quebec was to remain an agricultural colony, not a commercial one, and its workforce was to consist of French-speaking Catholics, not new Protestant arrivals. Maseres, the former attorney general of Quebec, had "[n]o doubt" that legal pluralism was meant to discourage "the population of it by the Protestant subjects."[63] The First Continental Congress reached the same conclusion, complaining that the Quebec Act "discourage[ed] the settlement of British subjects in that wide extended country," because potential settlers feared the "influence of civil [law] principles."[64]

Populists and paternalists agreed that legal pluralism would repel immigration and investment. But they disagreed about the merits of that goal. Populists' vision of the British Empire depended on making Quebec rich and populous—and, therefore, on transplanting English law in order to attract settlers and capital. The hoped-for benefits of this strategy were not only economic. If Quebec could attract immigrants from Britain and its older colonies, the new arrivals would accelerate the assimilation of Canadiens by modeling what it meant to be a British subject. That would create a virtuous cycle, in which an ever-more-anglicized Quebec would find it progressively easier to support English institutions, attract English settlers, and trade with English merchants. One memorialist, eager to accelerate the process, recommended founding a new provincial capital (subtly named "*British Town*") to be settled by Englishmen who would introduce "the English language, the English manners, & a Spirit of Industry, among the French Canadians."[65] Some observers thought this was unduly optimistic, but proponents of anglicization pointed to New Netherland's transformation into New York as an example of what English institutions could achieve.[66] In short, populists envisioned the total reconstruction of Quebec. "We are not now considering the law for an old province, but of a new," Thomas Townshend Jr. told the House of Commons. The purpose of that law should be "to assimilate as much as possible the manners, laws, and customs of Canada, and Great Britain."[67]

WHAT KIND OF LAW MATTERED?

Debates over the Quebec Act didn't treat all areas of law equally. The Act's opponents distinguished between topics that were essential to anglicize and those that might safely remain French. One group of Anglophone merchants, in a petition ghostwritten by Francis Maseres, said they were "most especially anxious" for English law related "to matters of navigation, commerce and personal contracts, and the method of determining disputes upon those subjects by the trial by jury, and likewise . . . to actions for the reparation of injuries received, such as actions of false imprisonment and of slander, and of assault, and whatever relates to the liberty of the person." In other words, they wanted English law for what lawyers today would call contract, tort, civil procedure, and public law. The merchants wished "most of all for the writ of habeas corpus." But they had no objection to French law for "tenures and descents of land."[68]

At first glance, this dichotomy isn't surprising. Comparative lawyers have long thought that some branches of law are easier to transplant than others. Family law, for example, is said to be uniquely embedded in particular societies, while commercial law is supposed to travel more easily.[69] That idea was present in Montesquieu's writings, and by the 1770s it had become familiar in England.[70] Perhaps Maseres and his clients were just trying to pick the low-hanging fruit: anglicizing law where it was relatively easy to do so, while acknowledging that it would be hard to transform every aspect of Quebec's legal system.

But on closer inspection, the merchants' position looks less intuitive. For one thing, scholars (then and now) disagree about the ease of transplanting different kinds of law. Montesquieu identified family law as especially transplant-resistant, but the historian Edward Gibbon reported that "the Roman laws . . . of marriage, testaments, and inheritances" had readily been taken up by that empire's new subjects. Similarly, it's far from obvious that civil procedure, which the British merchants wanted to see anglicized, is especially transplant-friendly.[71] And why did the merchants distinguish contract law (which they wanted to anglicize) from property law (which could remain French)? Later theorists, such as Friedrich Carl von Savigny (1779–1861), often lumped those branches of law together in their analyses of legal transplants.[72] Even more fundamentally, some scholars have rejected the premise that some kinds of law are easier to transplant than others.[73] Accordingly, we can't assume that Maseres and his merchant clients were responding to timeless truths when they came up with their hierarchy of anglicization.[74]

So where did they get their ideas? The notion that Britain might transplant only part of English law was advanced especially by a group of moderate lawyers.[75] In a 1766 report on Quebec's legal system, Attorney General Charles

Yorke and Solicitor General William de Grey proposed introducing English criminal law, retaining French laws for real property, and deciding disputes involving contracts and personal injuries according to "substantial maxims of law and justice [that] are every where the same"—which would mean, in practice, the principles familiar to the English lawyers running the system. Civil procedure would be modeled on the rules of "the supreme Courts of Westminster," as well as courts in Wales and older British colonies. William Hey, Quebec's chief justice, proposed something similar, as did Maseres.[76]

These lawyers didn't explain how they drew the line between acceptable and unacceptable legal pluralism, but three considerations seem to have shaped their thinking. First, the common law itself allowed for variation in property regimes. As the populist barrister John Dunning argued, English juries were competent to decide cases involving gavelkind or common socage; surely they could also handle French land tenures. "[N]o two things can be more distant," Dunning insisted, "than the laws and customs regulating the possession [of land], and the mode of trying questions which arose from those laws and customs."[77] John Lind, another barrister (and a friend of Jeremy Bentham), agreed: "the laws relating to succession" and "the laws relating to judicial proceedings" were "perfectly distinct and independent" from each other, so that Britain could introduce civil juries while retaining French inheritance law.[78]

Second, some moderate lawyers might have worried that it would be too hard for Canadiens to adapt to a new property regime. In 1763, in the course of commenting on a case from Bengal, Thurlow (the future attorney general) had suggested that property law was especially difficult to translate across cultures. In "cases of personal contracts," he explained, English courts often "receive evidence of the laws and customs of a country quite foreign and independent, in order to explain the terms and force of such a contract." But agreements "concerning a real subject" were much harder for English judges to understand: "in respect of the relative inability and incompetence of the court, it is extremely difficult for the greatest scholar, merely by reading, to have that expertness in the laws of a foreign country, which every citizen hath in his own."[79] That kind of thinking might have convinced lawyers in the 1760s that it would be easier for Canadiens to learn the English laws of contract and tort than to learn new rules of inheritance and property.

But while these considerations probably influenced moderates' thinking, they can't fully explain it. As an initial matter, not everyone agreed that substance and procedure were separable. Sir William Meredith insisted that "the civil law of France, and the trial by jury in England, are so dissonant, that the forms of one can never be blended into proceedings of the other."[80] This attitude was deeply embedded in the English legal tradition. The common law had originated not as a body of doctrines but as a system of writs. Each form of action (trespass, for example) was a "procedural pigeon-hole" that "contain[ed] its own rules of substantive law," as Maitland put it.[81] As a result, it made little sense to talk separately of substantive and procedure. By the 1770s, that conception of the common law was beginning to yield to a more substantive, doctrinal approach. But even Blackstone's *Commentaries* (1765–69), often described as the first major attempt to present English law in substantive terms, was a transitional work. Lawyers at the time would have had to work hard to find a transsubstantive "civil procedure" that could be neatly severed from the rules of contract and tort. To the extent that lawyers managed to do so, it was a choice, not a reflex.[82]

What might have encouraged moderates to make that effort? One important consideration was the perceived preference of Britain's new subjects. British officials believed that Canadiens were strongly attached to their "family customs, tenures of land, method of conveying," laws of marriage, and laws of "descent," but that they were more open to English "Forms of Judicature" and commercial law.[83] There was good evidence for that. One seigneur testified to the House of Commons that although Canadiens wanted "the circumstances of lands" to be "left to the Canadian laws," they "like the English judicature very well."[84] Even Governor Carleton, who opposed the introduction of English law, conceded that most Canadiens "would make no objection" to English commercial law.[85] According to Maseres, Francophone merchants had even come to accept arrest on mesne process in debt litigation, "a part of the English law that a good deal surprized and alarmed the Canadians upon its first introduction."[86] (Canadiens had also been open to receiving English bankruptcy laws—more willing, in fact, than many Anglophone merchants, whose objections were recounted in Chapter 2.) There's also evidence that most former French subjects would have welcomed civil juries.[87] In fact, the French-speaking residents of Illinois actively demanded them, much to the annoyance of General Gage.[88]

Another sign that moderates cared what Canadiens wanted was their willingness to refashion English institutions, especially juries, to make them more appealing to Francophone users. Maseres and Hey reported that Canadiens wanted jury verdicts based on majority vote rather than the traditional English requirement of unanimity.[89] Lind endorsed that proposal, suggesting that Canadiens' suggested reforms should be adopted even in England.[90] Just as

Lord Hardwicke had adapted English evidentiary law to accommodate Indian witnesses in *Omichund v. Barker,* perhaps Parliament could tweak jury trials to accommodate French Canadians.[91]

But there's also evidence that moderates weren't just thinking about the preferences of colonial subjects. Although Edmund Burke emphasized the need to give Canadiens a "Government which they like," he also insisted that Britain shouldn't blindly bow to their wishes. Conquerors had the duty to rule well; in Britain's case, that meant helping Canadiens appreciate the superiority of English law. Some institutions—such as juries—were so crucial for English liberty that Britain might be justified in disregarding Canadiens' prejudices against them.[92] Fowler Walker, a moderate barrister who served as the agent for Quebec's Anglophone merchants, took a similar position. He acknowledged that some Canadiens might object to the "tediousness" of English procedure. But he nonetheless suggested that "they should consider those *delays as the price which they pay for & the Criterion* of their liberty." (He cited Montesquieu for that claim.)[93] Moderates also showed little interest in preserving French criminal law or procedure, although there's evidence that some Canadiens would have preferred that.[94]

What seems to have mattered most to many moderates was not the perceived preferences of Canadiens, but moderates' own judgment about which kinds of law mattered most to Quebec's development. Moderates insisted on transplanting English procedure, even against the wishes of some Canadian subjects, because it was widely believed to be the branch of law most closely associated with a free English government. The dictum that procedural tedium was the price of liberty was a commonplace among English lawyers; Blackstone's *Commentaries* said it twice.[95] More surprisingly, even non-lawyers praised English procedure, or at least parts of it. Merchants, for example, insisted on "the Process for Imprisonment for Debts" as essential for protecting their investments in Canada.[96] This focus on the political and economic consequences of law also explains other aspects of moderates' taxonomy of legal transplants. Tort law mattered for redressing the misdeeds of government agents and great landowners. Contract law was self-evidently important for trade. Merchants had no special love for English law; they preferred to avoid courts altogether and to settle their differences informally. But that wasn't always possible, and to the extent that they had to sue each other, they wanted to do it using laws that were "generally known as understood"—which meant, for better or worse, the "Laws of England."[97]

In contrast, moderates were willing to keep French land tenures and inheritance rules because they weren't thought to have much effect on Quebec's growth. Moderates had several reasons to think so. First, some commentators doubted that English property and inheritance law was particularly good for colonial development. Smith's *Wealth of Nations,* published two years after the Quebec Act's passage, attributed the rapid growth of British North America to the "political institutions" that had encouraged "the improvement and cultivation" of land. But he was ambivalent about the common law's place in that story. On the one hand, he praised "free socage" because it "facilitates alienation" more than "the custom of Paris," thus making it easier to transfer land to more productive owners. On the other hand, he warned that English primogeniture tended to retard development by encouraging the accumulation of large and inefficient estates. English land law was therefore a mixed blessing. (The best system, according to Smith, was the law of Pennsylvania, which rejected primogeniture while also facilitating inter vivos transfers.)[98]

More importantly, English land law had a relatively weak political constituency. Merchants were among the loudest proponents of anglicizing Canadian law; and it didn't much matter to them whether Quebec's law of real property was drawn from France or England. The feature of real property that they cared about was its ability to function as collateral for colonial debts. The Debt Recovery Act, enacted in 1732 at the behest of English merchants, required that real property in the colonies be treated as equivalent to chattels for the purpose of satisfying debts. (Metropolitan law, in contrast, gave greater protection to real property from creditors, which increased the stability of land ownership but made land less useful as collateral.) Merchants wanted to ensure that the statute would also apply in Quebec, both out of self-interest and because it was thought to have spurred North America's development by making credit more readily available to colonists. But the application of the Debt Recovery Act didn't depend on the presence of English tenures.[99] Moreover, some British investors had a private economic interest in the persistence of French tenures. Although many Britons publicly denounced French land law as backward, some of them nonetheless found it attractive to acquire Canadian property under seigneurial forms, perhaps because of the exclusive mill, timber, and water rights they sometimes conferred. That made it harder to argue that French property law was a serious obstacle to British settlement.[100]

Not everyone agreed that land law was developmentally insignificant. As Chapter 2 explained, many politicians thought that feudal tenures, which linked wealth, loyalty, and political power, could be decisive. Lord Hillsborough and Governor Carleton, in particular, argued that the feudal character of French law was one of its most attractive aspects. An early draft of the Quebec Act would have allowed Canadians to convert their feudal seigneuries into free and common socage; that provision was struck out after Carleton and Hillsborough objected.[101] Nonetheless, even the Quebec Act's paternalist authors tended to see the French law of real property as a secondary feature—desirable, perhaps, but not essential to the Act's purpose. This comparatively relaxed attitude to property and inheritance was reflected in the final version of the Act itself, which preserved French inheritance law only as a default rule for intestate succession, while also providing that Canadians could devise "Lands, Good, or Credits" using either French- or English-style wills. That provision seems to have been uncontroversial, and it was generally ignored in debates about the Act.[102]

Politicians' focus on colonial development also helps to explain why paternalists showed little interest in preserving French criminal law. Some of them seem to have believed sincerely that it was too severe for Britons to administer in good conscience. Alexander Wedderburn, for example, declared that "the difference indeed between the certainty and mildness of the English, and the arbitrary Severity of the French criminal Law is so obvious, that the change of that Law is alone sufficient to repair all the necessary Evils of Conquest."[103] But paternalists also seem to have thought that criminal law would play a minor role in effecting their imperial agenda. They worried greatly about disorder, but their concerns focused on structural questions of social and political power, and their attitude to everyday crime was often indistinguishable from that of their political adversaries. Eighteenth-century England had a notoriously harsh criminal law—Parliament more than quadrupled the number of capital offenses between 1688 and 1820—but that wasn't a conspicuously partisan project. The same was true with respect to criminal law in the colonies. General Gage, for example, proposed a penal code for Illinois that was actually more lenient than England's, in that murder was the only capital offense. (One French merchant complained that Gage's approach was too lenient and demanded a criminal law more in line with "British principles.")[104]

Of course, criminal law mattered a lot for everyday life. Historians such as Douglas Hay and E. P. Thompson have shown its importance for social control in England; and in the nineteenth century, criminal justice would become an especially salient instrument for enforcing colonial hierarchies.[105] But in the eighteenth century, the rules of civil litigation had an especially visible role in structuring social, economic, and political life. "Whoever may think the criminal laws are alone the valuable parts of this Constitution," warned Dunning, "I beg leave to say the civil distribution of justice in this country is in my apprehension the pride, the boast, and glory of this country, and among the most valuable rights any country does enjoy."[106] It was civil justice that deterred illegal searches, civil justice that prevented the expropriation of property, and civil justice that would give merchants the confidence to invest in Britain's new colonies. For those reasons, it was civil law that became the focus of debates about legal pluralism in North America.

When moderate lawyers like de Grey first suggested that Quebec might retain some parts of French law, they had assumed that the laws of Canada would eventually become English. Partial legal pluralism was a route to eventual legal uniformity: as one official put it, preserving "the Coutume de Paris" in some particulars would be "a certain, though moderate, method to introduce our Laws . . . into the Province."[107] During the Quebec Act debates, moderates reframed their proposal. Instead of a stopover on the road to full anglicization, the partial transplantation of English law now offered a middle way between the more extreme positions of paternalists and populists.[108] As Chapter 5 will explain, paternalists argued that the complete elimination of French law would be cruel and intolerant. The Quebec Act's opponents responded by limiting their demands for anglicization. John Glynn conceded that Canadiens might retain "those particular usages, and customs that are so particularly" dear to them, as long as the "leading principle" of the colony remained "the laws of England." "Though I can't be so candid as to confess that would remove my objections to this Bill," Glynn continued, "I am certain it has a tendency to remove the objections of many, and to reconcile the minds of men in some degree, and to remove some of the most striking, and formidable objections to the Bill." His ally Isaac Barré likewise expressed support for a compromise that would introduce civil juries but allow Canadiens to retain "their customs of descent, and heritage."[109] Although populists continued to have qualms about allowing any French law to persist, they agreed with moderates that English laws of procedure, contract, and tort would be most important for Quebec's political and economic future.

Of course, paternalists rejected this intermediate position, the entire point of which was to neutralize the Quebec Act as a developmental policy. But even after the Act's passage, some policymakers continued to pursue a compromise. In 1775, Lord Dartmouth, the colonial secretary and president of the Board of Trade, drafted the instructions that were to guide Governor Carleton's implementation of the Quebec Act. Although Dartmouth was pleased that the Act had mollified Francophone elites, he also knew it had antagonized the Anglophone minority.[110] Accordingly, he encouraged Carleton to soften the Quebec Act's legal pluralism. Although the Quebec Act had preserved French law, it had also created a legislative council with the authority to alter that law. Dartmouth urged Carleton and the council to consider "whether the Laws of England may not be, if not altogether, at least in part the Rule for the decision in all Cases of personal Actions" for contracts and torts.[111]

Carleton rejected that suggestion. He not only blocked any attempt to anglicize private law but even questioned whether the Quebec Act had gone far enough in excluding the laws of England. "I have seen good Cause to repent my having ever recommended the Habeas Corpus Act and English criminal Laws," he wrote back to Dartmouth. "To render the Colony of that Advantage to Great Britain, it certainly is capable of, would require the reintroducing the French Criminal Law, and all the Powers of it's [sic] Government."[112] Carleton understood the Quebec Act's purpose, and he intended to see it through.

REMNANTS OF THE OLD SYSTEM

The Quebec Act was unusual. When it came to the other colonies Britain had acquired through the Treaty of Paris—the Floridas, the Ceded Islands, and Senegambia—paternalists agreed with moderates and populists that Britain should introduce English law. This difference in legal policy reflected a difference in developmental policy. There was a broad consensus that those other colonies needed to attract more Anglophone settlers and to develop commercial economies along the lines of older British possessions. There was also broad agreement that English law would facilitate that process.

Grenada (which also superintended St. Vincent, the Grenadines, Dominica, and Tobago) offers the clearest example of Britain's continuing appetite for legal uniformity. As Chapter 2 explained, Grenada's first British governor imposed English law only a few days after his arrival. This commitment to anglicized law reflected the widely shared belief that the Ceded Islands needed to be as economically productive as possible. Politicians didn't always agree about what that should look like, particularly when it came to the prudence and morality of slavery.[113] But everyone agreed that the sugar-rich West Indies needed to thrive for Britain's sake as well as their own.

Paternalists, in particular, treated Grenada quite differently from Quebec. Although the political satirist John Shebbeare supported the Quebec Act, he urged Britain to anglicize West Indian law, because "[o]ur laws and rules of government" would allow planters to be more productive than France's "cramping regulations."[114] Unlike in Quebec, there was no need to worry that excessive prosperity would made the West Indies self-sufficient and ungovernable. In Caribbean colonies, the threats of slave revolts and foreign invasion guaranteed planters' loyalty.[115] Those same security concerns made it imperative to introduce English law in order "to invite settlers and subjects" to reside there and bolster its defenses.[116] In short, English law survived in the Caribbean even as it was curtailed in Quebec because of a political consensus that the West Indies needed more settlers, who would only come if lured by English law. French Grenadians, for their part, seemed satisfied with the arrangement.[117]

Similar considerations led Britain to introduce English law to West and East Florida. There was broad agreement that those colonies would be useful buffers against Spanish or French aggression—but only if they had enough British settlers. Unlike in Quebec, there was little reason for paternalists to fear that the Floridas would even begin to approach economic self-sufficiency. They lacked enough colonists even to produce food and raw materials for export to Britain and its Caribbean colonies, much less to begin manufacturing. Underdevelopment, not autarky, was the leading concern.[118] The solution to the Floridas' underpopulation was, predictably, to transplant English law in order to attract immigrants.[119] As William Knox argued, British subjects would be more likely to move there if they knew that they would "have the Benefit of the Laws of Great Britain."[120] George Johnstone, the governor of West Florida, agreed. "Establishing the Civil Government of this Province agreeably to the laws of Great Britain & the precepts of her Constitution is one of the principal objects which his Majesty & his Ministers had in view in sending me here," he explained to a local army officer.[121] Johnstone liked to brag that he "sleeps with Montesquieu," which presumably gave him an osmotic appreciation for the theory that laws ought to conform to local circumstances.[122] But that didn't stop him from bringing English law to subtropical Pensacola, even though a small French population remained in the area around Mobile. (In East Florida, the evacuation of the colony's Spanish population made anglicization an even easier choice. Governor James Grant underscored the point by demolishing what remained of Spanish infrastructure and building an English-style courthouse in its place.)[123]

Perhaps the most surprising destination for English law in the 1760s was Senegambia, which Britain had taken from France during the war. When the Grenville administration came to power in 1764, it initially entrusted the management of Senegambia to the Company of Merchants Trading to Africa, the successor organization to the Royal African Company.[124] Because Britain intended its new West African outpost to be a trading station with "no perpetual Residencies or Planting," the administration saw no need for a "regular government." (Newfoundland provided the model for this kind of colonialism-lite.)[125] But in February 1765, the Board of Trade changed course, recommending that Senegambia be made into a Crown colony with a constitution and judiciary as similar as possible to those of "the American Colonies."[126] This new approach was partly a response to the failures of merchant-led government. But it also reflected a shift in the colony's purpose, from trading post to colony of settlement.[127]

Most scholars today would look skeptically on the claim that Britain really meant to bring English law to West Africa. The conventional wisdom among historians and social scientists is that European empires were unlikely to transplant their own institutions to places where their settlers faced high mortality rates.[128] And Senegambia was indeed a place of "extraordinary mortality" for Europeans, as contemporaries understood.[129] But despite their firsthand experience of disease and death, British officials assumed that Senegambia's climate was a surmountable challenge that didn't foreclose the introduction of English law.[130] West Africa was considered unhealthy for Europeans, but that didn't make it unusual. Indeed, many of Britain's American colonies were described at some point as unfit for settlement. New England and Nova Scotia now seem like quintessential settler colonies, but some eighteenth-century writers worried they might be too cold for colonization. The seventeenth-century Chesapeake killed perhaps 40 percent of immigrants within a few years of their arrival, and Philadelphia was a "demographic disaster" until the middle of the eighteenth century. The Floridas received English law despite the widespread perception that their climate was "extreme." In 1765, one soldier wrote from Mobile that West Florida was "good for nothing, but destroying Englishmen," and that it was even deadlier than Jamaica (another notoriously unhealthy common-law jurisdiction).[131] That Britons were likely to die in a particular place didn't always stop them from trying to live there.

Britain's persistence in settling unwholesome places was due partly to the belief that settlement itself would improve their climates over time. Physicians also argued that settlers' own constitutions would adapt—become "seasoned," in contemporary parlance—to their new surroundings. And there were a few tricks for sustaining colonies until those adaptations took place. One option was to seed them with criminals, deserters, or others whose lives were already forfeit. Officials with a greater regard for human life focused on the advice of medical experts, who argued that even intemperate regions had microclimates that were suitable for European habitation. And, of course, many tropical colonies had preexisting populations that Britain could incorporate into its own projects. Senegambia, in particular, had a thriving urban society on the island of St. Louis, dominated by the métis descendants of French merchants and African women.[132]

Eighteenth-century theories of climate and disease made the settlement of West Africa seem possible. What made it desirable was a broad consensus about its geopolitical and economic potential. It's unsurprising, perhaps, that the populists who wanted to anglicize Quebec wanted to do the same thing to Senegambia. But the idea of turning Senegambia into an anglicized Crown colony came from Grenville's paternalist administration, and specifically from the Board of Trade led by Lord Hillsborough—the same minister who wanted to block settlement in Illinois and to deter immigration to Quebec. Thomas Whately, a paternalist Treasury official, was another important supporter of the Senegambia project.[133] As with the West Indies, Senegambia's backers didn't always agree on the details. Some, including the populist leader William Pitt, assumed that the slave trade would play an important role.[134] Others, such as the political economist Malachy Postlethwayt, wanted to move Britain's West African trade away from the sale of enslaved persons. Instead, he argued, the colony's future lay in the gum trade, which was crucial for textile manufacturing.[135] But despite this fundamental disagreement about slavery, policymakers agreed that Senegambia's success depended on its ability to attract both British and free African inhabitants. The time-tested way to achieve that, of course, was to offer the benefits of English law.[136]

Charles O'Hara, Senegambia's first royal governor, understood his mission. He thought that his colony's success required him to turn West Africans into consumers of British manufactures, which they would buy using proceeds from raising cattle, cotton, tobacco, and other produce.[137] Creating such a colony would require Britain to attract and retain local inhabitants through the promise of secure property rights. That, in turn, would require a strong legal system. To that end, the Board of Trade had provided for the colony to have a chief justice, who would decide cases in a manner "agreeable to the Laws of England" and exercise powers based on those of the Westminster courts.[138] In 1766, O'Hara requested funds to construct a courthouse; notably, his budget included a line item for "Seats for the Jury." Although most of the materials for the courthouse were to be sourced locally, some items would

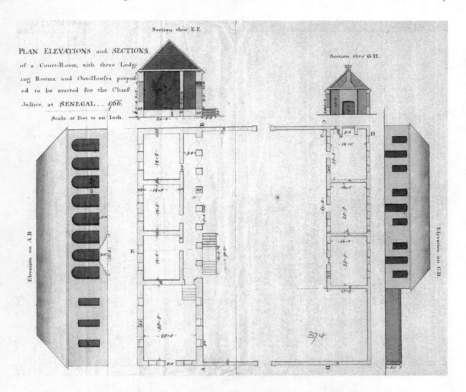

Plan, elevation, and sections for a courthouse at Senegal, T 1/445/374, TNA.
Courtesy of the National Archives, U.K.

have to be imported from England. Senegambian justice was literally to be built from English materials.[139]

O'Hara was by no means an egalitarian. On his watch, the métis population of St. Louis achieved greater political influence than it had enjoyed under French rule. But he knew that those prosperous Senegambian consumers had accumulated much of their wealth through urban slavery, a practice he showed no interest in ending.[140] Indeed, he cited his own experience as the part-owner of a plantation in Dominica when he argued for Senegambia's economic viability. Slavery was "the only means of working" West Indian plantations, he told the Board of Trade; but the purchase of enslaved people was expensive and "a considerable loss to England." Senegambia, if settled with "British planters," would avoid that unnecessary cost and therefore be able to produce commodities much more cheaply. He acknowledged that West Indian plant-

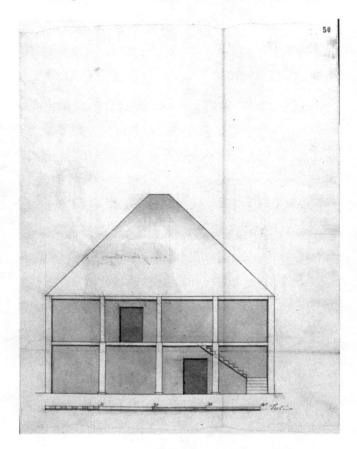

Elevation for a courthouse at St. Augustine (1770), MPG 1/979/2, TNA. Courtesy of the National Archives, U.K.

ers (including himself) might suffer as a result. But, he assured the board, the public would gain.[141]

Senegambia did indeed grow more prosperous under British rule. But it never fulfilled O'Hara's grander ambitions, thanks to a combination of diplomatic setbacks, bad luck, and his own maladministration. The colony's first chief justice, Christopher Milles, died in 1771 and was succeeded by Edward Morse, a barrister whose ill health forced him back to England less than a year after he arrived. As a result, the colony was mostly without a trained judge until Morse returned in 1776. During that time, O'Hara seems to have decided that West Indian slavery could compete with free labor in Senegambia after all. In 1776, a petition from the colony's inhabitants complained that his personal business ventures, which allegedly included a private slave trade to his own Caribbean plantation, were conflicting with his duties as governor. O'Hara was dismissed and sent to America, where he represented Lord Cornwallis in the surrender at Yorktown.[142]

O'Hara's successor, Matthias MacNamara, was no better. He had an appetite for nepotism—one of his brothers held ten different offices in the colony—and a distaste for legality.[143] He did, however, make one unwitting contribution to English law. After he returned to England, a subordinate sued him for false imprisonment, and the case gave Lord Mansfield an opportunity to define "bad malignant motive" and "corrupt abuse of authority." (Incidentally, Mansfield is not recorded as expressing any qualms about deciding the case according to English law.)[144] MacNamara was succeeded by John Clarke, an army officer and amateur classicist, who arrived in Senegambia in 1777. Horrified by the disorder he found, his "first step . . . was to establish the civil Constitution of the Province by erecting Courts of Judicature—a general Court of Pleas—Court of Oyer and Terminer,—and a Court of Admiralty." "Immediately after the courts were opened," he reported, "several suits were commenced against" MacNamara "for seizures of property, Acts of Violence, Debts, etc."[145] These developments gave the new governor some confidence in Senegambia's future: the judicial system was checking official abuses, just as it was supposed to. But Clarke didn't have a chance to see the fruit of his labors. He died in 1778, and France reconquered the colony the next year.[146]

In the 1760s and 1770s, Britain continued to transplant English law abroad, even to places that might seem inhospitable. Indeed, the only former French colonies *not* to receive English law—Illinois and Quebec—were those considered the most temperate and naturally suited for European settlement. The colonies that did receive English law—in West Africa, the West Indies, and North America—differed greatly from each other in terms of location, resources, and demography. But initial resource endowments did little to shape the kind of law that Britain installed in a particular jurisdiction. What mattered, rather, was whether British officials wanted to develop an American-style colony of settlement. Where that interest was absent, so, too, was much of the common law.

CHAPTER 4

Varieties of Pluralism in Bengal

In 1783, Edmund Burke concluded that the law of Bengal was too English and not English enough. The Regulating Act, passed a decade earlier, had authorized a new supreme court at Calcutta. But the statute had failed to tell the judges what body of law to apply. As a result, Burke explained, the court had oscillated between "too strict an Adherence to the Forms and Rules of English Practice" and "Principles perhaps too remote from the Constitution of English Tribunals."[1]

Burke, like most of his contemporaries, had concluded it would have been unwise and unjust to impose all of English law on the natives of India. But he also denied that Bengal was so alien as to make English law irrelevant. The purpose of the new supreme court was to provide "Security for the Natives against the Wrongs and Oppressions of British Subjects resident in Bengal." English law ordinarily checked "Oppressions of Power" through "Civil Actions"—such as trespass suits against abusive officials—of which "a Trial by Jury is a necessary Part." But Britain had denied civil juries to Bengal, partly on the assumption that its "Natives . . . were not capable of sharing in the Functions of Jurors." Burke warned that this assumption had been made "perhaps a little too hastily," and he admonished Parliament *"that the Use of juries is neither impracticable nor dangerous in Bengal."*[2]

Burke is often seen as a great defender of legal pluralism, and rightly so.

But his pluralism was profoundly ambivalent. As Chapter 3 showed, he had opposed the Quebec Act; and the same principles that had informed his opposition to legal pluralism in Canada led him to demand the partial introduction of English law in India. Although he recognized Hindu and Islamic law as worthy of respect, he worried about the political consequences of withholding English law from any subset of British subjects, and he retained throughout his career a conviction that British institutions were essential for a just and prosperous empire.[3]

Burke's ambivalence was the fruit of a decades-long debate about Indian laws. As Chapter 1 explained, the East India Company had a long history of administering English law in its South Asian factories. But although those courts were locally important, their reach was limited. For most of the eighteenth century, the Company was a mostly commercial enterprise with pretensions to sovereignty but little territorial power.[4] That changed starting in the 1750s. Following the Company's victories at the battles of Plassey (1757) and Buxar (1764), the Mughal emperor Shah Alam II granted it the *diwani* of Bengal, Bihar, and Orissa. By taking on the office of *diwan*, the Company acquired the right and obligation to collect taxes and administer civil justice for some thirty million residents of the region. Criminal justice technically remained in the hands of the Mughal nizam, Muhammed Reza Khan; but he was effectively under the Company's control. As a result, the Company now had to determine a legal policy not only for a handful of presidency towns, but for a region whose population dwarfed that of British North America.

Politicians and commentators disagreed about whether to extend English law to this newly acquired territory, just as they disagreed about anglicizing Quebec. On one side, a group of populists urged Britain to transplant English institutions in order to transform northeastern India into a neo-American plantation colony. On the other side, paternalists insisted on using legal pluralism to facilitate a more authoritarian and extractive form of colonialism. But there were also important differences between the debates over Quebec and Bengal. Moderates and populists continued to attack the Quebec Act throughout the 1770s and 1780s, and in 1791 they forced its repeal and replacement. In Bengal, the anti-pluralist argument lost ground more quickly. Although some politicians continued to urge anglicization, the primary debate after the 1770s was about what kind of legal pluralism Britain ought to support, not whether to have pluralism at all.

DISCIPLINE AND DOUBLE GOVERNMENT

Historians have sometimes described Britain's conquest of India as a very important accident.[5] But it was anything but inadvertent. Robert Clive, the Company's military commander, worked deliberately to build a territorial empire in South Asia. Backed by paternalist allies in England, especially George Grenville, he envisioned his conquests both as a solution to Britain's looming fiscal crisis and as an antidote to growing political radicalism throughout its empire. He hoped that tribute taken from Bengal would stabilize British finances without the need for controversial domestic tax hikes, while hierarchical governance in India would model (and provide opportunities for) the kind of aristocratic society paternalists hoped to reinvigorate in Britain and North America.[6] In other words, the Company's conquest of Bengal reflected many of the same concerns that drove paternalist policies in North America. Clive himself understood American and Asian developments to be connected, and he portrayed his work as a counterweight to the "great strides towards independency" in Ireland and America.[7] Commentators also saw similarities between Clive's program and the Quebec Act.[8]

Many of these similarities related to the kind of work that legal pluralism was meant to do. In both places, it was supposed to divide colonial subjects from each other and from their potential British allies, thus fragmenting colonial politics and inhibiting resistance to metropolitan control. In India, this meant separating Muslims from Hindus, castes from each other, and South Asians from Europeans. Demographic diversity, observed one senior Company employee, had facilitated Bengal's conquest and "prevent[ed] [Indians'] uniting to fling off the yoke" of foreign rule.[9] Another Company employee, James Grant, explained the implications of this insight for legal policy. Although he professed discomfort with creating "a most odious and invidious distinction" based on race or religion, he insisted on the "necessity that all British subjects in India . . . be separated from the native inhabitants" by keeping each group under a distinct legal system. Otherwise, Grant warned, "the unaccustomed dangerous draught" of English law "must infallibly produce intoxication & turn into a curse & our own destruction."[10]

As in North America, proponents of legal pluralism also worried about the emancipatory power of English law. Company officials repeatedly warned that English law would be incompatible with British dominance. Harry Verelst, the former governor of Bengal (and a close ally of Clive), thought that introducing English law would "instantly emancipate [Indians] from subjection to"

Britain.[11] An anonymous pamphleteer agreed: English law would "introduce[ ] a Levelling Principle among People accustomed to the most rigid Subordination of Rank and Character."[12] When exposed to the lenity of English institutions, officials in Calcutta warned, Indian natives "gradually acquire an independent and untractable Spirit." The best "remedy for these evils" was to keep Indians under their own laws.[13] Juries were particularly dangerous. Company officials had observed that jury service tended to arouse the political passions of European inhabitants, and they worried about the same thing happening to Indians.[14] "[I]f the natives should be actually endowed with the red cap of liberty in the jury room," warned one anonymous writer, "there is a danger, nay, there is a certainty, that they would make bold to wear it elsewhere; and then, adieu to the English dominion in Bengal."[15] Jury service was incompatible with the kind of superiority that the Company envisioned for itself.

Despite the similarities to the Quebec Act, legal pluralism in Bengal also reflected locally specific economic concerns. The *diwani* had fundamentally changed the Company's business model. In the early eighteenth century, the Company had imported bullion into Bengal to purchase local textiles, which it then resold for a profit. After 1765, however, the Company began using the taxes it collected in Bengal ("revenues," in Company jargon) to fund its purchases (the "investment"). As a result, the Company's procurement of textiles in Bengal became important less as a money-making enterprise on its own right than as a way to remit to London the tribute the Company extracted from its quasi-subjects. The projected scale of those extractions is worth emphasizing. In the early years of the *diwani*, Clive predicted that it would produce up to £4 million annually. That was about as much as the Company made from all of its commercial sales at the time, and one-third of the value of Bengal's total produce. It was enough, by all accounts, to transform the Company from a trading concern into a predatory tax collector.[16]

This reorientation from trade to tribute was controversial, both among politicians and within the Company itself. Between 1757 and 1763, Laurence Sulivan, the Company's most powerful director at the time, had blocked it from accepting the *diwani* and insisted that the Company remain a purely commercial enterprise. As we'll see, Sulivan's position had much in common with populists' distaste for hierarchical and extractive empire.[17] But Clive's supporters in the Company—including the paternalist politicians Grenville and Charles Jenkinson—ousted Sulivan in 1764. With the Company now controlled by his friends, Clive accepted the *diwani* the following year. Although it turned out to be less lucrative than he had promised, it quickly came to dominate the Company's priorities. As Warren Hastings observed at the time, "the investment which is the business of the factories is now but a secondary object of the company's attention."[18]

The change in business model led to a change in legal policy. When the Company had focused on trade, it had depended on its courts to attract Indian merchants to its factories. Rightly or wrongly, Company officials thought that its courts would be most attractive if they administered a locally appropriate form of English law. Calcutta had flourished, its aldermen explained in 1754, because of "the great Concourse of Indian Merchants" who desired "the Benefit of the Laws of England." (Verelst was among the signers of that letter.)[19] But once trade lost its priority, so, too, did the need to offer English-style justice.

In fact, English law would have threatened the Company's new business model by making it too easy for its new subjects to resist its tributary exactions. Eighteenth-century writers considered the common law a crucial bulwark against unjust taxation. Juries were especially important: criminal juries would refuse to convict anyone for violating illegitimate tax laws, while civil juries would award damages against tax collectors who abused their authority. (That's why American colonists were so appalled by efforts to have violations of the Sugar and Stamp Acts adjudicated in juryless vice-admiralty courts.)[20] Juries might even step in where Parliament failed to protect subjects from excessive taxation. In 1763, the inventor and moderate statesman David Hartley emphasized "the particular power of juries to protect us against the pernicious effects, or the farther extension, of a new, insidious, and unconstitutional mode of excise."[21] He assured readers that juries would never interfere with the collection of a proper, lawful tax. But his distinction between just and unjust taxes would hardly have comforted the East India Company, whose revenues depended on seizing the produce of landowners without their consent and using methods that would have horrified an English jury. Alexander Dalrymple, a Company employee (and, like Hartley, a man of science), insisted that it would have been impossible to collect the Bengal revenues without the aid of corporal punishment. His colleagues generally agreed. During the devastating famine that struck Bengal in 1769–70, the Company sustained its tax receipts by gibbeting the corpses of anyone who refused to pay.[22] This was not a system that would have thrived if tax collectors had been amenable to tort suits before panels of Bengali jurors. No wonder, then, that a senior Company official warned that trials by jury might "annihilate the Collections."[23]

Company officials generally agreed that the widespread availability of English law would have been incompatible with their new, tributary business model. But they disagreed about the right alternative. One faction, associated with Clive, wanted to create a relatively inexpensive colonial state that extracted wealth from Bengal but invested little money in governance. The Clivite vision was countered by Laurence Sulivan and Warren Hastings, whose reformist program sought to substantially improve the administration of Hindu and Islamic law beyond what the Mughal Empire had been able to achieve.[24] This chapter will consider each of those programs in turn.

As we've seen, Clive orchestrated the conquest of Bengal to create an extractive empire that would funnel revenue to Britain. "Bengal, like other subjected provinces, must yield its tribute," he reminded his colleagues in 1767.[25] His approach to governance reflected this purpose. Because the Company administered Bengal for profit, it was important to keep expenses low while ensuring a consistent tax revenue. But money wasn't Clive's only concern. As James Vaughn has shown, Clive and his paternalist allies worried that "licentiousness"—a capacious term that could mean anything from partisan conflict to military mutiny—posed an existential threat to the British Empire. The year the East India Company accepted the *diwani*—1765—also saw Parliament pass the Stamp Act. American resistance to that legislation confirmed Clive and his supporters in their view that the British Empire was at risk of disintegrating. The only way to reverse the empire's entropy was a thoroughgoing reformation of manners. In Bengal, this meant crafting a hierarchical and bureaucratic colonial state capable of controlling its own employees. In place of the old model of compensation, in which Company servants received low salaries but enjoyed the privilege of trading privately for their own benefit, Clive sought to create a corps of salaried professionals who would pursue the public's interest rather than their own. Of course, that project was in tension with his desire to minimize expenses, but one way to reconcile those goals was to minimize the number of Company employees. That, in turn, implied a limited mission for the Company state.[26]

These fiscal and political goals led Clive to insist that Bengal's future lay in a "double government," in which Indian elites continued to run day-to-day operations in the name of the old regime while the Company maintained ultimate control over the province's military and political affairs. Under this system, the Company would take no part in administering criminal justice, hearing the complaints of its de facto subjects, or appointing tax collectors.[27] For Clive, this arm's-length approach was a moral as well as a practical imperative. Even if it yielded worse governance than direct Company rule, he explained, "we ... shall have some satisfaction, in knowing that the Corruption is not among ourselves."[28] Doubting that Bengal would ever be governed properly, Clive sought at least to insulate himself and his colleagues from complicity. Modern readers might find it difficult to credit the scruples of a man who didn't hesitate to enrich himself at Bengal's expense. But his obsession with corruption nonetheless reflected a coherent and powerful concern, shared by his allies in England and India, that moral degeneration—and specifically a growing tension between public and private interests—threatened the success of Britain's South Asian empire. Limiting the Company's role in governance would limit its employees' opportunities for harmful self-dealing.[29]

Publicly, Clive presented his hands-off approach as a continuation of the Mughal system. "A sudden Revolution in Government," he argued, would have offended Bengali natives ("averse in the extreme, to any Innovation") and needlessly provoked foreign rivals, who might have felt threatened had the Company flaunted its new power too openly.[30] Privately, however, Clive and his colleagues understood that double government redefined the *diwani*. "We observe the account you give of the office and power of the King's Dewan in former times," the directors wrote to Clive in 1766. "This description of it is not the office we wish to execute." The *diwan* had traditionally combined powers of taxation and civil administration. But the Company wanted to separate those functions, controlling the former while outsourcing the latter to Indians. To the greatest extent possible, the directors hoped to leave "[t]he administration of justice" and "whatever comes under the denomination of civil administration" in the hands of the nawab, or Mughal provincial governor.[31] Clive agreed. "The power of supervising the Provinces, though lodged in us, should not ... be exerted," he explained. Cost was an important consideration: "Three times the present number of Civil Servants would be insufficient" to run Bengal properly; but "if we leave the Management to the old Officers of the Government, the Company need not be at the Expence of one additional Servant."[32]

Clive didn't favor this distanced style of governance because he found South Asia inscrutably alien or from a conviction that its inhabitants were innately unfit for British-style rule. Rather, his approach derived from his political and economic priorities. Indeed, part of what makes his commitment to exploiting Bengal so disturbing is his awareness that Indians would have been quite capable of equal government under English institutions. The best evidence for this comes from his treatment of Indian soldiers. Many eighteenth-century European writers described Indians in general, and sepoys in particular, as naturally less aggressive than their Western counterparts. Montesquieu and Voltaire, for example, both argued that India's climate tended to make its inhabitants docile; Clive's friend, the historian Robert Orme, advanced a similar claim.[33] But Clive disagreed. Although he denigrated Indians as "cowardly, beyond all conception," he insisted that India's martial spirit had been "broken by absolute and tyrannical Governments."[34] Institutions, not climate or complexion, had made sepoys unfit for war.

The Company's treatment of its native soldiers reflected this view. In the 1740s, British observers had disdained Indian soldiers as fit for little more than guard duty. Under Clive, however, the Company began treating them as an indispensable part of its army, and the Company increasingly sought to integrate them with European soldiers, train them according to European norms, and subject them to British martial law. By the 1760s, the conventional wisdom among British officers had shifted: sepoys were now assumed to be capable soldiers. Even as the Company moved toward greater pluralism in its civil law, it was drawing toward greater homogeneity in its army.[35]

As with other efforts to transplant British institutions, there were debates about how quickly and how thoroughly Indian soldiers should be brought under British military discipline. One such dispute arose in 1768, when Colonel Richard Smith, the commander in chief in Bengal, ordered that sepoys be held accountable under English law for "all capital crimes."[36] Clive's successor as governor, Harry Verelst, objected to Smith's orders, which he saw as usurping his own authority to set legal policy. As Bengal's civilian and military authorities jockeyed for supremacy, both sides insisted that their goal was to anglicize martial law. Smith argued that the British articles of war had applied to Indian soldiers (with local modifications) since he took command of the army in 1765.[37] Verelst and the members of the Fort William council disagreed. They acknowledged that "this government has long been endeavouring to introduce into the Sepoy corps such parts of the British martial laws as were not inconsistent with their customs and their religion," but the governor and council denied that this had already happened.[38] And while they agreed with Smith that British-style discipline "must tend to the better regulation of our army," they insisted on a more gradual introduction of English law than the general envisioned.[39] Nonetheless, both sides agreed that the question was how, not whether, to introduce English military law to the Indian army.[40]

Their shared enthusiasm for English military discipline puts Clive's policy of legal pluralism in a new light. Rather than a respectful attempt to maintain precolonial laws, it is more accurately described as the introduction of English-style restraints without English-style rights or remedies. Along the same lines, the Company didn't hesitate to introduce English practices of labor discipline, as Prasannan Parthasarathi has shown. Starting in the late 1760s, the Company introduced new, more coercive ways of controlling Indian weavers, which contravened South Asian labor practices. This disciplinary anglicization undermined what had been a thriving textile industry and helped transform Bengal into an economically extractive colony.[41]

In fact, Clive and his disciples seem to have been less interested in preserving Indian laws than in reducing the importance of law altogether. The most prominent feature of Clivite legal policy was not legal pluralism but a systematic attempt to suppress litigation. To be sure, a distaste for litigiousness had also been a feature of Mughal society, and one shouldn't exaggerate the novelty of Clive's program.[42] Before the Company took over Bengal's legal system, it had been customary for courts to levy a duty of between one-fourth and one-fifth of all judgments. As a result, many potential litigants avoided the courts and instead favored arbitration, which had been a staple of dispute resolution throughout precolonial and early colonial India.[43]

Under Clive and his successors, however, the Company took anti-litigiousness to a new level. Company-run cutchery courts started to levy "extraordinary" duties on suits they deemed frivolous or which demanded outrageously excessive damages. These aggressive new fines were designed to discourage meritless litigation, which Company officials described as an epidemic afflicting Bengal.[44] Meanwhile, Company officials also tried to make litigation less adversarial, transforming the courts of cutchery—the local tribunals that handled most civil litigation—into something more closely resembling conciliation courts. The centerpiece of this program was a new restriction on parties' right to be represented by counsel. In the early 1760s, litigants had often appeared by their vakils, or attorneys. In 1765, however, the court proposed to ban vakils unless the party was an orphan or widow or resided outside of Calcutta. Everyone else had to present their own arguments. The court also sought to limit the right of appeal.[45]

It's tempting to interpret these efforts as reflecting a caricature of Indians as unusually litigious. In the early 1750s, the mayor of Calcutta had warned that the inhabitants of his city "are beyond doubt the most litigious people existing."[46] Robert Orme agreed: "The Natives are as litigious and malicious a Race as any whatever."[47] But such stereotypes were not unique to India. In Quebec, Governor James Murray reported that "Canadians, mostly of a Norman Race, are in general of a litigious Disposition"; George Turnbull warned that the inhabitants of Detroit were "the most Licentious and most Litigious set in the world"; and Thomas Whately complained about "the litigiousness of the people" in other parts of North America.[48] During this time, officials throughout the British Empire adopted anti-litigation policies, including the Stamp Act (which was, among other things, a tax on litigation) and Gage's efforts to encourage arbitration in Illinois (discussed in Chapter 2).[49]

In time, the cliché of "the litigious Indian" would come to dominate colonial handbooks and historiography.[50] But in the 1760s and 1770s, the Company's attitude toward lawsuits in Bengal had less to do with local stereotypes than with a broader distrust of litigation common to paternalists in many parts of the British Empire. In response to what they saw as the destabilizing effects of litigation, officials in America, India, and England tried to reorient dispute resolution toward forms that were less adversarial and more amenable to the control of local elites. In both Bengal and Illinois, the failure of that project forced officials to seek new ways of administering civil justice. In North America, the result was Illinois's being folded into Quebec in 1774. In Bengal, the inadequacy of arbitration as a substitute for litigation contributed to the rise of a more ambitious program of Company-administered legal pluralism, as the next section will explain.

DISMANTLING DOUBLE GOVERNMENT

Clive's plan of double government was supposed to make the Company rich. Instead, it generated a series of crises. The "revenues" barely covered the cost of Bengal's civil and military establishment, and by 1768 it looked like the *diwani* might have produced a net loss. The Company's operations outside of Bengal were also struggling. In the Madras Presidency, the first Anglo-Mysore War (1767–69) produced rumors of military defeat that caused the Company's stock to plummet. Matters went from disappointing to catastrophic when a severe famine struck Bengal in 1769–70, killing perhaps a third of the population.[51]

Meanwhile, Company officials were finding it hard to make double government work. After Verelst succeeded Clive as governor in 1767, he determined that the Company needed to take a more active role in governing Bengal. Although the Company had previously sought to outsource civil administration to Mughal officials, Verelst and his advisors concluded "that the welfare of Bengal depends in a great degree upon the due execution of offices, and trust in which Europeans have never yet *formally* interfered."[52] Although the

Company persisted in its model of extracting wealth through taxation, it now sought to exercise more direct control over Bengal's administrative and legal affairs.

One aspect of this new attitude to governance was a greater willingness to change Indian law. Although the Company remained committed to legal pluralism, it had also become concerned that certain aspects of Mughal law were contrary to natural justice and economically counterproductive. One early target was Bengal's inheritance regime. In 1768, the Company's directors (still controlled by Clive's supporters) ordered the government at Calcutta to "introduce Laws of Inheritance . . . as near as possible to the Spirit of the Laws of this Country," and particularly "to introduce the Right of bequeathing by Will." The directors were under the impression that the Mughal state had customarily seized the estates of deceased persons, particularly those who died childless or who had been employed in government service. It's not clear that such seizures ever took place. But the directors feared that even the rumor of such a custom might cause property owners to hoard or conceal their wealth, thus rendering it economically useless.[53] At the same time, Company officials worried that escheatage of the sort allegedly practiced in Bengal was contrary to "the natural rights of inheritance."[54] Justice and corporate self-interest both demanded the abrogation of Mughal custom.

Mughal criminal law also came under greater scrutiny. In the early 1770s, the Council of Control at Murshidabad, which was chaired by Verelst's advisor Richard Becher, observed that Islamic criminal law as administered in Bengal violated several English norms. First, Mughal courts punished many crimes with fines, which were calculated not "according to the nature of the offence" but rather "the abilities and circumstances of the offender." As a result, a rich fornicator might be fined a thousand times more than a poor murderer. Moreover, because fines went chiefly to private prosecutors, not the public treasury, some inhabitants made their living from accusing "the rich and substantial" of crimes like "Witchcraft" or "Whoredom." Non-pecuniary punishments, such as the punishment of theft by amputation, also struck some Company servants as barbaric.[55]

In light of these apparent conflicts between Mughal criminal law and British sensibilities, the Council of Control considered "the propriety of deviating from the Letter of Mahometan Law, and of proportioning punishments to *our* notions of the nature and extent of crimes." This would not mean the wholesale application of English law, which was generally "unknown and in numberless instances repugnant to the Genius of the People and contrary to [the laws] already established." Nonetheless, it seemed essential to craft some discrete regulations, "formed from local knowledge," to curb what the Council saw as the most egregious abuses. The Council's report avoided proposing any definite solutions other than abolishing the office of *naib diwan,* which had formal responsibility for legal administration. Eliminating that position, the Council argued, would allow the power "of remedying very many evils" to "be vested formally in the Company's Servants," rather than their Mughal puppets.[56] This was, of course, antithetical to the notion of double government.

The Company also adjusted its efforts to discourage litigation. In 1769, the directors asked the Bengal government to investigate the administration of justice and to reform it as needed. They were particularly anxious to reduce taxes on recovered debts (although cutcherry courts could continue to fine plaintiffs who brought frivolous suits).[57] At the same time, however, the Company redoubled its efforts to encourage arbitration. It eliminated fees associated with court-annexed arbitration, started taxing appeals from arbitral awards, and began recording arbitral awards.[58]

In the early 1770s, however, some in the Company asked whether its preference for arbitration was worth the trouble. Litigants complained that arbitration was "dilatory, undecisive, and unsatisfactory."[59] Although Company officials "generally proposed to the parties in dispute to determine their causes by arbitration," Charles Stuart reported from Burdwan, "they nevertheless prefer the Enquiry & decision of the Cutcherry."[60] He attributed this "backwardness" to the "venality of the Natives," but other Company agents were more discerning. William Barton, the collector at Luckypore (Lakshmipur), agreed with Stuart that "[t]he original & laudable design of arbitrating causes . . . is strangely perverted," so that "what was intended as a relief to the Parties is now in fact no longer so." But he offered a more thoughtful explanation for arbitration's failure: a lack of enthusiasm among potential arbitrators.[61]

For a decade, the inhabitants of Bengal had complained about being asked by the Company to serve as uncompensated adjudicators of their neighbors' affairs.[62] This was particularly true of merchants, "who [were] obliged to neglect their own business" whenever they acted as arbitrators, "and who receive[d] nothing for their trouble."[63] People tapped as arbitrators frequently petitioned the Company to be excused—or, in some cases, just refused to show up. "[F]ew of the persons acting as arbitrators willingly perform this office," lamented Charles Bentley, the tax collector at Chittagong.[64] There was no obvious solution. If arbitration remained voluntary, arbitrators would "deem the cause referred to them as subservient to their leisure and to be postponed to all their private considerations."[65] As long as that was true, disputants would naturally prefer to go to law. Bentley's proposed solution was to fine delinquent arbitrators. He thought that some kind of "compulsion" was necessary—"persuasion will have little Effect"—and he couldn't think of anything "gentler" than a monetary penalty.[66] But some of his colleagues worried that conscripted adjudicators wouldn't perform their duties with care, and that drafting arbitrators would in any event be "an arbitrary and unjustifiable Exertion of Power."[67]

Another Company collector suggested a carrot instead of a stick: paying arbitrators for their work, in effect treating them as part-time magistrates.[68] But this also had pitfalls. In addition to the Company's aversion to new expenses, some local elites warned that paid arbitrators would "be the source of venality & Mal Practices."[69] At least in the eyes of some disputants, the legitimacy of arbitration depended on its seeming to be purely a matter of public service. After considering these objections, some Company employees concluded that there was no good option.[70] As Samuel Middleton and George Hurst reported from Murshidabad, "the Introduction of Arbitration on the extensive Plan laid down by our Honorable Masters, must, we think, be doubtful and precarious."[71]

Finding arbitrators wasn't the only challenge. The Company's arbitration program also faced political and theological objections from local elites. In 1772, Muhammed Reza Khan, the *naib diwan,* to whom the Company had delegated its duties under the *diwani,* complained that Company-sponsored arbitration contravened both Mughal custom and Islamic law. Several branches of law, he explained, had long been regulated "by the Laws of the Scripture according to the Orders of the Almighty and his Prophet." Those subjects included inheritance, family law, certain torts, and crimes. The *naib diwan* insisted that no devout Muslim could submit a dispute concerning those topics to arbitrators whose decision might "differ . . . widely from the peculiar Precepts of the Mussulman Faith."[72] The Company had initially been attracted to arbitration because it seemed to leave Indian society alone. But now, as Middleton and Hurst warned, the Company's efforts "suddenly to introduce the general Practice of the mode of arbitration in all Cases, would be looked on by [Mughal officials and Muslim inhabitants] as an Encroachment on their Laws, and consequently in some measure an Infringement on their Religion & Customs."[73] Mandatory arbitration was far more invasive than the Company had realized.

That didn't mean that every dispute had to be formally adjudicated under

Islamic law. Reza Khan conceded that "[t]here are a few Cases, . . . such as Debts and Commercial Matters," in which it might be appropriate for arbitrators to resolve disputes "according to Equity."[74] That exception led Middleton and Hurst to suggest that a more limited arbitration scheme might be salvaged. But in 1773, the Company's directors grudgingly conceded that their plan of arbitration had failed and that they needed a new strategy for civil justice. They continued to urge the government in Bengal to use their "best endeavours" to find "some method which may encourage the natives to take on themselves the office of arbitrators"; but the Company also acknowledged the need "for speedy and effectual administration of justice" through courts.[75] The task of constructing such a regime fell to Warren Hastings, who became governor of Bengal in 1772.

INTERVENTIONIST LEGAL PLURALISM

Hastings was an unlikely architect of Indian legal pluralism. He had entered the Company's service in 1750 at the age of seventeen, and his early years in India seem to have convinced him that the Company did best as a purely commercial enterprise. In the 1760s, he aligned himself with Laurence Sulivan (the influential Company director) and Henry Vansittart (another governor of Bengal), who resisted Clive's efforts to transform the Company into a territorial and extractive power. Sulivan, in particular, worried that Clive's conquests were a bad investment and that a mercantile corporation was poorly suited to the business of state-building. "It is extremely easy to parcel out upon paper Kingdoms that are infinitely larger than Great Britain," he warned William Pitt in 1761; "but to carry such schemes into execution might prove an arduous Task even to Government, surely then too bold and imprudent for a Trading Company."[76] In his view, the Company would thrive if it stuck to exploiting its longstanding commercial monopoly. Hastings articulated a similar vision from his position on the Calcutta council. Although he acknowledged the Company's rising military power in South Asia, he remained skeptical of the long-term benefits of conquest. The only advantage the Company ought to derive from the success of its armies was greater freedom to trade. Its only purpose in Bengal, he insisted, was to expand "commerce," from which both the Company and "the country" could "reap a benefit." Taxation and governance should remain in native hands.[77]

In other words, Hastings and his allies wanted the Company to continue its old business model. That, in turn, implied that the Company should also continue its earlier policy of using English law to attract local merchants. Thus, Governor Vansittart led Calcutta's justices of the peace in declaring that "a free and impartial administration of the Laws of England to the inhabitants in general of whatever cast or profession" would greatly benefit the city.[78] Just like it had before Plassey, the Company was to govern only a small slice of territory, and it would do so using English law. This approach remained viable as long as Vansittart controlled Bengal and Sulivan controlled the Company. In 1764, however, Clive's allies took control, and Clive himself returned to Bengal the following year. Within a few months, he had accepted the *diwani*, thus acquiring for the Company a formal role in territorial governance. Vansittart and Hastings resigned and returned to England.[79]

At that point, Sulivan shifted his strategy. The Company was stuck with the *diwani*, and he now considered it inevitable that Britons were going to rule Bengal. But he continued to insist that the business of the Company was business. The best way to reconcile these two realities was for the Company to surrender its territorial powers to the British state. That would free the Company to pursue "commerce alone," which Sulivan described as its "natural" mission.[80] In pursuit of this new project, he forged an alliance with populist politicians, including John Dunning (his longtime lawyer) and Lord Shelburne (who had previously secured Sulivan a seat in the House of Commons).

Sulivan's new alliance saw an opportunity in 1766, when the Chatham administration launched an ambitious inquiry into the Company. As we'll see below, some populists, such as William Beckford, wanted to use the inquiry as an excuse to dissolve the Company entirely. But Sulivan thought he could turn it to the Company's benefit. He hoped to persuade Parliament to take charge of Bengal's government and to compensate the Company for the privilege. (As Vansittart put it, "it will be best to look upon the King of England as Emperor of Bengal.")[81] That solution appealed to Sulivan, who would see his Company restored to commercial glory, and to populists who wanted to end Clive's extractions in Bengal.[82] But the inquiry failed to realize Sulivan's hopes (Chapter 5 will explain why), and he was forced once again to rework his ideas about the Company's purpose.

After the parliamentary inquiry fizzled out, Sulivan conceded that Clive's vision had prevailed and that the Company was now going to operate a tributary state in Bengal. At that point, he stopped trying to bring the Company back to its commercial roots. When he regained control of the Company in 1769, he and his allies instead focused on improving its approach to tax collection and governance.

In accepting Clive's business model, Sulivan and his allies also accepted his approach to legal policy. Since the Company now made more money from tribute than trade, it was no longer important to offer English law as an amenity to Indian merchants. Vansittart, who had once sought to make English law available to all, now thought it "advisable to let the Country people be govern'd by their own Chiefs and their own Laws just as they are at present." But although Sulivan and his friends now agreed with Clive on the need for legal pluralism, they had very different ideas about what it ought to look like. Clive's plan of double government had assumed that the old Mughal regime remained functionally intact, so that the Company could simply step into its shoes. Sulivanite officials, in contrast, started from the assumption that "[t]he Empire of India . . . is dissolved and shatter'd."[83] Building on reforms that had started under Verelst, Sulivan encouraged the Company to continue its reevaluation of double government, a process that culminated in the Company's decision in 1772 to "stand forth" as *diwan*—in other words, to assume direct responsibility for many of the functions it had previously delegated to Mughal officials.[84]

This decision had important implications for the Company's approach to law. When Hastings began his tenure as governor, he described Bengal as "a land which to this day exists without any Court or forms of Justice."[85] In making that statement, he didn't mean to disparage the substance of Hindu or Islamic law, but rather to describe a total breakdown of judicial administration. Because there was no Mughal legal system that the Company might plausibly claim to inherit, it had to build one. The central feature of this program was a firm assertion of the Company's sovereignty. Like Hardwicke's "Scotch Reformation," Hastings saw himself as engaged in a program of rationalization that sought to clear away rivals to the central government, whether heritable jurisdictions in Scotland or petty Mughal magistrates in Bengal.[86] He summarized his reforms as ensuring that "[e]very intermediate power is removed, and the sovereignty of this country wholly and absolutely vested in the Company."[87] Unlike Clive, who had tried to govern through local puppets, Hastings insisted on direct rule.

Like his vision of sovereignty, Hastings's ideas about the structure of government were rooted in the English Whig tradition. In a series of "Proposed Regulations" he drafted in 1772, he described his program as seeking "to make [Indians'] laws sit as light on them as possible, and to share with them the privileges of our own constitution, where they are capable of partaking of them consistently with their other Rights, and the Welfare of the State." While the substance of Bengal's laws would remain consistent with Clive's policy of legal pluralism, the institutions that administered them would gradually be anglicized. Revenue collection, for example, was to be organized into districts that "answer[ed] nearly to (a) Tithings, (b) Hundreds, & (c) Counties."[88] A similar desire to reproduce British institutions animated Hastings's efforts to distinguish more clearly between civil and criminal justice.[89]

Despite these anglicizing moves, Hastings and his colleagues insisted that they were maintaining the "ancient Usages and Institutions" of the Mughal Empire.[90] In practice, that meant repackaging Clive's program of litigation suppression as an enlightened revival of Mughal legality. In 1772, Hastings chaired a Committee of Circuit that drew up a new plan for the administration of justice in Bengal. The Committee purported to follow with "a scrupulous Exactness" "the constitutional forms of Judicature already established in this Province."[91] But although its language suggested careful adherence to Mughal tradition, the plan itself revealed great willingness to innovate when it suited the Company's purpose.

The 1772 plan created separate civil and criminal courts in each district, decisions from which would be appealable to a corresponding court of review in Calcutta. For civil cases, the district court would be known as the *mofussil diwani adalat*, with the district collector serving as judge. In those courts, litigation suppression remained a key feature of the Company's approach. The 1772 regulations included several provisions to combat "the Litigiousness . . . of the Natives of this Country." There would be a strict statute of limitations, as well as financial or corporal sanctions for anyone who filed "trivial and groundless Complaints," who filed groundless appeals, or who too flagrantly sought to play Bengal's competing jurisdictions against each other. In addition, local revenue farmers would decide small claims without appeal.[92]

The procedure for deciding higher-value cases would depend on the nature of the dispute. In cases involving "disputed Accounts, Partnerships, Debts, doubtful or contested Bargains, [or] Non-performances of Contracts," the collector was to recommend (but not compel) arbitration, which would be enforceable as a decree of the court. The parties themselves would choose the arbitrators, who were "to decide the Cause without Fee or Reward." Although the collector was "to afford every Encouragement in his Power to Inhabitants of Character and Credit to become Arbitrators," he could not "employ any coercive Means for that Purpose."[93]

Hastings thus declined to offer any response to widespread complaints about the difficulty of finding arbitrators. Indeed, by rejecting both compulsion and reward, he all but guaranteed that a lack of willing arbitrators would continue to clog the administration of justice. Hastings closed off another possible solution by forbidding the judge's own subordinates from serving as arbitrators—a practice that judges in England frequently used to facilitate dispute resolution.[94] Moreover, the new regulations said nothing about the substantive law that would govern such disputes. It seemed that in commercial cases, some kind of customary law was to apply, but only as determined ad hoc by the arbitrators or the court.[95] In contrast to these vague rules for commercial cases, "Suits regarding Inheritance, Marriage, Cast, and other religious Usages or Institutions" would "invariably" be decided according to religious law—namely, "the Laws of the Koran with respect to Mahometans, and those of the Shaster with respect to Gentoos."[96]

Historians have long been puzzled by this bifurcation between the so-called "listed subjects," for which Hindu or Islamic law would govern, and other areas of civil law, to which Hastings gave less attention. J. D. M. Derrett suggested that the boundary tracked contemporary Indian and English notions about the nature of religious law. (Ecclesiastical courts in England handled many of the same subjects that Hastings reserved for religious law in Bengal.) This interpretation aligns with Bernard Cohn's argument that Hastings viewed Indian society as fundamentally "theocratic." More recently, Robert Travers has linked Hastings's taxonomy to Muhammed Reza Khan's complaints about Company-sponsored arbitration. As we've seen, Reza Khan insisted that some kinds of disputes had to be decided according to Islamic law, while others could be handled more informally; and Hastings's plan of 1772 tracks the boundaries sketched out by Reza Khan.[97]

That explains why Hastings was so eager to provide for the formal adjudication of religiously charged disputes. But why *only* those disputes? Why didn't Hastings also specify that religious laws would govern commercial cases? The explanation lies in the purpose of legal pluralism. Despite his earlier qualms about Clive's agenda, Hastings had accepted that Bengal was going to become the tributary province Clive had envisioned. "The [Company's] System has within these few years undergone a total change," Hastings admitted in 1771: "From a merely commercial Body they are grown up into a military & Territorial Power, to which their Commerce is but a secondary concern."[98] On this view, English law was at best irrelevant and at worst unhelpful, for the reasons discussed above. Indeed, the Company had little to gain from encouraging any kind of litigation at all.

The 1772 regulations that Hastings drafted reflected a basic indifference about whether or how Indian litigants resolved certain kinds of disputes. Reza Khan had made it clear that Bengal's inhabitants (or at least some Mughal elites) would demand religious adjudication in some areas. But for those subjects over which Hastings had a freer hand, he declined to provide any workable system of adjudication at all. It cannot have escaped his attention that those were also the subjects of greatest importance to merchants. It was well known in Company circles that Indian merchants had for decades brought their cases before English courts, even after the Company's 1753 charter tried to keep them out.[99] In 1772, Alexander Wedderburn, who served both as solicitor general and as Clive's personal lawyer, learned of complaints by Indian merchants in Calcutta that "their own Country Judges" were corrupt, "very expensive," and "troublesome." As a result, native merchants often "chose to have their Disputes determined by the Chief of the Companies factory," whom they paid for that service, rather than resorting to the judiciary.[100]

In the early 1770s, British officials had ample evidence of a continuing demand for adjudication. Hastings responded by closing the courthouse door. Rather than specifying any sort of procedural or substantive framework on which litigants might have relied, he left the determination of their disputes entirely to the discretion of local Company officials. He then encouraged those officials to shunt commercial and other cases into a system of arbitration that had already proved ineffectual. This predictably unworkable system made sense only because Hastings had come to see the government of Bengal as a tributary enterprise meant to extract wealth from heavily policed inhabitants.

Hastings would continue to see courts as obstacles for the rest of his tenure as governor. "The court of justice is a dreadful clog on the government," Hastings grumbled in 1774, shortly after Parliament had authorized a new Supreme Court in Calcutta.[101] Like others in Bengal, he eventually adapted to the new institution. But it was often keener to hear Indians' complaints than he would have liked, and his alleged efforts to manipulate its judges would eventually contribute to his recall and impeachment. In the end, he would have been happier if the court hadn't been created at all.

PATHS NOT TAKEN

Hastings's antipathy to civil litigation reflected a new orthodoxy within the Company. Although he and Sulivan had once been skeptical of the Company's pivot toward a militarized and tributary form of colonialism, they now embraced it, along with a complementary strategy of legal pluralism. But not

The Old Court House, Calcutta. From Thomas Daniell,
Views in Calcutta (Calcutta: 1786–88). Courtesy of the Yale Center for
British Art, Paul Mellon Collection. The Supreme Court of Judicature sat for its
first seven years in the building on the right, which was also used by the Freemasons
and for public entertainments. After experimenting with other quarters (described
by Chief Justice Impey as posing a "manifest . . . danger to our constitutions and
lives"), the justices finally secured a new courthouse in 1782. The new building was an
improvement, although some residents thought that "there was not in the whole town
a meaner building externally." Quoted in H. E. A. Cotton, "Memories of the Supreme
Court: 1774–1862," *Bengal Past & Present* 30, no. 59 (1925): 150–98. The court's
physical infrastructure gives some indication of how the Company valued it.

everyone was willing to toe the new Company line. Britons had become accustomed to idealizing their empire as "Protestant, commercial, maritime, and free," in David Armitage's well-known formula.[102] Of course, that was a poor description of imperial reality, which included the domination of Catholic Ireland, the expropriation of indigenous land, and various forms of enslavement and unfree labor. But subjugating millions of non-Protestant Indians after 1757 was an exception that threatened to swallow the ideological rule.[103]

Unsurprisingly, then, the Company's post-Plassey transformation sparked a major backlash. As we've seen, one source of resistance came from within the Company itself, as Sulivan and others tried and failed to keep it a purely commercial enterprise. A group of external critics, mostly associated with populists, offered a more radical proposal: turn Bengal into a British province. This plan would have eliminated the Company entirely, instead turning northeastern India into a plantation colony like those in British North America. Although this group sometimes invoked North America as their model, Senegambia (discussed in Chapter 3) was a closer analogue to what they had in mind. In North America, British settlement had often presumed the expropriation or exclusion of natives. In Africa and Asia, however, settler-colonial projects imagined a combination of British immigration and the reconstruction of existing societies along British lines. The colonization of Bengal, in other words, was projected to involve the persistence of native labor and native title.

Despite that fundamental difference between Asian and American settler colonialism, populist writers often linked the two programs. Populists hoped that both places would share an economic model rooted in the colonial consumption of British goods rather than the extraction of wealth from tributary populations. In the words of one memorandum, "the Export of one thousand Pound in value of woollens manufactured [in Britain] is of more solid benefit to England than the Import of 10,000 [pounds] from our Revenues in the East."[104] Philip Francis, a member of Bengal's governing council, agreed. "Bengal should not, in my opinion, pay any direct Tribute to Great Britain," he told Lord North. "The Advantage to Great Britain will be much greater, and of a better Sort, if the People of India are gradually encouraged & enabled to purchase our Manufactures."[105] Only if Indians became consumers of British goods—and rich enough to sustain their consumption over time—would India benefit Britain.

Transplanting English law was at the core of this alternative vision of Indian empire. As Chapters 2 and 3 explained, policymakers generally agreed that British immigration was essential for developing anglicized colonies like those in North America. And the best way to lure new settlers was to promise English law.[106] As William Pulteney told Parliament, "the establishment of a proper system of laws" in Bengal would lead to more Britons residing there. In the same speech, he attacked the jurisdictional division between native and European litigants. Only a unified court system based on the laws of England, he suggested, would permit a free settlement based on trade rather than expropriation.[107]

Not everyone agreed that large-scale immigration to India was desirable or feasible. Company officials like Henry Vansittart insisted that Bengal was too large to "send over English Subjects in such numbers as to colonize" it, especially since its climate was unhealthy for Europeans.[108] But those sorts of claims were partisan talking points, not neutral statements of fact. Company officials gave varying assessments of Bengal's climate depending on what they wanted to accomplish. In the 1750s, the former mayor of Calcutta, John Zephaniah Holwell, had urged the Company to subsidize colonization for defensive purposes: "Embark 4 or 5 Familys, Farmers Laborers or handicrafts on each of their ships, under such Stipulations & contract, as will at once enlarge the Colony, give you in a short time a Standing Militia."[109] It seems that his earlier experience as the Company's chief physician and surgeon in Calcutta had failed to convince him that it was unfit for Europeans.

As P. J. Marshall has argued, India's "unique unfitness for 'colonization'" was a doctrine of politics, not science.[110] And Company officials knew it. Indeed, they believed that European settlement was plausible enough that it had to be discouraged—hence their decision in 1766 to prohibit Britons from owning land in Bengal.[111] The need for such measures suggests that many Britons would otherwise have found India to be a desirable place to live. Adam Smith reached the same conclusion in *The Wealth of Nations* when he sought to explain the discrepancy between settlement patterns in India and North America. Although he acknowledged that a densely settled region like Bengal was inherently less attractive to European settlers—"it was more difficult to displace the natives"—he didn't think that demography and climate were the main story. Instead, he argued that the Company's monopoly "has probably been the principal cause" of the absence of European colonization in India. As evidence, he cited Portuguese colonies in Africa and Asia, which were established "without any exclusive companies," and which more closely resembled "the colonies of America" than Britain's Indian outposts.[112] Asia and America were settled differently because they had been governed differently.[113]

Smith's analysis was plausible because, as Chapter 3 explained, there was no medical consensus that tropical colonies were categorically unfit for Europeans. To be sure, many contemporaries regarded Bengal as unhealthy. But prominent physicians also believed that Europeans could become "seasoned" to South Asia, so that they would eventually be "subject to as few diseases as those who reside at home."[114] Microclimates would facilitate the seasoning process. Cities like Calcutta might be unhealthy, but they usually had "healthy situations" nearby that could provide a refuge for new European arrivals.[115] And, as with Senegambia, commentators also predicted that British settlement would eventually improve the healthfulness of India's environment as a whole. Britons could adapt to India, and India could be adapted to Britons.[116] Even some opponents of colonization agreed. Clive told his father that "I enjoy my Health [in India] better than in England." When the Company's directors asked him whether a new fort at Calcutta was "unhealthy," he blamed soldiers' sickness on a poorly constructed pond nearby, rather than the regional climate.[117]

Contemporary views of climate and tropical medicine led many Britons to treat Bengal and North America as different but fundamentally commensurable. That explains, for example, why Smith could propose "a universal model of growth that could be extended across the British Empire from New Jersey to Bengal," as Fredrik Albritton Jonsson has summarized it.[118] According to Smith, the reason that Bengal suffered a catastrophic famine while other British colonies thrived was "[t]he difference between the genius of the British constitution which protects and governs North America, and that of the mercantile company which oppresses and domineers in the East Indies."[119] He wasn't alone in elevating institutions over environmental endowments as an explanation for colonial development. One of his acquaintances, the historian John Campbell, declared that Britain's South Asian outposts could "make as rich and as flourishing Colonies as *Virginia,* or *Jamaica,*" as long as Europeans and Indians were "incorporated" together under "*good laws.*" Campbell considered his theory of law and development to be a universal prescription for colonial growth, and he offered similar plans for improving Senegambia and Scotland's impoverished Western Isles.[120]

Proponents of colonizing Bengal agreed on the need to anglicize its legal system, but they weren't always clear about how fully English law would apply. George Johnstone, the former governor of West Florida, provides an example. In 1771, he wrote a pamphlet that encouraged transplanting English law to Bengal. But he shrank from imposing the full extent of it "at once." "What I chiefly wish to establish," he explained, "is the freedom and independence of our own countrymen, particularly in the pure administration of justice; so that the happy effects of a moderated government may extend to the native inhabitants of the country by due degrees."[121] But while his immediate focus was on providing English law for British immigrants, he ultimately intended his "plan for administration of justice abroad" to "extend to all inhabitants" in Bengal.[122] By gradually improving the administration of justice, Johnstone argued, Britain could increase the "wealth of the natives" and still "draw these immense sums" for its own benefit.[123]

Johnstone and his family were prominent in Company politics, and his work might have helped to inspire two other influential critiques of legal pluralism in Bengal. The first was by Alexander Dow, an orientalist, playwright, and army officer. Dow had links to a range of literary and political figures, and he intended his *History of Hindostan* as both a lasting scholarly contribution and an occasional attack on Company rule. Dow offered a sympathetic portrait of Mughal institutions, but his "Plan for Restoring Bengal to its Former Prosperity" urged Parliament to extend English law to Bengal—a demand rooted not in disdain for Indian legal traditions but in his understanding of law and development.[124] Like other critics of Clivite imperialism, Dow argued that Britain needed to focus less on extracting wealth from its subjects than on helping them thrive. "Bengal can . . . be useful," Dow insisted, "only in the prosperity and industry of its inhabitants." To bring that about, he prescribed several economic policies that were favored by populists, including a paper currency, the encouragement of immigration into Bengal, support for local manufacturing, the abolition of monopolies, and moderate taxes that would allow Indians to enjoy the rewards of their labor.[125]

Dow presented the partial introduction of English law as essential to his project. He thought that Bengalis would need to be "left in possession of some of their laws and usages" to ensure their loyalty. In particular, "regulations, with regard to their women and religion, must never be touched"; the same was true for most rules of inheritance. In that respect, his plan didn't diverge much from that of Hastings. In other areas, however, Dow's approach was quite different. Although existing inheritance laws might be retained for personal property, Dow proposed that "the spirit of the laws of a commonwealth be adopted" for land. "To prevent the accumulation of landed property," he wrote, lands should "be divided equally among all the male issue of the proprietor."[126] Although this deviated from the English rule of primogeniture, it reflected the practice of many American colonies, where partible inheritance was credited with encouraging productivity by allocating land to small-scale farmers.[127]

Dow also proposed other changes to Indian laws. British notions of "humanity" demanded a stop to sati and to punishing theft by amputation. And even insofar as Hindu or Islamic law were benign in themselves, a plurality of laws was inherently problematic: "To leave the natives entirely to their own laws, would be to consign them to anarchy, and confusion." If Britain retained separate laws for Hindus and Muslims, it would guarantee perpetual division between the two groups; and Dow's vision for Bengal demanded unification. "It is, therefore, absolutely necessary for the peace and prosperity of the country," Dow insisted, "that the laws of England, in so far as they do not oppose prejudices and usages which cannot be relinquished by the natives, should prevail."[128] Dow also wanted to anglicize the institutions that administered those laws. For example, he proposed to invest local revenue officers "with a commission similar to that of a justice of the peace." Mughal mayors could operate commercial tribunals modeled on English piepowder courts. Finally, he urged the creation of a supreme court in Calcutta that would be "the counterpart of the court of king's bench in England."[129]

Dow's approach was far from egalitarian. He was a critic of Clive's imperialism but not of imperialism itself. Indeed, he urged Lord Shelburne to expand the Company's territorial footprint, in part on the theory that Indians themselves wanted it. In Dow's view, the inhabitants of Bengal had little desire for political freedom as long as they enjoyed stability and economic security. Thus, only "British subjects"—a term that apparently excluded South Asians—needed to serve on juries or have a right to jury trials.[130] And yet, despite Dow's exclusionary views, there were important differences between his proposal and the Company's policies. Dow aimed to make the government of Bengal not only tolerable but genuinely attractive for Indians. He predicted that his proposal, if accepted, would generate an "influx of specie and inhabitants"—similar to what moderates and populists had hoped the introduction of English law would achieve in Quebec.[131] And while Dow envisioned Bengal's government as inevitably hierarchical, he also thought it could be participatory. As this chapter has shown, the Company's programs of legal pluralism reflected distaste for litigation. Dow, in contrast, accepted that his reforms would "introduce an ample harvest for men of the law; but it is better that they should live by litigiousness, than that the people should perish by tyranny."[132] His plan sought not only to make property secure, but to do so through a potentially contentious system that would give Bengalis (and their lawyers) a share in defending their own rights.

A more radical critique of Company rule came from William Bolts, a former Company trader. Bolts was less learned than Dow, and his book owed less to literary ambition than to his ongoing feud with Governor Verelst. But as a former alderman of Calcutta and member of its mayor's court, Bolts was well positioned to attack the Company's legal policy. Soon after returning to England, he published his *Considerations on Indians Affairs,* which attracted widespread attention.[133] Like Dow, he urged the partial introduction of English law. But Bolts's vision was more egalitarian, envisioning an integrated polity based on free trade and equal access to English justice.

One of his principal targets was the Company's claim to have preserved Mughal laws and institutions. Bolts, citing Dow as well as his own observations, insisted that the old Mughal regime was defunct: "the whole country is in a state of anarchy, where there is no law." This, in his view, was the fundamental cause of Bengal's distress: "In all countries the right administration of justice is the foundation of national prosperity." The solution, according to Bolts, was to renounce the fiction of Mughal continuity and for the Company to take direct control of the administration of justice. Up to this point, his diagnosis and prescription closely resembled the program that Hastings was executing at that very moment. But Bolts disagreed about the kind of law the Company ought to administer. He insisted on an English judiciary, including for Indians. Because Indians and Europeans in Bengal were equally "British subjects" and "members of the same body-politic," they deserved the protection of the same laws—namely, the "laws of England."[134]

Public reactions to the pamphlets of Bolts and Dow led some politicians to reevaluate Bengal's legal system.[135] At first, critics focused on the quality of Indian courts rather than the law they applied. This was largely due to the initiative of Laurence Sulivan, who had introduced, on behalf of the Company's directors, a bill to reform Bengal's judiciary. Like Hastings's regulations, the East India Judicature Bill of 1772 showed little concern for the law governing most transactions in Bengal. Instead, its purpose was to check abuses by Company officials. To that end, it proposed a supreme court in Calcutta staffed by professional judges whose tenure and independence would mirror those of judges in England, and who would hear suits concerning abuses by Company employees.[136]

Sulivan was proposing a fairly minor change, but George Johnstone took advantage of the ensuing debate to offer a broader critique of Indian legal pluralism. An early version of Sulivan's bill had limited the jurisdiction of the proposed court to "British subjects Europeans and Christians." Johnstone pointed out the absurdity of that limitation when he presented a petition from Gregore Cojamaul, an Armenian associate of Bolts who also alleged persecution at the hands of Verelst, and whom the bill would have excluded from the new court's protection. In response, the bill's sponsors dropped the "European" qualifier to make it clear that Armenian Christians like Cojamaul would have equal access to English law. But that missed the point, Johnstone complained. "[I]t was not because he was a Christian that I presented his petition, because he was a human being and fellow-creature," Johnstone told the Commons; "nor can the gentlemen who patronize this Bill shew me one reason for inserting the word Christian that does not equally apply for putting in the words Mussulman and Gentoo." Although he had previously expressed ambivalence about imposing English law on Indian natives, he now refused to countenance a court whose jurisdiction depended on religion. The laws and constitution of Bengal, he insisted, should be modeled on North America—specifically "Philadelphia, the most perfect government under the King."[137] Legal pluralism was no more appropriate for Bengal than for Pennsylvania.

Opponents of legal pluralism understood that their audience would be skeptical about the feasibility of their proposals. Dow confronted this challenge directly by offering an estimate of the number of personnel his plan would require, along with their salaries. "The expence of the judicial establishment is but trivial, if compared to the advantages which the kingdom of Bengal must derive from such a necessary institution," he concluded.[138] Part of what made his plan economical was its reliance on unpaid auxiliaries, in much the same way that English law depended on unpaid jurors and justices of the peace. Bolts had a similar strategy. In 1777, he published a second volume of his *Considerations on Indian Affairs,* which replied to criticisms of his earlier pamphlet. "Much has been said on the impossibility of introducing the *English* laws among the natives in *Bengal,*" he wrote. But such arguments were either made in bad faith—by those who "wished not to see any law at all introduced"—or under a misimpression about what Bolts intended. He had no interest in "transplanting the whole trunk" of English law to "the banks of the Ganges," "much less any of the decayed branches" that served only to enrich lawyers. Britain only had to introduce the "grand shoot and main support of the *British* full-grown oak"—namely, trial by jury—which "would take root and prosper in any climate." Jury trials, supervised by native judges and supplemented by a *voluntary* program of arbitration, would both limit the cost of British justice and allow it to spread "throughout the *Bengal* provinces."[139] Even Bolts didn't think that Bengal could be turned into Pennsylvania overnight. The point, rather, was to create institutions that might allow the colony to gradually approximate the American model. Laws, like settlers, needed time to become seasoned to the tropics.

Timothy Brecknock, a notoriously eccentric barrister, focused less on acclimating the British oak to the Ganges than on helping Indians grow accustomed to English justice. He worried not only about the dangers of withholding English justice from India but also about the costs of its imposition. "[W]hen the Spaniards conquered Mexico and Peru," he observed, "they held the laws of those two kingdoms *ipso facto,* absolutely abrogated and null."[140] By itself, that didn't trouble Brecknock. He had no qualms with the traditional doctrine that a conqueror could impose its laws on a conquered people, and he lacked anything like toleration for "pagan" religions. (A year earlier, he had urged the secretary of state to arrest a Tripoline diplomat on the theory "that the Law of Nations does not justify the Reception of an Infidel Ambassador.")[141] But Brecknock feared that if Britain followed Spain's example by abolishing Indian laws, it might end up committing the same "butcheries" and "inhumanity" as the conquistadors. To avoid reprising the Black Legend, he proposed a middle path between the Scylla of legal pluralism and the Charybdis of popish intolerance. Britain should introduce England's laws and religion to India, he argued, but "upon principles consistent with the exalted character of true-born Englishmen."[142]

Brecknock's plan was simple: "for every Englishman that goes to the Asiatic continent, let three or four Indian *infants* be brought over in the same vessel," to be raised in Britain or British America. "By thus being early habituated to the laws of England, and to the Christian persuasion," Brecknock continued, "the young Indians will become a valuable acquisition to us," whether they returned to India or remained in Britain's other dominions. "[H]aving imbibed the happy and irradicable prejudices of their own importance, as British subjects," these assimilated Indians would be ideal agents for conforming Bengal to British rule.[143]

Like many of Brecknock's projects, his proposal for integrating Bengal was unlikely to attract official support. (He had previously suggested that Parliament open a network of public breweries to supply the kingdom with better beer, the sale of which would finance the conquest of Spanish America.)[144] But it wasn't unthinkable. A few years later, Maurice Morgann, one of Lord Shelburne's top advisers, offered a remarkably similar proposal "for the introduction of free Negroes into some part of Florida." As Chapter 1 explained, Morgann wanted to replace West Indian slavery with a racially diverse coalition of free-labor colonies. To help achieve that, he proposed that Britain should buy West African children, educate them in Britain, and eventually grant them land in Florida, along with other "support proper to be given to new settlers."[145] Like Brecknock's project for India, Morgann's plan of abolition involved a striking combination of brutal coercion and racial optimism. Both men sought to construct a British Empire in which all colonists, whatever their racial or religious origins, had equal access to English law. And both men were willing to do disturbing things to bring that equality about.

CHAPTER 5

Despotic Humanitarianism and the New Imperial Common Law

When Sir Thomas Bernard died in 1818, he was one of Britain's most influential philanthropists. He had grown up in New Jersey and Massachusetts, where his father was governor; studied at Harvard; and then dropped out to help his father confront the budding Revolution. After returning to England, practicing law, and marrying well, the younger Bernard devoted his life to bettering English society. But although he was best known for the charities he founded or funded, his first foray into humanitarianism was an anonymous pamphlet in defense of the Quebec Act.[1]

Bernard's argument, written while he was studying at the Middle Temple, began with the citations that historians have taught us to expect from discussions of colonial law. There was *Calvin's Case* and its dicta about the law of conquest, invocations of Vattel and Montesquieu, and references to the legal pluralism of ancient Greece and Rome. Then, less expectedly, Bernard made an appeal to empathy. "Let us put ourselves, for a moment, in the situation of our conquered Canadian subjects," he urged his readers. They should imagine that some foreign power had conquered England and declared its legal system "void"—uprooting, at one blow, England's "laws, usages, [and] tenures," its writ of habeas corpus and trial by jury, its system of property rights. The "cruelty and injustice" of this "deadly edict" would have been self-evident to any English reader. What those readers might not have seen as readily was that Canadiens felt the same way about Britain's conquest of them: "*their* laws, *their* usages, *their* rights . . . are equally dear [to them] as *ours* are to us."[2]

In one sense, Bernard's invitation to empathy was routine. Since the early eighteenth century, latitudinarian theologians and Scottish academics had put fellow-feeling at the center of ethics—a trend popularized and reinforced by an explosion of sentimental literature. But Bernard's appeal to empathy also offers a striking contrast with Britain's older humanitarian tradition. In the seventeenth and early eighteenth centuries, humanitarianism had limited ambition. It sought only to stop unjust bodily violence. No imprisoning Jews for being Jewish or torturing Catholics for being Catholic; but no need to let them practice law or worship publicly, either. At best, religious and cultural minorities could hope to be left alone, or perhaps to see their corporal sufferings relieved.[3] Bernard, however, invoked humanitarian empathy to argue that the British state had an affirmative duty to administer the laws of its conquered subjects.

Bernard's rhetoric was part of a broader pattern in contemporary political discourse. Although policymakers thought about colonial law primarily as a question of political economy, that doesn't mean that other considerations were absent. Some paternalists, like Bernard, seem to have conceived of legal pluralism as a moral obligation. Others deployed humanitarian rhetoric merely to outflank their opponents. And still others changed their reasoning over time, first invoking humanitarianism out of convenience and later coming to defend it as a matter of principle. In the process, debates about colonial legal pluralism helped to change how Britons thought about the requirements of toleration and the nature of humanitarian sympathy.

By examining the role of humanitarian arguments in shaping imperial legal policy, this chapter also answers another crucial question: why did paternalists win? As previous chapters have emphasized, it was far from obvious that Britain would have turned to legal pluralism. Britain had a long tradition of building a unified imperial law, and that tradition continued to inspire moderates and populists. But by the end of the eighteenth century, legal pluralism was a standard part of Britain's imperial repertoire. This chapter argues that a new sense of humanitarianism—sometimes accompanied by invocations of natural rights—helped to cement the new pluralist orthodoxy.

In some ways, it's unsurprising that humanitarian arguments broke new ground in the context of colonial rule. A growing body of scholarship has emphasized the links between humanitarianism and empire. Nor is it shocking that rights-based or humanitarian arguments emerged from agents of the imperial state, as well as the petitions of subjects themselves. As Lauren Benton and Lisa Ford have shown for the nineteenth century, efforts to ameliorate colonial brutality often invoked, and enhanced, the power of the Crown.[4] Nonetheless, this chapter adds a new ingredient to received stories about humanitarianism and human rights. Although it agrees with historians who treat the late eighteenth century as an inflection point, it looks beyond the usual suspects, such as cultural trends in empathy, the rise of radical rights-talk, or reactionary efforts to buttress Britain's moral authority against revolutionary threats. Instead, it highlights debates about law and its role in structuring the British Empire.[5]

EMPATHY AND NATURAL RIGHTS

Most paternalists supported legal pluralism because of its projected effect on colonial development. But some also seemed to think that Britain had a duty to preserve local laws. Paternalists' deontological defenses of legal pluralism came in several varieties. One was ancient constitutionalism. As Robert Travers has shown, officials in Bengal translated the longstanding concept of an ancient English constitution into the claim that India enjoyed an ancient constitution of its own, which Britain had a duty to preserve or restore. Another style of argument was rooted in appeals to the rule of law. As I've argued elsewhere, British lawyers in the later eighteenth century became increasingly attracted to a formal, "thin" notion of legality, which elevated abstract ideals like legal certainty over specific institutions such as jury trials. In the 1760s and 1770s, paternalists sometimes used this new way of thinking about the rule of law to justify Britain's selective denial of English institutions to its empire.[6]

This chapter focuses on two other defenses of legal pluralism: humanitarian appeals to empathy and invocations of natural rights. Both of these approaches appeared in an exchange between Lord Mansfield and Warren Hastings. Hastings was one of the architects of legal pluralism in Bengal, as Chapter 4 explained, and he was worried that Parliament might unravel his work by mandating the application of English law in Indian courts. Eager to forestall any such legislation, he sought the help of Mansfield, Britain's most influential jurist (and, like Hastings, an alumnus of Westminster School). In a letter to Mansfield, Hastings described his policy of legal pluralism as securing "the rights of a great nation in the most essential point of civil liberty, the preservation of its own laws." In the same letter, Hastings twice more used the language of rights, insisting on Indians' "right to possess . . . the protection

William Murray, 1st Earl of Mansfield. By Francesco Bartolozzi.
Courtesy of the Metropolitan Museum of Art.
Morris K. Jesup Fund, 1955. Acc. No. 55.106.4.

of their own laws," which he described as "the most sacred and valuable of [their] rights."[7] Two years later, in another letter to Mansfield, Hastings again invoked "the rights of the people" to their own laws.[8]

It's not clear what kind of rights Hastings had in mind. In any event, they didn't move the lord chief justice. Despite agreeing with Hastings on the desirability of legal pluralism, his reply to Hastings used a different kind of rhetoric: humanitarian empathy. "[N]o measure could be more barbarous, in every sense of the Epithet," Mansfield wrote, "than to change the Laws of any People, except by very slow degrees, & in consequence of long Experience."[9] It's not clear why Mansfield avoided rights-talk. Perhaps he was thinking of the long line of judicial precedents—including his own opinion in *Campbell*

Warren Hastings. By Thomas Watson after
Sir Joshua Reynolds (c. 1777). Courtesy of the Yale Center
for British Art, Paul Mellon Fund. Acc. no. B1970.3.153.

v. Hall (1774)—that affirmed Britain's authority to abrogate the laws of conquered peoples.[10] In any event, Mansfield had used similar language a decade earlier, when he learned of Britain's (temporary) imposition of English law on Quebec. "The history of the world don't furnish an instance of so rash and unjust an act by any conqueror whatsoever," Mansfield fumed at the time, "much less by the Crown of England, which has always left to the conquered their own laws and usages." Mansfield acknowledged his historiographical hyperbole: he knew that England had imposed its law on Ireland and New York. But such changes, Mansfield explained, had "been the work of great length of time" and the result of "many emergencies." What troubled Mansfield was not the mere fact of legal uniformity but its imposition "all at once."[11]

Mansfield expanded on these statements in his 1775 letter to Hastings. His prescription against rapid legal change reflected his belief that "Positive Laws & Usages are, in themselves, indifferent." Laws might vary superficially, but an innate sense of natural justice led people "at all times and in all places" to agree about the basic principles of "Right & Wrong." When it came to filling in the details, it was more important that a rule be familiar than that it be optimal. This was, in part, because people become deeply devoted to the rules they know. "Time adapts [laws] to the Manners, Genius, and Modes of Religion and Government of every Country," Mansfield explained, "and interweaves them so strongly in the Habits of men's Minds, and the Prejudices of their Nature, that every People is attached to their own, in preference to all other." Change might sometimes be necessary, but only a "barbarous" conqueror would fail to recognize its emotional cost.[12]

In short, Mansfield offered two arguments for preserving local legal traditions. First, those traditions probably satisfied the requirements of natural law, so there was nothing wrong with retaining them; and second, uprooting them would be traumatic. This second argument, in particular, became a staple of paternalist rhetoric. Harry Verelst wrote that "humanity, justice, and sound police will equally demand" legal pluralism in Bengal.[13] Solicitor General Alexander Wedderburn argued that although Britain had the right to impose English law on Quebec, "it would be more humane" to leave Canadiens their accustomed laws.[14] Edward Thurlow, the attorney general, defended the Quebec Act in similar terms, telling the House of Commons that "humanity, justice, and wisdom equally conspire to advise you to leave [the laws] to the people just as they were." In contrast, "importing English laws into a country already settled, and habitually governed by other laws" would be "an act of the grossest, and absurdest, and cruellest tyranny, that a conquering nation ever practised over a conquered country."[15]

Few historians today would subscribe to Thurlow's ranking of imperial crimes; Britain inflicted far worse things on its colonial subjects than writs of trespass and trials by jury. But his argument seemed plausible to contemporaries because it played on well-established notions of humanitarianism. Since the early eighteenth century, British diplomats had intervened on behalf of persecuted religious minorities in other countries. For example, during negotiations to end the War of the Spanish Succession (1701–14), Britain had lobbied to free a group of Huguenot prisoners condemned to slavery on French galleys. In seeking their release, British diplomats deployed arguments based on natural law and empathy for the oppressed. At first, these kinds of interventions usually focused on persecuted Protestants. But as Catherine Arnold has shown, British politicians soon broadened their focus. Between 1720 and 1750, British officials helped Marrano refugees find asylum from persecution in Portugal, pressured Empress Maria Theresa to reverse her expulsion of Jews from Bohemia and Moravia, and interceded with the French government on behalf of Jansenists.[16]

In one sense, then, paternalists' appeal to natural rights and humanitarian empathy simply extended this foreign-policy framework to Britain's own possessions. In another respect, however, paternalist arguments marked a crucial innovation. Earlier appeals to humanitarian norms had focused on physical violence to religious minorities. That focus on bodily harm—particularly imprisonment, torture, or exile—had allowed Britons to expand their humanitarian imaginations beyond their coreligionists. (Embodiment is, after all, a universal human experience.) But this focus on physical violence had also exempted certain kinds of persecution from scrutiny. The loss of civil privileges, such as the right to enter a particular profession or to worship publicly, didn't much matter for early humanitarians. And the loss of a community's customary laws didn't seem to matter at all. Although eighteenth-century commentators often described rights of conscience as absolute, those rights were limited to freedom from persecution for mere belief. In their view, a state had no affirmative duty to protect the traditions of minority communities. This helps to explain why the same British ministry that intervened on behalf of persecuted Jews in Bohemia aggressively worked to anglicize Scotland, as Chapter 1 described. The difference wasn't a matter of hypocrisy; it was the faithful implementation of their constrained but coherent understanding of what minorities deserved.[17]

Paternalists in the 1760s and 1770s broke with that narrow approach by equating the imposition of English law with violent religious persecution. Of course, paternalists didn't invent the idea of sympathizing with non-physical distress.[18] But they were pioneers in using it to shape policy. A letter in the *Public Advertiser* warned that "with equal Justice, we might endeavour to force the Protestant Religion on the Canadians, as the Trial by Jury."[19] Thomas Bernard agreed, arguing that introducing English law to Quebec would be akin to proselytizing heretics "by *fire* and *faggot*." Readers might have found it odd to conflate the forms of action with autos-da-fé, but this is why his appeal to empathy was so important. Only by imaging the loss of their own laws could Britons understand why Canadiens might want to keep theirs.[20]

Paternalists' analogy between legal and religious uniformity elevated the importance of subjects' consent in crafting colonial laws. The Church of England and trial by jury might both be superior to foreign alternatives, but they lost their goodness when adopted under duress. Lord Clare argued that no matter how wonderful the common law might be at home, its imposition on Quebec would be a form of tyranny: "You make those people free to whom you give that form of government they like."[21] Sir William Meredith made the same point in a more scholarly way, citing Grotius and Solon and pointing out that "[e]ven the law of God, as proposed by Moses, was submitted to the judgment of the people before it was adopted by them."[22] "Trial by Jury is a Blessing" in England, agreed the letter to the *Public Advertiser,* "but it is no Blessing in a Kingdom of Frenchmen; and . . . the Question is not what we think a Blessing, but what the Canadians think a Blessing."[23] Francis Lind, an East India Company lawyer, even invoked complaints about taxation without representation to oppose the introduction of English law to Bengal. The "intricacy of our Civil Law," as well as its delays and expenses, "are taxes & those no light ones, which we pay for our political freedom," Lind explained. "[I]t must be wrong to force [Indians] to submit to the burdens of" such a tax against their will. This was a remarkable twist on the Montesquieu-Blackstone dictum (discussed in Chapter 3) that procedural tedium was the price of liberty.[24]

According to this logic, the demand for legal uniformity was nothing less than tyranny. English law, Thurlow declared, "would so completely confound [Canadiens] as to be more tyrannical than can be easily imagined."[25] Hastings agreed. "It would be a grievance to deprive the people of the protection of their own laws," he told Mansfield, "but it would be a wanton tyranny to require their obedience to others of which they are wholly ignorant, and of which they have no possible means of acquiring a knowledge."[26] Imposing English law on Bengal, an anonymous pamphlet asserted, would "be Tyranny in its most dreadful form."[27]

This argument had a crucial premise: that Britain's conquered subjects didn't actually want English law. As previous chapters have shown, that wasn't always true. Edmund Burke, among others, tried to point that out. "I have not yet evidence, [Canadiens] do not like [English] law," he protested. "Until I know the people of Canada condemn the British law, I shall not impose another."[28] At most, there was evidence that the Canadien nobility opposed English law—but, in Burke's view, that was a small minority that Britain could "sacrifice" to "make the majority of the people happy." (This, from the future critic of the French Revolution!) Moreover, Burke continued, even the noblesse would have been happy under English law. They professed to dislike it only because of their misunderstanding that it was incompatible with their religious liberty. If Britain could "remove those prejudices which the Noblesse had imbibed from misrepresentations," Burke predicted, "they would not only admire our laws, but petition to have them." After all, French writers had produced "mountains of books" praising "the justness and excellency of [English] laws," and particularly trial by jury. Surely their countrymen might be brought to agree?[29]

Other opponents of the Quebec Act blamed Canadiens' alleged dislike of English law on the poor quality of its administration. Isaac Barré found it unsurprising that Canadiens hated English courts. "You have insulted them with the worst of men, the bench of justices, men who deserve to stand at the bar of justice here as criminals," he told the House of Commons.[30] The solution was not to revert to French law but to implement an English legal system worthy of the name. George Johnstone agreed. "What idea must the Canadians have of laws thus administered?" he asked the House of Commons. "And from bringing them, by series of such infamous impressions, to hate the law, was it not natural that they should petition against it? . . . Have I not accounted satisfactorily for this dislike?"[31] Properly administered, English law would be perfectly acceptable.

Unfortunately for populists and moderates, these arguments were hard to substantiate. The relevant colonial governors, Carleton in Quebec and Hastings in Bengal, both supported legal pluralism, and they used their positions to control the flow of information back to England. Carleton, in particular, crafted a view of Canadien preferences that gave excessive weight to the views of seigneurs while ignoring the majority of his province's inhabitants.[32] Although he cited popular opinion when it suited his purpose, he had little interest in what local subjects actually thought. "If in tumultuous meetings, or by dint of numbers only, laws were to be made or abrogated," he chided the authors of one petition, "the lowest dregs of the people, and the most ignorant among them, would, of course, become the law-givers of the country."[33] Indeed, he seems to have resented even petitions that aligned with his views. In 1769, he "quashed" a petition "for the re-establishment of the antient Laws of the Country," because he thought it better that legal pluralism should emerge from the king's "paternal attention to [Canadiens'] Interests" rather "than proceed from any solicitations on their part."[34] As a result, Parliament legislated for Canada in the dark. Only after the Quebec Act was law would officials in London learn that, rather than "gratifying" ordinary Canadiens, it had "become the first object of their discontent & dislike."[35]

East India Company officials also misrepresented, or at least misunderstood, the attitude of many Indians toward English law. In the 1750s, the Company had cited Indians' aversion to English law when it obtained a new charter that excluded them from the mayor's courts. There were dissenting voices even at the time, and a few decades later, Company lawyers suspected that only a minority of Indian elites, acting "from private motives and not from public Policy," had demanded exclusion from English law.[36] By the 1780s, "[t]he Attachment of the natives of Bengal to the English laws" had even become a source of amusement for British commentators in Calcutta.[37] That's not to say that English law was beloved in Bengal. (It wasn't always loved in England, either.) But the supposed antipathy of non-Britons to English law wasn't universal.

In fact, British law in India was more rigidly plural than the Mughal system it replaced. As a practical matter, Mughal law was far from uniform. The Mughal state didn't have a monopoly on dispute resolution, and the state itself accommodated a wide range of local norms, institutions, and legal practices. But neither did the Mughals administer discrete systems of Hindu and Islamic law, as the Company did under Hastings. Instead, everyone in the old regime could and did participate in a single system, which was officially Islamic but also willing to accommodate local and communal custom.[38] In other words, the Mughal approach to law had looked more like the law of the first British Empire than of the second: a global legal language with lots of local dialects. The post-1772 system of personal laws in Bengal had more to do with Hastings's own priorities—including his desire to divide Indian communities from each other—than faithfully preserving the Mughal system.[39]

THE SINCERITY OF PATERNALIST ARGUMENTS

These misrepresentations (or, at least, misunderstandings) invite questions about paternalists' sincerity. This book has argued that paternalists favored legal pluralism because they thought it would advance their vision of colonial development. Were humanitarian arguments just window-dressing? Or did they also play a causal role in motivating the paternalist position?

There are a few reasons to doubt the sincerity of paternalists' humanitarian arguments. One is that they were sometimes more protective of Canadian and Indian laws than were Canadiens and Indians themselves. Paternalists claimed that conquered subjects would find it impossible, or at least traumatic, to learn English law. But as historians of colonial law have repeatedly shown, colonial subjects have generally proved more than capable of adapting to new legal institutions. That also seems to have been the case in eighteenth-century Quebec and Bengal. Indeed, complaints about colonial litigiousness suggest that the new British subjects were exploiting English courts more enthusiastically than the conquerors would have liked. And some subjects expressly petitioned for greater access to English law, particularly trials by jury.[40] This is how Quebec's chief justice, William Hey, summarized the preferences of most Canadiens in 1775: "English officers to command them in time of war, & English Laws to govern them in time of Peace, is the general wish."[41]

Hey exaggerated. In all parts of the empire, including Quebec, local elites were wary of abandoning the laws and institutions that defined their social and political preeminence. Moreover, some areas of law, such as inheritance, were closely tied to religious or cultural practices that would have been threatened by anglicization (as Chapters 3 and 4 described). All things being equal, many ordinary people would have preferred to keep the laws they knew. But all things weren't equal. Colonial subjects faced a choice between their accustomed laws and the economic and political opportunities that English law offered. In many cases, they chose the latter:

> Q [FROM A MEMBER OF PARLIAMENT]. Would the Canadians rather admit a part of the English law, rather than lose those benefits they find from the introduction of English merchants among them?
> A [FRANCIS MASERES]. I am persuaded they would. I apprehend if the option was, that the English merchants should cease to trade there, or that they should submit to have part of the law, trial by jury, they would undoubtedly choose the latter.[42]

Canadiens might have disliked English law, but they disliked the consequences of legal pluralism even more.

Paternalists' claim to speak for the rights of conquered subjects is plausible only on a selective reading of the evidence. Nonetheless, some paternalists seem to have believed their own rhetoric. This was true of Mansfield, in particular. Both as a judge and as a politician, he consistently defended the rights of religious minorities in Britain.[43] His attitude toward legal pluralism also fit with his general skepticism about radical reform, whether in Britain or the colonies. When he was asked in 1787 about the potential introduction of civil juries to his home country of Scotland, he warned that "[g]reat alterations in the course of the administration of justice ought to be sparingly made, and by degrees"—the same argument he had made about Bengal.[44] Mansfield's jurisprudence also revealed a consistent concern with the costs of changing the law. In commercial cases, he often remarked that "it is of more consequence that a rule should be certain, than whether the rule is established one way or the other."[45] This was thanks partly to his appreciation of the practical benefits of legal certainty.[46] But he also seems to have believed that unnecessary change was morally problematic. As an advocate before the House of Lords, for example, he had warned that any innovation was potentially "unjust" if it upset settled expectations.[47]

But there were limits to Mansfield's conservatism. His principles established only a rebuttable presumption against innovation. Although he acknowledged the cost of uprooting established rules, he was willing to do so if there were sufficient benefits—too willing, in the eyes of those who criticized his judicial decisions for undervaluing precedent.[48] In that respect, Mansfield was not very different from the lawyers who opposed legal pluralism. John Glynn, for example, responded to paternalist invocations of "inhumanity" and "cruelty" by conceding that "new laws must certainly be a *temporary* evil." But he urged his listeners to weigh it against the "permanent, and lasting advantage" that English law would bring. Just as Ireland and Wales "are indebted [to England] for all the happiness they enjoy" (one assumes he meant this sincerely), Canada would one day thank Britain for its new legal system.[49] Glynn thus agreed with Mansfield on the need to tally the costs and benefits of legal change. But they made different marks on each side of the ledger; and their different answers reflected their different assumptions about the goals of empire.

Even for paternalists, moreover, the cost-benefit calculus changed depending on the colony. Although Mansfield reacted with shock to the elimination of French law in Quebec, he showed no concern about analogous developments in Grenada.[50] Paternalists were also selective about what kinds of imposed law they considered troubling. As Chapter 3 explained, they had no compunction about thrusting English criminal law and criminal procedure on Quebec, even though many Canadiens expressed discomfort with it. It's not clear whether paternalists knew about this ambivalence, or whether they would have cared if they had known. Alexander Wedderburn, for example, wrote in 1772 that French criminal law would have been "incompatible with an English Government of any sort"; two years later, however, he insisted that he "would not have compelled the Canadians to adopt the criminal law [of England], if they had found it a hardship."[51]

In short, paternalists' tenderness for the laws of conquered subjects had at best an imperfect relationship to what those subjects wanted. Two additional considerations support the hypothesis that political economy, not humanitarianism, was the main driver of paternalist legal policy. First, some paternalists—most notably Warren Hastings—didn't offer a humanitarian or rights-based defense of legal pluralism until after they had adopted that policy for expressly instrumental reasons. In the first couple of years after crafting his judicial reforms for Bengal, Hastings and his allies stressed their practical value. In 1773, when the council at Fort William censured an employee for suing an Indian landowner under English law, it argued not that the landowner's rights had been violated, but that such suits might reduce tax revenues.[52] At the same time, Hastings emphasized that the Company's preservation of Hindu and Islamic law did not "preclude the Right . . . to establish new regulations upon any occasion where they may be required."[53] It was only in 1774, when he began to suspect that Parliament might countermand his decisions, that he articulated a rights-based defense of legal pluralism.

But despite the instrumental origins of Hastings's defense, it soon took on a life of its own, moving from public-relations talking points into the Company's own approach to governance. By the 1780s, the Company's lawyers referred routinely to the "natural rights" of Indians to their customary laws.[54] Any attempt to introduce English law became a campaign "to deprive the natives of those rights, which they have hitherto enjoyed under every change of Government."[55] Company lawyers also clarified what kind of rights were at stake. Because Indian laws were religious laws, legal pluralism was fundamentally about protecting religious liberty. Hindu and Islamic laws, explained Archibald Macdonald, "are interwoven with . . . their respective religions and are therefore matter[s] of conscience." As a result, any alteration of those laws is "in reality an attempt to force the minds and consciences of Men." Macdonald reinforced this argument from conscience by an appeal to native suffering: violating the religious rights of Muslims and Hindus was not merely wrong but "an absolute cruelty."[56]

This kind of language had concrete effects on Company policy, most notably in its administration of Hindu ordeal trials. For Enlightenment writers, ordeals represented the very essence of barbarism, and many Britons were horrified that the Company permitted them to persist in its territories.[57] William Tennant, a military chaplain in Bengal, declared "the cruel trial by ordeal" to be "not merely hurtful to the police of the country, but incompatible with the exercise of the judicial power."[58] Joseph Priestley had few peers in his dedication to religious liberty, but even he balked. "A superstitious respect for the elements of fire and water seems at first perfectly harmless," Priestley wrote. "But when we find that the same ideas . . . led likewise to the drowning and burning alive of innocent persons, we find that they deserve a serious examination."[59] And James Forbes, a Company servant who supervised several ordeals during his time in India, described them as "measure[s] to which [he] was very averse."[60] Muslim magistrates also raised religious and practical objections to administering Hindu ordeals.[61]

And yet, despite these concerns, the Company not only permitted ordeals to continue but incorporated them into its law. As Forbes explained, a person undergoing an ordeal

> is immediately put into close confinement under a guard of the English East India Companies Soldiers, who are ordered to keep a constant watch over his actions. . . . His hand too, is also sealed up in the presence of the Gentlemen of the Factory, and clean washed, to prevent their being imposed upon by any external application. After a certain limited Time, the prisoner is brought out to undergo this fiery Trial . . .

The seal in question was in fact "the Companies Seal," which was affixed "both before, and after the Ceremony."[62] The Company not only tolerated the persistence of ordeals but actively facilitated their administration—notwithstanding the qualms that its Christian or Muslim servants might have had about the proceedings.

This new view of conscience represented an important shift in the Company's relationship to Mughal rule. In 1772, the *naib diwan* Muhammed Reza Khan had objected to Hastings's proposal that Hindu pandits assist Muslim magistrates. "The Gentoos are subject to the true Faith," Reza Khan insisted, "and to order a Magistrate of the Faith to decide in Conjunction with a Brahmin would be repugnant to the Rules of the Faith." In a country ruled by a Muslim emperor, "it is improper that any order should be issued inconsistent with the Rules of his Faith, or that Innovation should be introduced in the administration of Justice." The Mughal Empire had always administered a "System of Justice, which has for a long Series of time been binding on the whole Body of the People whether Mussulmen or Gentoos." If the East India Company implemented Hastings's proposal, "a confusion subversive of the maxims of our Judicial System & the Rules of our Religion must take place."[63]

By the 1780s, Reza Khan's prediction had come true. The East India Company, which had once sought legitimacy from the "ancient constitution" of the Mughal Empire, now sought not merely to preserve the preexisting laws of Bengal but to offer Hindus a degree of religious freedom that surpassed what they had enjoyed under the previous regime. Robert Travers has attributed this shift to several causes, including the internal logic of ancient constitutionalism (which readily analogized the Mughals to tyrannical Norman invaders) and the fruitless debates of the 1770s and 1780s over the precise nature of the Mughal constitution (which encouraged Company officials to seek other sources of legitimacy).[64] This chapter has suggested an additional factor: the Company's internalization of a rhetoric of rights that had first been developed to win a partisan conflict over legal pluralism.

HOW PATERNALISTS WON: QUEBEC

The growing power of humanitarian and rights-based arguments helps explain how paternalists steered Britain away from its traditional pursuit of an imperial common law. Their victory was not just a matter of raw political power. In the 1760s and 1770s, when the crucial debates took place, paternalists controlled the government but remained a minority in Parliament. Partisan identities were fluid, and there is no agreed-upon list of paternalist MPs; but it's unlikely that committed paternalists made up more than a third of the House of Commons during that time. The balance of power remained with a sizeable group of political independents, whose support had to be won measure by measure. The outcome of votes also depended on attendance. Just getting one's own side to show up, or persuading opponents that attendance wasn't worth the trouble, could make all the difference.[65]

These considerations proved crucial in securing the Quebec Act's passage. As we've seen, prominent moderate and populist politicians attacked the bill, and their criticisms were amplified in print. But the opposition faced several obstacles in trying to rally support. Because the Quebec Act had been introduced by the North Ministry, its supporters had the advantage of clear leadership, which carefully choreographed its drafting and introduction in Parliament. The opposition was comparatively disorganized, which led to some tactical errors.[66] More fundamentally, opponents of the Quebec Act couldn't agree about what, exactly, they opposed.

This was particularly true with respect to the Quebec Act's religious policy. Religious bigotry was unfashionable by the 1770s, as Chapter 2 explained, and overt anti-Catholicism rarely appeared in the parliamentary debates. But

Paul Revere, *The Mitred Minuet* (1774). Engraved for the *Royal American Magazine* (1774). The devil joins Lord Bute, Lord North, and four Anglican bishops in celebrating the Quebec Act's passage. Revere copied this print from the *London Magazine*. Courtesy of the National Gallery of Art, Washington, D.C. Corcoran Collection (Museum Purchase, Mary E. Maxwell Fund). Acc. No. 2015.19.783.

that doesn't mean it was absent. Thomas Hollis, Lord Chatham's friend and Harvard College's benefactor, had warned in the 1760s that Catholics were growing in numbers and power. To calm the panic that Hollis helped stoke, Anglican bishops felt compelled to take a census of English Catholics in 1767. When they found only a modest increase in the Catholic population, Hollis and his friends refused to believe the results, which they cited as evidence of a pro-Catholic conspiracy within the Church of England.[67] A few years later, the Quebec Act seemed to validate their bigoted paranoia. Invoking long-standing tropes that linked Catholicism to arbitrary government, Hollis warned that Britain's supposed policy of toleration was really a ploy to establish Catholic absolutism in Canada—and, eventually, throughout the British Empire. American populists were especially susceptible to this sort of argument. We've already seen (in Chapter 3) John Adams's alarm about "Romish Superstition" and "Orders of military Monks" descending from Quebec. Alexander Hamilton warned that if Britain could establish "popery and arbitrary dominion" in Canada, New York might suffer the same fate.[68] Other colonists portrayed

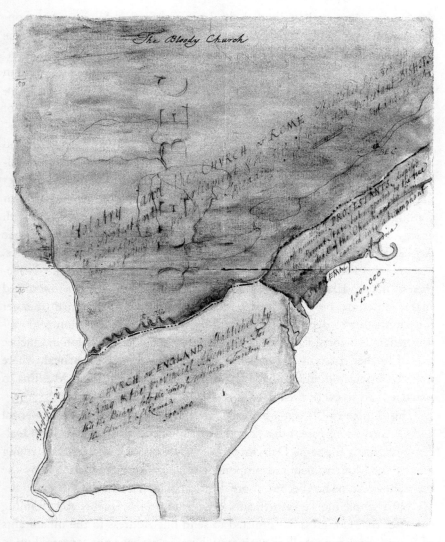

Ezra Stiles, "The Bloody Church" (August 1774), Ezra Stiles Papers, MVP 627, BRBML. Courtesy of the Beinecke Rare Book and Manuscript Library, Yale University. Stiles, the future president of Yale University, drew this map in which the Quebec Act has turned Canada into a bloody mass that threatens to swallow Protestant New England.

the Quebec Act as a literally diabolical project. Samuel Sherwood, a Connecticut minister (and Aaron Burr's cousin), warned of the "flood of the dragon that has been poured forth to the northward, in the Quebec bill," while Paul Revere reproduced for American readers an English print of Satan celebrating the Act's passage.[69] But it wasn't just Americans. Chatham, populists' leader in the House of Lords, warned of "the return of popery and of popish influence."[70]

Populists' anti-Catholic rhetoric alienated some of their allies. Edmund Burke, who helped lead moderates' opposition to the Quebec Act, was a well-known proponent of religious toleration (and the son, husband, and brother of Catholics). Sir George Savile, who also opposed the bill, would sponsor Catholic relief legislation in 1778. They sometimes seemed to spend as much energy attacking populist intolerance as they spent going after the Quebec Act itself. Not all populists embraced religious bigotry; and some moderates, most notably Francis Maseres, had their own qualms about toleration.[71] Nonetheless, the moderate/populist split over religion was sufficiently pronounced that it sometimes obscured the debate about legal policy—and made it easier for paternalists to depict opposition to French law as an extension of populists' religious bigotry. Paternalists' invocation of religious toleration in Quebec gained further strength from contemporary developments in Bengal, where nobody seriously doubted that Britain must allow Hindus and Muslims to practice their respective religions.[72]

This double conflation—between law and religion, and between Bengal and Quebec—is apparent in a pamphlet by the Scottish lawyer Sir John Dalrymple. This is the same Dalrymple who appeared in Chapter 1 as a young admirer of Montesquieu and proponent of anglicizing Scottish law. By the 1770s, however, he had become more skeptical of legal transplants. The middle-aged Dalrymple mocked Americans' opposition to the Quebec Act, feigning surprise "that Congress has omitted to send one Address to the inhabitants of Bengal, to rise in rebellion against us, because we have not conferred upon them all the honours of English liberty, which they are not asking; and another to their fellow-subjects in England, to reproach them for permitting the Gentoo religion to exist in that part of their dominions."[73] Those sorts of analogies didn't persuade the Quebec Act's most committed opponents. (As Horace Walpole archly asked, "Is abolition of juries part of the spirit of toleration?")[74] But paternalists didn't need to persuade Walpole. They only had to reorient the debate away from controversial questions of colonial development and toward the far safer issue of religious toleration, so that the great mass of independents might find the Quebec Act insufficiently alarming to oppose. And that's what happened. The Quebec Act passed the House of Commons by a vote of 56 to 20—in a chamber of 558 members.[75]

Eventually, some of the Quebec Act's more bigoted opponents came to regret their religious rhetoric. The author of a pamphlet urging the Quebec Act's repeal felt compelled to "apologize for any Strictures with regard to Popery, which may appear too severe to some Persons."[76] Even some Americans experienced a conversion. As the colonies moved toward independence, the Continental Congress began looking at Catholic Canadiens not as religious enemies but as political allies. When the congress sent the inhabitants of Quebec a letter trying to recruit them to the revolutionary cause, it not only declined to criticize the Quebec Act's policy of toleration but even insisted that religious liberty was a natural right given by God and guaranteed by the Treaty of Paris.[77] On the cusp of revolution, American populists realized what paternalists had known all along: that the Quebec Act's emancipatory religious policy really was severable from its authoritarian use of legal pluralism.

HOW PATERNALISTS WON: BENGAL

Legal pluralism in Bengal had an easier path but a messier victory. As Chapter 4 explained, several influential pamphlets in the early 1770s had urged Parliament to anglicize Bengal's legal system at least in part. Paternalists reacted with alarm to those proposals. Alexander Wedderburn complained to his brother that "[t]he publick attention" had fixed on "a variety of wild Projects of introducing the Laws & Constitution of England into that Part of the Globe which Providence seems to have preordained for the seat of absolute Power."[78] On the other side of the empire, Warren Hastings worried that the House of Commons was poised to overturn his policies. "It is a little strange that we should be framing Laws, and Establishing new Courts of Justice for Bengal, at the same time that you are busied in Parliament on the like work," he wrote to Laurence Sulivan. "[I]t will grieve me to see the structure which we have raised, destroyed to make room for any that shall subject the Natives of Bengal to the Laws of England, or make them amenable to our Courts or Forms of Justice."[79] But although it seemed plausible at the time that Parliament might have decided to anglicize Bengal's laws, the project turned out to lack a substantial constituency. For different reasons, the two groups that led opposition to the Quebec Act—populists and moderates—failed to mount a substantial challenge to legal pluralism in Bengal.

Populists should have been the staunchest opponents of Clive's brand of authoritarian conquest and the legal policies it engendered. While populists wanted an empire based on commercial exchange, anglicization, and a global common law, Clive envisioned a tributary, militarized empire that departed sharply from earlier models of British colonialism. But the divergence between Clive and populists wasn't always so obvious. When Horace Walpole looked back in 1772 at the rise of the Company's territorial empire, he thought populists had been complicit from the start: "Lord Chatham begot the East India Company; the East India Company begot Lord Clive."[80]

When Clive first made his name in the 1750s, many populists welcomed him as one of their own. They shared a view of the old Whig order as corrupt, and they agreed that Britain's security demanded a muscular approach to geopolitics.[81] Clive also seemed to share populists' ideas about what British aggression should look like. In the 1740s, Britain had embarked on a controversial effort to professionalize its armed forces. This program culminated in the Mutiny and Navy Acts of 1749, which sought to create a more hierarchical and disciplined British military whose members would be increasingly set apart from civilians. Populists distrusted that project, which they (correctly) viewed as the first step of a broader campaign to discipline British society. Instead of a professionalized military, populists wanted Britain to rely on privateers and militias, whose part-time members would be less inclined to see themselves as distinct from the civilians they might otherwise oppress.[82]

Accordingly, populists rejoiced when, at the siege of Arcot (1751), Clive not only defeated the French but did so with mostly non-professional forces. A few years later, the writer John Campbell contrasted "two Kinds of Soldiers": "the regular one, who is curb'd by the Mutiny and Desertion Act, and another Kind of Soldier, who serves, because he chuses to defend the Laws, Liberties and Properties of the Community of which he is a Member." Soldiers of the second type, "led by the *valiant* Clive," "fight for Freedom, because they are free, and would not bear to live under slavish Rule." The success of Clive's "irregulars" at Arcot was the best argument Campbell could muster for an English militia, which would be governed by ordinary English law rather than the distinctive strictures of military discipline. This was the political context in which William Pitt extolled Clive as the "heaven-born general."[83]

Clive's honeymoon with the populists ended when it was time to decide what to do with his conquests. As Chapter 4 explained, Clive saw Bengal as a source of tribute. Pitt and many of his allies disagreed. In 1759, when Clive first proposed to Pitt his scheme for acquiring the *diwani*, Pitt reacted skeptically, warning that it would "endanger our liberties" to entrust such massive revenues either to the Crown or to the Company.[84] But circumstances changed again after 1765, when Clive had taken control of the Company and accepted the *diwani* on its behalf. At that point, the question became not whether Bengal's revenues should flow to Britain but who would control them once they arrived. And that led some populists to see an opportunity to use Bengal to subsidize other parts of their imperial agenda.

During the Seven Years' War, Britain's public spending had tripled, and its public debt had increased by 86 percent. Parliament had three options for sustaining this new fiscal burden. First, it might have raised taxes within Britain. That turned out to be politically impossible. In 1767, moderates and paternalists forced the Chatham administration, against its wishes, to cut the land tax by a quarter. The move was politically astute—it put populists on the wrong side of Britain's electorally important landowners—and aligned with moderates' and paternalists' interest in shoring up the position of landed gentlemen. But the tax cut also exacerbated Britain's budget woes. The Chatham administration could have compensated by raising taxes on trade or consumption. But populists generally disfavored those sorts of taxes, which fell most heavily on the consumers and manufacturers who were at the center of populists' plans for British prosperity (and of their political coalition). Britain's second option—taxing the American colonies—was unattractive to populists for similar reasons.[85] And even politicians who supported colonial taxes doubted that they would be enough to cure Britain's fiscal ills. The 1767 land-tax reduction cost the government £500,000 in revenue; by comparison, even Charles Townshend's controversial colonial tax scheme was projected to generate at most £40,000. (In practice, it raised even less.) Something more was needed.[86]

That led some populists to explore a third option: the *diwani,* which Chatham (using his favorite figure of speech) now described as a "gift from heaven."[87] It wasn't entirely clear how populists meant to use that gift. Chatham himself never articulated a coherent plan for Bengal, and by the late 1760s he was too ill to put any of his contradictory statements into effect. ("I am not sure that his Lordship has any *or ever had any* fixed plan or Idea on" India, Rockingham told Burke in 1772.)[88] But the general idea was to redirect some of the Company's newfound wealth into the public treasury. That, at least, was how many observers explained the Chatham ministry's decision in 1766 to launch an ambitious parliamentary inquiry into the Company. In the words of William Beckford, the London alderman who led the inquiry, "Look to the rising sun . . . Your Treasury coffers are to be filled from the east, not the west."[89] For populists, taxing Bengal had a clear political advantage. Although it was controversial—many Britons remained skeptical about this new font of riches—it was unlikely to provoke the same kind of uproar as taxing North America, whose colonies had older and deeper ties to British politicians in general and populist figures in particular. (Beckford himself had served in Jamaica's assembly.) Although it was hard to square a tributary Bengal with populists' enthusiasm for a free and commercial empire, the Bengal revenues struck many of them as the least-bad solution.[90]

Not all populists shared Beckford's willingness to make Bengal bear the weight of imperial finances.[91] Some populists agreed that Britain should take over the Company's revenues in Bengal, but they hoped that this seizure would be linked to a broader program of reform that treated Bengal more like the rest of the empire. (Chatham himself, in one of his many inconsistencies, apparently wanted to introduce an independent judiciary in Bengal.) But while prominent outsiders like William Bolts and well-connected insiders like George Johnstone continued to urge more radical reforms, including the anglicization of Indian institutions, their proposals were increasingly in tension with the state's dependency on Company payments. As a result, debates about Bengal in the 1760s and 1770s tended to focus on who would enjoy its spoils—the Company's shareholders or the state—rather than the propriety of spoils at all.[92] And that meant there was less interest in questioning the legal institutions that made Bengal's tribute possible.

Moderates had their own reasons for avoiding serious debate about Indian law. Especially between 1767 and 1773, they were less concerned with how Bengal was governed than who would govern it. In large part, this was because they viewed populists' threatened abolition of the Company as an attack on the rights guaranteed to it by its charter—and, therefore, a precedent for attacks on other chartered rights, including those that protected the North American colonies. From this perspective, Chatham's attempt to seize the Company's revenues was not an alternative to taxing America but another, more extreme version of the same oppression.[93] Populists denied any connection— "those who seriously compare the two Cases do nothing more than discover their Ignorance of the Subject," wrote one of Shelburne's correspondents— but moderates remained adamant that colonial and Company rights would stand or fall together.[94]

Moderates' procedural focus on corporate rights dominated their response to the parliamentary inquiry of 1766–67. A central issue in that inquiry was whether Bengal should be considered as a "conquered" or "ceded" colony. The distinction had legal significance. A decade earlier, the Company had petitioned the King to recognize its right to all "plunder and booty" it seized during the war (that is, moveable property taken from the enemy), as well as all "fortresses, districts, and Territories" it might acquire. In response, two of the Crown's law officers, Charles Pratt (later Lord Camden) and Charles Yorke, prepared an opinion about the relationship between sovereignty and ownership in Bengal. Although their opinion was ambivalent about granting territorial rights to the Company, it proposed a distinction between conquered and ceded territories. In the former case, the Crown obtained both "property" and "dominion"; in the latter case, the Company gained "property of the soil," subject only to the Crown's right of sovereignty.[95]

Under the Pratt-Yorke framework, much depended on whether the *diwani* had been taken by force or voluntarily granted by the Mughal emperor. A finding that the *diwani* was the fruit of conquest would automatically place millions of pounds into the Treasury each year. In 1767, the question came before Parliament, where Chatham and Beckford urged legislators to declare the revenues of Bengal to be the property of the Crown. Moderates not only opposed the request on the merits but also objected to its being put to Parliament at all. "We are to set ourselves up as Judges upon a Point of Law, to decide between the Subject and the Crown a matter of property of the greatest concern and magnitude without the least colour of right; at once Judge and party!" Burke wrote with horror.[96] Through the early 1770s, moderates continued to focus on the procedural and constitutional dimensions of the debate while paying less attention to substantive questions about Bengal's governance. In fact, they almost reflexively opposed any attempt to regulate the Company's operations, whether by Chatham's populists or by the later administration of Lord North, as cynical maneuvers to acquire power and dispense patronage. To the extent that moderates did offer substantive suggestions, they focused on empowering the Company's directors to better control their own agents, rather than intervening in the law of Bengal itself.[97]

Thus, as with the Quebec Act, disagreements between moderates and populists prevented a successful challenge to legal pluralism in Bengal. The ambitious inquiry of 1766–67 terminated in a modest settlement: the Company retained control of Bengal and its revenues in exchange for an annual payment to the Treasury of £400,000. By that point, Chatham had ceased to exercise any meaningful leadership, and his administration's East Indian affairs had fallen under the direction of Townshend, a paternalist who enthusiastically supported the Company's transformation into an extractive territorial power.[98]

By the time the North ministry introduced the Regulating Act in 1773, the question of English law in Bengal had fallen off the table. As the statute's name suggests, it was an attempt to regulate the East India Company's operations—but not to transform Bengal into a British province, as some populists had proposed.[99] Because the Regulating Act didn't challenge the Company's right to run an extractive territorial state in Bengal, there was little reason to question the legal pluralism that made the arrangement possible.

The Regulating Act did, however, make a substantial change to Bengal's legal institutions. Among other provisions, it empowered the Crown to charter a Supreme Court of Judicature at Calcutta. As Chapter 4 observed, the Act failed to say anything about what law the court should apply. Its authors seem to have meant for the court to have plenary jurisdiction over suits against British subjects of European descent and Company employees. The Act also provided for contract suits by Europeans against Indians who had expressly consented in the original contract to the Supreme Court's jurisdiction, provided that the claim was for more than 500 rupees.[100] The court would, therefore, have no jurisdiction over suits between non-Europeans or over most suits by Europeans against Indians. Those jurisdictional limitations might explain why the Act's drafters gave little thought to the court's rules of decision: if it was to be a court primarily for Britons, it could simply apply English law. But that might be giving the authors too might credit: on reading a late version of the bill, Lord Mansfield complained that "he [did] not understand many Clauses," which suggests it had been hastily drafted.[101]

In any event, the omission of substantive law turned out to be a crucial oversight, which inadvertently resurrected the question of introducing English law to India. The Regulating Act left the details of the Supreme Court to be defined by a royal charter, the drafting of which fell primarily to Attorney General Edward Thurlow and several other lawyers, including Elijah Impey, soon to be the new court's first chief justice. Thurlow seems to have intended to deny English law to India, just as he was in the process of doing for Quebec. But he failed to make that clear in the charter itself, which, like the Regulating Act, failed to specify the law that the Supreme Court would apply.[102]

Impey and the court's three puisne judges were all English barristers, and they arrived in India under the impression that they were supposed to conduct themselves as English judges. This led to a series of conflicts with Company officials, who had imagined a much narrower place for English law in Bengal.[103] During those conflicts, Impey made three arguments that challenged the foundations of paternalist legal policy. First, he rejected the assumption that India was radically different from other parts of the British Empire. Just as England courts could apply the common law to a Spanish-born resident of Gibraltar, the Supreme Court could apply English law to a Bengal-born resident of Calcutta. "There is nothing in the quality of an Hindoo that makes the law of the country wherein he was born more attached to him than to a Frenchman or Spaniard," he told the House of Commons a decade later. "All must be obedient to the law that protects them." Second, because "he had always conceived of India . . . to be greatly commercial," it was suitable to introduce those aspects of English law that safeguarded commercial exchange. Finally, English law was a crucial check against official misconduct. Even if his court couldn't apply that law indiscriminately across Bengal, it was important that Indian litigants have access to English remedies, such as habeas corpus, that would protect them against mistreatment by the Company and its agents.[104]

Unfortunately for Impey, his efforts to extend English law lacked a constituency in Britain. Thanks in part to paternalists' new rhetoric of humanitarianism, the introduction of English law into India was seen not only as damaging to the Company's business but as an assault on the rights of the very people he claimed to protect. In 1781, Parliament passed the Bengal Judicature Act, which sharply reduced the Supreme Court's powers. The statute stripped the Supreme Court of jurisdiction over revenue collections, thus ensuring that it would offer no check on alleged abuses in that department. The court could still hear suits among Indian natives living in Calcutta, but it was now directed to apply Hindu or Islamic law to all inheritance and contract disputes, depending on the religion of the parties. Traditional rules governing family and religious matters would remain in place, "although the same may not be held justifiable by the laws of England." And civil procedure would be accommodated to "the Religion and Manners" of the natives, rather than adhering to English practice.[105] According to the Act's proponents, "humanity" demanded these changes: Parliament had to consider "the situation of the miserable natives," for whom "it would be a consolation to their hearts to have their old laws."[106] It would be cruel, in other words, to treat Bengal like the rest of the British Empire.

THE NEW IMPERIAL COMMON LAW

Even as Parliament was ejecting Bengal and Quebec from the common-law world, England's courts were knitting the empire more closely together.

As this book has emphasized, Britain's turn to legal pluralism was the product of politics, not precedent. Legal doctrine had little to say about the laws that Parliament might choose to govern the colonies.[107] Nonetheless, the courts of Westminster Hall played an important role in facilitating Britain's new colonial legal policy. They did so, ironically, by developing a new imperial common law that gave English judges a greater role in policing colonial affairs.

As Chapter 1 explained, decisions such as *Calvin's Case* gave British monarchs the right, and sometimes the duty, to abrogate the laws of conquered territories. That doctrine retained its force in the eighteenth century. Just a few months after the Quebec Act was enacted, Mansfield's opinion in *Campbell v. Hall* reiterated the legitimacy of Britain's decision to impose English law on Grenada.[108] The case arose when Alexander Campbell, a newly arrived planter, challenged a duty on sugar exports on the ground that it had been imposed unlawfully. The Crown had imposed the duty by letters patent (and before Grenada's assembly had convened to authorize any taxes), and Campbell sued customs collector William Hall for taking his money without legal authority. (That a colonist could raise fundamental constitutional questions through an action for money had and received is another reminder of why private law loomed so large in debates about colonial legal pluralism.) The case was tried before Mansfield on July 2, 1773, and, after the jury gave a special verdict, "was very elaborately argued four several times" before the Court of King's Bench.[109]

The core of Campbell's argument was that the Proclamation of 1763 had promised the inhabitants of Grenada "the laws of liberty and of England," and that a tax imposed solely by Crown prerogative violated those laws.[110] Naturally, Hall disagreed. But while the two parties offered competing accounts of the Crown's power, they agreed that it had the authority to introduce English law to Grenada, at least until Parliament decided otherwise. The populist barrister John Glynn, generally mistrustful of prerogative, argued for Campbell that the King had the power of "promulging and introducing administration of the laws of England." On the other side, Attorney General Thurlow agreed that "[t]he King by his conquest acquired a power to provide laws for his subjects."[111] That doctrine hadn't been contested since the days of Coke, and it remained well known when *Campbell* was being argued. In 1772, a minor official in West Florida had applied it to the inhabitants of Illinois: "the King may direct that they shall be governed by their old Laws and Customs, or alter and change those Laws at his pleasure."[112]

The question in *Campbell*, then, was not what the Crown could do to

Grenada's law but what it had actually done. James Wallace, arguing for the tax collector, suggested that the Proclamation of 1763 had introduced only English criminal law (and perhaps English civil procedure) but had left untouched the French laws of marriage, property, and inheritance. Campbell's lawyers disagreed, insisting that the Proclamation had introduced English law more fully.[113] But this was a debate about how to interpret a particular legal text, not about legal policy in the abstract. Unsurprisingly, Mansfield's opinion agreed with the parties that the King "has a power to alter the old and to introduce new laws in a conquered country."[114] He then interpreted the Proclamation to mean that the Crown had in fact introduced English law to Grenada. In doing so, George III had deprived himself of the power to tax by prerogative, even if Grenada's old laws would have allowed it. The sugar duty he had imposed by fiat was therefore void.

At the same time, Mansfield emphasized the contingency of that outcome. Campbell's lawyers had suggested that English law automatically followed the flag. Glynn had argued that the very act of conquest had "annihilated" the "ancient law" of Grenada; another lawyer, John Alleyne, had insisted that British Grenadians enjoyed the laws of England "as a necessary consequence of the country being a part of the British Empire." Mansfield rejected those arguments, declaring instead that the "Laws of a conquered country continue until they are altered by the conqueror."[115] Legal pluralism, not English law, was the default.

Mansfield presented this principle as "too clear to be denied"; but in the 1770s it had come under pressure. The same issue had emerged in *Mostyn v. Fabrigas,* in which a native of Minorca sued the island's British governor for imprisoning and deporting him unlawfully. The governor, John Mostyn, argued that his actions had been permissible under the "ancient laws of Minorca"—that is, the laws of Spain, which had governed the island before its acquisition by Britain in 1713.[116] The Court of Common Pleas rejected Mostyn's argument, finding in an opinion by Chief Justice William de Grey that "the old law of Minorca"—at least insofar as it authorized torture and banishment—"fell of course when it came into our possession."[117] His description of Minorcan law gave credibility to the argument that Glynn and Alleyne presented in *Campbell.* (Not coincidentally, Glynn represented the plaintiff in both cases.)

The idea that Minorcan law had fallen was news to Governor Mostyn, and he challenged the verdict in King's Bench.[118] The court heard argument just two weeks before it decided *Campbell,* and Mansfield understood the two cases to be related. In the course of explaining his decision in the Grenada case, he pointed to Minorca as "another proof that the constitution of England does not necessarily follow a conquest by the king of England." He expanded on this point in *Mostyn*. He began by observing "[t]hat the Minorquins are governed by the Spanish laws, but when it serves their purpose plead the English laws." So, contrary to what de Grey had suggested, Governor Mostyn might have justified his actions under Spanish law. To do so, however, he would have had to introduce the relevant laws into evidence, because the content of foreign law had to be proved as a fact. Because he had failed to do so in this case, English law would still decide the case.[119]

In short, *Campbell* made it clear that the Crown could impose English law on a conquered colony; *Mostyn* established that doing so was optional. Taken together, the two cases reiterated the longstanding rule that policy, not precedent, determined what laws applied in conquered colonies. This was not a new idea—dicta in *Calvin's Case* had pointed in a similar direction—but it disposed of the notion that English law required its own propagation. At the same time, *Campbell* and *Mostyn* emphasized that foreign legal systems were just that—systems of *laws*. When Britain was deciding what law to apply in its colonies, the choice was not between English law and tyranny, but between competing legal systems, any of which might be appropriate in the right circumstances.

Mostyn made another contribution to Britain's new imperial constitution by amplifying the overseas jurisdiction of English courts. Much of the argument in that case focused not on what law that the court should apply, but on whether a court in England had jurisdiction over a trespass committed overseas. There were reasons to doubt whether King's Bench could even hear a case like *Mostyn*. A decade earlier, Chief Justice Charles Pratt had suggested that London-based courts lacked jurisdiction over cases arising in Minorca or applying Minorcan law.[120] *Mostyn* held otherwise, making it clear that colonial officials could be sued in the Westminster courts for torts committed overseas, even if those officials raised local laws in their defense. (This turned out to be an enduring legacy of *Mostyn:* well into the twentieth century, unfortunate law students encountered the case as their introduction to the concepts of jurisdiction and venue.)[121] Other cases reinforced this jurisdictional point. Previously, Mansfield had found jurisdiction in a case involving a naval officer's destruction of property in Nova Scotia.[122] Throughout the 1770s and 1780s, judges in King's Bench and Common Pleas adjudicated trespass actions against officials who had abused their authority in Quebec, Bengal, Senegambia, and elsewhere.[123] Parliament encouraged this trend, authorizing criminal prosecutions in London against governors and other officials for their actions overseas.[124] Even in an era of legal pluralism, the exercise of British power remained under the eye of metropolitan courts.

The enduring relevance of the Westminster courts had an important consequence for how legal pluralism worked in practice. *Mostyn* had explained that local customs might excuse actions that were unjustifiable under the laws of England; as such, it had blessed the divergence between metropolitan and colonial law. But *Mostyn* had also provided that English law remained the default rule in English courts. To invoke local laws as a defense, a defendant had to prove them as facts. And facts, of course, were ultimately the province of the jury—whose members might look skeptically on a governor's claim to rule by alien laws.[125] Something like that seems to have happened in *Rafael v. Verelst* (1774–76), in which two Armenian merchants sued Harry Verelst in Common Pleas for imprisoning them when he was governor of Bengal. After the jury returned a substantial verdict for the plaintiffs, one of Verelst's friends complained that it had "made no allowance for the Situation of a Gov[ernor] or the Custom of the People, but treated it intirely as an act of trespass [by] an Englishman towards another."[126] It's possible that the jury's verdict reflected ignorance or knee-jerk parochialism. But the jury might also have been making a deliberate statement about the kind of law that ought to govern the actions of a British governor, no matter where he was.[127]

Whatever the jurors' reasoning, cases like *Rafael* tempered the effect of legal pluralism, at least when it came to high-profile cases about official misconduct. Colonial governors and their subordinates knew that their actions might one day come before an English court, and that it would therefore be safest to keep their behavior within the lines marked by the sensibilities of an English jury. Governors acted otherwise at their peril. In 1806, for example, Governor Thomas Picton of Trinidad was tried in King's Bench for illegally ordering the judicial torture of a free woman of color. As in *Mostyn,* the governor argued that his actions had been authorized by the laws of Spain, which had survived Trinidad's conquest by Britain. Picton's counsel had learned from *Mostyn,* and this time the governor introduced evidence to prove that judicial torture had been part of Trinidadian law when Britain acquired the island. Under *Mostyn*'s framework, this could have shielded Picton from punishment. The prosecution, however, countered with an argument founded in *Calvin's Case* and *Campbell v. Hall:* that some foreign laws were so odious that they were necessarily abrogated by conquest; that judicial torture was such a law;

and, therefore, that the law of Trinidad had not authorized Picton's actions. Because Picton and the prosecution presented rival accounts of Trinidadian law, it fell to the jury to decide what that law actually said. And the jury convicted Picton. Even in a colony like Trinidad, where Spanish law officially persisted, domestic legal and moral ideals could still shape imperial governance.[128]

Ironically, this residual availability of English law might have helped to secure colonial legal pluralism. Cases like *Mostyn* reassured domestic audiences that an English tribunal would be available to punish egregious abuses of British authority, even in legally plural colonies.[129] That perhaps made it easier for Britons to accept the more general withdrawal of English law that paternalists were engineering. Clive had suggested as much in 1772. "The Idea of introducing the English Laws throughout our Possessions is absurd and impracticable," Clive wrote, shortly after William Bolts had criticized legal pluralism in Bengal. Bolts had argued, among other things, that English law was the soundest means of policing Company officials. Clive replied that English law could do that necessary work if it stayed in England: "If a Governor or any Man oppresses another in the East Indies . . . Redress may be had in the Court of King's Bench."[130] Governor Verelst made the same argument. "It is utterly incredible," he exclaimed, that Company officials "would risque their own fortunes" by abusing their power, when "[t]he experience of every day evinces, that an innocent and injured man would obtain ample compensation from an English jury."[131] He fulfilled his own prophecy when the jury in *Rafael v. Verelst* decided against him a few years later.

But cases like *Mostyn* and *Rafael* were necessarily rare. They required a plaintiff with the resources to travel to England and a defendant with the bad luck to be found there at the same time. Political connections helped, too. Anthony Fábrigas had arrived in England with the encouragement of Lord George Henry Lennox, a high-ranking officer who had himself crossed Mostyn in Minorca. Among other support, Lennox introduced Fábrigas to his influential brother, the Duke of Richmond. In *Rafael*, too, the plaintiffs had outside backing—in their case, from William Bolts, who had helped arrange the plaintiffs' passage to England, and who used the case to advance his own personal and political agenda.[132] English law remained available, but only in exceptional cases, and for those able to work within the hierarchies paternalists hoped to maintain.

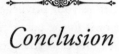

Conclusion

In October 1774, the First Continental Congress resolved that "the respective colonies are entitled to the common law of England."[1] After condemning the Quebec Act as "impolitic, unjust, and cruel," the delegates called for a boycott of British goods until Parliament repealed it. Later that month, Congress warned French Canadians that the Quebec Act was "'a whited sepulchre,' for burying [their] lives, liberty and property" under the guise of toleration. Invoking Montesquieu, Congress urged Canadiens to set aside religious differences and to unite with Protestant North Americans in resisting Britain's turn to legal pluralism.[2] A year and a half later, Americans justified their independence by citing, among other grievances, Britain's "abolishing the free System of English Laws in a neighbouring Province."[3] The United States—the "Empire of Liberty," as Thomas Jefferson christened it—would take up the old project of forging a common-law empire.[4]

Back in England, the notion of a common imperial law already seemed like the relic of another age. If one had to pick a date to mark its passing, one could do worse than March 22, 1775, when Edmund Burke delivered his "Speech on Conciliation with the Colonies." Burke spoke primarily to avert the impending war of American independence, but he also eulogized the legal framework that had governed the first British Empire. In expounding his vision for British North America, Burke compared it to Ireland, Wales, Durham, and Chester. Each of those jurisdictions had retained some degree of autonomy; but they had all remained under the mantle of English law and government. In each of those places, Burke told the House of Commons, Britain's success had depended on its extension of English law and liberty: "Your standard could never be advanced an inch before your privileges." But that was the old dispensation, and Burke spoke of it in the past tense. His plan for conciliating America required Parliament to repeal a string of statutes to which the colonists objected, including the hated tax on tea.[5] But he spared the Quebec Act, which some colonists had described as "the worst grievance" of all, and which Burke himself had opposed only a year earlier.[6] Even as Burke fought to maintain the boundaries of the first British Empire, he conceded that its constitution had lapsed. In the new empire, English law would no longer follow the flag.

Britain was coalescing around a new approach to colonial legal policy. But its details remained in doubt. Although legal pluralism had become part of the imperial repertoire, its use remained a matter of debate for as long as Britain kept its colonies. Policymakers and colonial subjects continued to dispute the issues that had given rise to legal pluralism in the first place, including the purpose of colonial economies, the nature of toleration, and the feasibility of legal transplants. Those arguments were repeatedly refashioned as Britain gained new territory, developed new understandings of empire, and reacted to new crises. The result was a second British Empire that took legal pluralism for granted but continued to contest its contours.

This concluding chapter considers these developments from several perspectives. It begins with a glance toward the later career of legal pluralism in the British Empire. This book has focused on the critical years between the Seven Years' War and the American Revolution, but it might be helpful to consider whether its approach—of examining legal policy as an instrument of colonial development—has broader application. My goal is not to present a definitive account of law in the later empire but to suggest how future work might carry forward the story told here.

The conclusion then revisits the book's central claim. This book has insisted that Britain had a choice about the kind of law that would govern its colonies. But it's also acknowledged that Britain faced a variety of constraints, including the preferences of colonial subjects. The conclusion weighs the relative importance of these considerations and argues that Britain really did have meaningful and consequential choices to make about colonial law. To reinforce this point, the conclusion then takes a comparative perspective, asking how other empires (especially France and Spain) have approached colonial legal policy. Without attempting to offer a universal history of colonial law, the conclusion highlights the range of attitudes that other empires have displayed toward legal pluralism—from encouragement to suppression. The diversity of imperial legal strategies further suggests that Britain could have picked a different path. The book ends by considering some broader implications of that finding, particularly with respect to theories of law and economic development.

A PLURALIST EMPIRE

Britain adopted legal pluralism to build a particular kind of empire in Bengal and Quebec. As circumstances evolved in the 1770s and 1780s, many Britons revised their thinking about those colonies' place in the British Empire—which, in turn, led to a reevaluation of legal pluralism as a colonial strategy. At the same time, earlier debates had convinced most policymakers that legal pluralism of some sort was obligatory and perhaps inevitable. The result was an ongoing debate that assumed some degree of pluralism but continued to question its parameters.

The shifting shape of legal pluralism was most evident in Quebec. Parliament had passed the Quebec Act in part to discourage Canada from joining a possible American rebellion. When that rebellion came to pass, it transformed the politics of English law in Canada. The reasons were partly demographic. After the war, the influx of Loyalist refugees made it harder to dismiss the Anglophone population as an insignificant minority, as Governor Carleton and others had done in the early 1770s. American independence also led Parliament to revisit the geopolitical and economic calculations that had made legal pluralism attractive. Instead of suppressing the colony's growth, as the Quebec Act's authors had intended, it now seemed desirable to build up the colony as a counterweight to the United States. It therefore no longer made sense to use French law to discourage immigration. French law had also lost some of its luster as a guarantor of loyalty and obedience, thanks to Canadiens' unenthusiastic resistance to the American invasion in 1775.[7]

In light of these new circumstances, some revision of Canadian law seemed inevitable. But there was no consensus about what the new system should look like. Some populists continued to urge wholesale anglicization.[8] Other politicians sought to revive the moderate compromise—in other words, to introduce English commercial law and civil juries while leaving other parts of French law in place. In 1777, Quebec's legislative council had taken a step in that direction by introducing English evidentiary law for commercial cases. In 1791, however, Parliament decided on a different compromise. The Constitutional Act split Quebec into two provinces: Upper Canada, which would have English law, and Lower Canada, which retained French law. In some respects, that looked like a big departure from the old paternalist program. Even in Lower Canada, English freehold tenures would be available, and the 1791 act provided more support for Anglican clergy. But Canada's commercial hub, Montreal, was in Lower Canada and remained subject to French law. The Constitutional Act thus represented a compromise in political economy as well as a compromise in law. It continued the Quebec Act's plan of trying to create a fundamentally agricultural and non-commercial colony, while also accommodating the interests of Anglophone farmers.[9]

The discussions leading up to the Constitutional Act revealed how thoroughly paternalists had managed to shape the public's understanding of colonial law. By the 1780s, even many proponents of anglicization agreed that Britain had some obligation to administer the laws of conquered subjects and that colonial legal policy should be framed in humanitarian terms. Francis Maseres, for instance, warned against the "*cruelty* of introducing or supporting the whole of either the English or French laws, in a country inhabited by two classes of people."[10] This kind of rhetoric facilitated some remarkable conversions. Edmund Burke, who had vigorously opposed the Quebec Act in 1774, declared in 1791 that he "most heartily agree[d] in the propriety of governing the ancient Canadian by those laws that he has been taught from his infancy to venerate."[11] Paternalists hadn't just won the debate over legal pluralism—they had set the debate's very terms.

In Bengal, too, the conversation unfolded within the framework that paternalists had laid out in the 1770s. As Chapter 5 explained, the Bengal Judicature Act of 1781 solidified Britain's commitment to legal pluralism in India, creating a dual legal system that would endure until 1861 (and in some respects even after the end of the Raj). But that's not to say that Indian law was settled. Continuing problems with the Company's finances and administration led in 1784 to Pitt's India Act, which restructured Company government, and in 1786 to the appointment of Charles Cornwallis, second Earl Cornwallis, as governor general.

In some respects, Cornwallis was an unlikely agent of paternalist empire. Although Americans tend to remember him for his defeat at Yorktown, his politics in the 1760s had been populist and supportive of colonists. (He had voted, for example, against the Stamp and Declaratory Acts.) His politics survived the war and shaped his approach to India, where he showed some sympathy for the old populist project of transplanting English institutions. His most enduring policy as governor general was the "permanent settlement" of 1793, which established *zamindars* as landowners who paid taxes to the Company at a fixed rate. As Ranajit Guha has argued, Cornwallis's system reflected his belief that it was possible to introduce into Bengal a set of English institutions—in this case, a particular notion of property rights—that would remodel Indian agriculture along British lines. In a departure from the approach under Warren Hastings, Cornwallis's reforms didn't depend for their legitimacy on their supposed continuity with Mughal institutions. Instead, he frankly described his approach as a break with the past.[12]

But Cornwallis's program of anglicization had limited ambitions. Rather than transforming India into a neo-American colony, as some populists had once hoped, his chief concern was to limit the harm inflicted by British rule. In the 1760s and early 1770s, the populist program for India had presupposed a colonial state that would transform Indian society by introducing a new legal culture. Cornwallis was far more pessimistic that British power could be used for good, and his reforms sought to create a limited government that would necessarily lack the capacity to transform Bengal in any significant way. His goal was not to anglicize Bengal's law but to introduce a few quasi-English practices that might improve the administration of Hindu and Islamic laws. And even Cornwallis's rather conservative program of reform faced criticism from arch-pluralists like Sir Thomas Munro, who would have gone even further in leaving Indian law alone.[13]

As with Quebec, Cornwallis's administration revealed the extent to which paternalists had redefined the debate over colonial law. His chief legal adviser was Sir William Jones, a justice of the Supreme Court of Judicature who in England had been well known for his populist politics and his radical defense of common-law institutions. In India, however, Jones insisted on the necessity of legal pluralism, writing to Burke that it would be "cruel tyranny" to force English liberties on India. "Any system of judicature affecting the natives in Bengal, and not having for its basis the old Mogul constitution," Jones warned, "would be dangerous and impracticable."[14]

Jones's acceptance of legal pluralism revealed a new understanding of the nature of law. In his *Essay on the Law of Bailments* (1781), written a few years before he arrived in Calcutta, Jones had insisted on the fundamental similarity between Asian and European legal systems, at least when it came to "*contracts* and the common intercourse between man and man." The universality of basic legal principles suggested that legal transplants would be easy. "I cannot help thinking," Jones wrote, that a treatise in Persian or Arabic "on the law of *Contracts,* and evincing the general conformity between the *Asiatick* and *European* systems, would contribute . . . to bring our *English* law into good odour among those, whose fate it is to be under our dominion." Even if the East India Company was constrained in the short term to "a strict observance" of Indian laws, that policy didn't need to be permanent. And even if the Company felt compelled to leave certain religious laws untouched, it might still anglicize laws related to commerce. That, of course, was similar to the compromise that moderates had proposed for Quebec. It was also consistent with what Muhammed Reza Khan had demanded from Hastings.[15]

Jones's legal universalism evaporated in India. Although he continued to insist that Indians deserved some English legal rights—especially trial by jury in criminal cases—he became more pessimistic about transplanting English law in general. This was not because he started to think of Bengal as fundamentally more alien. In some respects, his time there led him in the opposite direction. It was while in Bengal, for example, that he developed his famous hypothesis that European and Indian languages had a common origin.[16] His new view of Indian law had less to do with a generic embrace of colonial difference than his acceptance of a new political reality. It had become clear that legal pluralism was practically irradicable, and there was little point in clinging to a view of law that held otherwise. In the nineteenth century, even liberal reformers like Thomas Babington Macaulay took legal pluralism for granted. Although more willing than paternalists to anglicize Indian laws, Macaulay nonetheless dismissed legal uniformity as an "unattainable" fantasy. "We do not mean that all the people of India should live under the same law; far from it," Macaulay declared in 1833.[17]

There were dissenters from the new orthodoxy. One critique came from utilitarians such as Jeremy Bentham. As the introduction explained, Bentham and his disciples had little love for English law in England and even less interest in allowing it to spread overseas. But they also resisted the prevailing tendency to treat India and Europe as radically different. Even into the 1780s, after legal pluralism had a solid hold over British policy, Bentham continued to write to politically connected friends—especially populists like Shelburne and John Dunning—urging them to reconsider their views on colonial law.[18]

Perhaps the most radical critique of legal pluralism came from Granville Sharp. Best known as an opponent of slavery, his evangelical Anglicanism and sympathy for populist causes led him to believe that Britain had a moral ob-

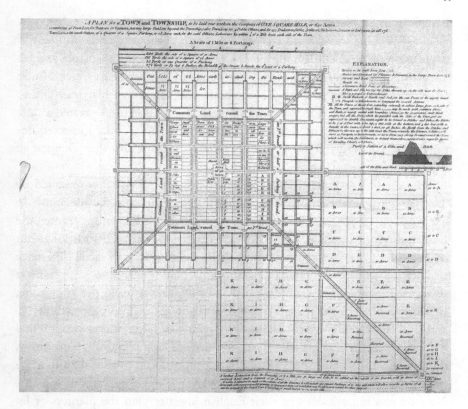

Granville Sharp argued that the same institutions (such as this town plan) could be used "in the East Indies, America and elsewhere." Granville Sharp, *A General Plan for Laying Out Towns and Townships, on the New-Acquired Lands in the East Indies, America, or Elsewhere* ([London]: n.p., 1794). Courtesy of the British Library, digitized by the Google Books project.

ligation to transplant its laws across its empire.[19] His campaign to spread the common law abroad was linked to his efforts to revitalize it at home. Starting in the 1780s, he urged Parliament to revive the Anglo-Saxon institution of frankpledge, which had required male commoners to organize themselves into ten-man "tithings." Although the Normans had used frankpledge for disciplinary purposes—each member of a tithing was on the hook for the others' good behavior—Sharp reimagined it as a way to secure participatory government across the Anglophone world. In a series of tracts and letters, he urged that frankpledge become the basis of reconstructed societies in Britain, Africa, "the East Indies, America, or Elsewhere."[20] This universal institution, "equally beneficial to all Nations and Countries," would eventually enable the entire English-speaking world to converge on a common model of English liberty.[21]

Sharp was unusual in both his optimism about legal transplants and his antipathy toward non-English law. He went out of his way to attack Hindu law, which he linked to Catholicism (both were satanic, in his view) and to slavery, which he described as "English Gentoo-ism" because it created a caste system. In continuing to defend a common-law empire, Sharp rejected not only paternalists' extractive vision of colonial rule but also their rhetoric of humanitarian toleration.[22]

His unapologetic defense of Protestant superiority was accompanied by another unusual feature of his thinking: his rejection of racial hierarchy. In the 1760s and 1770s, the debate over legal pluralism had taken for granted the universality of human nature and the formative power of institutions. But by the end of the eighteenth century, more rigid notions of racial difference had started to predominate, and white supremacy became so important as to sometimes seem like the very purpose of empire. Around the same time, British administrators became more pessimistic about Europeans' ability to thrive in tropical climates.[23] These two trends—of racial and environmental determinism—helped to ossify the new regime of legal pluralism. Conversely, differences in law made it easier for white Britons to rationalize their increasingly racialized empire. To be sure, English law had never guaranteed equality. Nobody was more jealous of their English liberties than the planters of Jamaica, who relied on the common law to turn people into property.[24] Nonetheless, the implicit egalitarianism of a shared law had been useful to antislavery advocates.[25] Slavery itself involved a sort of legal pluralism, as Chapter 1 observed.[26] Policymakers like Maurice Morgann, activists like Sharp, and judges like Mansfield all assumed, despite their different political views, that a universal common law would be incompatible with racialized slavery. As an East India Company lawyer observed in 1781, to give white and black subjects "equally the benefit of English laws would be to abolish the relation of master & slave."[27]

The selective denial of English law to certain groups of people eased the way for the racial and other hierarchies that structured the age of high imperialism.[28] A vicious cycle emerged in which the sharpening of racial divisions made it ever harder to imagine a truly uniform system of laws. In 1811, Henry Brougham, the future lord chancellor and a committed abolitionist, warned that it was "a mockery to talk of transplanting the English law to the West Indies," where the venerable system of trial by jury would become nothing more than an occasion for "twelve white planters" to bless the barbarities of their friends. "The British constitution was to be found in no other part of the world but in this country," he concluded.[29] In the nineteenth century, abolitionists and other reformers looked less often to the common law for aid and more frequently to parliamentary legislation, Crown prerogative, and bureaucratic supervision. In an empire structured by difference, the question became not whether to eliminate legal pluralism but how to use it.[30]

CONTINGENCY AND CONSTRAINT

This brief sketch of a postscript suggests that Britain's range of choices narrowed after 1780. Paternalists' humanitarian rhetoric, increasingly potent ideologies of difference, and the brute fact of pluralism on the ground all combined to make a common-law empire seem less plausible over time. But how much choice did Britain ever have when it came to colonial law? Although politicians sometimes spoke as if they could alter legal systems "at the scratch of a pen," they usually knew better.[31] Their papers were filled with the details of making the law work: building courthouses, appointing judges, paying lawyers. And while their understanding of the colonies was often imperfect, they knew that Britain had a limited ability to coerce its far-flung subjects. By the 1780s, these considerations led some lawmakers to insist that legal pluralism had been the only realistic option all along. Now that all the evidence is on the table, it's worth reconsidering the true range of British options.

Perhaps the most enduring argument against the possibility of a common-law empire has been the sheer number of new British subjects after 1763, particularly in India. In 1781, a Member of Parliament doubted that it was "agreeable to common sense" for "five thousand British in Bengal" to impose English law on millions of native Indians.[32] There was also a lopsided population in Quebec after its conquest: sixty or seventy thousand French Catholics, versus a few hundred Anglophone merchants and traders (plus the military).[33] The places where English law did take root were much smaller. There were fewer than two thousand free Grenadians in 1763, and perhaps nine thousand New Yorkers in 1664. Surely size mattered?

Yes and no. It seems clear that the introduction of English law would have happened less quickly and more unevenly in Bengal than in Grenada or New York. But we shouldn't exaggerate the difficulties. When populists talked about anglicizing the laws of Bengal, they didn't imagine that every transaction would immediately be conducted according to the formalities of the common law. That wasn't even true in England.[34] Instead, populists had in mind the kinds of big cases that ended up in Chancery or King's Bench, such as trespass actions against government officials or high-value contract disputes. From the perspective of colonial development, those were the cases that mattered. The rest could be entrusted to arbitrators, small-claims courts (similar to those found in England), or minor officials (analogous to English justices of the peace).[35]

Policymakers understood that Britain would rarely be able to force English law on an unwilling populace. Indeed, they were painfully aware of the weakness of the imperial state.[36] Recall Chapter 3, for example, when Lord Hillsborough declared it "impracticable" to ban manufacturing in Quebec. It was that same weakness that made legal pluralism so attractive as a regulatory strategy: rather than forcing colonial subjects to pay a new tax or follow new rules, it merely withheld certain English institutions. At the same time, we shouldn't exaggerate the challenges of transplanting English law, even for an empire with limited power. One of the enduring themes of legal history has been the eagerness of litigants to exploit whatever courts helped them win the dispute at hand. Plaintiffs sometimes took a principled stand about what law ought to govern their lives. But they were usually willing to shop for a favorable forum, no matter whose law it applied. Litigants' flexibility had political consequences. When litigants invoked a particular tribunal or body of law, they implicitly endorsed its legitimacy. Repeated over many cases, this process could make even the most alien institutions a familiar part of the colonial legal landscape. As Lauren Benton and other historians have shown, colonial law was not just something the conqueror imposed. It was also a potential resource. For that reason, Britain's new subjects didn't need to like English law for it to take root. They just had to find it useful—and it often was.[37]

This starts to make the introduction of English law to Bengal (or other colonies) sound less daunting. At first, English law would have been a relatively elite phenomenon (just as it was in the 1740s, when Omichund brought his case in Chancery). Like their English counterparts, Bengali elites would have relied on English lawyers for advice and representation, which would have further facilitated their adaption to the new system. (It's easier to hire a new lawyer than to learn a new law.) It wouldn't have been hard to find lawyers to do the job: there was an oversupply of them in England at the time, and in the 1770s more barristers sought passage to Bengal than the Company was willing to admit.[38] Nor would it have been difficult to find staff to handle a greater caseload in common-law courts. For better or worse, English law got by with remarkably few personnel. Until the nineteenth century, the central courts of Westminster Hall rarely had more than fifteen judges; much of the legal system's work depended on lay adjuncts, such as jurors. These considerations made it plausible for writers like Alexander Dow to project that it would cost a "trivial" amount to establish an English judiciary in Bengal.[39]

Even the most ardent devotees of anglicization assumed that Bengal's courts were going to look different from those of New York or Pennsylvania. Demographics and the limited power of the imperial state placed real constraints on the changes that Britain could hope to effect, especially in the short term. But those constraints still left Britain with a meaningful choice about its legal policy. Everyone, including populists, assumed that some Hindu and Islamic norms would persist, especially since many disputes would be resolved by native arbitrators. But populists nonetheless proposed a legal system that was fundamentally English, particularly in its use of English judges and trials by jury. Rather than forcing legal pluralism on India, populists proposed instead to make English law available to all, under the assumption that local litigants would flock to it voluntarily. The later acceptance of English law in India suggests that their assumption was reasonable.[40]

COMPARISONS

Perhaps the best evidence that Britain might have taken a different course is that other empires did so. To be sure, no empire had perfectly uniform laws. As Jane Burbank and Frederick Cooper explain, the size and internal complexity of empires has generally meant that "[t]he option of one law for all ... was sure to fail."[41] But the strategic legal pluralism that emerged in the British Empire went well beyond the mundane variations in law that one would expect in any large, complex polity.[42] A comparison with other empires will help us see the distinctiveness of Britain's approach.

Let's start with Rome, which later empires so often took as their model. For much of its history, the Roman Empire was formally legally plural: Roman citizens lived under Roman civil law, while non-citizens used the laws of their own communities. But that changed in AD 212, when the emperor Caracalla extended Roman citizenship to nearly all of the empire's free-born inhabitants. Because Roman citizens were by definition subject to Roman law, Caracalla's edict entailed the universalization of Roman law; as a formal matter, there was now only one law for the empire. Historians debate the extent to which 212 was really a watershed. Rome's *ius civile* had influenced local laws before that year, and local customs still mattered afterwards, so that "Roman law" still varied from place to place. But legal pluralism—in the sense of an explicit policy fostered by the imperial state—ceased to be Rome's way of managing difference.[43] Similarly, law in Mughal India, while internally complex, didn't depend on the tidy application of different laws to different communities. As Nandini Chatterjee has recently put it, Mughal subjects didn't experience the law as an "eclectic" regime composed of strikingly different systems. Instead, "they saw it all as 'law.'"[44] Law varied by place and social status, but there wasn't "manifest legal pluralism" of the kind that Britain later engineered.[45]

As in Britain, the rulers of other empires thought of themselves as having to choose how pluralistic their empire should be. Clifford Ando reports "dynamic debate within the Roman population" about the boundaries of citizenship (and, by implication, the boundaries of Roman law).[46] The Dutch also debated the merits of uniform law, both in the colonies and within the Netherlands.[47] Their answers changed over time. In the seventeenth century, the inhabitants of New Netherland expected, and the Dutch West India Company required, that colonial courts follow "the custom and order of fatherland."[48] The same rule applied in early Batavia, where the first law code applied many of the "statutes and customs of the United Netherlands" to everyone who came under the rule of the Dutch East India Company (VOC). Over time, the VOC reversed course, formalizing a separate system of native courts in the Netherlands Indies and parceling non-European communities into separate jurisdictions.[49] But not everyone agreed with that policy, and the propriety of legal pluralism remained a matter of debate in the nineteenth century.[50] In the end, the pluralists won—sometimes to the frustration of local inhabitants, one of whom observed that "the admiration of [indigenous customary] law is to be found more among Europeans than among Indonesians."[51]

To appreciate the distinctiveness of Britain's legal policy, the most illuminating comparison is with Britain's chief eighteenth-century rivals, France and Spain. All three empires embarked on ambitious programs of reform during and after the Seven Years' War. In all three empires, reformers sought to centralize imperial administration and to boost tax revenues. And in all three, those centralizing reforms sparked protest and even revolt.[52] But only Britain made legal pluralism a central plank of its postwar program.

The story of Spanish imperial law is one of gradual (and imperfect) homogenization. Early modern Spain, like many contemporary kingdoms, was a legal patchwork. "Spain" itself was a composite of kingdoms and provinces, each of which had its own laws, which were further punctuated by local and corporate privileges. The Americas added further layers to Spanish legal pluralism by building a distinct body of colonial law and separate courts for Indian litigants.[53] But there were also centripetal pressures. Pursuing the maxim of "many kingdoms but one law" (a favorite saying of the Count-Duke of Olivares), Spain gradually imposed Castilian law on conquered territories in Europe and the Americas.[54] Legal actors throughout the Spanish Atlantic saw themselves as participating in what was fundamentally a single legal system—albeit one that made room for local exceptions in Iberia and Spanish America alike.

The push for legal uniformity gained momentum during the Bourbon reforms. The process started when Felipe V (1683–1746) imposed Castilian law on Aragon. After the Seven Year' War, Carlos III extended this homogenizing program to the New World. Inspired by an Enlightenment ideal of "one law for all," Spain curtailed the jurisdiction of special Indian tribunals and, in the words of one contemporary, sought to craft "a universal body of legislation for both Americas."[55] (In that sense, Carlos was acting like other enlightened absolutists, such as Frederick II, who sought to impose a uniform code on Prussia and its growing territory.)[56] These efforts were not always successful. As in the British Empire, attempts to standardize imperial governance generated resistance and debate among royal officials and colonial subjects, and improvisation remained an important part of Spain's imperial legal culture.[57] But the dominant thrust of Spanish policy—at least in aspiration—was toward uniformity.[58]

France entered the eighteenth century with a relatively centralized imperial law, which became more uniform over time. In fact, French colonial law was more uniform than the law of France itself: in the metropole, the law varied across provinces, but the colonies all applied the *coutume de Paris*. To be sure, there were some areas of law, especially concerning slavery and taxation, that varied across the empire. And, as in Britain, there was a robust debate about the promises and perils of "legal universalism."[59] The general direction of reform, however, was toward greater similarity between metropolitan and colonial law—a trend reinforced by the circulation of lawyers among metropolitan and colonial postings.[60] Indeed, legal uniformity struck some French elites as the *sine qua non* of imperial rule. (The Abbé Raynal, writing in the 1770s, warned against conquering Spanish America because its inhabitants would "never conform to new laws.")[61] The Revolution intensified this trend. "Under the Directory," Pernille Røge argues, "French revolutionaries endorsed a model of empire which sought to preserve France's remaining colonies through integration, abolition, and legal universalism."[62]

Why did Britain and its Bourbon rivals take such different paths? Their divergence was partly a matter of circumstance. Britain first deployed colonial legal pluralism in the territories it gained from the Seven Years' War. France and Spain, the war's losers, lacked an equivalent opportunity for experimentation. But circumstances alone don't explain the difference. Spain did gain one new colony, Louisiana, from France in 1762. There, Spain imposed its own law, at least on paper.[63] One might also ask whether the civil-law systems of France and Spain were inherently easier to export—for example, because civil codes travel more easily than common-law precedents.[64] But while that notion has some currency with today's comparative lawyers, it wasn't obvious to eighteenth-century writers.[65] Indeed, some English lawyers thought that their law was especially easy to ship abroad. As we saw with *Omichund v. Barker* (discussed in Chapter 1), judges habitually tweaked common-law rules to reflect new circumstances; and local juries could interpret the common law in light of local conditions. Civil-law systems, in contrast, lacked these mechanisms for quick adaptation.[66] That's why Burke, citing Mansfield's argument in *Omichund,* could praise the common law's superiority over statutes for keeping pace with "the Growth of our Commerce and of our Empire."[67] For proponents of legal pluralism, the common law's problem was not that it was too hard to send overseas; it was that it was too hard to control after it arrived. Common-law adjudication—especially jury trials—gave the English law a degree of local autonomy that was poorly suited to paternalists' hierarchical project. Codified legal systems, in contrast, have long been seen as friendlier to political centralization.[68] In other words, the common law was fine for an expanding empire—just not the kind of empire paternalists wanted to run.

THE COMMON LAW AND COLONIAL DEVELOPMENT

This brings us back one last time to the question of choice. The last section confirmed what this book has been arguing: the mere fact of being an empire didn't drive Britain willy-nilly toward legal pluralism. Nor did anything inherent in the common law, or in the climate, or in contemporary assumptions about human difference. Certainly, the laws of Britain's far-flung possessions would never have been identical to each other. But the particular variety of strategic legal pluralism that emerged in the eighteenth-century British Empire was anything but inevitable. Instead, policymakers made a choice about the kind of empire they wanted and what sort of legal system they thought would sustain it.

The story is at odds with how scholars across a range of disciplines tend to talk about imperial law—and about empire in general. The usual story depicts European colonialism as following an inexorable logic. Where Europeans could settle in large numbers, such as North America, they sought to eliminate the indigenous population and to erect a "neo-Europe" in its place. Where a dense indigenous population and a high rate of settler mortality made that impossible, Europeans instead tried to extract wealth and labor from the existing inhabitants.[69] Empire was always destructive, but demographic and environmental conditions determined what form that destruction would take.

As this book has tried to make clear, eighteenth-century readers wouldn't have recognized that story. Instead, they understood that initial conditions were only one factor in fixing the shape of colonial rule. In "modern European colonies," Sir John Dalrymple explained in the 1750s, "principles of settlement are not determined by the natural circumstances attending a settlement, but by the particular views with which they are settled."[70] As he and his contemporaries understood, political and economic calculations often mattered more than demography or the disease environment. Neither the deadliness of Senegambia's climate nor the presence of a dense African and métis community stopped Britain from trying to transplant English institutions there. Similarly, the healthy environments of Illinois and Quebec failed to inspire automatic anglicization.

The contingency of colonial institutions reflected the contested character of empire itself. During the eighteenth century, the nature and purpose of empire was still being worked out. Consider, for example, Edmund Burke's definition of empire as "the aggregate of many states under one common head."[71] That definition (taken from his "Speech on Conciliation") was deliberately thin. It permitted difference but didn't demand it, nor did it say anything about the nature of imperial headship. But even that minimalist account was polemical. By insisting on the subordination of colonies to a common head, Burke was rejecting other proposals for imperial union, such as the confederation of Britain's territories as a league of equal states or their incorporation into a unitary British kingdom.[72] No wonder, then, that authors seeking a neutral definition of empire sought refuge in bigness. Dr. Johnson's dictionary, for example, borrowed a definition of empire as a nation or kingdom "extended over vast tracts of land, and numbers of people."[73] Size was all that mattered. Johnson's definition might seem a little *too* stripped down for modern academic purposes, but it's more useful than it might seem, at least for legal historians. On the one hand, it allows us to avoid the question-begging assumption that imperial law is necessarily defined by difference. On the other hand, it helps us appreciate what made imperial law unique: the need to respond to issues arising from scale, including the challenge of governing diverse ethnic, religious, and geographic communities. Imperial law, in other words, is characterized by the kinds of problems it must address, rather than a particular set of solutions.[74]

This book is not the first to point out that empires could take many forms. Burbank and Cooper, among others, argue that imperial strategies have run the gamut from "homogenization" to "recognition of difference."[75] But scholars have been slow to appreciate the importance of that insight for how we evaluate legal systems.

In the past few decades, a consensus has emerged that a country's welfare depends at least partly on the quality of its institutions. But there's less agreement about which institutions matter most—and especially the extent to which a country's legal tradition, such as civil or common law, influences economic and political development.[76] For example, economists and legal scholars continue to debate whether the common law is uniquely suited to promoting liberty, the rule of law, or economic growth.[77]

One of the most influential attempts to answer this question is known as the legal-origins theory. Starting in the 1990s, a number of economists have argued that common-law countries enjoyed various advantages over their civil-law counterparts, including more secure property rights, greater judicial independence, and superior economic performance. Furthermore, these economists purported to show that the common law *caused* those advantages. The argument goes like this: Most countries today used to be colonies. As such, they didn't get to choose the common or civil law; instead, they inherited their legal system from their former colonial rulers. Because legal inheritance was mostly a historical accident—Britain usually happened to impose English law, France imposed French law, and so on—it was exogenous to later economic development. In other words, countries didn't choose to adopt the common law because they were rich; rather, Britain imposed the common law wherever it happened to rule, and those places grew richer as a result.

The policy prescription of this work was clear: countries that aspire to economic success ought to import elements of the common law.[78] Perhaps because of its significant real-world implications, the legal-origins thesis quickly attracted critiques from several directions.[79] This isn't the place to rehash the debate, but one problem with the thesis should strike readers immediately. In its classic form, the legal-origins theory assumes that European empires spread their own laws uniformly across their possessions. But, of course, that didn't always happen. Instead, European empires transplanted their own institutions more fully to some colonies than to others.

While that might be a problem for the legal-origins theory, it's the key feature of an alternative approach championed by economists including Daron Acemoglu, Simon Johnson, and James Robinson (AJR). Like the legal-origins theorists, AJR think that institutions matter for a country's prosperity. AJR agree, too, that colonial institutions often persisted after independence, so that they have played an important role in shaping postcolonial prosperity. But instead of focusing on whether a country inherited civil or common law, AJR focus on whether it inherited institutions that are "extractive" (restricting power and wealth to a narrow elite) or "inclusive" (allowing for broader participation in political and economic life). To explain why a particular colony received inclusive or exclusive institutions, AJR adopt the deterministic model of empire that so many historians have favored. In colonies where Europeans could settle in relatively large numbers, they built "neo-Europes" with inclusive institutions meant to protect the colonizers. But where Europeans had trouble settling (due to high mortality or denser indigenous populations), they tended to build extractive institutions that funneled wealth back home.[80]

AJR and the legal-origins theorists reach different conclusions about the importance of a country's legal tradition, and they rely on different stories about how empires typically operated. But they both treat colonial legal institutions (and, by extension, many postcolonial institutions) as the predictable product of initial conditions. The legal-origins theory assumes that European empires brought their own laws everywhere.[81] AJR make the opposite move: by tying a colony's institutional outcomes to its environmental and demographic endowments, their theory suggests that legal pluralism was practically inevitable.[82] Both theories, however, assume that empires had a certain tendency—either toward difference or sameness—that played out in predictable ways.

What is missing from both of these theories is choice. As this book has shown, a colony's legal system didn't flow automatically from the identity of the colonizer or the conditions the colonizer encountered. Instead, it reflected the empire's political and economic agenda. That agenda, in turn, emerged from political debates—among politicians, soldiers, bureaucrats, and subjects across the empire—about the nature and purpose of colonial rule. The existence of those debates matters for how we gauge the quality of different kinds of law today.

Most attempts to evaluate legal traditions (such as the common law) have focused on their intrinsic characteristics. Economists and comparative lawyers have been particularly attracted to the idea that common-law systems both reflected and encouraged a less statist approach to governance than did code-based systems, particularly the civil law.[83] And if the common law does indeed boost a country's economic prospects, it's perhaps plausible that it would do so by offering greater sympathy for market-based approaches. But there might be another explanation. In the British Empire, English law mattered not only because of what it was, but also because of what it said. Britons and their colonial subjects did sometimes speak about the common law as uniquely protective of liberty; and they sometimes had good reason to do so. Common-law suits were the chief means of redressing official misconduct, and juries played an important part in protecting colonial subjects and their property. It's also true, however, that many Britons had little love for their supposedly glorious legal heritage. This was particularly true of members of the business community—the very people who should have been most attuned to the common law's supposed tendency to support free markets. Merchants complained about the law incessantly in their letters to each other; advice manuals urged them to avoid litigation; and political economists argued that England's legal institutions were stunting its economy. When the merchant John Levett wrote to his partner in the 1770s, he used the occasion to fantasize about governing a kingdom without common lawyers, or at least getting to throw a few of them off a cliff. His ideal legal system, he told Richard Oswald, would fit into "a pocket volume" based on "the Prussian code."[84] Levett was hardly alone in finding the common law unfit for business. Metropolitan and colonial lawmakers repeatedly proposed ways to free commercial litigation from the deadening grip of the common law, such as by creating specialized merchant courts or facilitating arbitration.[85]

And yet, when Britain had to choose what law to apply in a new colony, merchants almost universally demanded English law. That wasn't because they thought its rules were especially fair or its procedures notably efficient. Nor did they think that its philosophy was more laissez-faire. To the contrary, most observers assumed that transplanting English law would require aggressive state intervention. (Think back to Hardwicke's "Scotch Reformation"; to Brecknock's plan of transporting Indian children to England; or to the anonymous proposal to found a "British Town" in Quebec.) Instead, merchants and their allies focused on what it meant to have a common imperial law.

Britain's decision to transplant English law to a particular place sent a message that it was trying to build a certain kind of colony—one that included, among other things, a vibrant commercial economy with a robust Anglophone population. Thus, when Britain initially imposed English law on Quebec, the barrister Fowler Walker described it as "a royal Invitation to his Majesty's subjects to settle" there.[86] Observers understood that such an invitation would be hard to rescind. Under the framework announced in *Campbell v. Hall,* the Crown could grant English law by proclamation, but only Parliament could take it away, and only at great political cost. Sometimes politicians chose to pay the price, as with the Quebec Act. But the presence of the common law in a colony was usually a reliable guide to the long-term plans of the imperial state. Withholding English law sent a very different message: that Britain was planning an extractive colony in which Anglophone settlement and investment would be unwelcome and unwise. Of course, a well-informed merchant or settler would take the hint and would naturally prefer those places that the British state had blessed with English law. The result was a self-fulfilling prophesy. Even if English law was intrinsically neutral for a colony's economic or political development, its presence might still have been helpful thanks to the preferences, prejudices, and assumptions of British subjects.[87]

The signaling function of the eighteenth-century common law might illuminate its role in economic development today. Katharina Pistor has observed that "[t]wo legal systems dominate the world of global capital: English common law and the laws of New York State."[88] It's not just that private parties often choose those bodies of law when crafting contracts. A growing list of sovereign nations, including Kazakhstan, the United Arab Emirates, and France, have erected common-law courts meant to attract international business. Perhaps these actors all think that the common law is intrinsically superior.[89] But there's another possibility. International business uses common law so frequently because it's a *common* law. This is true at the level of legal personnel: transnational lawyers have disproportionately been educated in England or the United States, and they like to work with the law they know best. But it's also about the message that the common law sends. By creating common-law courts, countries can declare themselves open for business.[90]

Would it have been possible for Britain to apply the same laws to everyone in its empire? Would it have been just? In 1760, most Britons would have answered "yes" to both questions. By 1780, the typical answer was "no." This book has offered a new explanation for that revolution in legal policy. British officials elected to administer different kinds of law as a way of shaping what kind of colony each place would become.

Britain's reimagining of imperial law has left an enduring and ambiguous legacy. On the one hand, economists have found evidence that colonial legal pluralism often functioned just as paternalists had intended: to slow economic development. Colonies that received legally plural systems often became less prosperous than those places where Britain imposed English law.[91] On the other hand, paternalists justified their economically destructive legal policy by creating a rhetoric of toleration and humanitarianism whose liberatory potential still resonates today. Britain's empire of laws has been buried, but it continues to rule us from its grave—for better and for worse.

Acknowledgments

This book grew out of an unexpected encounter in Yale's Beinecke Library. Shortly after starting graduate school, I read a letter from a young East India Company employee to a relative back home. The author, James Forbes, described his occasional duty of supervising trials by ordeal. He made it clear that ordeals were an unsound way to decide cases—but also that they ought to be done properly. He (and his employer) not only tolerated ordeals but actively aided in their administration, even authenticating ordeal proceedings with the Company's seal. I was intrigued by the Company's decision to administer a procedure it disdained, and this book eventually followed. My first thanks therefore go to the staffs of the Beinecke and the other libraries and archives whose collections made this book possible. Archivists at Scone Palace and the University of Dundee helped me access manuscripts belonging to the present Earl of Mansfield, whose permission to consult them I gratefully acknowledge.

This book owes a special debt to Steve Pincus, who advised the dissertation on which it's based, and who has more than anyone else shaped how I think about writing history. John Langbein, Claire Priest, Jim Whitman, and John Witt were indispensable guides to the field of legal history, and their advice has shaped not only this project but my broader approach to writing and teaching. I gratefully remember the advice of David Lieberman, and I'm sorry that his tragic and untimely death has prevented me from showing him the fruit of his encouragement. Conversations with Julia Adams, Lauren Benton, Ned Blackhawk, Richard Bourke, Benjamin Brady, Nancy Christie, Joanne Freeman, Richard Huzzey, Emily Kadens, Karuna Mantena, Michel Morin, Richard Ross, Jennifer Wells, and Nicholas Wilson sharpened my thinking during this book's long gestation. Heather Welland kindly shared a late draft of her own excellent book. My classmates at Yale, especially Catherine Arnold, Amanda Behm, Jadzia Biskupska, Megan Cherry, Amy Dunagin, Elizabeth Herman, Lucy Kaufman, Matthew Lockwood, Agnieszka Rec, and Alec Zuercher Reichardt, made me both smarter and saner. Justin du Rivage, Eliga Gould, Patrick Griffin, and Mitra Sharafi provided valuable guidance as I first thought about turning my thesis into a book.

Many people have read partial drafts at various stages. I'm especially grateful for the perceptive comments of Tiraana Bains, Christina Bambrick, Christopher Casey, Zachary Herz, James Vaughn, and Amy Watson, and for those of audiences at Notre Dame, Penn State Law–University Park, the Northwestern University Pritzker School of Law, the Chicagoland Junior Scholars conference, Steve Pincus's virtual British and Imperial History Workshop, and Bill Nelson's virtual legal history colloquium. Parts of my argument have been previewed in the *Virginia Law Review* and *Entangling the Quebec Act: Transnational Contexts, Meanings, and Legacies in North America and the British Empire* (McGill-Queen's University Press, 2020). The editors of the latter volume, François Furstenberg and Ollivier Hubert, were enthusiastic and helpfully critical as I was first putting together my thoughts about the Quebec Act.

I'm still astounded by the generosity of the scholars who agreed to read a full draft of this book as part of a virtual manuscript workshop: T. T. Arvind, Holly Brewer, Barry Cushman, Dan Hulsebosch, Amalia Kessler, Michael Lobban, Steve Pincus, and Phil Stern. Their voluntarily enduring yet another (long) Zoom meeting is a model of academic charity, and their advice immensely improved the final thing.

My colleagues at Notre Dame Law School have been exceptionally supportive. I was pleased but unsurprised when my fellow legal historians, Barry Cushman and David Waddilove, showed interest in my work. But I didn't expect that my acknowledgments would need to incorporate by reference the whole faculty directory. Particular thanks go to Deans Nell Newton and Marcus Cole, who arranged funding for research in London; Beth Smith, who provided outstanding administrative support; and my first-rate research assistants (Sophia Aguilar, Elisabeth Crusey, Natalie Fulk, Tom Hellenbrand, Michael Polito, Jensen Rehn, Michael Snyder, David Spicer, and Nikolai Stieglitz). Of course, this book simply wouldn't exist without the wonderful staff at Yale University Press, especially Bill Frucht, Amanda Gerstenfeld, Joyce Ippolito, and Jill Twist.

My last and greatest thanks go to my family. My parents' unflagging support gave me the courage to start down this path and then to keep going. My wife, Alex, has patiently endured long archival absences and too many stories about Lord Mansfield; but that's hardly the start of why I'm grateful for her. Our sons are too young to know why their father was working so much. When they're older, I hope they'll understand that this book was for them, too.

Notes

ABBREVIATIONS

BL	British Library
Blackstone, *Commentaries*	William Blackstone, *Commentaries on the Laws of England*. Edited by Wilfrid Prest (individual volumes edited by David Lemmings, Simon Stern, Thomas P. Gallanis, and Ruth Paley). Oxford: Oxford University Press, 2016. Page numbers refer to the original pagination of the *Commentaries*.
BRBML	Beinecke Rare Book and Manuscript Library, Yale University
DNB	*Oxford Dictionary of National Biography*. Oxford: Oxford University Press, 2004; online ed., https://oxforddnb.com
FWIHC	*Fort William–India House Correspondence and Other Contemporary Papers Relating Thereto*. 21 vols. Delhi: Published for the National Archives of India by the Manager of Publications, 1957–69
KA	Kent Archives, Maidstone, United Kingdom
LIL	Lincoln's Inn Library
NLS	National Library of Scotland
NRO	Norfolk Record Office, Norwich, United Kingdom
NRS	National Records of Scotland

PH	William Cobbett, ed., *The Parliamentary History of England, from the Earliest Period to the Year 1803*, 36 vols. London: Printed by T. C. Hansard for Longman, Hurst, Rees, Orme & Brown, 1806–20
Proceedings and Debates	R. C. Simmons and P. D. G. Thomas, eds., *Proceedings and Debates of the British Parliaments Respecting North America, 1754–1783*. Millwood, N.Y.: Kraus International Publications, 1982
SA	Sheffield Archives, Sheffield, United Kingdom
TNA	The National Archives, Kew, United Kingdom
WLCL	William L. Clements Library, University of Michigan

INTRODUCTION

1. Jeremy Bentham, "Place and Time [1782]," in *Selected Writings*, ed. Stephen G. Engelmann (New Haven, Conn.: Yale University Press, 2011), 153–54, 179–80.
2. Ibid., 154, 173, 181; see also Bentham to Lord Ashburton (June 3, 1782), in *The Correspondence of Jeremy Bentham*, ed. Timothy L. S. Sprigge and Ian R. Christie (London: UCL Press, 2017), 3:127 ("Some parts of a perfect body of law [would] be equally adapted to all times and places: others not."); Stephen G. Engelmann and Jennifer Pitts, "Bentham's 'Place and Time,'" *Tocqueville Review/La Revue Tocqueville* 32, no. 1 (2011): 46; Gerald J. Postema, *Bentham and the Common Law Tradition*, 2d ed. (Oxford: Oxford University Press, 2019), 164–65.
3. See Bentham, "Place and Time," 156 n.(a).
4. The Seven Years' War gets its name from the interval between the formal declaration of war in 1756 and the signing of the Treaty of Paris in 1763. But Britain and France started fighting in 1754 in North America, where the conflict was known as the French and Indian War. Fred Anderson, *Crucible of War: The Seven Years' War and the Fate of Empire in British North America, 1754–1766* (New York: Vintage Books, 2001), 505–6; Daniel A. Baugh, *The Global Seven Years War 1754–1763: Britain and France in a Great Power Contest*, 2d ed. (London: Routledge, 2021); Colin G. Calloway, *The Scratch of a Pen: 1763 and the Transformation of North America* (New York: Oxford University Press, 2006), 152; P. J. Marshall, "The British in Asia: Trade to Dominion, 1700–1765," in *The Oxford History of the British Empire: The Eighteenth Century*, ed. P. J. Marshall (Oxford: Oxford University Press, 2001), 492.
5. Scholars debate the extent to which "Hindu law" was a British invention. See, e.g., Donald R. Davis Jr., "Law and 'Law Books' in the Hindu Tradition," *German Law Journal* 9, no. 3 (2008): 318–19; Nandini Bhattacharyya Panda, *Appropriation and Invention of Tradition: The East India Company and Hindu Law in Early Colonial Bengal* (New Delhi: Oxford University Press, 2008), 10; Chandra Mallampalli, "Escaping the Grip of Personal Law in Colonial India: Proving Custom, Negotiating Hindu-Ness," *Law and History Review* 28, no. 4 (2010): 1046–50; cf. William T. Cavanaugh, *The Myth of Religious Violence: Secular Ideology and the Roots of Modern Conflict* (Oxford:

Oxford University Press, 2009), 87–92 (arguing that "Hinduism" was a colonial construction). This book uses "Hindu law" to refer to what British officials described themselves as administering. Similarly, "Islamic law" as deployed by European empires was at least partly a colonial creation. See Nurfadzilah Yahaya, *Fluid Jurisdictions: Colonial Law and Arabs in Southeast Asia* (Ithaca, N.Y.: Cornell University Press, 2020), 29–32, 169–70.

6. Broader studies of legal pluralism include Lauren Benton, *Law and Colonial Cultures: Legal Regimes in World History, 1400–1900* (Cambridge: Cambridge University Press, 2002); and Lauren Benton and Richard J. Ross, eds., *Legal Pluralism and Empires, 1500–1850* (New York: New York University Press, 2013). On Britain's imperial constitution, see, e.g., Mary Sarah Bilder, *The Transatlantic Constitution: Colonial Legal Culture and the Empire* (Cambridge, Mass.: Harvard University Press, 2004); and Daniel J. Hulsebosch, *Constituting Empire: New York and the Transformation of Constitutionalism in the Atlantic World, 1664–1830* (Chapel Hill: University of North Carolina Press, 2005). For imperial histories of particular doctrines or institutions, see, e.g., Paul D. Halliday, *Habeas Corpus: From England to Empire* (Cambridge: Belknap Press of Harvard University Press, 2010); and Hannah Weiss Muller, *Subjects and Sovereign: Bonds of Belonging in the Eighteenth-Century British Empire* (Oxford: Oxford University Press, 2017).

7. J. R. Seeley, *The Expansion of England: Two Courses of Lectures* (London: Macmillan, 1883), 8–9; see also ibid., 179 ("Nothing great that has ever been done by Englishmen was done so unintentionally, so accidentally, as the conquest of India."); Amanda Behm, *Imperial History and the Global Politics of Exclusion: Britain, 1880–1940* (London: Palgrave Macmillan, 2018), 31–33 (discussing Seeley's remark).

8. Seeley, *Expansion of England*, 8.

9. L. B. Namier, *The Structure of Politics at the Accession of George III*, 2d ed. (London: Macmillan, 1957), 2. For discussions and critiques of Namier's influence, see Quentin Skinner, "Meaning and Understanding in the History of Ideas," *History and Theory* 8, no. 1 (1969): 42 n.177; Nancy Christie, *The Formal and Informal Politics of British Rule in Post-Conquest Quebec, 1760–1837: A Northern Bastille* (Oxford: Oxford University Press, 2020), 18; Patrick Griffin, *The Townshend Moment: The Making of Empire and Revolution in the Eighteenth Century* (New Haven, Conn.: Yale University Press, 2017), 18–19; and James M. Vaughn, *The Politics of Empire at the Accession of George III: The East India Company and the Crisis and Transformation of Britain's Imperial State* (New Haven, Conn.: Yale University Press, 2019), 9–12.

10. See, e.g., James A. Henretta, *"Salutary Neglect": Colonial Administration under the Duke of Newcastle* (Princeton, N.J.: Princeton University Press, 1972), 344; Trevor Burnard, "Beyond Salutary Neglect: A Reflection on 'Thinking the Empire Whole,'" *History Australia* 16, no. 4 (2019): 642–43 (describing and critiquing this tendency). Notable exceptions to this trend include David Armitage, *The Ideological Origins of the British Empire* (Cambridge: Cambridge University Press, 2000); C. A. Bayly, *Imperial Meridian: The British Empire and the World, 1780–1830* (London: Longman, 1989); and P. J. Marshall, *The Making and Unmaking of Empires: Britain, India, and America C. 1750–1783* (Oxford: Oxford University Press, 2005).

11. See, e.g., Christopher L. Tomlins and Bruce H. Mann, eds., *The Many Legalities of Early America* (Chapel Hill: University of North Carolina Press, 2001); Hendrik Hartog, "Pigs and Positivism," *Wisconsin Law Review* 1985 (1985): 899; James Willard Hurst, *Law and the Conditions of Freedom in the Nineteenth-Century United States* (Madison: University of Wisconsin Press, 1964); cf. Lauren Benton, "Beyond Anachronism: Histories of International Law and Global Legal Politics," *Journal of the History of International Law* 21, no. 1 (2019): 18–21 (highlighting the influence of social history on legal history).

12. See Laura F. Edwards, "Law as Social History," in *The Oxford Handbook of Legal History*, ed. Markus D. Dubber and Christopher Tomlins (Oxford: Oxford University Press, 2018), 118–34; Charles L. Barzun, "Causation, Legal History, and Legal Doctrine," *Buffalo Law Review* 64 (2016): 81–99; Catherine L. Fisk and Robert W. Gordon, "Forward: 'Law As . . .': Theory and Method in Legal History," *UC Irvine Law Review* 1, no. 3 (2011): 519–41; cf. Shyamkrishna Balganesh and Taisu Zhang, "Legal Internalism in Modern Histories of Copyright," *Harvard Law Review* 134 (2021): 1090–91 (noting that "historical analyses routinely deny the existence of a causal emphasis," but that "causality remains an inevitable part of any historical analysis that presents itself as a narrative account").

13. See Benton, *Law and Colonial Cultures*, 21 n.28 (warning that an excessive focus on "causality . . . leads us away from investigating interconnections"); Paul D. Halliday, "Legal History: Taking the Long View," in *The Oxford Handbook of Legal History*, ed. Dubber and Tomlins, 332, 335.

14. See, e.g., Steven Pincus, Tiraana Bains, and A. Zuercher Reichardt, "Thinking the Empire Whole," *History Australia* 16, no. 4 (2019): 610–37; Vaughn, *Politics of Empire*, 3; Kavita Saraswathi Datla, "The Origins of Indirect Rule in India: Hyderabad and the British Imperial Order," *Law and History Review* 33, no. 2 (2015): 324.

15. F. W. Maitland, *The Constitutional History of England* (Cambridge: Cambridge University Press, 1908), 340 (emphasis added).

16. See, e.g., Mark Fathi Massoud, *Law's Fragile State: Colonial, Authoritarian, and Humanitarian Legacies in Sudan* (Cambridge: Cambridge University Press, 2013), 22, 32, 37 (using "legal pluralism" to describe both the internal complexity of state law in Sudan and the uneven reach of state law in rural areas).

17. Brian Z. Tamanaha, "The Promise and Conundrums of Pluralist Jurisprudence," *Modern Law Review* 82, no. 1 (2019): 163–64; cf. Lawrence M. Friedman, *A History of American Law*, 4th ed. (Oxford: Oxford University Press, 2019), 16 (describing "colonial legal dialects" of American law).

18. Lauren Benton describes this as "state-centered legal pluralism." Benton, *Law and Colonial Cultures*, 29–30; see also M. B. Hooker, *Legal Pluralism: An Introduction to Colonial and Neo-Colonial Laws* (Oxford: Clarendon Press, 1975); Sally Engle Merry, "Legal Pluralism," *Law & Society Review* 22, no. 5 (1988): 871 (defining "juristic" legal pluralism as occurring "when the sovereign commands different bodies of law for different groups of the population . . . and when the parallel legal regimes are all dependent on the state legal system") (citing John Griffiths, "What Is Legal Pluralism?," *Journal of Legal Pluralism and Unofficial Law* 24 [1986]: 5). For other definitions of

"legal pluralism," see Paul D. Halliday, "Laws' Histories: Pluralisms, Pluralities, Diversity," in *Legal Pluralism and Empires,* ed. Benton and Ross, 263–67; and Mitra Sharafi, "Justice in Many Rooms since Galanter: De-Romanticizing Legal Pluralism through the Cultural Defense," *Law and Contemporary Problems,* 71 (2008): 142.

19. Charles Tilly, *Coercion, Capital, and European States, AD 990–1992* (Cambridge, Mass.: Blackwell, 1992), 1 (emphasis added). Ancient empires were usually more pluralistic than Tilly's anecdote suggests. See Clifford Ando, "Pluralism and Empire: From Rome to Robert Cover," *Critical Analysis of Law* 1 (2014): 9; cf. Seth Richardson, "Early Mesopotamia: The Presumptive State," *Past & Present* 215, no. 1 (2012): 9 (questioning whether Hammurabi could really enforce his code).

20. Max Weber, *Economy and Society: An Outline of Interpretive Sociology,* ed. Guenther Roth and Claus Wittich (Berkeley: University of California Press, 1978), 694–704; Robert M. Cover, "Foreword: Nomos and Narrative," *Harvard Law Review* 97 (1983): 40–41 (quoting *The Federalist* no. 22 [A. Hamilton]); see also James C. Scott, *Seeing Like a State: How Certain Schemes to Improve the Human Condition Have Failed* (New Haven, Conn.: Yale University Press, 1999), 10; Ralf Michaels, "The Re-*state*-ment of Non-State Law: The State, Choice of Law, and the Challenge from Global Legal Pluralism," *Wayne Law Review* 51 (2005): 1214; James Tully, *Strange Multiplicity: Constitutionalism in an Age of Diversity* (Cambridge: Cambridge University Press, 1995), 58–98 (defining "modern constitutionalism" as tending [regrettably, in his view] toward an "empire of uniformity"); Brett Bowden, *The Empire of Civilization: The Evolution of an Imperial Idea* (Chicago: University of Chicago Press, 2009), 5, 100.

21. Bilder, *Transatlantic Constitution,* 31; see also P. G. McHugh, *Aboriginal Societies and the Common Law: A History of Sovereignty, Status, and Self-Determination* (Oxford: Oxford University Press, 2004), 129; J. H. Elliott, *Empires of the Atlantic World: Britain and Spain in America, 1492–1830* (New Haven, Conn.: Yale University Press, 2006), 144.

22. Niall Ferguson, *Empire: The Rise and Demise of the British World Order and the Lessons for Global Power* (New York: Basic Books, 2003), xxii; see also P. J. Cain and A. G. Hopkins, *British Imperialism: Innovation and Expansion, 1688–2015,* 3d ed. (London: Longman, 2016), 91.

23. Jean-Laurent Rosenthal and Roy Bin Wong, *Before and Beyond Divergence: The Politics of Economic Change in China and Europe* (Cambridge, Mass.: Harvard University Press, 2011), 32–33.

24. Tamanaha, "The Promise and Conundrums of Pluralist Jurisprudence," 165; see also Harold J. Berman, *Law and Revolution: The Formation of the Western Legal Tradition* (Cambridge, Mass.: Harvard University Press, 1983), 38–39; Ralf Michaels, "On Liberalism and Legal Pluralism," in *Transnational Law: Rethinking European Law and Legal Thinking,* ed. Miguel Maduro, Kaarlo Tuori, and Suvi Sankari (Cambridge: Cambridge University Press, 2014), 133; Richard J. Ross and Philip Stern, "Reconstructing Early Modern Notions of Legal Pluralism," in *Legal Pluralism and Empires,* ed. Benton and Ross, 112–13; R. C. Van Caenegem, *Legal History: A European Perspective* (London: Hambledon Press, 1991), 119.

25. See, e.g., Michael A. Helfand, "Religious Arbitration and the New Multiculturalism:

Negotiating Conflicting Legal Orders," *New York University Law Review* 86, no. 5 (2011): 1231–1305; Victor Muñiz-Fraticelli, *The Structure of Pluralism* (Oxford: Oxford University Press, 2014), 25–28.

26. Jane Burbank and Frederick Cooper, *Empires in World History: Power and the Politics of Difference* (Princeton, N.J.: Princeton University Press, 2010), 8; see also Karen Barkey, *Empire of Difference: The Ottomans in Comparative Perspective* (New York: Cambridge University Press, 2008), 83; cf. Christina Duffy Burnett and Burke Marshall, "Between the Foreign and the Domestic: The Doctrine of Territorial Incorporation, Invented and Reinvented," in *Foreign in a Domestic Sense: Puerto Rico, American Expansion, and the Constitution,* ed. Christina Duffy Burnett and Burke Marshall (Durham: Duke University Press, 2001), 11–12; Mahmood Mamdani, *Neither Settler Nor Native: The Making and Unmaking of Permanent Minorities* (Cambridge, Mass.: Harvard University Press, 2020), 5–14.

27. See, e.g., Alison Games, *The Web of Empire: English Cosmopolitans in an Age of Expansion, 1560–1660* (Oxford: Oxford University Press, 2008), 7, 291; Eliga H. Gould, *Among the Powers of the Earth: The American Revolution and the Making of a New World Empire* (Cambridge, Mass.: Harvard University Press, 2012), 27–28; Marshall, *Making and Unmaking of Empires,* 205–6.

28. Partha Chatterjee, *The Nation and Its Fragments: Colonial and Postcolonial Histories* (Princeton, N.J.: Princeton University Press, 1993), 10, 15–16; cf. Jörg Fisch, *Cheap Lives and Dear Limbs: The British Transformation of the Bengal Criminal Law, 1769–1817* (Wiesbaden: F. Steiner, 1983), 20–26; Pekka Hämäläinen, *The Comanche Empire* (New Haven, Conn.: Yale University Press, 2008), 350; Timothy Parsons, *The Rule of Empires: Those Who Built Them, Those Who Endured Them, and Why They Always Fall* (New York: Oxford University Press, 2010), 15.

29. Benton, *Law and Colonial Cultures,* provides the most important account of the ubiquity of colonial legal pluralism, and her work has transformed how historians write about colonial law. Of course, she was not alone in generating interest in legal difference. See, e.g., Tomlins and Mann, *The Many Legalities of Early America.* But her emphasis on "jurisdictional politics"—and, more broadly, on the centrality of local conflict in shaping colonial legal orders—has been especially influential. See, e.g., Craig Bryan Yirush, "Claiming the New World: Empire, Law, and Indigenous Rights in the Mohegan Case, 1704–1743," *Law and History Review* 29, no. 2 (2011): 339; Eliga H. Gould, "Zones of Law, Zones of Violence: The Legal Geography of the British Atlantic, circa 1772," *William and Mary Quarterly* 60, no. 3 (2003): 475 n.15, 496.

30. See, e.g., Philip Lawson, *The Imperial Challenge: Quebec and Britain in the Age of the American Revolution* (Montreal: McGill-Queen's University Press, 1989), 139.

31. England had overseas territories before the mid-seventeenth century, but there was no *British Empire* until those territories became subject to an imperial state (rather than being merely subject to the monarch). Historians disagree about when that happened, but their answers generally fall somewhere in the second half of the seventeenth century. See, e.g., P. J. Marshall, "The First British Empire," in *The Oxford History of the British Empire: Historiography* (Oxford: Oxford University Press, 1999), 46–47 (identifying the Navigation Act of 1651 as a key moment); Abigail L. Swingen, *Competing*

Visions of Empire: Labor, Slavery, and the Origins of the British Atlantic Empire (New Haven, Conn.: Yale University Press, 2015), 32–55 (the Western Design of 1654–55); William E. Nelson, *The Common Law in Colonial America: The Chesapeake and New England, 1607–1660* (New York: Oxford University Press, 2008), 6–7 (the Restoration in 1660); Jack P. Greene, *Peripheries and Center: Constitutional Development in the Extended Polities of the British Empire and the United States, 1607–1788* (Athens: University of Georgia Press, 1986), 13 (the creation of the Lords of Trade in 1675); Steve Pincus and James Robinson, "Wars and State-Making Reconsidered: The Rise of the Developmental State," *Annales* 71, no. 1 (2016): 33 (the creation of the Board of Trade in 1696).

32. William E. Nelson, *E Pluribus Unum: How the Common Law Helped Unify and Liberate Colonial America, 1607–1776* (Oxford: Oxford University Press, 2019), 3; J. G. A. Pocock, *The Ancient Constitution and the Feudal Law: A Study of English Historical Thought in the Seventeenth Century,* rev. ed. (New York: Cambridge University Press, 1987), 30–69.

33. See, e.g., Gould, *Among the Powers of the Earth,* 80–108.

34. See, e.g., Pauline Maier, "Whigs against Whigs against Whigs: The Imperial Debates of 1765–76 Reconsidered," *William and Mary Quarterly* 68, no. 4 (2011): 578–82; J. C. D. Clark, "A General Theory of Party, Opposition and Government, 1688–1832," *Historical Journal* 23, no. 2 (1980): 305; Lord Edmond Fitzmaurice, *Life of William, Earl of Shelburne, Afterwards First Marquess of Lansdowne* (London: Macmillan, 1875), 238–39; cf. James J. Sack, *From Jacobite to Conservative* (Cambridge: Cambridge University Press, 1993), 64–74.

35. See Justin du Rivage, *Revolution against Empire: Taxes, Politics, and the Origins of American Independence* (New Haven, Conn.: Yale University Press, 2017), 5–6; Max Skjönsberg, *The Persistence of Party: Ideas of Harmonious Discord in Eighteenth-Century Britain* (Cambridge: Cambridge University Press, 2021), especially 236. For contemporary assessments of partisanship, see Edmund Burke, "On Parties" (1757), in Richard Bourke, "Party, Parliament, and Conquest in Newly Ascribed Burke Manuscripts," *Historical Journal* 55, no. 3 (2012): 644–47; and [Maurice Morgann], [Papers Considering Problems Facing England in Political Divisions in Parliament, Scotland, Ireland, India and America, West Indies] ([1766]), Shelburne Papers, vol. 168, box 2, WLCL.

36. Daron Acemoglu and James A. Robinson, *Why Nations Fail: The Origins of Power, Prosperity and Poverty* (New York: Crown Publishers, 2012), 74, 82.

37. "Patriot" generally had a positive connotation, and so it was widely claimed. Thus the "patriot king" (George III) was sometimes at odds with his "patriot minister" (William Pitt) and the "patriots" who led the American revolution. John Brewer, *Party Ideology and Popular Politics at the Accession of George III* (Cambridge: Cambridge University Press, 1976), 101–2. Nonetheless, by the 1770s, the term had acquired a more precise partisan meaning, and even populists' opponents sometimes referred to them as "patriots." See, e.g., "News from America, or the Patriots in the Dumps," *London Magazine,* November 1776, 599.

38. For links between the Grenville and Bedford sets, see, e.g., Lord Rockingham to William Dowdeswell (August 11, 1768), WWM/R/1/1083, SA.

39. Rockingham to Joseph Harrison (May 19, 1769), WWM/R/1/1186, SA; Fowler Walker, Considerations on the Present State of the Province of Quebec (March 1, 1766), Add MS 35915, 24, BL. Historians have described these groups by other names: populists as "Patriots" or "radical Whigs"; moderates as "establishment Whigs"; and paternalists as "authoritarian Whigs," "authoritarian reformers," or "new Tories." du Rivage, *Revolution against Empire;* Sarah Kinkel, *Disciplining the Empire: Politics, Governance, and the Rise of the British Navy* (Cambridge, Mass.: Harvard University Press, 2018), 13–14; Steve Pincus, *The Heart of the Declaration: The Founders' Case for an Activist Government* (New Haven, Conn.: Yale University Press, 2016); Vaughn, *Politics of Empire,* 114; Heather Welland, "Commercial Interest and Political Allegiance," in *Revisiting 1759: The Conquest of Canada in Historical Perspective,* ed. Philip Buckner and John G. Reid (Toronto: University of Toronto Press, 2012), 167.

Those labels have some advantages for political historians, and I've used them myself in earlier work. Nonetheless, there are good reasons to avoid them here. "Authoritarian" accurately invokes paternalists' obsession with authority, but it invites unwarranted comparisons to more recent authoritarian regimes. Paternalists were not "authoritarian" in a straightforward sense. For example, Lord Mansfield, the leading paternalist judge, was an unmatched proponent of using habeas corpus to free those who were unjustly confined, including impressed sailors and enslaved people. Halliday, *Habeas Corpus,* 55. I've also avoided some historians' tendency to describe paternalists as conservative and populists as progressive. Neither of those groups embraced positions that were uniformly right- or left-wing by today's standards. Edmund Burke is the most famous "conservative" of the period, but he often advanced policies that were "liberal" or "progressive" by the standards of his time. Compare Daniel O'Neill, *Edmund Burke and the Conservative Logic of Empire* (Berkeley: University of California Press, 2016), with Richard Bourke, "What Is Conservatism? History, Ideology and Party," *European Journal of Political Theory* 17, no. 4 (2018): 449–75.

40. See, e.g., Nelson, *The Chesapeake and New England, 1607–1660,* 26; Dan Hulsebosch, "English Liberties outside England: Floors, Doors, Windows, and Ceilings in the Legal Architecture of Empire," in *The Oxford Handbook of English Law and Literature, 1500–1700,* ed. Lorna Hutson (Oxford: Oxford University Press, 2017), 762.

41. See O'Neill, *Edmund Burke,* 1–18 (summarizing "orientalist" and "ornamentalist" modes of justifying empire).

42. See, e.g., Patrick Wolfe, "Settler Colonialism and the Elimination of the Native," *Journal of Genocide Research* 8, no. 4 (2006): 387–409; Patrick Wolfe, "Land, Labor, and Difference: Elementary Structures of Race," *American Historical Review* 106, no. 3 (2001): 868; E. Tendayi Achiume, "Migration as Decolonization," *Stanford Law Review* 71 (2019): 1541–42; Jeffrey Ostler and Nancy Shoemaker, "Settler Colonialism in Early American History: Introduction," *William and Mary Quarterly* 76, no. 3 (2019): 361–68; see also Renisa Mawani, "Law, Settler Colonialism, and 'the Forgotten Space' of Maritime Worlds," *Annual Review of Law and Social Science* 12, no. 1 (2016): 115 (describing critiques of the dichotomy).

43. See, e.g., Alfred W. Crosby, *Ecological Imperialism: The Biological Expansion of Europe, 900–1900,* 2d ed. (Cambridge: Cambridge University Press, 2004), 134, which argues

that "[t]he rule (not the law) is that although Europeans may conquer in the tropics, they do not Europeanize the tropics."
44. See, e.g., Lorenzo Veracini, "Understanding Colonialism and Settler Colonialism as Distinct Formations," *Interventions* 16, no. 5 (2014): 618; Daron Acemoglu, Simon Johnson, and James A. Robinson, "The Colonial Origins of Comparative Development: An Empirical Investigation," *American Economic Review* 91, no. 5 (2001): 1370.

CHAPTER 1. FORGING A COMMON-LAW EMPIRE

1. Thomas More, *Utopia*, ed. Edward Surtz (New Haven, Conn.: Yale University Press, 1964), 76.
2. See Stephanie Elsky, "Common Law and the Commonplace in Thomas More's *Utopia*," *English Literary Renaissance* 43, no. 2 (2013): 181–210. On the importance of humanistic thought for early English colonization, see Andrew Fitzmaurice, *Humanism and America: An Intellectual History of English Colonisation, 1500–1625* (Cambridge: Cambridge University Press, 2003), 1–2, 190.
3. See, e.g., Jeremy Waldron, "One Law for All? The Logic of Cultural Accommodation," *Washington and Lee Law Review* 59 (2002): 3–34.
4. Sir John Baker, *An Introduction to English Legal History*, 5th ed. (Oxford: Oxford University Press, 2019), 33 & n.98; Brodie Waddell, "Governing England through the Manor Courts, 1550–1850," *Historical Journal* 55, no. 2 (2012): 279–315.
5. Blackstone, *Commentaries*, 1:64–92; Edmund Burke, "An Essay towards an History of the Laws of England" (c. 1757), in *The Writings and Speeches of Edmund Burke*, ed. T. O. McLoughlin and James T. Boulton (Oxford: Clarendon Press, 1997), 1:325; Halliday, *Habeas Corpus*, 262; Ken MacMillan, *Sovereignty and Possession in the English New World: The Legal Foundations of Empire, 1576–1640* (Cambridge: Cambridge University Press, 2006), 25–26; Christopher L. Tomlins, *Freedom Bound: Law, Labor, and Civic Identity in Colonizing English America, 1580–1865* (New York: Cambridge University Press, 2010), 209–11; J. H. Baker, *The Law's Two Bodies: Some Evidential Problems in English Legal History* (Oxford: Oxford University Press, 2001), 23–24; cf. Philip Loft, "A Tapestry of Laws: Legal Pluralism in Eighteenth-Century Britain," *Journal of Modern History* 91, no. 2 (2019): 276–310.
6. Matthew Hale, *The History of the Common Law* (London: James Moore, 1792), 58.
7. See Pocock, *The Ancient Constitution and the Feudal Law*, 30; Hartog, "Pigs and Positivism," 914–16; Bilder, *Transatlantic Constitution*, xiii; George L. Haskins, "The Beginnings of Partible Inheritance in the American Colonies," *Yale Law Journal* 51, no. 8 (1942): 1299; Terry Reilly, "King Lear: The Kentish Forest and the Problem of Thirds," *Oklahoma City University Law Review* 26 (2001): 383; see also Marianne Constable, *The Law of the Other: The Mixed Jury and Changing Conceptions of Citizenship, Law, and Knowledge* (Chicago: University of Chicago Press, 1994), 126–27 (using changes in juries *de medietate linguae* to document the ascendance of a national common law starting in the sixteenth century).
8. Adam Donald Pole, "Customs in Conflict: Sir John Davies, the Common Law, and the Abrogation of Irish Gavelkind and Tanistry" (master's thesis, Queen's University,

1999), 40–41; John M. Collins, *Martial Law and English Laws, c. 1500—c. 1700* (Cambridge: Cambridge University Press, 2016), 29–30, 114 n.117, 251; Lords Debates (May 24, 1756), *PH*, 15:720.
9. Chantal Stebbings, "Bureaucratic Adjudication," in *Judges and Judging in the History of the Common Law and Civil Law*, ed. Paul Brand and Joshua Getzler (Cambridge: Cambridge University Press, 2011), 159; John Brewer, *The Sinews of Power: War, Money, and the English State, 1688–1783* (New York: Alfred A. Knopf, 1989), 113–14; Edward Hughes, *Studies in Administration and Finance, 1558–1825: With Special Reference to the History of Salt Taxation in England* (Manchester: Manchester University Press, 1934), 333; Peter Mathias, *The Brewing Industry in England, 1700–1830* (Cambridge: Cambridge University Press, 1959), 354–55; Jay Tidmarsh, "The English Fire Courts and the American Right to Civil Jury Trial," *University of Chicago Law Review* 83 (2016): 1893–1941.
10. Voltaire, *The Works of M. de Voltaire*, trans. T. Smollett and T. Francklin, vol. 17 (London: J. Newbery, R. Baldwin, W. Johnston, S. Crowder, T. Davies, J. Coote, G. Kearsley, and B. Collins, 1762), 42.
11. Laws in Wales Act 1542, 35 Henry 8, c. 26; Laws in Wales Act 1535, 27 Henry 8, c. 26; Michael Braddick, *State Formation in Early Modern England, c. 1550–1700* (Cambridge: Cambridge University Press, 2000), 347–48; Matthew Lockwood, *The Conquest of Death: Violence and the Birth of the Modern English State* (New Haven, Conn.: Yale University Press, 2017), 34.
12. Nicholas P. Canny, "The Ideology of English Colonization: From Ireland to America," *William and Mary Quarterly* 30, no. 4 (1973): 588 (quoting Sir Thomas Smith, an Elizabethan diplomat, lawyer, and politician); see also Hans S. Pawlisch, *Sir John Davies and the Conquest of Ireland: A Study in Legal Imperialism* (Cambridge: Cambridge University Press, 1985), 55–83; John Miller, "Britain," in *Absolutism in Seventeenth-Century Europe*, ed. John Miller (London: Macmillan, 1990), 221; F. H. Newark, "Notes on Irish Legal History," *Northern Ireland Legal Quarterly* 7 (1947): 126–38; cf. W. N. Osborough, "Letters to Ireland—Professional Enlightenment from the English Bench," *Irish Jurist* 31 (1996): 226–54 (describing how English judges advised Irish counterparts about the proper application of English law).
13. Edward Coke, *The First Part of the Institutes of the Laws of England; Or, a Commentary upon Littleton*, ed. Francis Hargrave (London: G. Kearsly & G. Robinson, 1775), 141.b (1628); see also Hale, *The History of the Common Law*, 58. Coke and Francis Bacon agreed on very little, but they agreed that a union of kingdoms was impossible without a union of laws. See Edward Coke, *The Fourth Part of the Institutes of the Laws of England* (London: E. Brooke & R. Brooke, 1797), 347; Francis Bacon, Speech (February 14, 1606), *PH*, 1:1088.
14. Blackstone, *Commentaries*, 1:94; Robert Chambers, *A Course of Lectures on the English Law: Delivered at the University of Oxford 1767–1773*, ed. Thomas M. Curley (Madison: University of Wisconsin Press, 1986), 1:276–77; see also Julia Rudolph, *Common Law and Enlightenment in England, 1689–1750* (Woodbridge, U.K.: Boydell Press, 2013), 239.
15. Quoted in Daniel J. Hulsebosch, "The Ancient Constitution and the Expanding Em-

pire: Sir Edward Coke's British Jurisprudence," *Law & History Review* 21, no. 3 (2003): 439, 448–49, 454–58.

16. Gaillard Thomas Lapsley, *The County Palatine of Durham: A Study in Constitutional History* (London: Longmans, Green, 1900), 210–16; W. S. Holdsworth, *A History of English Law* (London: Methuen, 1903–1966), 1:111–12; John Baker, *The Oxford History of the Laws of England: Volume VI, 1483–1558* (Oxford: Oxford University Press, 2003), 291–98. For palatinates as a model for colonial charters, see Tim Thornton, "The Palatinate of Durham and the Maryland Charter," *American Journal of Legal History* 45, no. 3 (2001): 235–55; and Tomlins, *Freedom Bound*, 170–71. On the circulation of legal personnel, see Lauren Benton and Kathryn Walker, "Law for the Empire: The Common Law in Colonial America and the Problem of Legal Diversity," *Chicago-Kent Law Review* 89, no. 3 (2014): 944–45.

17. Nelson, *The Chesapeake and New England, 1607–1660*, 6–7; Hulsebosch, "English Liberties Outside England," 766–68; David Thomas Konig, "Virginia and the Imperial State: Law, Enlightenment, and 'the Crooked Cord of Discretion,'" in *The British and Their Laws in the Eighteenth Century*, ed. David Lemmings (Woodbridge, U.K.: Boydell Press, 2005), 210; Agnes M. Whitson, *The Constitutional Development of Jamaica: 1660–1729* (Manchester: Manchester University Press, 1929), 71–72.

18. Bilder, *Transatlantic Constitution*; Joseph Henry Smith, *Appeals to the Privy Council from the American Plantations* (New York: Columbia University Press, 1950), 656; William E. Nelson, *The Common Law in Colonial America: The Middle Colonies and the Carolinas, 1660–1730* (New York: Oxford University Press, 2012), 3; William E. Nelson, *The Common Law in Colonial America: The Chesapeake and New England, 1660–1750* (New York: Oxford University Press, 2016), 132; Cornelia Hughes Dayton, *Women before the Bar: Gender, Law, and Society in Connecticut, 1639–1789* (Chapel Hill: University of North Carolina Press, 1995), 11; John M. Murrin, "The Legal Transformation: The Bench and Bar of Eighteenth-Century Massachusetts," in *Colonial America: Essays in Politics and Social Development*, ed. Stanley N. Katz (Boston: Little, Brown, 1971), 415–49.

19. See, e.g., Richard S. Dunn, *Sugar and Slaves: The Rise of the Planter Class in the English West Indies, 1624–1713* (Chapel Hill: Published for the Omohundro Institute of Early American History and Culture, Williamsburg, Va., by the University of North Carolina Press, 1972), 3–45.

20. See Tomlins, *Freedom Bound*, 439, 444, 450, 484–85, 495, 500; Lee B. Wilson, *Bonds of Empire: The English Origins of Slave Law in South Carolina and British Plantation America, 1660–1783* (Cambridge: Cambridge University Press, 2021), 60; Holly Brewer, "Creating a Common Law of Slavery for England and Its New World Empire," *Law and History Review* 39, no. 4 (2021): 765–834; Jack P. Greene, "Liberty, Slavery, and the Transformation of British Identity in the Eighteenth-Century West Indies," in *Creating the British Atlantic: Essays on Transplantation, Adaptation, and Continuity* (Charlottesville: University of Virginia Press, 2013), 308–13; [Edward Long], *Candid Reflections upon the Judgement Lately Awarded by the Court of King's Bench . . . on What Is Commonly Called the Negroe-Cause, by a Planter* (London: T. Lowndes, 1772). Of the 236 American-born members of the Inns of Court before 1815, nearly two-thirds came

from South Carolina (74), Virginia (49), or Maryland (29). E. Alfred Jones, *American Members of the Inns of Court* (London: Saint Catherine Press, 1924), xxviii. For the high number of West Indians at the Inns, see Andrew Jackson O'Shaughnessy, *An Empire Divided: The American Revolution and the British Caribbean* (Philadelphia: University of Pennsylvania Press, 2000), 25.

21. Calvin's Case (1608) 77 Eng. Rep. 377, 397–98; 7 Co. Rep. 1a, 17b. Coke was working within a long tradition of theorizing about conquest. See Anthony Pagden, *Lords of All the World: Ideologies of Empire in Spain, Britain and France, c. 1500–c. 1850* (New Haven: Yale University Press, 1995), 94; Richard Tuck, *The Rights of War and Peace: Political Thought and the International Order from Grotius to Kant* (Oxford: Oxford University Press, 1999), 122–23.

22. Blankard v. Galdy (1693) 90 Eng. Rep. 1089; 2 Salk. 411 (K.B.) (Holt, C. J.); Blackstone, *Commentaries*, 1:107; Kathleen Davis, *Periodization and Sovereignty: How Ideas of Feudalism and Secularization Govern the Politics of Time* (Philadelphia: University of Pennsylvania Press, 2012), 56–57 ("A conqueror is bound by no law but has power *dare leges*" [quoting a 1628 speech in the House of Commons]).

23. Charles E. Reis, "Spanish Law in the British Empire," *Journal of the Society of Comparative Legislation* 14, no. 1 (1914): 28. Later lawyers described the Spanish evacuation as so complete that Jamaica was effectively a newly settled colony. See *Campbell*, 98 Eng. Rep. at 1049; 1 Cowp. at 211–12. Of course, this elided Spanish resistance in the immediate aftermath of conquest, not to mention maroon communities of African descent. See Carla Gardina Pestana, *The English Conquest of Jamaica* (Cambridge, Mass.: Harvard University Press, 2017), 207–8.

24. Whitson, *The Constitutional Development of Jamaica*, 17–18.

25. Nelson, *The Middle Colonies and the Carolinas, 1660–1730*, 43; Alan Taylor, *American Colonies: The Settling of North America* (New York: Penguin Books, 2002), 260; Robert C. Ritchie, *The Duke's Province: A Study of New York Politics and Society, 1664–1691* (Chapel Hill: University of North Carolina Press, 1977), 185; David William Voorhees, "English Law through Dutch Eyes: The Leislerian Understanding of the English Legal System in New York," in *Opening Statements: Law, Jurisprudence, and the Legacy of Dutch New York*, ed. Albert M. Rosenblatt and Julia C. Rosenblatt (Albany: Excelsior Editions/State University of New York Press, 2013), 210–11.

26. Donna Merwick, *Death of a Notary: Conquest and Change in Colonial New York* (Ithaca, N.Y.: Cornell University Press, 1999); Herbert A. Johnson, "The Advent of Common Law in Colonial New York," in *Essays on New York Colonial Legal History* (Westport, Conn.: Greenwood Press, 1981), 38; Hulsebosch, *Constituting Empire*, 47–48; Jaap Jacobs, *The Colony of New Netherland: A Dutch Settlement in Seventeenth-Century America* (Ithaca, N.Y.: Cornell University Press, 2009), 100–101; Megan Lindsay Cherry, "The Imperial and Political Motivations behind the English Conquest of New Netherland," *Dutch Crossing: Journal of Low Countries Studies* 34, no. 1 (2010): 77–94; Simon Middleton, "Legal Change, Economic Culture, and Imperial Authority in New Amsterdam and Early New York City," *American Journal of Legal History* 53, no. 1 (2013): 89–120.

27. Opinion of Thomas Corbett (1677?), quoted in William A. Pettigrew and George W.

Van Cleve, "Parting Companies: The Glorious Revolution, Company Power, and Imperial Mercantilism," *Historical Journal* 57, no. 3 (2014): 622; see also Memorandum of August 9, 1722 (reporting a Privy Council determination to the same effect), quoted in 99 Eng. Rep. 398 n. (K).

28. Gabriel Glickman, "Empire, 'Popery,' and the Fall of English Tangier, 1662–1684," *Journal of Modern History* 87, no. 2 (2015): 267.

29. Edwin Chappell, ed., *The Tangier Papers of Samuel Pepys* (Colchester: Navy Records Society, 1935), 97; see also Philip J. Stern, "The Corporation and the Global Seventeenth-Century English Empire: A Tale of Three Cities," *Early American Studies* 16, no. 1 (2018): 54, 56–57 (noting complaints about governance in Tangier).

30. Tristan M. Stein, "The Mediterranean in the English Empire of Trade, 1660–1748" (PhD. diss., Harvard University, 2012), 102–3; Arthur Mitchell Fraas, "'They Have Travailed into a Wrong Latitude': The Laws of England, Indian Settlements, and the British Imperial Constitution 1726–1773" (PhD. diss., Duke University, 2011), 52–53; see also Linda Colley, *Captives: Britain, Empire and the World, 1600–1850* (London: Jonathan Cape, 2002), 25–28 (describing efforts to anglicize Tangier); Games, *The Web of Empire*, 294–98 (noting plans to settle Tangier on the model of North American colonies).

31. William Dalrymple, *The Anarchy: The East India Company, Corporate Violence, and the Pillage of an Empire* (London: Bloomsbury Publishing, 2019), 46–87; Philip Lawson, *The East India Company: A History* (London: Longman, 1993), 47.

32. Quoted in Philip J. Stern, *The Company-State: Corporate Sovereignty and the Early Modern Foundations of the British Empire in India* (Oxford: Oxford University Press, 2011), 27.

33. Ibid., 26–29.

34. Fraas, "'They Have Travailed into a Wrong Latitude,'" 12.

35. See Mitch Fraas, "Making Claims: Indian Litigants and the Expansion of the English Legal World in the Eighteenth Century," *Journal of Colonialism and Colonial History* 15, no. 1 (2014); Smith, *Appeals to the Privy Council*, 170; John Shaw, *Charters Relating to the East India Company from 1600 to 1761: Reprinted from a Former Collection with Some Additions and a Preface for the Government of Madras* (Madras: R. Hill at the Government Press, 1887), 234–36; Gagan D. S. Sood, "Sovereign Justice in Precolonial Maritime Asia: The Case of the Mayor's Court of Bombay, 1726–1798," *Itinerario* 37, no. 2 (2013): 51; Niels Brimnes, "Beyond Colonial Law: Indigenous Litigation and the Contestation of Property in the Mayor's Court in Late Eighteenth-Century Madras," *Modern Asian Studies* 37, no. 3 (2003): 513–50; cf. Stern, "The Corporation and the Global Seventeenth-Century English Empire," 62–63 (comparing municipal corporations in England, Tangier, Philadelphia, and Madras). For examples of how eighteenth-century lawyers understood procedure in the mayor's courts as a variation on English procedure, see Charles Sayer, Case: East India Co. upon Proceedings in the Mayor's Court (October 30, 1763), IOR/L/L/7/69, BL; and EIC Court of Directors to President & Council of Ft. William (February 22, 1764), *FWIHC*, 4:30–31.

36. Dalrymple, *The Anarchy*, 73–74; see, e.g., Petition of the Gentoo Merchants in Bombay ([1746]), IOR/H/432, 45, 47–48, BL (complaining that the Bombay mayor's court

had ignored English law); John Browne, EIC Counsel, to President and Council of Madras (February 3, 1738), IOR/H/427, 27–28, BL (reminding local officials that they were bound to apply English law); Extract of a Letter from Fort St. George (September 20, 1642), IOR/H/427, 1, BL (noting that a local Hindu ruler had requested that the Company "should do justice upon [murderers], according to the Custom of England"); Benton, *Law and Colonial Cultures*, 132–33.

37. Sood, "Sovereign Justice in Precolonial Maritime Asia," 55; Fraas, "'They Have Travailed into a Wrong Latitude,'" 336–81.
38. For examples, see Fraas, "'They Have Travailed into a Wrong Latitude,'" 368–69.
39. Sood, "Sovereign Justice in Precolonial Maritime Asia," 51.
40. Shaw, *Charters Relating to the East India Company*, 230, 252 (emphasis added).
41. Reasons against That Part of a Bill Now Depending in Parliament . . . ([1772]), IOR/A/2/8, 245–46, BL.
42. Brimnes, "Beyond Colonial Law"; Fraas, "'They Have Travailed into a Wrong Latitude,'" 378; Entry of December 12, 1752, PC 2/103, 249, TNA; Charles Yorke, Powers of the Mayor's Court at Fort St. George (February 2, 1761), IOR/L/L/7/54, BL.
43. Entry of March 25, 1756, in B. S. Baliga, ed., *Diary and Consultation Book (Public Department) 1756*, vol. 85, Records of Fort St. George (Madras: Printed by the Superintendent, Government Press, 1943), 80.
44. EIC Court of Directors to President & Council of Ft. William (January 31, 1755), in *FWIHC*, 1:70.
45. See, e.g., Smith, *Appeals to the Privy Council*, 3; Bilder, *Transatlantic Constitution*, 73.
46. Hulsebosch, "Ancient Constitution," 440; Muller, *Subjects and Sovereign*, 17–33; Henry Sumner Maine, *Ancient Law: Its Connection with the Early History of Society and Its Relation to Modern Ideas*, 10th ed. (London: John Murray, 1906), 30; Baker, *Law's Two Bodies*, 34–35; Holdsworth, *History of English Law*, 5:118, 140–42. Because judges received fees for each case they heard, they had an incentive to expand the reach of their courts. See Daniel Klerman, "Jurisdictional Competition and the Evolution of the Common Law," *University of Chicago Law Review* 74 (2007): 1179–1226; Adam Smith, *Lectures on Jurisprudence*, ed. Ronald L. Meek, D. D. Raphael, and Peter Stein (Indianapolis: Liberty Fund, 1978), 280–81.
47. Mostyn v. Fabrigas (1774) 98 Eng. Rep. 1021, 1031; 1 Cowp. 161, 178 (K.B.) (Mansfield, C. J.) (citing Robert v. Harnage (1704) 92 Eng. Rep. 192; 2 Lord Raymond 1043 (K.B.)); see also Parker v. Crook (1714) 88 Eng. Rep. 716; 10 Modern 255 (K.B.).
48. See Hulsebosch, "Ancient Constitution," 473–74; Alexander N. Sack, "Conflicts of Laws in the History of the English Law," in *Law: A Century of Progress, 1835–1935*, vol. 3 (New York: New York University Press, 1937), 388–89; Smith, *Appeals to the Privy Council*, 325–26.
49. Omychund v. Barker (1744) 26 Eng. Rep. 15, 15; 1 Atkyns 21, 22. Note that the reporter of this case, John Tracy Atkyns, was the lawyer for Barker's estate. Webb would later serve as a member of Parliament and as solicitor of the treasury. Geoffrey Treasure, "Webb, Philip Carteret (1702–1770)," in *DNB*, https://doi.org/10.1093/ref:odnb/28929. For background on Omichund himself (also transliterated as "Omychund," "Amir

Chand," or "Umichund"), see Somendra C. Nandy, "Amir Chand (*d.* 1758)," in *DNB*, https://doi.org/10.1093/ref:odnb/63551. For background on the litigation, see Fraas, "Making Claims"; and Jud Campbell, "Testimonial Exclusions and Religious Freedom in Early America," *Law and History Review* 33 (2019): 438–43.
50. John Browne to President and Council of Madras (February 3, 1738), IOR/H/427, 27–28, BL.
51. Quakers Act 1695, 7 & 8 Will. 3, c. 34; Omichund v. Barker (1744) 125 Eng. Rep. 1310, 1312–13; 1 Willes 542–44 (Willes, C. J.); Ramkissenseat v. Barker (1739) 26 Eng. Rep. 13, 13; 1 Atkyns 19, 19.
52. John H. Langbein, *The Origins of Adversary Criminal Trial* (Oxford: Oxford University Press, 2003), 246.
53. The Quaker Affirmation Act of 1696 didn't permit Quakers to give evidence in criminal cases. Another issue was that a false oath was punishable as perjury at common law; punishing a false *affirmation*, however, required statutory authorization. See Joseph H. Smith, "Administrative Control of the Courts of the American Plantations," *Columbia Law Review* 61, no. 7 (1961): 1239–45; Charles Yorke, Instructions for Alterations in Draft of New Charter (November 12, 1752), IOR/H/411, 11–13, BL; see also Esther Sahle, "Law and Gospel Order: Resolving Commercial Disputes in Colonial Philadelphia," *Continuity and Change* 35, no. 3 (2020): 289 (noting that controversies over Quaker oath-taking occasionally shut down courts in colonial Pennsylvania).
54. Browne to President and Council of Madras (February 3, 1738), IOR/H/427, 27–28.
55. The common law had provided for compulsory process in civil cases since the sixteenth century; Chancery had compelled testimony by subpoena for two centuries before that. John H. Langbein, Renée Lettow Lerner, and Bruce P. Smith, *History of the Common Law: The Development of Anglo-American Legal Institutions* (New York: Aspen Publishers, 2009), 246–47.
56. Sir Dudley Ryder, Sir John Strange, and John Browne, "Opinion Relating to the Company's Charter" (December 31, 1741), in *Despatches from England, 1740–1743*, Records of Fort St. George (Madras: Printed by the Superintendent, Government Press, 1911), 81, 85.
57. *Ramkissenseat*, 26 Eng. Rep. at 13; 1 Atkyns at 19.
58. *Omychund*, 1 Atkyns at 48 (Hardwicke, L. C.); see also ibid., 1 Atkyns at 41 (Parker, C. B.); Omichund and Barker, Coxe MSS, vol. 53 (BB), ff. 252–361, LIL (giving another version of Chief Baron Parker's opinion).
59. Campbell, "Testimonial Exclusions," 442–43.
60. See, e.g., David Lieberman, *The Province of Legislation Determined: Legal Theory in Eighteenth-Century Britain* (Cambridge: Cambridge University Press, 1989), 93–94 (discussing the effect of Hardwicke's opinion and Murray's argument on ideas about common-law reasoning).
61. Petition of the Gentoo Cast in General to William Wake, Governor of Bombay (April 26, 1746), IOR/H/432, 33, BL. Oaths in India remained controversial throughout the eighteenth century. See Radhika Singha, *A Despotism of Law: Crime and Justice in Early Colonial India* (Delhi: Oxford University Press, 1998), 46–49.

62. Leonard Hodges, "Between Litigation and Arbitration: Administering Legal Pluralism in Eighteenth-Century Bombay," *Itinerario* 42, no. 3 (2018): 491 (quoting IOR/P/341/15, 506–11, BL).

63. The Petition of the Gentoo Merchants in Bombay as Representatives of their Several Castes in General to William Wake ([1746]), IOR/H/432, 45, BL.

64. Ibid.

65. Bombay Council to EIC Court of Directors (September 14, 1746), IOR/H/432, 53–54, BL.

66. Ryder, Murray, John Browne, and Jonathan Browning, [Opinion] (November 11, 1747), IOR/H/432, 81, 87, BL.

67. *Omichund*, 125 Eng. Rep. at 1317; 1 Willes at 552 (Willes, C. J.) ("I do not at all rely upon the books which were cited and which give an account of the Gentoo religion. But it is plain from the certificate itself that they believe and worship a god."); see also Omichund v. Barker, 22 Eng. Rep. 339, 345; 2 Eq. Ca. Abr. 397, 405 (Willes, C. J.) ("Authors that write of Things so far distant have seldom Veracity enough to be depended upon in Courts of Justice."). Hardwicke was more willing to rely on secondary literature. See Omichund v. Barker, 22 Eng. Rep. at 347; 2 Eq. Ca. Abr. at 407–8.

68. *Omychund*, 26 Eng. Rep. at 22–23; 1 Atkyns at 33.

69. See Lieberman, *Province of Legislation Determined*, 90–94.

70. Jack P. Greene, "The Perils of Success," in *Revisiting 1759*, 97; Stephen Conway, "The Consequences of Conquest: Quebec and British Politics, 1760–1774," in *Revisiting 1759*, 145–46; [Thomas Bernard], *An Appeal to the Public Stating and Considering the Objections to the Quebec Bill*, 2d ed. (London: T. Payne and M. Hingeston, 1774), 19.

71. Jerry Bannister, *The Rule of the Admirals: Law, Custom, and Naval Government in Newfoundland, 1699–1832* (Toronto: Published for the Osgoode Society for Canadian Legal History by University of Toronto Press, 2003), 4, 15, 96, 104–33.

72. Lubbock v. Potts (1806) 103 Eng. Rep. 174, 176; 7 East. 449, 455 (K.B.) (Ellenborough, C. J.); see also ibid. ("The term plantation in its common known signification . . . have never in fact been applied to a place like Gibraltar.").

73. Stephen Constantine, *Community and Identity: The Making of Modern Gibraltar since 1704* (Manchester: Manchester University Press, 2013), 23–24, 76–77; Hannah Weiss Muller, "The Garrison Revisited: Gibraltar in the Eighteenth Century," *Journal of Imperial and Commonwealth History* 41, no. 3 (2013): 359; Geoffrey Plank, "Making Gibraltar British in the Eighteenth Century," *History* 98, no. 331 (2013): 355–56; Smith, *Appeals to the Privy Council*, 268.

74. Constantine, *Community and Identity*, 78; Lord Barrington to Thomas Gage (August 1, 1768), Gage Papers, vol. ES 13, WLCL.

75. Dudley Ryder and William Murray, Opinion of Attorney and Solicitor General (January 22, 1752), CO 91/62, TNA (discussing criminal law and procedure).

76. Francis Maseres, *The Canadian Freeholder: Volume II* (London: B. White, 1779), 279, 360; see also William Knox, *The Justice and Policy of the Late Act of Parliament for Making More Effectual Provision for the Government of the Province of Quebec, Asserted and Proved* (London: J. Wilkie, 1774), 27 (Minorca "has never been attempted to be made a colony"); Peter Marshall, "The Incorporation of Quebec in the British Empire,

1763–1774," in *Of Mother Country and Plantations: Proceedings of the Twenty-Seventh Conference in Early American History,* ed. Virginia Bever Platt and David Curtis Skaggs (Bowling Green, Ohio: Bowling Green State University Press, 1971), 44.

77. Desmond Gregory, *Minorca, the Illusory Prize: A History of the British Occupation of Minorca Between 1708 and 1802* (Rutherford, N.J.: Fairleigh Dickinson University Press, 1990), 86; Conway, "The Consequences of Conquest," 144; Queries Relating to Minorca [n.d.], Shelburne Papers, vol. 82, 399, WLCL.

78. [Richard Kane], Minutes on the Laws and Constitution of Minorca to Be Taken under Consideration ([1727–1736?]), Add MS 23638, 32, BL. For the document's authorship, see Gregory, *Minorca, the Illusory Prize,* 101. See also Copy of the Report of Mr Attorney and Mr Sollictor General . . . about Erecting a Court of Appeals in That Island, &c. (August 17, 1731), Shelburne Papers, vol. 82, 29, WLCL (discussing whether Minorca's terms of cession permitted the Crown to establish a new legal system). These proposed legal reforms had ecclesiastical parallels: in 1720, Archbishop of Canterbury William Wake and Bishop of London Thomas Gibson authored a proposal for how to turn the island toward Protestantism. Heather Welland, *Political Economy and Imperial Governance in Eighteenth-Century Britain* (New York: Routledge, 2021), 192.

79. Considerations upon Heads of Instructions to the Governor of Minorca Submitted to the Privy Council ([1753?]), Add MS 23638, 120, 125–26, BL; Kane, Minutes on the Laws and Constitution of Minorca to be taken under Consideration, Add MS 23638, 70, BL.

80. See, e.g., John Campbell, *A Political Survey of Britain: Being a Series of Reflections on the Situation, Lands, Inhabitants, Revenues, Colonies, and Commerce of This Island* (London: Printed for the author, and sold by Richardson [and nine others], 1774), 2:583; ibid., 2:582 note h ("The Natives of the Island . . . would reap much greater Benefits from . . . having their Choice to seek Relief in our Courts or in their own."); Aaron Willis, "The Standing of New Subjects: Grenada and the Protestant Constitution after the Treaty of Paris (1763)," *Journal of Imperial and Commonwealth History* 42, no. 1 (2014): 15–16; [Thomas] Hope to Henry Seymour Conway (July 30, 1765), Shelburne Papers, vol. 82, 41–45, WLCL; [Francis Maseres], *A Review of the Government and Grievances of the Province of Quebec, since the Conquest of It by the British Arms* (London: J. Stockdale, 1788), 59.

81. Petition of British and Minorcan Merchants (May 26, 1764), CO 174/3, 175–76, TNA. A prominent exception was Governor James O'Hara, second Baron Tyrawley, who insisted that Minorca "can only be kept under Subjection" "under an arbitrary government." Tyrawley to Henry Fox (May 23, 1753), Add MS 23638, 95, BL.

82. King James VI and I, *Political Writings,* ed. Johann P. Sommerville (Cambridge: Cambridge University Press, 1994), 162.

83. Brian P. Levack, *The Formation of the British State: England, Scotland, and the Union, 1603–1707* (Oxford: Clarendon Press, 1987), 68–97.

84. See Daniel Defoe, *The History of the Union of Great Britain* (Edinburgh: Printed by the Heirs and Successors of Andrew Anderson, 1709), 57–58.

85. Colin Kidd, *Union and Unionisms: Political Thought in Scotland, 1500–2000* (Cam-

bridge: Cambridge University Press, 2008), 57–59; Jim Smyth, "Empire-Building: The English Republic, Scotland and Ireland," in *Varieties of Seventeenth- and Early Eighteenth-Century English Radicalism in Context*, ed. Ariel Hessayon and David Finnegan (Surrey: Ashgate, 2011), 142–43; Allan I. Macinnes, *Union and Empire: The Making of the United Kingdom in 1707* (Cambridge: Cambridge University Press, 2007), 75–77, 321–22; John W. Cairns, "Natural Law, National Laws, Parliaments, and Multiple Monarchies: 1707 and Beyond," in *Law, Lawyers, and Humanism: Selected Essays on the History of Scots Law* (Edinburgh: Edinburgh University Press, 2015), 123–25; John W. Cairns, "Scottish Law, Scottish Lawyers and the Status of the Union," in *A Union for Empire: Political Thought and the British Union of 1707*, ed. John Robertson (Cambridge: Cambridge University Press, 1995), 247–48; J. D. Ford, "The Legal Provisions in the Acts of Union," *Cambridge Law Journal* 66, no. 1 (2007): 117, 139–40; A. J. MacLean, "The 1707 Union: Scots Law and the House of Lords," *Journal of Legal History* 4, no. 3 (1983): 67–68; Conrad Russell, "Topsy and the King: The English Common Law, King James VI and I, and the Union of Crowns," in *Law and Authority in Early Modern England: Essays Presented to Thomas Garden Barnes*, ed. Buchanan Sharp and Mark Charles Fissel (Newark: University of Delaware Press, 2007), 71–73; Rudolph, *Common Law and Enlightenment*, 184.

86. See, e.g., William Logan, *A View of the Present State of Scotland in Regard to the Tenures and Slavish Dependencies of the Subjects of That Part of North Britain: In a Memorial* (London: J. Wilford, 1733), 1–22; Alexander Murray, *The True Interest of Great Britain, Ireland and Our Plantations* (London: Printed for the author, 1741), vi; John Willison, *A Letter to an English Member of Parliament, from a Gentleman in Scotland: Concerning the Slavish Dependencies, Which a Great Part of That Nation Is Still Kept under, by Superiorities, Wards, Reliefs, and Other Remains of the Feudal Law, and by Clanships and Tithes* (Edinburgh: J. McEuen, 1721). Feudal tenures had been abolished in England in 1646. Parliament confirmed that decision soon after the Restoration. Tenures Abolition Act, 1660, 12 Charles 2, c. 24; Christopher Hill, *The English Revolution, 1640: An Essay*, 3d ed. (London: Lawrence & Wishart, 1972), 58.

87. Linda Colley, *Britons: Forging the Nation, 1707–1837*, 3d ed. (New Haven, Conn.: Yale University Press, 2005), 71–84; Marshall, *Making and Unmaking of Empires*, 34; Paul Langford, *A Polite and Commercial People: England 1727–1783* (Oxford: Oxford University Press, 1998), 216–18; Allan I. Macinnes, *Clanship, Commerce and the House of Stuart, 1603–1788* (East Linton, U.K.: Tuckwell Press, 1996), 211–21. On the Jacobites, see Daniel Szechi, *The Jacobites: Britain and Europe, 1688–1788* (Manchester: Manchester University Press, 1994). For the connection between legal pluralism and the 1745 rebellion, see Gould, *Among the Powers of the Earth*, 27.

88. Charles Erskine, Lord Tinwald, The Alterations Proposed to Be Made in the Criminal Law of Scotland (January 21, 1747), Add MS 35446, 127, BL; Lord Hardwicke, Lords Debates (February 17, 1747), *PH*, 14:18–25; Julian Hoppit, "Compulsion, Compensation and Property Rights in Britain, 1688–1833," *Past & Present* 210, no. 1 (2011): 108–14. The Heritable Jurisdictions (Scotland) Act, 1747, 20 Geo. 2, c. 43, eliminated those local courts. The Tenures Abolition Act 1746, 20 Geo. 2, c. 50, abolished some feudal tenures, but others survived until 2004. Abolition of Feudal Tenure (Scotland) Act

2000, (ASP 5). The circuit courts were created as part of the Heritable Jurisdictions Act, §§ 31–40. Lindsay Farmer, *Criminal Law, Tradition, and Legal Order: Crime and the Genius of Scots Law, 1747 to the Present* (Cambridge: Cambridge University Press, 2005), 64.

89. Lord Hardwicke to Duke of Cumberland (April 16, 1747), in Philip C. Yorke, *The Life and Correspondence of Philip Yorke, Earl of Hardwicke, Lord High Chancellor of Great Britain* (Cambridge: Cambridge University Press, 1913), 1:607; see also A Short Description of the Nature of the Jurisdictions to Be Abolished ([c. 1747]), Newcastle Papers, Add MS 33049, ff. 228–29, BL.

90. *Observations upon a Bill, Entitled, an Act for Taking Away, and Abolishing the Heritable Jurisdictions in That Part of Great Britain Called Scotland . . .* (Edinburgh: n.p., 1747), 28; see also Bob Harris, *Politics and the Nation: Britain in the Mid-Eighteenth Century* (Oxford: Oxford University Press, 2002), 14; Kidd, *Union and Unionisms*, 178–89, 210.

91. See Alexander Murdoch, *Making the Union Work: Scotland, 1651–1763* (New York: Routledge, 2020), 148–49.

92. James Erskine, Lord Grange, to Lord Hardwicke (March 1, 1747), Add MS 35446, 148, BL; see also ibid., 101 ("Gentem unam faciam eos [I will make of them one people], is my ultimate view and Aim in all such things.").

93. Memorial in Relation to Service Duties according to the Present Practice in Scotland (July 1, 1746), Add MS 35446, 137–43, BL; see also Corbyn Morris to Charles Yorke (August 20, 1754), Add MS 35634, f. 20, BL (lamenting "the constant artifices us'd, to keep the forms of Law in Scotland distinct from those in England, and to defeat their coincidence").

94. See, e.g., John W. Cairns, "Watson, Walton, and the History of Legal Transplants," *Georgia Journal of International & Comparative Law* 41 (2012): 637; O. Kahn-Freund, "On Uses and Misuses of Comparative Law," *Modern Law Review* 37, no. 1 (1974): 6–7; Brian Z. Tamanaha, "Understanding Legal Pluralism: Past to Present, Local to Global," *Sydney Law Review* 30 (2008): 2241–44.

95. Bentham, "Place and Time," 156 n.(a).

96. Charles-Louis de Secondat, Baron de La Brède et de Montesquieu, *The Spirit of the Laws*, ed. Anne M. Cohler, Basia Carolyn Miller, and Harold Samuel Stone (Cambridge: Cambridge University Press, 1989), 329. On Montesquieu's ambiguities, see Isaiah Berlin, "Montesquieu," in *Against the Current*, ed. Henry Hardy (Princeton, N.J.: Princeton University Press, 2013), 194–97; and Jacob T. Levy, *Rationalism, Pluralism, and Freedom* (New York: Oxford University Press, 2015), 147.

97. Peter Stein, *Legal Evolution: The Story of an Idea* (New York: Cambridge University Press, 1980), 23–25; Charles Yorke to Lord Hardwicke (October 31, 1749), in Yorke, *Hardwicke Correspondence*, 1:172–73.

98. Dalrymple to Charles Yorke (February 14, 1758), Add MS 35635, 102, BL; David Hume to Montesquieu (April 10, 1749), in *The Letters of David Hume*, ed. J. Y. T. Greig (Oxford: Clarendon Press, 1932), 1:134; cf. Montesquieu, *The Spirit of the Laws*, 18–19; David Hume, *The History of England, from the Invasion of Julius Caesar to the Revolution in 1688* (Indianapolis: Liberty Fund, 1983), 174 ("The Highlands of Scotland have

long been entitled by law to every privilege of British subjects; but it was not till very lately that the common people could in fact enjoy these privileges.").

99. John Dalrymple, *An Essay towards a General History of Feudal Property in Great Britain*, 4th ed. (London: A. Millar, 1759), iv; Dalrymple to Charles Yorke (April 12, 1757), Add MS 35635, 100, BL.
100. Dalrymple to Lord Hardwicke (February 14, 1756), Add MS 35449, 91, BL.
101. Henry Home, Lord Kames, *Sketches of the History of Man*, ed. James A. Harris (Indianapolis: Liberty Fund, 2007), 1:163; Henry Home, Lord Kames, *Historical Law-Tracts*, 2d ed. (Edinburgh: A. Kincaid, 1761), xii. For similarities between Kames's and Montesquieu's approaches, see Lieberman, *Province of Legislation Determined*, 147–49.
102. John Campbell, Baron Glenorchy (afterward 3d Earl of Breadalbane and Holland) to Hardwicke (July 3, 1746), Add MS 35450, ff. 118–120, BL; see Glenorchy to Hardwicke (June 20, 1747), Add MS 35450, f. 128, BL.
103. Humphrey Bland to Lord Hardwicke (November 26, 1754), Add MS 35448, 210, BL.
104. Cairns, "Natural Law, National Laws, Parliaments, and Multiple Monarchies," 124; Dalrymple, *Feudal Property*, viii–ix; Kames, *Historical Law-Tracts*, xii; John Finlay, "Scots Lawyers and House of Lords Appeals in Eighteenth-Century Britain," *Journal of Legal History* 32, no. 3 (2011): 250–51; see also Lieberman, *Province of Legislation Determined*, 159–75 (explaining Kames's preference for judicial rather than legislative change).
105. John Perceval [later 2d Earl of Egmont], Draft of a Speech on the Proposed Feudal Tenures Bill ([1747?]), Add MS 47097, 1–2, BL.
106. [Duncan Forbes,] Some Thoughts concerning the State of the Highlands of Scotland ([1746]), in *Culloden Papers*, ed. H. R. Duff (London: T. Cadell & W. Davies, 1815), 297, 298.
107. Anonymous letter to Lord Hardwicke (October 9, 1755), Add MS 35448, 305–06, BL.
108. See Matthew P. Dziennik, "'Under Ye Lash of Ye Law': The State and the Law in the Post-Culloden Scottish Highlands," *Journal of British Studies* 60, no. 3 (2021): 609–31.
109. Chatterjee, *The Nation and Its Fragments*, 10; see also Elizabeth Kolsky, "Codification and the Rule of Colonial Difference: Criminal Procedure in British India," *Law and History Review* 23, no. 3 (2005): 637.
110. See, e.g., Elizabeth Kolsky, "The Colonial Rule of Law and the Legal Regime of Exception: Frontier 'Fanaticism' and State Violence in British India," *American Historical Review* 120, no. 4 (2015): 1222; Kunal M. Parker, "The Historiography of Difference," *Law and History Review* 23, no. 3 (2005): 688; cf. Samera Esmeir, "On the Coloniality of Modern Law," *Critical Analysis of Law* 2, no. 1 (2015): 20; Peter Fitzpatrick, *The Mythology of Modern Law* (London: Routledge, 1992), 108.
111. The "rule of colonial difference" is perhaps more apt for the nineteenth-century British Empire. But see Lauren A. Benton and Lisa Ford, *Rage for Order: The British Empire and the Origins of International Law, 1800–1850* (Cambridge, Mass.: Harvard University Press, 2016), 83 (showing how, in the early nineteenth century, commissions of inquiry "worked to partially and conditionally enfold new subjects as well as

to discriminate against them," in a process that "helped to compose the empire as a single legal administrative framework").

112. Jennifer Pitts, *Boundaries of the International: Law and Empire* (Cambridge, Mass.: Harvard University Press, 2018), 24; see Holly Brewer, "Subjects by Allegiance to the King?," in *State and Citizen: British America and the Early United States*, ed. Peter Thompson and Peter S. Onuf (Charlottesville: University of Virginia Press, 2013), 25–51; Wolfe, "Land, Labor, and Difference," 880; Patrick Griffin, *American Leviathan: Empire, Nation, and Revolutionary Frontier* (New York: Hill and Wang, 2007), 26–31; Fredrik Albritton Jonsson, *Enlightenment's Frontier: The Scottish Highlands and the Origins of Environmentalism* (New Haven, Conn.: Yale University Press, 2013), 69–92; Dror Wahrman, *The Making of the Modern Self: Identity and Culture in Eighteenth-Century England* (New Haven, Conn.: Yale University Press, 2004), 86–87.

113. [Maurice Morgann], *A Plan for the Abolition of Slavery in the West Indies* (London: William Griffin, 1772). For the date of composition, see Christopher Leslie Brown, *Moral Capital: Foundations of British Abolitionism* (Chapel Hill: Published for the Omohundro Institute of Early American History and Culture, Williamsburg, Va., by the University of North Carolina Press, 2006), 217. On Morgann, see du Rivage, *Revolution against Empire*, 154; and Hilda Neatby, *Quebec: The Revolutionary Age, 1760–1791* (Toronto: McClelland and Stewart, 1966), 101.

114. Morgann, *Plan for the Abolition of Slavery*, 5, 25 (emphasis added), 27.

115. Brown, *Moral Capital*, 219.

116. See Mark Harrison, *Climates and Constitutions: Health, Race, Environment and British Imperialism in India, 1600–1850* (Oxford: Oxford University Press, 1999), 215; cf. William Doyle, *Some Account of the British Dominions beyond the Atlantic* (London: J. Browne, 1770), 61 ("[O]ne universal code should be made for every the smallest part of the dominions of the greatest state. . . . Why a Japernese governed by one system of laws; and a Spaniard, or Britton, an Indian, or Russian, by another? is not the human nature every where alike?").

117. See George M. Fredrickson, *Racism: A Short History* (Princeton, N.J.: Princeton University Press, 2015), 49; Brown, *Moral Capital*, 302–5; Nicholas Guyatt, *Bind Us Apart: How Enlightened Americans Invented Racial Segregation* (Oxford: Oxford University Press, 2016), 22–28. On Hume, compare F. T. H. Fletcher, *Montesquieu and English Politics (1750–1800)* (London: E. Arnold, 1939), 95–96, with Silvia Sebastiani, "Hume versus Montesquieu: Race against Climate," in *The Scottish Enlightenment: Race, Gender, and the Limits of Progress* (New York: Palgrave Macmillan, 2013), 24.

118. We should also keep in mind that racial thinking varied geographically, and that it responded to local events as well as broader intellectual trends. See, e.g., Vincent Brown, *Tacky's Revolt: The Story of an Atlantic Slave War* (Cambridge, Mass.: The Belknap Press of Harvard University Press, 2020), 216; Alejandro de la Fuente and Ariela J. Gross, *Becoming Free, Becoming Black: Race, Freedom, and Law in Cuba, Virginia, and Louisiana* (Cambridge: Cambridge University Press, 2020).

119. Roxann Wheeler, *The Complexion of Race: Categories of Difference in Eighteenth-Century British Culture* (Philadelphia: University of Pennsylvania Press, 2000), 177–233; Brooke N. Newman, *A Dark Inheritance: Blood, Race, and Sex in Colonial Ja-*

maica (New Haven, Conn.: Yale University Press, 2018), 22; Sharon Block, *Colonial Complexions: Race and Bodies in Eighteenth-Century America* (Philadelphia: University of Pennsylvania Press, 2018); Brown, *Tacky's Revolt,* 121–23; Patrick Wolfe, *Traces of History: Elementary Structures of Race* (New York: Verso Books, 2016), 6–7; Bruce Buchan and Silvia Sebastiani, "'No Distinction of Black or Fair': The Natural History of Race in Adam Ferguson's Lectures on Moral Philosophy," *Journal of the History of Ideas* 82, no. 2 (2021): 207–29; Suman Seth, *Difference and Disease: Medicine, Race, and the Eighteenth-Century British Empire* (Cambridge: Cambridge University Press, 2018), 208–40; see also Wolfe, "Land, Labor, and Difference," 878 (describing the possibility of becoming legally white in colonial Georgia). A similar hardening of racial lines occurred with respect to Native Americans. Starting in the 1760s, colonists of European descent increasingly described themselves as "white" to distinguish themselves from Native Americans. But it was only in the 1780s that whiteness took on a genuinely racial connotation; and even then, U.S. elites continued to disagree about "the innateness of Native difference." Gregory Ablavsky, "'With the Indian Tribes': Race, Citizenship, and Original Constitutional Meanings," *Stanford Law Review* 70 (2018): 1050–53; see also Peter Silver, *Our Savage Neighbors: How Indian War Transformed Early America* (New York: W. W. Norton, 2008), xxi, 116–24.

120. See Langford, *A Polite and Commercial People,* 292; Robert Kent Donovan, "The Military Origins of the Roman Catholic Relief Programme of 1778," *Historical Journal* 28, no. 1 (1985): 83.

121. Jonathan I. Israel, "Spinoza, Locke and the Enlightenment Battle for Toleration," in *Toleration in Enlightenment Europe,* ed. Ole Peter Grell and Roy Porter (Cambridge: Cambridge University Press, 2000), 102–13; Toleration Act 1689, 1 W. & M., c. 18; Michael W. McConnell, "The Origins and Historical Understanding of Free Exercise of Religion," *Harvard Law Review* 103, no. 7 (1990): 1422; Alexandra Walsham, *Charitable Hatred: Tolerance and Intolerance in England, 1500–1700* (Manchester: Manchester University Press, 2006), 228–79; Dana Rabin, "The Jew Bill of 1753: Masculinity, Virility, and the Nation," *Eighteenth-Century Studies* 39, no. 2 (2006): 157–71; Justin Champion, "Toleration and Citizenship in Enlightenment England: John Toland and the Naturalization of the Jews, 1714–1753," in *Toleration in Enlightenment Europe,* ed. Grell and Porter, 138–39.

122. Blackstone, *Commentaries,* 4:54; Rebecca Probert, *Marriage Law and Practice in the Long Eighteenth Century: A Reassessment* (Cambridge: Cambridge University Press, 2009), 164–65, 234–35, 328–30, 337; Benjamin J. Kaplan, *Divided by Faith: Religious Conflict and the Practice of Toleration in Early Modern Europe* (Cambridge, Mass.: Harvard University Press, 2007), 348; see also Jeremy Pfeffer, *"From One End of the Earth to the Other": The London Bet Din, 1805–1855, and the Jewish Convicts Transported to Australia* (Brighton: Sussex Academic Press, 2009), 90.

123. See Katherine A. Hermes, "'Justice Will Be Done Us': Algonquin Demands for Reciprocity in the Courts of European Settlers," in *The Many Legalities of Early America,* ed. Tomlins and Mann, 123–49; Yirush, "Claiming the New World"; McHugh, *Aboriginal Societies and the Common Law,* 102–3; Mark D. Walters, "Mohegan Indians v. Connecticut (1705–1773) and the Legal Status of Aboriginal Customary Laws and

Government in British North America," *Osgoode Hall Law Journal* 33 (1995): 785–829; Bradley J. Dixon, "'His One Netev Ples': The Chowans and the Politics of Native Petitions in the Colonial South," *William & Mary Quarterly* 76, no. 1 (2019): 50–52.
124. John Locke, *Political Essays*, ed. Mark Goldie (Cambridge: Cambridge University Press, 1997), 59. My reading of Locke is indebted to Teresa M. Bejan, *Mere Civility* (Cambridge, Mass.: Harvard University Press, 2017), 117–19.
125. See J. C. Walmsley and Felix Waldman, "John Locke and the Toleration of Catholics: A New Manuscript," *Historical Journal* 62, no. 4 (2019): 1110.
126. John Locke, *Two Treatises of Government*, ed. Peter Laslett (Cambridge: Cambridge University Press, 1988), 387.
127. Michael G. Kammen, "Virginia at the Close of the Seventeenth Century: An Appraisal by James Blair and John Locke," *Virginia Magazine of History and Biography* 74, no. 2 (1966): 159, 167; Holly Brewer, "Slavery, Sovereignty, and 'Inheritable Blood': Reconsidering John Locke and the Origins of American Slavery," *American Historical Review* 122, no. 4 (2017): 1071–72.
128. Edmund Burke, "An Essay Towards an History of the Laws of England" (c. 1757), in *Writings and Speeches*, ed. McLoughlin and Boulton, 1:325–36; see Richard Bourke, *Empire & Revolution: The Political Life of Edmund Burke* (Princeton, N.J.: Princeton University Press, 2015), 161. Burke reached the same conclusion in "An Essay towards an Abridgment of the English History" (started in 1757 but never completed). When Rome conquered Britain, it initially made some concessions to British manners; but it eventually "subdued the Britains by civilizing them." This was "the most perfect model for those employed in the unhappy, but sometimes necessary task of subduing a rude and free people." *Writings and Speeches*, ed. McLoughlin and Boulton, 1:368.

CHAPTER 2. EXPERIMENTING WITH LAW AND DEVELOPMENT

1. These quotations come from the letters as published in *Letters from the Marquis de Montcalm, Governor-General of Canada; to Messrs. de Berryer & de La Molé, in the Years 1757, 1758, and 1759* (London: J. Almon, 1777), 25–27. Slightly different versions are in William Knox Papers, box 9, folder 1, WLCL; and *The Manuscripts of the Earl of Dartmouth* (London: Printed for H.M.S.O. by Eyre and Spottiswoode, 1887–96), 2:546. This book uses "Canadien" to refer to the former subjects of France in Quebec; "Canadian" refers more generally to the inhabitants of the province.
2. Some contemporaries questioned the authenticity of the letters, but the forgeries fooled others, including Lord Mansfield. See, e.g., "Review of New Publications," *London Magazine, or Gentleman's Monthly Intelligencer*, June 1777, 328; Lord Weymouth, Lords Debates (May 30, 1777), *PH*, 19:346; Lord Mansfield, Lords Debates (May 30, 1777), *PH*, 19:351; "Supplement," *London Review*, July 1777, 153; "Books: America," *Scots Magazine*, April 1777, 206; "Monthly Catalogue," *Critical Review*, April 1777, 315. For Roubaud and his fabrications, see Caroline Masse, "Pierre Roubaud, polygraphe et faussaire au Siècle des lumières," *Voix et Images* 20, no. 2 (1995): 319–20; Auguste Vachon, "Roubaud, Pierre-Joseph-Antoine," in *Dictionary of Canadian Biography*, 22 vols. (Toronto: University of Toronto/Université Laval, 1966–2005), http://www

.biographi.ca/en/bio/roubaud_pierre_joseph_antoine_4E.html; and Bronwen McShea, *Apostles of Empire: The Jesuits and New France* (Lincoln: University of Nebraska Press, 2019), 236–38.

3. Articles of Capitulation (September 8, 1760), in *Documents Relating to the Constitutional History of Canada, 1759–1791*, ed. Adam Shortt and Arthur G. Doughty, 2d ed. (Ottawa: J. L. Taché, 1918), 1:33–34; cf. George III, Observation upon the Projet d'Articles Preliminaires, & Lord Egremont's [Draft] ([1762]), PRO 30/47/6, TNA (approving of the term *sujets* in the Treaty of Paris, because "*sujets* takes in *Canadiens*, as well as *English*," and "expressing the *Canadiens* as well as *English* would imply a difference, & therefore is wrong"). In contrast, Major General John Barrington allowed Guadeloupe to retain French law in its capitulation—but only because the military situation didn't allow for protracted negotiations, and because he didn't expect the island to remain a British colony for long. See P. J. Marshall, *Edmund Burke and the British Empire in the West Indies: Wealth, Power, and Slavery* (Oxford: Oxford University Press, 2019), 28, 34.

4. Royal Proclamation of 1763, in *Constitutional History*, ed. Shortt and Doughty, 1:165.

5. Ordinance Establishing Civil Courts (1764), in *Constitutional History*, ed. Shortt and Doughty, 1:205; see also Neatby, *Quebec*, 49; Instructions to Governor Murray (1766), in *Constitutional History*, ed. Shortt and Doughty, 1:181–205; Commission of Chief Justice William Hey (1766), in *Constitutional History*, ed. Shortt and Doughty, 1:273–76.

6. Campbell v. Hall (1774) 98 Eng. Rep. 848, 850; Lofft 655, 658 (K.B.); *The Annual Register, or, a View of the History, Politicks, and Literature for the Year 1762* (London: R. & J. Dodsley, 1763), 251–54; Marshall, "The Incorporation of Quebec in the British Empire," 48; [James Harris], Hints Relative to the Division and Government of the Conquered and Newly Acquired Countries in America (June 1, 1763), Shelburne Papers, vol. 48, folder 45, 543, WLCL. For Grenada's population, see Robert V. Wells, *The Population of the British Colonies in America before 1776: A Survey of Census Data* (Princeton, N.J.: Princeton University Press, 1975), 253; and Mark Quintanilla, "The World of Alexander Campbell: An Eighteenth-Century Grenadian Planter," *Albion* 35, no. 2 (2003): 236.

7. See Heather Freund, "When French Islands Became British: Law, Property and Inheritance in the Ceded Islands," in *Voices in the Legal Archives in the French Colonial World: "The King Is Listening,"* ed. Nancy Christie, Michael Gauvreau, and Matthew Gerber (New York: Routledge, 2021), 309.

8. Griffin, *The Townshend Moment*, 134–35; Aaron Willis, "Rethinking Ireland and Assimilation: Quebec, Collaboration, and the Heterogeneous Empire," in *Entangling the Quebec Act: Transnational Contexts, Meanings, and Legacies in North America and the British Empire*, ed. Ollivier Hubert and François Furstenberg (Montreal: McGill-Queen's University Press, 2020), 177; [John Pownall], General Propositions: Form and Constitution of Government to Be Established in the New Colonies [1763], Shelburne Papers, vol. 48, folder 46, WLCL; Harris, Hints Relative to the Division and Government of the Conquered and Newly Acquired Countries; A Sketch of a Report with Observations on the Commission and Instructions for the Governor of Granada ([1763?]), Shelburne Papers, vol. 49, folder 20, 293, WLCL; [Observations on Granada],

Charles Townshend Papers, box 8, folder 52/2, 6, WLCL; M. C. Mirow, "The Thistle, the Rose, and the Palm: Scottish and English Judges in British East Florida," in *Networks and Connections in Legal History*, ed. Ian Williams and Michael Lobban (Cambridge: Cambridge University Press, 2020), 90; see also Royal Proclamation Issued by Governor Robert Melvill (December 19, 1764), in *Laws of Grenada and the Grenadines, 1766–1875*, ed. Sanford Freeling (London: George Phipps, 1875), 6–8. On "periphery-to-periphery legal transplants" elsewhere in the British Empire, see Assaf Likhovski, "Peripheral Vision: Polish-Jewish Lawyers and Early Israeli Law," *Law and History Review* 36, no. 2 (2018): 235–66.

9. [Pownall], General Propositions; Dates of Certain Proceedings Relating to Canada ([after 1766]), Shelburne Papers, vol. 64, 497, WLCL.
10. Colley, *Britons*, 101–2; Armitage, *Ideological Origins*, 8.
11. Langford, *A Polite and Commercial People*, 549; Szechi, *The Jacobites*, 120; Michael D. Breidenbach, *Our Dear-Bought Liberty: Catholics and Religious Toleration in Early America* (Cambridge, Mass.: Harvard University Press, 2021), 116–46; Jessica L. Harland-Jacobs, "Incorporating the King's New Subjects: Accommodation and Anti-Catholicism in the British Empire, 1763–1815," *Journal of Religious History* 39, no. 2 (2015): 203–23; see also Caitlin Anderson, "Old Subjects, New Subjects and Non-Subjects: Silences and Subjecthood in Fédon's Rebellion, Grenada, 1795–96," in *War, Empire, and Slavery, 1770–1830*, ed. Richard Bessel, Nicholas Guyatt, and Jane Rendall (New York: Palgrave Macmillan, 2010), 207 (arguing that Gallican theology's apparent resemblance to Anglicanism made French Catholicism less threatening).
12. Poor Old England [Anon.], "To the Printer of the Public Advertiser," *Public Advertiser*, June 22, 1774.
13. *Thoughts on the Act for Making More Effectual Provision for the Government of the Province of Quebec* (London: T. Becket, 1774), 23–25. Sir William Meredith even connected Catholicism with the foundations of English liberty, pointing out that Magna Carta had been produced by Catholics. William Meredith, *A Letter to the Earl of Chatham, on the Quebec Bill*, 2d ed. (London: T. Cadell, 1774), 22.
14. [William Knox], Hints Respecting the Settlement of Florida ([1763?]), William Knox Papers, box 9, folder 3, WLCL; [John Shebbeare], *One More Letter to the People of England* (London: J. Pridden, 1762), 17–18; Langford, *A Polite and Commercial People*, 224; see also Sylvana Tomaselli, "Intolerance, the Virtue of Princes and Radicals," in *Toleration in Enlightenment Europe*, ed. Grell and Porter, 86–101 (discussing Enlightenment arguments for toleration on pragmatic grounds).
15. O'Shaughnessy, *An Empire Divided*, 124–25; Alexander Wood Renton, "French Law Within the British Empire," *Journal of the Society of Comparative Legislation* 10, no. 1 (1909): 93–119; Ordinance Establishing Civil Courts (1764), in *Constitutional History*, ed. Shortt and Doughty, 1:205.
16. Maurice Morgann, An Account of the State of Canada from Its Conquest to May 1766 ([1766–1767?]), Shelburne Papers, vol. 64, 525, WLCL; see David Lemmings, *Professors of the Law: Barristers and English Legal Culture in the Eighteenth Century* (New York: Oxford University Press, 2000), 41 n.64, 227–29.
17. Alteration of Quebec Judiciary Ordinance (February 24, 1766), in *Royal Instructions*

to *British Colonial Governors, 1670–1776,* ed. Leonard Woods Labaree (New York: D. Appleton-Century, 1935), 1:300–301. The ordinance is reprinted in *Constitutional History,* ed. Shortt and Doughty, 1:249.
18. The same report also proposed limiting the number of Catholic seminarians and replacing the bishop of Quebec with a royally appointed superintendent. Report of Lords Commissioners for Trade and Plantations Relative to the State of the Province of Quebec (July 10, 1767), in *Constitutional History,* ed. Shortt and Doughty, 1:377–93.
19. Presentments of the Grand Jury of Quebec (October 16, 1764), in *Constitutional History,* ed. Shortt and Doughty, 1:212, 214–16. A prominent merchant named Thomas Walker made the same argument a few months later. In December 1764, a group of soldiers with blackened faces broke into Walker's home, beat him, and cropped one of his ears. Walker insisted that the offenders be tried by an all-Protestant jury. The affair of Walker's ear quickly became a transatlantic controversy, and Governor Murray's inability to bring the offenders to justice contributed to his recall. The affair also raised several technical but consequential legal issues, including the applicability in Canada of the Coventry Act, 1670 Charles 2, c. 1, which made ear-cutting a felony. See Thomas Walker, [Protest against a Regulation of the Governor and Council] (March 14, 1765), CO 42/2, 287, TNA; Neatby, *Quebec,* 38–39; Board of Trade to George III (September 2, 1765), CO 43/1, 209, TNA; Lisa Ford, *The King's Peace: Law and Order in the British Empire* (Cambridge, Mass.: Harvard University Press, 2021), 58–99; Thomas Gage to Ralph Burton (January 31, 1765), Gage Papers, vol. AS 30, WLCL; Guy Carleton to Thomas Gage (January 31, 1767), Gage Papers, vol. AS 61, WLCL.
20. Muller, *Subjects and Sovereign,* 140.
21. O'Shaughnessy, *An Empire Divided,* 124–25.
22. PC 2/115/299–304, TNA; Smith, *Appeals to the Privy Council,* 493–95.
23. Fletcher Norton and William de Grey, Report of Attorney and Solicitor General Re Status of Roman Catholic Subjects (June 10, 1765), in *Constitutional History,* ed. Shortt and Doughty, 1:236; Mr. Yorke's Opinion Relative to the Grenades (June 12, 1767), Shelburne Papers, vol. 61, 697, WLCL; Smith, *Appeals to the Privy Council,* 494. For earlier discussions of this issue, see Ned Landsman, "The Episcopate, the British Union, and the Failure of Religious Settlement in Colonial British America," in *The First Prejudice: Religious Tolerance and Intolerance in Early America,* ed. Christopher S. Beneke and Christopher S. Grenda (Philadelphia: University of Pennsylvania Press, 2011), 75–97; and Lord Egremont to James Murray (August 13, 1763), Amherst Papers, vol. 1, WLCL.
24. See Christian R. Burset, "Advisory Opinions and the Problem of Legal Authority," *Vanderbilt Law Review* 74 (2021): 621; and George Chalmers, *Opinions of Eminent Lawyers, on Various Points of English Jurisprudence, Chiefly Concerning the Colonies, Fisheries, and Commerce of Great Britain* (London: Reed and Hunter, 1814), xxi–xxii.
25. Smith, *Appeals to the Privy Council,* 495; Rex v. Vaughan (1765) 98 Eng. Rep. 308, 311; 4 Burrow 2494, 2500; cf. Mansfield to George Grenville (December 24, 1764), in *The Grenville Papers,* ed. William James Smith (London: J. Murray, 1852), 2:477–78 ("A colony which goes from hence to settle in a waste country . . . carries with them such

part of the laws of England as is adapted to, and proper for their situation. A very small part of the Common or Statute Law of England is law there by this maxim.... Penal Laws, and a thousand other heads, do not bind there by implication.").

26. Smith, *Appeals to the Privy Council*, 495; Mary Sarah Bilder, "Colonial Constitutionalism and Constitutional Law," in *Transformations in American Legal History: Essays in Honor of Morton J. Horwitz*, ed. Daniel W. Hamilton and Alfred L. Brophy (Cambridge, Mass.: Harvard University Press, 2009).

27. James Oldham, "Wilmot, Sir John Eardley (1709–1792)," in *DNB*, https://doi.org/10.1093/ref:odnb/29624; Charles Yorke to Lord Rockingham (July 30, 1766), WWM/R/1/668, SA; Lord Bathurst to Sir John Eardley Wilmot (January 1774), OSB MSS File 921, BRBML. Smith acknowledges that Francis Maseres held out Wilmot as an authority on the law of Quebec. Smith, *Appeals to the Privy Council*, 495. Wilmot was also consulted frequently on legal matters in India. See, e.g., Laurence Sulivan to Warren Hastings (April 14, 1775), Add MS 29136, 171, BL; Charles Jenkinson to John Clavering (December 13, 1776), MSS Eur E16, 33, BL; Lord Bathurst to Sir John Eardley Wilmot (November 1773), OSB MSS File 919, BRBML.

28. Appellant's Case, Scott v. Brebner, William Samuel Johnson Collection, Diamond Law Library, Columbia University, https://amesfoundation.law.harvard.edu/ColonialAppeals/CaribAppeals/CLLImageList_mysqli.php?report_no=GRE_1770_01. Dunning made his name in the early 1760s as an advocate for the EIC. Wedderburn rose to prominence partly as a legal adviser to Lord Clive. John Cannon, "Dunning, John, first Baron Ashburton (1731–1783)," in *DNB*, https://doi.org/10.1093/ref:odnb/8284; Alexander Murdoch, "Wedderburn, Alexander, first earl of Rosslyn (1733–1805)," in *DNB*, https://doi.org/10.1093/ref:odnb/28954.

29. See Freund, "When French Islands Became British," 320.

30. See Michael Lobban, *The Common Law and English Jurisprudence, 1760–1850* (Oxford: Clarendon Press, 1991), 83, 104–5; James Oldham, *English Common Law in the Age of Mansfield* (Chapel Hill: University of North Carolina Press, 2004), 365–67. Compare Smith, *Appeals to the Privy Council*, 464 (noting the "judicial isolation" of the Privy Council), with George L. Haskins, "Appeals to the Privy Council from the American Plantations" (Book Review), *University of Pennsylvania Law Review* 100 (1952): 1271 (noting "a consistent reliance almost exclusively upon English cases and form books" in briefs before the Privy Council).

31. See Smith, *Appeals to the Privy Council*, 495.

32. Johnson, note of decision on page 5 of brief.

33. See Chapter 1.

34. See, e.g., Haskins, "Appeals to the Privy Council from the American Plantations," 1271–72. Wilmot would have been eager to avoid any suggestion that Parliament couldn't legislate for the empire. In 1765 or 1766, he had written a defense of Britain's right to tax the colonies. See John Wilmot, *Memoirs of the Life of the Right Honourable Sir John Eardley Wilmot, Knt.*, 2d ed. (London: J. Nichols & Son, 1811), 217–26.

35. Muller, *Subjects and Sovereign*, 146; Smith, *Appeals to the Privy Council*, 465; O'Shaughnessy, *An Empire Divided*, 124–25.

36. Francis Maseres to Charles Yorke (November 15, 1766), Add MS 35638, 43, BL (em-

phasis added). Under the new procedure, a creditor initiated a case with a summons. The creditor could then procure a writ of distringas to seize goods equivalent to the value of the debt. Those goods would be held as security until a jury decided the case. If the creditor prevailed, and the goods seized were insufficient to cover the debt, the court would issue a writ for the sale of the debtor's lands. Finally, if the combined value of the seized goods and land was still insufficient to repay the debt, the chief justice was empowered to issue a writ of capias to authorize the debtor's imprisonment—but only upon the affidavit of the plaintiff or some other "credible person" that the debtor was concealing assets. Moreover, imprisonment would be of limited duration. After a period of no more than six months, the prisoner could swear that he had no assets and regain his freedom. (The writs against his property would remain in effect.)

37. It seems the summary procedure was never introduced. See Francis Maseres to Fowler Walker (April 4, 1768), in *The Maseres Letters, 1766–1768*, ed. W. Stewart Wallace (Toronto: Oxford University Press, 1919), 84. Instead, in 1779, the colonial secretary ordered Quebec's governor to create a court of requests—another kind of small-debt tribunal modeled on existing courts in England and several of its colonies.

38. Blackstone, *Commentaries*, 4:424; Oldham, *English Common Law*, 107. Historians have been similarly divided. Compare Holdsworth, *History of English Law*, 5:492 (describing England's bankruptcy regime as "a disgrace to a civilized community"), with Julian Hoppit, *Risk and Failure in English Business, 1700–1800* (Cambridge: Cambridge University Press, 1987), 19–41 (noting contemporary critiques but concluding that "the strength and fairness of bankruptcy recommended it to eighteenth-century businessmen").

39. Oldham, *English Common Law*, 108–11.

40. Sheldon J. Godfrey and Judith C. Godfrey, *Search Out the Land: The Jews and the Growth of Equality in British Colonial America, 1740–1867* (Montreal: McGill-Queen's Press, 1995), 88–91; Jacob Rader Marcus, *Early American Jewry* (Philadelphia: Jewish Publication Society of America, 1951), 1:232.

41. Memorial of the Subscribing Merchants (November 17, 1767), CO 42/6, 206, TNA.

42. Francis Maseres, "A Draught of an Intended Report . . . Concerning the State of the Laws and the Administration of Justice in that Province" (February 27, 1769), in *Constitutional History*, ed. Shortt and Doughty, 1:347.

43. Memorial of the Subscribing Merchants. For attempts to enact bankruptcy laws in other American colonies during this period, see Bruce H. Mann, *Republic of Debtors: Bankruptcy in the Age of American Independence* (Cambridge, Mass.: Harvard University Press, 2002), 51–77.

44. Robert Craigie to Lord Hardwicke (January 2, 1755), Add MS 35448, 226, BL.

45. The Petition of the Montreal Merchants (January 1768), CO 42/6, f. 212, TNA.

46. Francis Maseres to Fowler Walker (November 19, 1767), in *Maseres Letters*, ed. Wallace, 55, 59 (emphasis added).

47. Smith, *Appeals to the Privy Council*, 489–93.

48. "A Friend to Liberty, Tho' not a Merchant," to the Printer of the *Quebec Gazette*, "A Seasonable Answer to the 'Short View of the Laws of England Now in Force relating to Bankrupts' . . . " (December 19, 1767), reprinted in *Maseres Letters*, ed. Wallace, 125.

49. Guy Carleton to Lords Commissioners for Trade and Plantations (November 21, 1767), CO 42/6, 204, TNA; Lord Hillsborough to Guy Carleton (March 6, 1768), in *Constitutional History,* ed. Shortt and Doughty, 1:297–98.
50. Brewer, *Party Ideology,* 3–25; Steve Pincus, *1688: The First Modern Revolution* (New Haven, Conn.: Yale University Press, 2009), 393–96; Swingen, *Competing Visions of Empire,* 153–55.
51. See Amy Watson, "Patriot Empire: The Rise of Party Politics in the British Atlantic, 1716–1748" (PhD diss., Yale University, 2018); Pincus, *Heart of the Declaration.*
52. du Rivage, *Revolution against Empire,* 6, 78–79; Vaughn, *Politics of Empire,* 77.
53. George Grenville to Duke of Bedford (September 5, 1763), in *Grenville Papers,* ed. Smith, 2:109. On the realignment of partisan politics after Pitt's appointment as prime minister, see Clark, "General Theory of Party," 303–5.
54. Norman S. Poser, *Lord Mansfield: Justice in the Age of Reason* (Montreal: McGill-Queen's University Press, 2013), 33; W. S. Holdsworth, "Lord Mansfield," *Law Quarterly Review* 53 (1937): 228; Langford, *A Polite and Commercial People,* 222.
55. Wedderburn (later Baron Loughborough and first Earl of Rosslyn) was the son of an Anglophilic Scottish advocate who had served the Whig establishment as secretary to the board of excise and as lord of session. The younger Wedderburn started his career in Edinburgh, but he moved to London after refusing to apologize for insulting the Jacobite dean of the Faculty of Advocates. In England, he became increasingly concerned about "popular licentiousness" and grew attracted to paternalist politics. Vaughn, *Politics of Empire,* 175–76; Alexander Allardyce, ed., *Scotland and Scotsmen in the Eighteenth Century* (Edinburgh: William Blackwood and Sons, 1888), 1:142; Brewer, *Party Ideology,* 232; Murdoch, "Wedderburn, Alexander," *DNB;* Lord Rockingham to [William Dowdeswell] (January 13, 1771), WWM/R/1/1348, SA.
56. Linda Colley, *In Defiance of Oligarchy: The Tory Party 1714–60* (Cambridge: Cambridge University Press, 1985); Kinkel, *Disciplining the Empire,* 94–95.
57. Gage to Frederick Haldimand (June 12, 1774), Gage Papers, vol. AS 120, WLCL.
58. Kinkel, *Disciplining the Empire,* 169–80.
59. [Robert Orme] ([1766–1778]), MSS Eur Orme OV 303/4, BL. Analogies between the American crisis and the *lex Julia* were common in contemporary Scottish thought. See Iain McDaniel, *Adam Ferguson in the Scottish Enlightenment* (Cambridge, Mass.: Harvard University Press, 2013), 186.
60. Charles-Louis de Secondat, Baron de La Brède et de Montesquieu, *Reflections on the Causes of the Rise and Fall of the Roman Empire,* 4th ed. (Glasgow: Robert Urie, 1758), 94–96.
61. T. H. Breen, *The Marketplace of Revolution: How Consumer Politics Shaped American Independence* (New York: Oxford University Press, 2004); du Rivage, *Revolution against Empire,* 192; Thomas Gage to Lord Barrington (March 10, 1768), Gage Papers, vol. ES 11, WLCL.
62. Lord Mansfield, Lords Debates (March 11, 1766), in *Proceedings and Debates* 2:342.
63. See, e.g., George Grenville to William Knox (June 27, 1768), William Knox Papers, box 1, folder 27, WLCL.
64. Edmund Burke to Committee of Correspondence of the General Assembly of New

York (August 2, 1774), in *The Correspondence of Edmund Burke*, ed. Thomas W. Copeland (Cambridge: Cambridge University Press, 1958–1978), 3:13; cf. Welland, "Commercial Interest and Political Allegiance."

65. See Hulsebosch, "English Liberties Outside England," 761–62; Nelson, *The Chesapeake and New England, 1607–1660*, 8–9.
66. Clarence Edwin Carter, *Great Britain and the Illinois Country, 1763–1774* (Washington, D.C.: American Historical Association, 1910), 15; Hillsborough to Thomas Gage (February 5, 1772), Gage Papers, vol. ES 21, WLCL (noting that if Indian hostilities "should have the effect to induce the Inhabitants of the Ilinois Country to remove into the Province of Quebec, that of West Florida, or any other of the settled Colonies, it would in my opinion be a happy Event"); Gage to Hillsborough (May 6, 1772), Gage Papers, vol. ES 22, WLCL (agreeing with Hillsborough).
67. Hillsborough to Gage (November 4, 1771), Gage Papers, vol. ES 21, WLCL.
68. Carter, *Great Britain and the Illinois Country*, 30, 103–9, 118–19; A. Zuercher Reichardt, "War for the Interior: Imperial Conflict and the Formation of North American and Transatlantic Communications Infrastructure, 1727–1774" (PhD diss., Yale University, 2017), 382–83; Griffin, *American Leviathan*, 38–39; *The Expediency of Securing Our American Colonies by Settling the Country Adjoining the River Mississippi, and the Country upon the Ohio, Considered* (Edinburgh: n.p., 1763); Phineas Lyman, Plan . . . for Settling Louisiana, and for Erecting New Colonies between West Florida and the Falls of St. Anthony ([1763–69]), Shelburne Papers, vol. 50, WLCL; George Morgan, In Behalf of the Inhabitants at the Illinois, Some Reasons Why the Distillation of Spirits from Grain Ought to Be Encouraged at the Illinois ([1769]), Gage Papers, vol. AS 88, WLCL; Lord Shelburne, Minutes Submitted to the Cabinet in the Beginning of Summer 1767 (September 11, 1767), 12, WLCL; Ephraim Biggs to Lord Chatham (April 2, 1759), PRO 30/8/96, 198, TNA; see also William Johnson to Henry Seymour Conway ([c. 1763]), Shelburne Papers, vol. 48, folder 7, WLCL; William Franklin, Reasons for Establishing a Colony in the Illinois (1766), in *The New Régime, 1765–1767*, ed. Clarence Walworth Alvord and Clarence Edwin Carter (Springfield: Illinois State Historical Library, 1916), 252.
69. Thomas Gage to George Croghan (April 4, 1766), Gage Papers, vol. AS 50, WLCL; Gage to Robert Farmar (March 14, 1766), Gage Papers, vol. AS 49, WLCL; Gage to Farmar (July 7, 1766) Gage Papers, vol. AS 54, WLCL.
70. Fletcher Norton, Report of the Attorney General on the Subject Whether Those Subjects of the Crowns of France and Spain Who Remain in the Ceded Countrys in America Are to Be Considered as Aliens (July 27, 1764), Shelburne Papers, vol. 61, 685–88, WLCL.
71. George Turnbull to Thomas Gage (January 10, 1767), Gage Papers, vol. AS 61, WLCL; Gage to Hillsborough (November 10, 1770), Gage Papers, vol. ES 19, WLCL.
72. Representation of the Lords of Trade to the Principal Secretary of State (March 7, 1768), Gage Papers, vol. ES 11, WLCL; see also Robert Farmar to Thomas Gage (March 18, 1766), Gage Papers, vol. AS 49, WLCL; Captain Gordon Forbes, State of the Commerce and Country of the Illinois &c. (January 6, 1769), Gage Papers, vol. AS 83, WLCL.

73. Richard White, *The Middle Ground: Indians, Empires, and Republics in the Great Lakes Region, 1650–1815* (Cambridge: Cambridge University Press, 1991), 305–9; Lord Dartmouth to Thomas Gage (November 4, 1772), vol. ES 23, WLCL; Lord Dartmouth to Frederick Haldimand (October 14, 1773), Add MS 21695, 40, BL.
74. Stuart Banner, *How the Indians Lost Their Land: Law and Power on the Frontier* (Cambridge: Belknap Press of Harvard University Press, 2005), 100–104; Alan Taylor, *American Revolutions: A Continental History, 1750–1804* (New York: W. W. Norton & Company, 2016), 72–75.
75. Thomas Gage to Lord Hillsborough (May 6, 1772), Gage Papers, vol. ES 22, WLCL; see also Gage to Captain James Stevenson, May 15, 1772, Gage Papers, vol. AS 111, WLCL (stating that it would be "no great loss" if colonists were driven to settle elsewhere).
76. Lord Barrington to Thomas Gage (August 1, 1768), Gage Papers, vol. ES 13, WLCL; see also Lord Dartmouth to Thomas Gage (November 4, 1772), Gage Papers, vol. ES 23, WLCL (supporting Gage's plan to deny civil juries to Illinois).
77. Thomas Gage, Instructions to Captain Sterling of the 42d Regiment Ordered with a Detachment to Take Possession of the Ilinois (May 20, 1765), Gage Papers, vol. AS 36, WLCL.
78. Lord Hillsborough to Thomas Gage (December 9, 1769), Gage Papers, vol. ES 16, WLCL; Frederick Haldimand to Lord Dartmouth (November 3, 1773), Add MS 21695, 42, BL; Thomas Gage to Ralph Burton (January 31, 1765), Gage Papers, vol. AS 30, WLCL; Thomas Gage to Robert Farmar (February 18, 1765), Gage Papers, vol. AS 31, WLCL. For the illegality of using martial law to govern civilians, see Ford, *The King's Peace*, 69–73.
79. Thomas Gage to Colonel John Reed (July 22, 1767), Gage Papers, vol. AS 67, WLCL; see also Thomas Gage to Lt. Colonel John Wilkins (June 16, 1771), Gage Papers, vol. AS 104, WLCL; Thomas Gage to Major John Bruce (August 6, 1770), Gage Papers, vol. AS 94, WLCL (recommending that all disputes in Detroit be settled by arbitration).
80. Frederick Haldimand to Captain Hugh Lord (October 24, 1773), Add MS 21693, 211, BL; see also M. Scott Heerman, *The Alchemy of Slavery: Human Bondage and Emancipation in the Illinois Country, 1730–1865* (Philadelphia: University of Pennsylvania Press, 2018), 54–55 (showing that Gage's actions "bolstered French local authority").
81. Thomas Gage to Lord Hillsborough (August 6, 1771), Gage Papers, vol. ES 20, WLCL.
82. Jeremy Krikler, "The Zong and the Lord Chief Justice," *History Workshop Journal* 64 (2007): 35 (quoting Rex v. Inhabitants of Harberton [1785]); see also Oldham, *English Common Law*, 72 (describing Mansfield's "relentless efforts to get parties to settle their disputes").
83. Guy Carleton to Lord Hillsborough (March 28, 1770), CO 42/7, 261, TNA; see also James Marriott, *Plan of a Code of Laws for the Province of Quebec* (London, 1774), 61–62; *Proceedings of the Governor and Council at Fort William, Respecting the Administration of Justice amongst the Natives in Bengal* (London: J. Almon, 1775), 18; Douglas Hay, "Moral Economy, Political Economy and Law," in *Moral Economy and Popular*

Protest: Crowds, Conflict and Authority, ed. Adrian Randall and Andrew Charlesworth (New York: St. Martin's Press, 2000), 98–99.

84. See Christian R. Burset, "Arbitrating the England Problem: Litigation, Private Ordering, and the Rise of the Modern Economy," *Ohio State Journal on Dispute Resolution* 36 (2020): 1–64.

85. du Rivage, *Revolution against Empire*, 115 (quoting Letter from William Allason [September 8, 1765], in *Richmond College Historical Papers*, ed. D. R. Anderson [Richmond, Va.: n.p., 1915–1917], 2:137–38).

86. Edmund S. Morgan and Helen M. Morgan, *The Stamp Act Crisis: Prologue to Revolution* (Chapel Hill: University of North Carolina Press, 1995), 177; see also Jay F. Alexander, "Legal Careers in Eighteenth Century America," *Duquesne Law Review* 23 (1985): 656 (noting another Philadelphia merchant's inability to recover debts or obtain credit during the Stamp Act crisis). Similar complaints came from other commercial centers. du Rivage, *Revolution against Empire*, 114–15.

87. Edmund Burke, *Observations on a Late State of the Nation*, 3d ed. (London: J. Dodsley, 1769), 113; see also James Otis, [Oration on the Stamp Act (December 20, 1765)], in *Reports of Cases Argued and Adjudged in the Superior Court of Judicature of the Province of Massachusetts Bay, between 1761 and 1772*, ed. Josiah Quincy (Boston: Little, Brown, 1865), 204–5 (describing "[t]he shutting up of the courts" as "a total dissolution of government" and "a dissolution of society").

88. See Clarence Walworth Alvord, *The Illinois Country, 1673–1818* (Springfield: Illinois Centennial Commission, 1920), 266.

89. John Wilkins, Commission to the Court, Chartres, Illinois (March 4, 1770), in *Trade and Politics, 1767–1769*, ed. Clarence Walworth Alvord and Clarence Edwin Carter (Springfield: Trustees of the Illinois State Historical Library, 1921), 455; Carter, *Great Britain and the Illinois Country*, 65–66, 72; Thomas Gage to John Wilkins (March 24, 1769), Gage Papers, vol. AS 84, WLCL.

90. Robert Michael Morrissey, *Empire by Collaboration: Indians, Colonists, and Governments in Colonial Illinois Country* (Philadelphia: University of Pennsylvania Press, 2015), 228–29; Thomas Gage to Lord Barrington (May 15, 1768), Gage Papers, vol. ES 12, WLCL.

91. Hints for the Forming Courts of Judicature at the Ilinois, for the Decision of Disputes amongst the Inhabitants, or betwixt the Inhabitants and Traders, Gage Papers, vol. AS 106, WLCL; see also Thomas Gage to John Wilkins (March 9, 1772), Gage Papers, vol. AS 109, WLCL; ibid. (specifying that "[l]es anciennes Loix et Coutumes du Pais" would specify the basis of future laws); Gage to Lord Hillsborough (April 13, 1772), Gage Papers, vol. ES 22, WLCL (reporting this proposal to his superiors).

92. Extract of Letter from Major John Hamilton, 18th Regiment, to General Gage (August 8, 1772), Gage Papers, vol. ES 23, WLCL; Daniel Blouin & William Clajon, Recueil de Pièces traduites de l'Anglais . . . (July 8, 1771), Gage Papers, vol. AS 138, folder 17, WLCL; Morrissey, *Empire by Collaboration*, 228.

93. Thomas Gage to Lord Hillsborough (September 2, 1772), Gage Papers, vol. ES 23, WLCL; Isaac Hamilton to Thomas Gage (August 8, 1772), Gage Papers, vol. AS 113, WLCL.

94. See Roger L. Severns, *Prairie Justice: A History of Illinois Courts under French, English, and American Law* (Carbondale: Southern Illinois University Press, 2015), 20–22.
95. Lords of Trade to George III (September 3, 1766), in *The New Régime*, ed. Alvord and Carter, 371; Thomas Gage to Henry Seymour Conway (March 28, 1766), in *The New Régime*, ed. Alvord and Carter, 197; see also S. Max Edelson, *The New Map of Empire: How Britain Imagined America before Independence* (Cambridge, Mass.: Harvard University Press, 2017), 186–88.
96. See, e.g., Francis Stoughton Sullivan, *An Historical Treatise on the Feudal Law and the Constitution and Laws of England* (London: J. Johnson and J. Payne, 1772) (printing lectures given at the University of Dublin in the early 1760s); Blackstone, *Commentaries*, 2:43; see also Susan Reynolds, *Fiefs and Vassals: The Medieval Evidence Reinterpreted* (Oxford: Clarendon Press, 1996), 6–8 (noting differences between medieval law and eighteenth-century notions of "feudalism").
97. Davis, *Periodization and Sovereignty*, 64–66; Pocock, *The Ancient Constitution and the Feudal Law*; John W. Cairns and Grant McLeod, "Thomas Craig, Sir Martin Wright, and Sir William Blackstone: The English Discovery of Feudalism," *Journal of Legal History* 21, no. 3 (2000): 54–66; John Salter, "Adam Smith on Feudalism, Commerce and Slavery," *History of Political Thought* 13, no. 2 (1992): 219–41; Kames, *Historical Law-Tracts*, 186; see also Dalrymple, *Feudal Property*, 332 (noting "the declensions of almost every part of the feudal system").
98. Chambers, *Lectures on the English Law*, 1:268, 279–80; Granville Sharp, MS annotation on [Edward Long], *Candid Reflections upon the Judgement Lately Awarded by the Court of King's Bench . . . on What Is Commonly Called the Negroe-Cause, by a Planter* (London: T. Lowndes, 1772), 5 (copy in BRBML); see also Brewer, "Slavery, Sovereignty, and 'Inheritable Blood,'" 1042–43; Granville Sharp, *A Representation of the Injustice and Dangerous Tendency of Tolerating Slavery, or of Admitting the Least Claim of Private Property in the Persons of Men, in England* (London: Benjamin White and Robert Horsfield, 1769), 4 (praising the abolition of heritable jurisdictions); cf. Davis, *Periodization and Sovereignty*, 22–23 (discussing early modern attempts to identify feudalism "as characteristic of Europe's past and a non-European present").
99. Tim Mowl, "'Against the Time in Which the Fabric and Use of Gunpowder Shall Be Forgotten': Enmore Castle, Its Origins and Its Architect," *Architectural History* 33 (1990): 102–19; J. M. Bumsted, *Land, Settlement, and Politics on Eighteenth-Century Prince Edward Island* (Kingston, Ont.: McGill-Queen's University Press, 1987), 15–16; Clive Wilkinson, "Perceval, John, second earl of Egmont (1711–1770)," in *DNB*, https://doi.org/10.1093/ref:odnb/21912; Horace Walpole, *Memoirs of the Reign of King George III* (London: Richard Bentley, 1845), 1:387.
100. Draft of a Speech on the Proposed Feudal Tenures Bill ([1746?]), Add MS 47097, 1, BL.
101. [Lord Egmont], [Feudal Tenures] ([1763?]), Add MS 47012B, 187–89, 191, BL; cf. Lord Morton to Duke of Newcastle, "With Respect to a Boundary to Be Settled between Great Britain & France in North America (January 15, 1760), Add MS 35910, 18–19r, BL (estimating that the Ohio Country could support, "with moderate cultivation," about fifty million inhabitants). Egmont's calculations excluded the West Indies.

102. Egmont, "Feudal Tenures."
103. Ibid., 191.
104. Charles Yorke and William de Grey, [Reference on the Grant of Lands in the Island of St. John] ([1766]), Add MS 35914, 87, BL. Yorke and de Grey also noted that Egmont's proposal to limit the alienability of land in St. John's ran afoul of another statute, 5 Geo. 2, c. 7.
105. Henry Seymour Conway played a particularly important role in crushing the feudal dreams of both Egmont and Gage. See Walpole, *Memoirs of the Reign of King George III*, 1:387; Bumsted, *Land, Settlement, and Politics*, 16–17, 24–25.
106. [Maurice Morgann] to Lord Shelburne, [Paper on Trade] ([1766?]), Shelburne Papers, vol. 168, box 2, WLCL; see also Plan Proposed by Gen[era]l Phineas Lyman, for Settling Louisiana, and for Erecting New Colonies between West Florida and the Falls of St. Anthony ([1763–69]), Shelburne Papers, vol. 50, 170–71, WLCL ("The Period will doubtless come when North America will no longer acknowledge a Dependence on any part of Europe, but that Period seems to be so remote as not to be at present an Object of national Policy or human Prevention."); du Rivage, *Revolution against Empire*, 50, 59–60, 188–89; [William] Bollan, *A Succinct View of the Origin of Our Colonies with Their Civil State* (London: n.p., 1766), 33–36.
107. Camden to Robert Stewart (August 21, 1777), U840/C173/18, KA.
108. Dundas to Eden (September 7, 1775), in C. R. Fay, *Adam Smith and the Scotland of His Day* (Cambridge: Cambridge University Press, 1956), 10–14; Jonsson, *Enlightenment's Frontier*, 39–40.
109. See Randall Lesaffer, *European Legal History* (Cambridge: Cambridge University Press, 2009), 448; Richard B. Sher, *Church and University in the Scottish Enlightenment: The Moderate Literati of Edinburgh* (Princeton, N.J.: Princeton University Press, 1985), 179–80, 189, 265–66; Jonsson, *Enlightenment's Frontier*, 25; Donald Winch, *Adam Smith's Politics: An Essay in Historiographic Revision* (Cambridge: Cambridge University Press, 1978), 103–8; see also Levy, *Rationalism, Pluralism, and Freedom*, 141–211. For Ferguson's pervasive concern with disorder, see, e.g., Ferguson to Sir John Macpherson (June 12, 1780), GD51/1/2, Melville Papers, NRS; and Ferguson to William Pulteney (November 7, 1769), in *The Correspondence of Adam Ferguson*, ed. Vincenzo Merolle (London: Pickering & Chatto, 1995), 1:81–83.
110. [Alexander Wedderburn], "Preface," *Edinburgh Review*, 1755; Alexander Wedderburn to Sir Gilbert Eliot (July 2, 1757), MS 11008, Minto Papers, 58r–58v, NLS; David Hume to Adam Smith (April 1759), in *The Correspondence of Adam Smith*, ed. Ernest Campbell Mossner and Ian Simpson Ross, 2d ed. (Oxford: Clarendon Press, 1986), 33; Alexander Wedderburn to Lord Milton (September 21, 1757), Ms. 16702, Milton Papers, 210, NLS; Sher, *Church and University*, 129. For the "heterogeneity" of the Scottish Enlightenment, see Skjönsberg, *Persistence of Party*, 316; and Buchan and Sebastiani, "No Distinction of Black or Fair," 208 & n.3.
111. See Hulsebosch, *Constituting Empire*, 75–83; Sarah Kinkel, "The King's Pirates? Naval Enforcement of Imperial Authority, 1740–76," *William and Mary Quarterly* 71, no. 1 (2014): 9; Marshall, *Making and Unmaking of Empires*, 176; Jonsson, *Enlightenment's Frontier*, 248–51.

112. See, e.g., Holly Brewer, "Entailing Aristocracy in Colonial Virginia: 'Ancient Feudal Restraints' and Revolutionary Reform," *William and Mary Quarterly* 54, no. 2 (1997): 307 (describing the abolition of entail by Revolutionary elites in Virginia as a radical campaign against feudalism).
113. Jonsson, *Enlightenment's Frontier*, 40; Robert Joseph Taylor, ed., *Papers of John Adams* (Cambridge: Belknap Press of Harvard University Press, 1977), 1:113; "Sui Juris," *Boston Gazette*, May 23, 1768, in *Papers of John Adams*, ed. Taylor, 1:211–14; L. Kinvin Wroth and Hiller B. Zobel, eds., *Legal Papers of John Adams* (Cambridge: Belknap Press of Harvard University Press, 1965), 1:228; Catharine Macaulay to John Adams, July 19, 1771, in *Papers of John Adams*, ed. Taylor, 1:250; James Muldoon, "John Adams, Canon Law, and the Ghost of Thomas Becket," in *Empire and Revolutions* (Washington, D.C.: Folger Institute, 1993), 237; "To the *Boston Gazette*," February 15, 1773, in *Papers of John Adams*, ed. Taylor, 1:294–303. The *Dissertation*, originally published serially in the *Boston Gazette*, was republished in the *London Chronicle*.

CHAPTER 3. THE QUEBEC ACT AND ITS ALTERNATIVES

1. [Notes of Debates in the Continental Congress, 17? October 1774], in John Adams, *Diary and Autobiography of John Adams*, ed. L. H. Butterfield (New York: Atheneum, 1964), 2:154.
2. On contemporary anti-Catholicism, see Pauline Maier, "The Pope at Harvard: The Dudleian Lectures, Anti-Catholicism, and the Politics of Protestantism," *Proceedings of the Massachusetts Historical Society*, Third Series, 97 (1985): 16–41; and Breidenbach, *Our Dear-Bought Liberty*, 116–17, 136–37. As Breidenbach points out, the Quebec Act's religious policy wasn't especially innovative; instead, it built on earlier accommodations in Minorca, Gibraltar, and Maryland. Breidenbach, *Our Dear-Bought Liberty*, 147–53. See also Thomas Paine, "Dialogue between General Wolfe and General Gage in a Wood near Boston" (January 4, 1775), in *The Complete Writings of Thomas Paine*, ed. Philip S. Foner (New York: Citadel Press, 1945), 2:47–49. In that imaginary dialogue, Paine had the ghost of a British military hero warn that "popery and French laws in Canada are but a part of that system of despotism, which has been prepared for the colonies." As for John Adams, the threat of "popery" depended on its ties to French law.
3. Quebec Act 1774, 14 Geo. 3 c. 83.
4. See, e.g., Peter N. Miller, *Defining the Common Good: Empire, Religion, and Philosophy in Eighteenth-Century Britain* (Cambridge: Cambridge University Press, 1994), 305–6.
5. See, e.g., Gould, *Among the Powers of the Earth*, 99; Lawson, *Imperial Challenge*, 139–40; Aziz Rana, *The Two Faces of American Freedom* (Cambridge, Mass.: Harvard University Press, 2010), 75–76; Tully, *Strange Multiplicity*, 145–64.
6. See, e.g., Lord Lyttelton, Lords Debates, *PH*, 17:1406; Marriott, *Laws for the Province of Quebec*, 46–48; Meredith, *Letter to the Earl of Chatham*, 35; cf. Benton, *Law and Colonial Cultures*, 12–15 (explaining that jurisdictional differences can reinforce cultural boundaries).

7. See, e.g., Colley, *Britons*, 101–3.
8. [Benjamin Franklin], *The Interest of Great Britain Considered, with Regard to Her Colonies, and the Acquisitions of Canada and Guadaloupe* (London: T. Becket, 1760), 39–41; cf. John Simcoe to Lord Barrington (June 1, 1755), in *Thirteenth Report of the Bureau of Archives for the Province of Ontario*, ed. Alexander Fraser (Toronto: A. T. Wilgress, 1917), 142–43 ("[T]he diversity of Manners, customs, modes of religion, and interests . . . consequent to the difference of climates, provincial laws, products & situation . . . will render a coalition of political views not easily practicable . . . [and] would very solidly establish British dominion."). For the debate over keeping Canada, see Lawson, *Imperial Challenge*, 9–14.
9. Benjamin Franklin, "Join, or Die," *Pennsylvania Gazette*, May 9, 1754, http://loc.gov/pictures/item/2002695523; Francis Maseres to Richard Sutton (August 14, 1768), in *Maseres Letters*, ed. Wallace, 110.
10. See Benjamin Franklin, "Notes on Britain's Intention to Enslave America" ([1774–75?]), in *The Papers of Benjamin Franklin*, ed. Leonard Woods Labaree et al. (New Haven, Conn.: Yale University Press, 1959), 21:608.
11. Marriott, *Laws for the Province of Quebec*, 46–48.
12. Guy Carleton to Lord Hillsborough (November 20, 1768), in *Constitutional History*, ed. Shortt and Doughty, 1:325–26.
13. *PH*, 17:1406.
14. Meredith, *Letter to the Earl of Chatham*, 35.
15. See, e.g., *The Expediency of Securing Our American Colonies by Settling the Country Adjoining the River Mississippi* . . . , 7–8; John Glynn, Commons Debates (May 26, 1774), in *Proceedings and Debates*, 4:464. Participants in the Quebec Act debate disagreed about how quickly England had imposed its law on Ireland and Wales, with each party interpreting the historical record to favor its own cause. See Richard Bourke, "Edmund Burke and the Politics of Conquest," *Modern Intellectual History* 4, no. 3 (2007): 415–20.
16. *A Letter to Sir William Meredith, Bart., in Answer to His Late Letter to the Earl of Chatham* (London: G. Kearsly, 1774), 27.
17. Charles James Fox, Commons Debates (May 26, 1774), in *Proceedings and Debates*, 4:471; see also Articles of Association (October 20, 1774), in *Journals of the Continental Congress*, ed. Worthington Chauncey Ford (Washington, D.C.: G.P.O., 1904), 1:76 (warning that "civil [law] principles" would "dispose the inhabitants [of Quebec] to act with hostility against" other American colonies).
18. Edmund Burke to Sir Charles Bingham (October 30, 1773), in *Burke Correspondence*, ed. Copeland, 2:474–76 (emphasis added). This was a new position for Burke, who had supported a similar tax as a young man. See Bourke, *Empire & Revolution*, 393–94; Thomas F. Moriarty, "The Irish Absentee Tax Controversy of 1773: A Study in Anglo-Irish Politics on the Eve of the American Revolution," *Proceedings of the American Philosophical Society* 118, no. 4 (1974): 381, 400–404.
19. See Burke to Committee of Correspondence of the General Assembly of New York (August 2, 1774), in *Burke Correspondence*, ed. Copeland, 3:14; see also Burke, Speech on Conciliation with America (March 22, 1775), in *Writings and Speeches*, ed. Mc-

Loughlin and Boulton, 3:161 & n.1 (warning that the ministry was pursuing a policy of *divide et impera*).
20. Carleton to Lord Shelburne (December 24, 1767), in *Constitutional History*, ed. Shortt and Doughty, 1:289; see also Carleton to Shelburne (April 12, 1768), in *Constitutional History*, ed. Shortt and Doughty, 1:303 ("The Canadian Tenures . . . will ever secure a proper Subordination from this Province to Great Britain.").
21. Edward Thurlow, Report of the Attorney General (January 22, 1773), in *Constitutional History*, ed. Shortt and Doughty, 1:305. Historians of New France have shown that its legal system was indeed more focused on preserving order than protecting individual rights. See Alexandra Havrylyshyn, "Troublesome Trials: How a Parisian Legal Practitioner Disrupted the Order of New France," *William & Mary Quarterly* 78, no. 1 (2021): 45–78.
22. See, e.g., Blackstone, *Commentaries*, 3:2, 22–24.
23. See Pincus, *1688*, 192–97; Amy Watson, "The New York Patriot Movement: Partisanship, the Free Press, and Britain's Imperial Constitution, 1731–39," *William and Mary Quarterly* 77, no. 1 (2020): 56–62.
24. See David Feldman, "The Politics and People of *Entick v Carrington*," in *Entick v Carrington: 250 Years of the Rule of Law*, ed. Adam Tomkins and Paul Scott (Oxford: Hart Publishing, 2017), 23; John Brewer, "The Wilkites and the Law, 1763–74: A Study of Radical Notions of Governance," in *An Ungovernable People: The English and Their Law in the Seventeenth and Eighteenth Centuries*, ed. John Brewer and John Styles (New Brunswick, N.J.: Rutgers University Press, 1980), 128–71; Stephan Landsman, "The Rise of the Contentious Spirit: Adversary Procedure in Eighteenth Century England," *Cornell Law Review* 75 (1990): 583–89.
25. Francis Bernard to Board of Trade (August 6, 1761), in *The Papers of Francis Bernard: Governor of Colonial Massachusetts, 1760–69*, ed. Colin Nicholson (Boston: Colonial Society of Massachusetts, 2007), 1:134; see John Phillip Reid, *In a Defiant Stance: The Conditions of Law in Massachusetts Bay, the Irish Comparison, and the Coming of the American Revolution* (University Park: Pennsylvania State University Press, 1977), 30–32.
26. Thomas Gage to Henry Bouquet (June 2, 1765), Gage Papers, vol. AS 36, WLCL.
27. John Wilkins to Thomas Gage (June 9, 1771), Gage Papers, vol. AS 103, WLCL.
28. See Oldham, *English Common Law*, 299–300 (noting that Mansfield was "far less tolerant" than his predecessors of sheriffs who mistakenly seized goods); Halliday, *Habeas Corpus*, 55.
29. Hector Theophilus Cramahé, Lieutenant Governor of Quebec, to [Lord Rochford], Secretary of State (July 25, 1772), CO 43/13, 43, TNA.
30. See Brewer, "Wilkites and the Law," 154; cf. Akhil Reed Amar, *The Bill of Rights: Creation and Reconstruction* (New Haven, Conn.: Yale University Press, 1998), 94–96 (describing eighteenth-century views of "jurors as political participants").
31. See Presentments of the Grand Jury of Quebec (October 16, 1764), in *Constitutional History*, ed. Shortt and Doughty, 1:212–13; Mr. Gridley, Answer to the Presentments of the Grand Jury (1764), CO 42/2, 33, TNA. Grand juries also claimed representative functions in East Florida and South Carolina. Mirow, "The Thistle, the Rose, and the Palm," 91.

32. Entry of October 8, 1765, in *Acts of the Privy Council of England: Colonial Series*, ed. W. L. Grant, James Munro, and Sir Almeric W. Fitzroy (Hereford: Printed for H.M.S.O., by the Hereford Times, 1908–1912), 4:722.
33. See Marriott, *Laws for the Province of Quebec*, 62.
34. Lord North, Commons Debates (June 10, 1774), in *Proceedings and Debates*, 5:219.
35. John Glynn, Commons Debates (June 10, 1774), in *Proceedings and Debates*, 5:185, 186; see also John Dunning, Common Debates (May 26, 1774), in *Proceedings and Debates*, 4:451.
36. See T. T. Arvind and Christian R. Burset, "A New Report of *Entick v. Carrington* (1765)," *Kentucky Law Journal* 110 (2022): 281–85. On the importance of tort suits against government officials, see James E. Pfander, *Constitutional Torts and the War on Terror* (New York: Oxford University Press, 2017), 4–5; and Jerry L. Mashaw, *Creating the Administrative Constitution: The Lost One Hundred Years of American Administrative Law* (New Haven, Conn.: Yale University Press, 2012), 63, 76.
37. Jed Handelsman Shugerman, *The People's Courts: Pursuing Judicial Independence in America* (Cambridge, Mass.: Harvard University Press, 2012), 17–19.
38. See, e.g., Francis Maseres, *Additional Papers concerning the Province of Quebeck* (London: W. White, 1776), 298–300.
39. John Glynn, Commons Debates (June 10, 1774), in *Proceedings and Debates*, 5:186.
40. Government of Quebec Bill: Committee (May 31, 1774), in *Proceedings and Debates*, 4:498–99.
41. Marriott, *Laws for the Province of Quebec*, 47–48.
42. Hillsborough to Guy Carleton (November 15, 1768), CO 43/8, 56, TNA; see also George Grenville to William Knox (June 27, 1768), William Knox Papers, box 1, folder 27, WLCL ("[N]or do I think it possible to prevent all manufactures entirely in our colonies, & the attempting to do it by force . . . would be most violent & unjust, as well as impracticable."); "Sunday's and Monday's Posts," *York Chronicle and Weekly Advertiser* (January 8, 1773), 26; Francis Maseres to Fowler Walker (November 19, 1767), in *Maseres Letters*, ed. Wallace, 61; Lawson, *Imperial Challenge*, 113–14.
43. Griffin, *American Leviathan*, 19–96; Taylor, *American Revolutions*, 72–75.
44. Adam Smith, *An Inquiry into the Nature and Causes of the Wealth of Nations*, ed. R. H. Campbell and Andrew S. Skinner (Indianapolis: Liberty Fund, 1976), 2:582.
45. Hillsborough to Carleton (November 15, 1768), CO 43/8, 56, TNA.
46. See, e.g., Thomas Gage to Lord Barrington (December 2, 1772), Gage Papers, vol. ES 23, WLCL.
47. Pincus, *Heart of the Declaration*, 117–21, 150–51; Declaration of Independence para. 9 ("[George III] has endeavoured to prevent the population of these States.").
48. Lawson, *Imperial Challenge*, 113–14; *Constitutional History*, ed. Shortt and Doughty, 1:57–59.
49. Proponents of the Stamp Act had followed a similar logic: because unstamped documents lacked legal effect, they argued, "the tax would be largely self-enforcing." P. D. G. Thomas, *British Politics and the Stamp Act Crisis: The First Phase of the American Revolution 1763–1767* (Oxford: Clarendon Press, 1975), 91. For the imperial state's weakness in the colonies, see Ford, *The King's Peace*, 22–99.

50. Memorial & Petition from the Merchants & Traders of the City of London Trading to Canada on Behalf of Themselves & Others (April 18, 1765), CO 42/2, 102, TNA; Memorial of Fowler Walker, Agent on Behalf of the Merchants, Traders, and Others the Principal Inhabitants of the Cities of Quebec and Montreal (1765), CO 42/2, 113, TNA; Memorial of the Merchants and Other Inhabitants of the City of Quebec (April 10, 1770), CO 42/8, 7–8, TNA.
51. Case of the British Merchants Trading to Quebec (1774), in Francis Maseres, *An Account of the Proceedings of the British, and Other Protestant Inhabitants, of the Province of Quebeck, in North-America: In Order to Obtain an House of Assembly in That Province* (London: Sold by B. White, 1775), 202–9.
52. Smith, *Wealth of Nations*, 1:419.
53. Testimony to the House of Commons (June 2, 1774), in *Proceedings and Debates* 5:20 (question from Mr. Baker to Francis Maseres).
54. Edmund Burke, Commons Debates (June 10, 1774), in *Proceedings and Debates*, 5:208; see also Captain Phipps, Commons Debates (May 31, 1774), in *Proceedings and Debates*, 4:486.
55. Alexander Wedderburn, Report (December 6, 1772), in *Constitutional History*, ed. Shortt and Doughty, 1:430.
56. Knox, *Justice and Policy*, 42–43; see also [Bernard], *Appeal to the Public*, 55; Dartmouth to Hillsborough (May 1, 1774), in *Constitutional History*, ed. Shortt and Doughty, 1:554 ("[I]f it is not wished that British Subjects should settle [the interior,] nothing can more effectually tend to discourage such attempts.").
57. See Jack M. Sosin, *Whitehall and the Wilderness: The Middle West in British Colonial Policy, 1760–1775* (Lincoln: University of Nebraska Press, 1961), 4; Calloway, *The Scratch of a Pen*, 92–100.
58. Remarks on the State of Newfoundland, Cape Breton, Nova Scotia, and Canada, collected by Wm. Vaughan (January 3, 1745), PRO 30/8/98/1, 126–27, TNA.
59. Report of the Board of Trade (June 8, 1763), Add MS 35913, 232, BL.
60. See Marriott, *Laws for the Province of Quebec*, 14–15; Commission of Captain-General & Governor in Chief of the Province of Quebec (November 28, 1763), in *Constitutional History*, ed. Shortt and Doughty, 1:173–81; Board of Trade to George III (June 8, 1763), in *Constitutional History*, ed. Shortt and Doughty, 1:142–47; John Dunning, Commons Debates, (May 26, 1774), in *Proceedings and Debates*, 4:452; Willis, "Rethinking Ireland and Assimilation," 168–69; Edelson, *The New Map of Empire*, 59–61.
61. Commons Debates (June 2, 1774), in *Proceedings and Debates*, 5:4–5.
62. Commons Debates (June 13, 1774), in *Proceedings and Debates*, 5:226; Charles James Fox, Commons Debates (June 2, 1774), in *Proceedings and Debates*, 5:4–5.
63. Commons Debates (June 2, 1774), in *Proceedings and Debates*, 5:18.
64. Continental Association (October 20, 1774), in *Papers of John Adams*, ed. Taylor, 2:397; see also Silas Deane to Patrick Henry (January 2, 1775), Schoff Revolutionary War Collection, box 1, WLCL (arguing that the Quebec Act was meant to block "Settlements of True and well principled Protestants Westward"); Benjamin Franklin to Jonathan Shipley (March 10, 1774), in *The Papers of Benjamin Franklin*, ed. Labaree et al., 21:138–40.

Some populists expressed a different concern: that the Quebec Act would discourage Protestant immigration while also attracting Catholics. See, e.g., Alexander Hamilton, Remarks on the Quebec Bill (June 22, 1775), in *The Papers of Alexander Hamilton*, ed. Harold C. Syrett and Jacob E. Cooke (New York: Columbia University Press, 1961), 1:175; John Jay, Address to the People of Great Britain (October 21, 1774), in *The Selected Papers of John Jay*, ed. Elizabeth M. Nuxoll (Charlottesville: University of Virginia Press, 2010–2015), 1:101–07; *Observations and Reflections on an Act Passed in the Year, 1774, for the Settlement of the Province of Quebec: Intended to Have Been Then Printed for the Use of the Electors of Great Britain, but Now First Published* (London: J. Stockdale, 1782), 24. But such an outcome would have been inconsistent with paternalists' efforts to limit Quebec's population. Conversely, paternalists sometimes accused populists of wanting to expel Catholics. See, e.g., James Murray to Lords of Trade (October 29, 1764), in *Constitutional History*, ed. Shortt and Doughty, 1:231. There was precedent for that with the expulsion of the Acadians. But by the late 1760s, populists were more interested in assimilation than expulsion.

65. Memorandum to the Board of Trade, Some Thoughts on the Settlement and Government of Our Colonies in North America (March 10, 1763), Shelburne Papers, vol. 48, folder 44, 523–27, WLCL; see also *Letter to Sir William Meredith*, 5; Maurice Morgann, An Account of the State of Canada from Its Conquest to May 1766 ([1766–67?]), Shelburne Papers, vol. 64, 548–50, WLCL.
66. Case of the British Merchants Trading to Quebec, 210.
67. Thomas Townshend Jr., Commons Debates (June 7, 1774), in *Proceedings and Debates*, 5:106; see also Commons Debates (June 10, 1774), in *Proceedings and Debates*, 5:200.
68. Case of the British Merchants Trading to Quebec, 211. The Quebec Act didn't exclude the writ of habeas corpus, but until 1784 there was some doubt about its availability. Halliday, *Habeas Corpus*, 275–81.
69. See, e.g., Ron Harris and Michael Crystal, "Some Reflections on the Transplantation of British Company Law in Post-Ottoman Palestine," *Theoretical Inquiries in Law* 10, no. 2 (2009): 562–63, 568; Fernanda G. Nicola, "Family Law Exceptionalism in Comparative Law," *American Journal of Comparative Law* 58, no. 4 (2010): 787–89; see also Yun-chien Chang and Henry E. Smith, "An Economic Analysis of Civil versus Common Law Property," *Notre Dame Law Review* 88 (2012): 20–21 (arguing that property law is especially resistant to change); Ryan Bubb, "The Evolution of Property Rights: State Law or Informal Norms?," *Journal of Law and Economics* 56 (2013): 589 (suggesting that it might be easier to change inheritance practices than property rights).
70. See, e.g., Harry Verelst, *A View of the Rise, Progress, and Present State of the English Government in Bengal* (London: J. Nourse, 1772), 133–35.
71. Edward Gibbon, *The History of the Decline and Fall of the Roman Empire*, ed. J. B. Bury (New York: Fred de Fau, 1906), 1:46. Some comparative lawyers today cite family law as a leading example of transnational convergence. See, e.g., Nicola, "Family Law Exceptionalism in Comparative Law," 805–9; cf. Ivana Isailovic, "Same Sex but Not the Same: Same-Sex Marriage in the United States and France and the Universalist Narrative," *American Journal of Comparative Law* 66, no. 2 (2018): 267–315 (de-

scribing and questioning the dominant assumption that same-sex marriage laws are "homogenous" and "transferable across jurisdictions"). Compare Kahn-Freund, "On Uses and Misuses of Comparative Law," 19–20 (arguing that procedural law is transplant-resistant), with Guy I. Seidman, "Comparative Civil Procedure," in *The Dynamism of Civil Procedure: Global Trends and Developments*, ed. Colin B. Picker and Guy I. Seidman (Cham, Switzerland: Springer International Publishing, 2016), 6–7 (rejecting that claim). See also Mitra J. Sharafi, *Law and Identity in Colonial South Asia: Parsi Legal Culture, 1772–1947* (New York: Cambridge University Press, 2014), 235; Anna Dolganov, "Reichsrecht and Volksrecht in Theory and Practice: Roman Justice in the Province of Egypt," *Tyche* 34 (2019): 39 (noting that the Roman Empire preserved a distinctive Egyptian family law).

72. See Duncan Kennedy, "Savigny's Family/Patrimony Distinction and Its Place in the Global Genealogy of Classical Legal Thought," *American Journal of Comparative Law* 58, no. 4 (2010): 811–41.

73. Alan Watson, *Legal Transplants: An Approach to Comparative Law* (Charlottesville: University Press of Virginia, 1974), 98; Toby S. Goldbach, "Why Legal Transplants?," *Annual Review of Law and Social Science* 15, no. 1 (2019): 592–93.

74. Several scholars have noted that the British Empire was more likely to transplant some kinds of English law than others, particularly in the nineteenth and twentieth centuries. E.g., T. O. Elias, *British Colonial Law: A Comparative Study of the Interaction between English and Local Laws in British Dependencies* (London: Stevens, 1962), 287; Adam S. Hofri-Winogradow, "Zionist Settlers and the English Private Trust in Mandate Palestine," *Law and History Review* 30, no. 3 (2012): 815; Assaf Likhovski, *Law and Identity in Mandate Palestine* (Chapel Hill: University of North Carolina Press, 2006), 55–56. Paul Halliday notes that property law was more likely to vary among colonies than laws dealing with personal rights. Halliday, *Habeas Corpus*, 263. The distinctive treatment of commercial law in Quebec is narrated in Edouard Fabre-Surveyer, "The Struggle for English Commercial Law in Canada," *Commercial Law League Journal* 34 (1929): 616–24.

75. This was not the first time that English lawyers thought about selective legal uniformity. Edward Coke and Matthew Hale had emphasized the importance of a uniform property and inheritance law for economic and political integration. Francis Bacon, in contrast, thought that a uniform public law was more important than uniform land tenures. Bilder, *Transatlantic Constitution*, 32–34; Hulsebosch, *Constituting Empire*, 27–28. A provincial ordinance of November 6, 1764, had provided for the temporary retention of French tenures and inheritance rights. See *Constitutional History*, ed. Shortt and Doughty, 1:331–32.

76. Charles Yorke and William de Grey, Report of Attorney and Solicitor General Regarding the Civil Government of Quebec (April 14, 1766), in *Constitutional History*, ed. Shortt and Doughty, 1:255–56; Francis Maseres to Fowler Walker (November 19, 1767), in *Maseres Letters*, ed. Wallace, 55, 58; Francis Maseres to Richard Sutton (August 14, 1768), in *Maseres Letters*, ed. Wallace, 108; [Francis Maseres], *The Canadian Freeholder: A Dialogue, Shewing, the Sentiments of the Bulk of the Freeholders of Canada Concerning the Late Quebeck-Act* (London: B. White, 1776), 19–25; Francis Maseres to

Sir John Eardley Wilmot (August 16, 1773), OSB MSS File 9999, BRBML; Neatby, *Quebec*, 106; see also William de Grey to Lord Rockingham (February 10, 1774), WWM/R/1/1481, SA ("[T]he General Idea . . . was to leave to the Canadians their own Laws relative to Land, to give them the Criminal Laws of England as far as they were applicable to that Country, and upon personal Rights and Contracts to determine by the general Principles of Justice which are, to some degree, the same in most European Countries.").

77. John Dunning, Commons Debates (June 10, 1774), in *Proceedings and Debates*, 5:221. Some commentators argued that the Proclamation of 1763 should be read against this background. Michel Morin, "The Discovery and Assimilation of British Constitutional Law Principles in Quebec, 1764–1774," *Dalhousie Law Journal* 36 (2013): 611–12.

78. John Lind, *Remarks on the Principal Acts of the Thirteenth Parliament of Great Britain* (London: T. Payne, 1775), 471. Such blends of local substance and centrally dictated procedure were a common feature of European law. James Q. Whitman, "Western Legal Imperialism: Thinking about the Deep Historical Roots," *Theoretical Inquiries in Law* 10, no. 2 (2009): 328.

79. Edward Thurlow, Opinion on Lord Clive's Jaghire (December 1763), in *Collectanea Juridica: Consisting of Tracts Relative to the Law and Constitution of England*, ed. Francis Hargrave (London: E. and R. Brooke, 1791), 1:253–54; see also Pike v. Hoare (1763) 28 Eng. Rep. 867, 867; 2 Eden 182, 184 (Ch.) (Henley, L. C.) (drawing a similar contrast).

80. See Meredith, *Letter to the Earl of Chatham*, 15.

81. F. W. Maitland, *Equity, Also the Forms of Action at Common Law*, ed. A. H. Chaytor and W. J. Whittaker (Cambridge: Cambridge University Press, 1910), 295–301; see also Henry Sumner Maine, *Dissertations on Early Law and Custom* (London: John Murray, 1883), 384.

82. Duncan Kennedy, "The Structure of Blackstone's Commentaries," *Buffalo Law Review* 28, no. 2 (1979): 231–33; William E. Nelson, *Americanization of the Common Law: The Impact of Legal Change on Massachusetts Society, 1760–1830* (Athens: University of Georgia Press, 1975), 69–88; Daniel J. Hulsebosch, "Writs to Rights: Navigability and the Transformation of the Common Law in the Nineteenth Century," *Cardozo Law Review* 23 (2002): 1068; see also Amalia D. Kessler, *Inventing American Exceptionalism: The Origins of American Adversarial Legal Culture, 1800–1877* (New Haven, Conn.: Yale University Press, 2017), 11–12 (arguing that "the category of procedure did not exist in any meaningful way before the mid-nineteenth century").

83. Francis Maseres, Testimony to the House of Commons (June 2, 1774), in *Proceedings and Debates*, 5:18; [William Dowdeswell], Observations on Mr Maseres['s] letters to Mr T. Townshend (November 11, 1766), William Dowdeswell Papers, folder 10, WLCL; Philip Yorke, 2d Earl of Hardwicke to Lord Rockingham (June 30, 1766), WWM/R/1/638, SA.

84. Testimony of the Marquis de Lotbinière (June 3, 1774), in *Proceedings and Debates*, 5:61; see also Michel Morin, "Blackstone and the Birth of Quebec's Legal Culture 1765–1867," in *Re-Interpreting Blackstone's Commentaries: A Seminal Text in National and International Contexts*, ed. Wilfrid Prest (Oxford: Hart Publishing, 2014), 114.

85. Commons Debates (June 2, 1774), in *Proceedings and Debates*, 5:3.
86. Francis Maseres, Draught of an Intended Report . . . (1769), in *Constitutional History*, ed. Shortt and Doughty, 1:347.
87. Marriott, *Laws for the Province of Quebec*, 27; Donald Fyson, "The Conquered and the Conqueror: The Mutual Adaptation of the Canadiens and the British In Quebec, 1759–1775," in *Revisiting 1759*, 205; Notes on the Affairs of Quebec ([1767?]), Shelburne Papers, vol. 64, 471, WLCL; (May 31, 1774), Committee Discussion of Quebec Bill, in *Proceedings and Debates*, 4:498; Willis, "Rethinking Ireland and Assimilation," 172–73.
88. Thomas Gage to John Wilkins (March 9, 1772), Gage Papers, vol. AS 109, WLCL; Gage to Lord Hillsborough (April 13, 1772), Gage Papers, vol. ES 22, WLCL; Gage to Lord Hillsborough (September 2, 1772), Gage Papers, vol. ES 23, WLCL; Isaac Hamilton to Gage (August 8, 1772), Gage Papers, vol. AS 113, WLCL.
89. Testimony of William Hey in the House of Commons (June 2, 1774), in *Proceedings and Debates*, 5:30; Francis Maseres, Statement to the Commons (June 2, 1774), in *Proceedings and Debates*, 5:18; see also "London," *Quebec Gazette*, December 26, 1771 ("[A] proposition now lies before government, to make the majority of a jury sufficient to acquit or condemn, instead of requiring the verdict to be unanimous, which is productive of many consequences equally repugnant to reason and humanity."). Canadiens also suggested that there be an odd number of jurors (to make a tied vote impossible) and that jurors be compensated for their time.
90. Lind, *Remarks on the Principal Acts*, 473–74.
91. Paternalists countered that it would be fraudulent to give Canadians the appearance of an English jury without its substance. "That is not an English jury," Alexander Wedderburn told the Commons. "Better [for them to] be without a jury until they are fitted to receive such a jury." Commons Debates (June 10, 1774), in *Proceedings and Debates*, 5:198; see also Lord North, Commons Debates (June 10, 1774), in *Proceedings and Debates*, 5:219; Meredith, *Letter to the Earl of Chatham*, 11–14 ("[A]n English jury . . . in an imperfect state . . . would be the worst way of trial upon earth.").
92. Burke, Notes for Speech on the Canada Bill (1774), WWM/Bk P/6/5, SA; Burke, Commons Debates (June 10, 1774), in *Proceedings and Debates*, 5:204; Bourke, *Empire & Revolution*, 466–67.
93. Fowler Walker, Considerations on the Present State of the Province of Quebec (March 1, 1766), Add MS 35915, 45, BL; see also "To the Printer," *Quebec Gazette*, July 25, 1767; Montesquieu, *The Spirit of the Laws*, 74. For some differences between Walker's position and that of other moderate lawyers, see Michel Morin, "Choosing between French and English Law: The Legal Origins of the Quebec Act," in *Entangling the Quebec Act*, ed. Hubert and Furstenberg, 107–8.
94. Canadiens worried about the difficulty of securing convictions under English law. Some also worried that the publicity of English trials might humiliate innocent defendants, especially since private parties often brought prosecutions. See Douglas Hay, "The Meanings of the Criminal Law in Quebec, 1764–1774," in *Crime and Criminal Justice in Europe and Canada*, ed. Louis A. Knafla (Waterloo, Ont.: Published for Calgary Institute for the Humanities by Wilfrid Laurier University Press, 1981), 89–96; Morin, "Discovery and Assimilation," 586 n.18.

95. Blackstone, *Commentaries*, 3:423–24, 4:344; cf. Kennedy, "Structure of Blackstone's Commentaries," 247.
96. *Observations and Reflections on an Act Passed in the Year, 1774*, 19–20; see also Maseres, *Additional Papers Concerning the Province of Quebeck*, 297–98; "To the Printer," *Public Advertiser* (May 19, 1774), 6 ("How are Debts to be proved by People residing in Great Britain against People in Quebec? What is the Interest of Money in that Country, and what Damages on Bills of Exchange?").
97. Petition of Merchants for Repeal of the Quebec Act (April 2, 1778), in *Constitutional History*, ed. Shortt and Doughty, 2:694. On merchants' preference for arbitration (and their inability to rely on it exclusively), see Burset, "Arbitrating the England Problem."
98. Smith, *Wealth of Nations*, 2:572–73.
99. Indeed, as Claire Priest has emphasized, the Debt Recovery Act itself had departed from English practice by making land vulnerable to the claims of unsecured creditors. An Act for the More Easy Recovery of Debts in His Majesty's Plantations and Colonies in America, 5 Geo. 2, c. 7 (1732); "To the Printer," *Public Advertiser* (London), May 19, 1774, 6; Claire Priest, *Credit Nation: Property Laws and Institutions in Early America* (Princeton, N.J.: Princeton University Press, 2021), 74–89. Although nothing in the Quebec Act prohibited applying the Debt Recovery Act to Quebec, the issue remained unsettled until the early nineteenth century. John C. Weaver, "While Equity Slumbered: Creditor Advantage, A Capitalist Land Market, and Upper Canada's Missing Court," *Osgoode Hall Law Journal* 28 (1990): 877–78.
100. Christie, *Formal and Informal Politics*, 3; Françoise Noël, *The Christie Seigneuries: Estate Management and Settlement in the Upper Richelieu Valley, 1760–1854* (Montreal: McGill-Queen's University Press, 1992), 13, 49, 136; Allan Greer, *Property and Dispossession: Natives, Empires and Land in Early Modern North America* (Cambridge: Cambridge University Press, 2018), 400; Hector Theophilus Cramahé to Lord Hillsborough (May 5, 1772), CO 42/8, 79, TNA.
101. Lord Hillsborough's Objections to the Quebec Bill in Its Present Form, in *Constitutional History*, ed. Shortt and Doughty, 1:552–54; see also Carleton to Lord Shelburne (April 12, 1768), in *Constitutional History*, ed. Shortt and Doughty, 1:300. Conversely, some of the Quebec Act's opponents were wary of retaining Canadian land law. Although Fowler Walker conceded that Britain should preserve "[s]uch of the ancient laws of Canada which concern real property as are found to coincide with the genius and spirit of the english laws," he found it harder to accept the persistence of laws that "greatly differ" from the laws of England. But even he conceded that land tenures "repugnant" to the laws of England should "not be wantonly abrogated but rather corrected and alter'd with much care & deliberation." Fowler Walker, Considerations on the Present State of the Province of Quebec (March 1, 1766), Add MS 35915, 45, BL. For real property in New France, see Greer, *Property and Dispossession*, 144–89.
102. Quebec Act 1774, 14 Geo. 3, c. 83, § 10; see Alexander Wedderburn, Commons Debates (May 26, 1774), in *Proceedings and Debates*, 4:469. The Act also exempted lands that had been granted "in free and common Soccage" from the requirements of French property law. Quebec Act, § 9.

103. Alexander Wedderburn ([1772]), R2903-0-4-E, Edmund Burke Fonds, National Archives (Canada); see also Lord North, Commons Debates (May 26, 1774), in *Proceedings and Debates* 4:447 (describing English criminal law as "a more refined, a more merciful law, than the law of France").

104. Oldham, *English Common Law*, 40–41; Peter King and Richard Ward, "Rethinking the Bloody Code in Eighteenth-Century Britain: Capital Punishment at the Centre and on the Periphery," *Past & Present* 228, no. 1 (2015): 172 & n.40; Langford, *A Polite and Commercial People*, 494; Ford, *The King's Peace*, 58–99; Thomas Gage to John Wilkins (March 9, 1772), Gage Papers, vol. AS 109, WLCL; Morrissey, *Empire by Collaboration*, 229; Daniel Blouin to Lord Dartmouth (October 6, 1773), CO 5/74, 175–76, TNA. In 1782, Lord Shelburne's (populist) government responded to a rise in crime by refusing to pardon anyone convicted of robbery—a severe departure from the usual operation of criminal law. Three years later, Shelburne's ally James Townsend criticized the (paternalist) government of William Pitt the Younger for executing too few criminals. Simon Devereaux, "Inexperienced Humanitarians? William Wilberforce, William Pitt, and the Execution Crisis of the 1780s," *Law and History Review* 33, no. 4 (2015): 844–46, 861.

105. Douglas Hay, "Property, Authority and the Criminal Law," in *Albion's Fatal Tree: Crime and Society in Eighteenth-Century England*, ed. Douglas Hay, Peter Linebaugh, and Cal Winslow (New York: Pantheon Books, 1975); E. P. Thompson, *Whigs and Hunters: The Origin of the Black Act* (New York: Pantheon Books, 1975); Catherine L. Evans, "Heart of Ice: Indigenous Defendants and Colonial Law in the Canadian North-West," *Law and History Review* 36, no. 2 (2018): 199–234; Ford, *The King's Peace*, 137–75; Kolsky, "The Colonial Rule of Law and the Legal Regime of Exception."

106. John Dunning, Commons Debates (May 26, 1774), in *Proceedings and Debates* 4:451. In the nineteenth century, jurists would also emphasize the importance of private litigation in preserving English liberty. See, e.g., A. V. Dicey, *The Law of the Constitution*, ed. J. W. F. Allison (Oxford: Oxford University Press, 2013); Rudolph von Jhering, *The Struggle for Law*, trans. John J. Lalor, 2d ed. (Chicago: Callaghan, 1915), 99–100; cf. John H. Langbein, "Albion's Fatal Flaws," *Past and Present* 98, no. 1 (1983): 119 (arguing that "the criminal justice system occupies a place not much more central than the garbage collection system" in promoting the agenda of the ruling class).

107. Paulus Aemilius Irving to the Lords of Trade (August 20, 1766), in *Constitutional History*, ed. Shortt and Doughty, 1:269–70; see also Francis Maseres to Charles Yorke (November 15, 1766), Add MS 35638, 43, BL; Francis Maseres, *Considerations on the Expediency of Procuring an Act of Parliament for the Settlement of the Province of Quebec* (London: n.p., 1766), 363 (arguing that "the revival of the French laws in these particulars" would promote the eventual anglicization of the colony by encouraging Canadiens to "acquiesce very chearfully in the general establishment of the laws of England"); cf. Morin, "Choosing between French and English Law," 103 ("[U]p to the final stages of the drafting of the Quebec Act, it was assumed that . . . the laws in force prior to the Conquest would eventually disappear.").

108. For examples of the extreme populist position, see "To the Members of the House of

Commons," *Public Ledger,* May 31, 1774; Alexander Hamilton, "Remarks on the Quebec Bill: Part One" (June 15, 1775), in *Hamilton Papers,* ed. Syrett and Cooke, 1:165.

109. John Glynn, Commons Debates (June 10, 1774), in *Proceedings and Debates,* 5:185; Isaac Barré, Commons Debates (June 2, 1774), in *Proceedings and Debates,* 5:3; see also John Faulkner, "Burke's First Encounter with Richard Price: The Chathamites and North America," in *An Imaginative Whig: Reassessing the Life and Thought of Edmund Burke,* ed. Ian Crowe (Columbia: University of Missouri Press, 2005), 93.

110. See, e.g., Lawson, *Imperial Challenge,* 71–72 (noting Dartmouth's support for an elected assembly in Quebec); Dartmouth to Guy Carleton (December 10, 1774), in *Constitutional History,* ed. Shortt and Doughty, 2:585 (chiding Carleton for being "silent as to the Sentiments of His Majesty's Natural born Subjects in Canada respecting the late Act").

111. Instructions to Governor Carleton (January 3, 1775), in *Constitutional History,* ed. Shortt and Doughty, 2:599. The same instructions directed Carleton to form courts in Illinois.

112. Guy Carleton to Lord Dartmouth (June 7, 1775), in *Constitutional History,* ed. Shortt and Doughty, 2:665.

113. See Brown, *Moral Capital,* 33–206; Pincus, *Heart of the Declaration,* 121–27; Sebastiani, "Hume versus Montesquieu," 41–42.

114. Shebbeare, *One More Letter to the People of England,* 16–17. For Shebbeare's support of the Quebec Act, see John Shebbeare, *An Answer to the Queries, Contained in a Letter to Dr. Shebbeare, Printed in the Public Ledger, August 10* (London: S. Hooper, 1774).

115. See O'Shaughnessy, *An Empire Divided;* cf. Brown, *Tacky's Revolt,* 218–19 (discussing Jamaica's obedience).

116. Campbell v. Hall (1774) 98 Eng. Rep. 1045; 1 Cowp. 204 (K.B.) (Mansfield, C. J.).

117. Objects to Be Attended to in Granting Lands in the Newly Acquired Islands ([after 1763]), Shelburne Papers, vol. 74, 63, WLCL; Some Hints for the Better Settlement of the Ceded Islands ([1763]), Shelburne Papers, vol. 48, folder 46, 567, WLCL; Some Hints for the Better Settlement of the Ceded Islands, 567; Robert Melvill, Some General Heads Submitted concerning the Most Eligible Plan of Government for the New Acquired Islands . . . , Shelburne Papers, vol. 74, 51, WLCL; O'Shaughnessy, *An Empire Divided,* 124–25; Marshall, *Edmund Burke and the British Empire in the West Indies,* 67; Karen Stanbridge, "Quebec and the Irish Catholic Relief Act of 1778: An Institutional Approach," *Journal of Historical Sociology* 16, no. 3 (2003): 396; Wood Renton, "French Law within the British Empire," 103; Anderson, *Crucible of War,* 490.

118. Calloway, *The Scratch of a Pen,* 155–57; Carter, *Great Britain and the Illinois Country,* 135; Robin F. A. Fabel, *The Economy of British West Florida, 1763–1783* (Tuscaloosa: University of Alabama Press, 1988), 6–7, 138–40.

119. See, e.g., [James Harris], Hints Relative to the Division and Government of the Conquered and Newly Acquired Countries in America (June 1, 1763), Shelburne Papers, vol. 48, folder 45, 552–53, WLCL (arguing that because the Floridas would

likely "be settled either by foreign Protestants, or the King's natural born subjects," the colonial constitution should be modeled on that of "Georgia, or Nova Scotia").
120. [William Knox], Hints Respecting the Settlement of Florida 8 ([1763]), William Knox Papers, box 9, folder 3, WLCL. Knox also argued for freedom of religion, so that Britain could more easily recruit non-Anglican settlers.
121. George Johnstone to Major Robert Farmar (January 7, 1765), Gage Papers, vol. AS 30, WLCL.
122. Emma Rothschild, *The Inner Life of Empires: An Eighteenth-Century History* (Princeton, N.J.: Princeton University Press, 2011), 42 (quoting Charles-Philippe Aubry, French governor of Louisiana, to the French minister of the navy [April 24, 1765]).
123. Calloway, *The Scratch of a Pen*, 152–56; Edelson, *The New Map of Empire*, 256; M. C. Mirow, "The Court of Common Pleas of East Florida 1763–1783," *Legal History Review* 85 (2017): 544; Richmond F. Brown, "Colonial Mobile, 1712–1813," in *Mobile: The New History of Alabama's First City*, ed. Michael V. R. Thomason (Tuscaloosa: University of Alabama Press, 2001), 42–44.
124. Joshua D. Newton, "Naval Power and the Province of Senegambia, 1758–1779," *Journal for Maritime Research* 15, no. 2 (2013): 129–30; Anderson, *Crucible of War*, 306; Christopher Leslie Brown, "1763 and the Genesis of British Africa," in *Envisioning Empire: The New British World from 1763 to 1773*, ed. James M. Vaughn and Robert A. Olwell (London: Bloomsbury, 2019), 113–16; see also Joseph E. Inikori, "Gentlemanly Capitalism and Imperialism in West Africa: Great Britain and Senegambia in the Eighteenth Century," in *Africa, Empire, and Globalization: Essays in Honor of A. G. Hopkins*, ed. Toyin Falola and Emily Brownell (Durham: Carolina Academic Press, 2011), 226–27.
125. Report of the Board of Trade in Answer to Lord Egremont's Letter of May the 5th (June 8, 1763), Add MS 35913, 230–231v, BL.
126. Newton, "Naval Power," 131 (quoting Board of Trade to George III [February 21, 1765], CO 389/31, TNA); see also Smith, *Appeals to the Privy Council*, 268–69; Eveline C. Martin, *The British West African Settlements, 1750–1821: A Study in Local Administration* (London: Published for the Royal Colonial Institute by Longmans, Green, 1927), 67–70; Hillsborough to Governor of Senegambia (April 26, 1771), CO 268/3, TNA (noting that Senegambia had been placed under the control of the colonial secretary—the same office responsible for the American colonies).
127. Newton, "Naval Power," 130; Bryan Rosenblithe, "Empire's Vital Extremities: British Africa and the Coming of the American Revolution," in *The American Revolution Reborn*, ed. Patrick Spero and Michael Zuckerman (Philadelphia: University of Pennsylvania Press, 2016), 165; Matthew P. Dziennik, "'Till These Experiments Be Made': Senegambia and British Imperial Policy in the Eighteenth Century," *English Historical Review* 130, no. 546 (2015): 1146–47.
128. See, e.g., Acemoglu, Johnson, and Robinson, "Colonial Origins"; Crosby, *Ecological Imperialism*, 134–41.
129. Entry of April 1767, in *Calendar of Home Office Papers of the Reign of George III*, ed. Joseph Redington and Richard Arthur Roberts (London: Longman, 1878–1899), 2:169; see also James Lind, *An Essay on Diseases Incidental to Europeans in Hot Climates:*

With the Method of Preventing Their Fatal Consequences, 2d ed. (London: T. Becket and P. A. De Hondt, 1771), 249–50; State of the British Settlements &ca. in Africa in 1765, Kings MS 200, ff. 2, 11v–12r, BL; Crosby, *Ecological Imperialism*, 138–39.

130. In the 1760s, the French Crown also explored a "plan to create a self-sustaining settler colony in Senegal." The hope of conquering the local climate might have been delusional, but it was widely shared. See Pernille Røge, *Economistes and the Reinvention of Empire: France in the Americas and Africa, c. 1750–1802* (Cambridge: Cambridge University Press, 2019), 170.

131. "[Review of] A Summary, Historical and Political, of the First Plantings . . . in North America. By William Douglas, M.D. . . . ," *Edinburgh Review*, 1756; Anya Zilberstein, *A Temperate Empire: Making Climate Change in Early America* (Oxford: Oxford University Press, 2016), 5–6, 94; Tomlins, *Freedom Bound*, 64 n.121, 583–84; "Extract of a Letter from West Florida," *Scots Magazine*, May 1766, 271; Brown, "Colonial Mobile," 44; Trevor Burnard, "Not a Place for Whites? Demographic Failure and Settlement in Comparative Context: Jamaica, 1655–1780," in *Jamaica in Slavery and Freedom: History, Heritage, and Culture*, ed. Kathleen E. A. Monteith and Glen L. Richards (Barbados: University of the West Indies Press, 2002), 73–88; cf. Eric Williams, *Capitalism and Slavery* (Chapel Hill: University of North Carolina Press, 1994), 20–23 (critiquing historians' overemphasis on climate in explaining West Indian slavery).

132. Christopher Leslie Brown, "The Origins of 'Legitimate Commerce,'" in *Commercial Agriculture, the Slave Trade and Slavery in Atlantic Africa*, ed. Robin Law, Suzanne Schwarz, and Silke Strickrodt (Woodbridge, U.K.: Boydell and Brewer, 2013), 150–51; Jonsson, *Enlightenment's Frontier*, 73; Zilberstein, *A Temperate Empire*, 148–69; Guy Carleton to Thomas Gage (September 20, 1766), Gage Papers, AS 57, WLCL; Mattias McNamara to Lord ? (August 5, 1776), CO 268/4, TNA; Lind, *Essay on Diseases*, 247–48; Katherine Johnston, "The Constitution of Empire: Place and Bodily Health in the Eighteenth-Century Atlantic," *Atlantic Studies* 10, no. 4 (2013): 443–66; P. D. Curtin, "'The White Man's Grave': Image and Reality, 1780–1850," *Journal of British Studies* 1, no. 1 (1961): 98–99; James F. Searing, *West African Slavery and Atlantic Commerce: The Senegal River Valley, 1700–1860* (Cambridge: Cambridge University Press, 1993), 106, 114; Seth, *Difference and Disease*, 5–6; see also Sven Outram-Leman, "Mapping Senegambia: Legacies of Ambition and the Failure of an Early Colonial Venture," *Britain and the World* 11, no. 2 (2018): 220 (noting the Governor of Senegambia's proposal in 1766 to settle a "healthier" mountainous region of his colony).

133. Conway to Rockingham (October 10, 1765), WWM/R/1/502, SA; Board of Trade to George III (February 21, 1765), PC 1/7/139, 1–15, TNA.

134. Considerations on a Future Peace &ca as It Relates to Great Britain Only (October 30, 1759), PRO 30/8/96, 238, TNA; Inikori, "Gentlemanly Capitalism and Imperialism in West Africa," 232–33; see also Emma Christopher, "A 'Disgrace to the Very Colour': Perceptions of Blackness and Whiteness in the Founding of Sierra Leone and Botany Bay," *Journal of Colonialism and Colonial History* 9, no. 3 (2008) (arguing that in the 1780s, policymakers turned against settlement because of concerns about interfering with the slave trade).

135. Brown, *Moral Capital*, 272–73; Brown, "Legitimate Commerce," 145–50.
136. It's not clear whether the framers of Senegambia's legal system envisioned the equal participation of subjects of African descent. There were black jurors in Sierra Leone in the 1780s and 1790s; perhaps something similar was planned for Senegambia. See Martin, *The British West African Settlements*, 122, 130; cf. Bronwen Everill, "'All the Baubles That They Needed': 'Industriousness' and Slavery in Saint-Louis and Gorée," *Early American Studies* 15, no. 4 (2017): 722 (noting that urbanization "helped desegregate" Saint-Louis during British rule).
137. Minute on Gen. O'Hara's report on the Province of Senegambia (1766), Kings MS 200, ff. 35–45, BL; Charles O'Hara to Board of Trade (May 28, 1766), CO 267/1, TNA.
138. O'Hara to Board of Trade (May 28, 1766); Dziennik, "'Till These Experiments Be Made,'" 1146; Board of Trade to George III (February 21, 1765), PC 1/7/139, 1–15, TNA; Everill, "'All the Baubles That They Needed,'" 728–29.
139. Governor O'Hara, Plan and Estimate for the building of a court room and house for the Chief Justice at Fort Lewis, Senegal (August 2, 1766), T 1/445/372–378, TNA; see also Christopher Milles, Petition for the Building of a Courthouse and Residence (March 21, 1766), PC 1/8/11, TNA.
140. See Everill, "'All the Baubles That They Needed'"; Searing, *West African Slavery and Atlantic Commerce*, 114–16; Cheikh Sène, "From Slaves to Gum: Colonial Trade and French-British Rivalry in Eighteenth-Century Senegambia," in *British and French Colonialism in Africa, Asia and the Middle East*, ed. James R. Fichter (Cham, Switzerland: Palgrave Macmillan, 2019), 31.
141. Charles O'Hara to Board of Trade (July 25, 1766), CO 267/1, TNA. For O'Hara's investment in the Rosalie estate in Dominica, see Anthony Mullan, "A Web of Imperial Connections: Surveyors and Planters in Eighteenth-Century Dominica," *Terrae Incognitae* 48, no. 2 (2016): 202–3. For the estate itself—part of another ambitious plan to anglicize a former French territory—see Edelson, *The New Map of Empire*, 211–15. For further evidence of O'Hara's racial attitudes, see Charles O'Hara to Board of Trade (May 28, 1766), CO 267/1, TNA (resisting an order to integrate African soldiers into the units under his command, because white soldiers would object and because integration "would at once destroy that Subordination, to which the negroes submit").
142. See Searing, *West African Slavery and Atlantic Commerce*, 114–17.
143. Martin, *The British West African Settlements*, 80, 93; Edward Morse, *Case of Edward Morse, Esq.* ([London]: n.p., 1787); Michael King Macdona, "Lieutenant John Clarke: An Eighteenth-Century Translator of Vegetius," *Journal of the Society for Army Historical Research* 95, no. 382 (2017): 124–25.
144. See Sutton v. Johnstone (1786) 99 Eng. Rep. 1215, 1239; 1 Term Rep. 493, 536 (quoting Wall v. McNamara [1779] [unreported] [Mansfield, C. J.]).
145. John Clarke to Richard Cumberland, Secretary to the Board of Trade (July 26, 1777), CO 267/3, TNA.
146. Dziennik, "'Till These Experiments Be Made,'" 1149–50; Newton, "Naval Power," 131; Paul E. Lovejoy, "Forgotten Colony in Africa: The British Province of Senegambia

(1765–83)," in *Slavery, Abolition and the Transition to Colonialism in Sierra Leone*, ed. Paul E. Lovejoy and Suzanne Schwarz (Trenton, N.J.: Africa World Press, 2014), 116–17.

CHAPTER 4. VARIETIES OF PLURALISM IN BENGAL

1. Ninth Report from the Select Committee, Appointed to Take into Consideration the State of the Administration of Justice in the Provinces of Bengal, Bahar and Orissa (1783), in *Writings and Speeches*, ed. McLoughlin and Boulton, 5:205–6.
2. Ibid.
3. See Bourke, *Empire & Revolution*, 661–62.
4. See Stern, *The Company-State*.
5. See, e.g., Seeley, *The Expansion of England*, 179.
6. See generally Spencer A. Leonard, "'A Theatre of Disputes': The East India Company Election of 1764 as the Founding of British India," *Journal of Imperial and Commonwealth History* 42, no. 4 (2014): 593–624; Vaughn, *Politics of Empire*.
7. Clive to Claud Russell (February 10, 1769), in John Malcolm, *The Life of Robert, Lord Clive: Collected from the Family Papers Communicated by the Earl of Powis* (London: J. Murray, 1836), 3:241.
8. See, e.g., Verelst, *A View of the Rise*, 143; "London. Continuation of the India Debate," *Gazetteer and New Daily Advertiser*, December 20, 1771; "Postscript, London," *St. James's Chronicle or the British Evening Post*, June 28, 1774 (sarcastically comparing the Quebec Act to "a Bill . . . for establishing the Gentoo Religion among his Majesty's Subjects in the Kingdom of Bengal, Bahar, and Orixa"); Lord Lyttelton, Lords Debates (June 17, 1774), in *Proceedings and Debates*, 5:230.
9. Luke Scrafton, *Reflections on the Government of Indostan with a Short Sketch of the History of Bengal from MDCCXXXVIIII to MDCCLVI: And an Account of the English Affairs to MDCCLVIII* (1763; repr., London: W. Strahan, 1770), 26. Legal pluralism was not the only way in which the East India Company sought to rule through division. Hastings also wanted to make the Indian army a high-caste service to divide Indian elites from their social inferiors. G. J. Bryant, "Indigenous Mercenaries in the Service of European Imperialists: The Case of the Sepoys in the Early British Indian Army, 1750–1800," *War in History* 7, no. 1 (2000): 12; see also Lord Clive to EIC Court of Directors (August 28, 1767), MSS Eur F218/4, 14, BL (describing efforts to divide Hindus and Muslims from each other in the army).
10. James Grant to Lord Shelburne, State of the British Affairs in India (November 30, 1780), Shelburne Papers, vol. 99, 340, WLCL.
11. Verelst, *A View of the Rise*, 144; see also Harry Verelst to John Cartier and Gentlemen of the Council at Fort William (June 5, 1769), IOR/P/1/44, 216, BL.
12. *Observations upon the Administration of Justice in Bengal; Occasioned by Some Late Proceedings at Dacca* ([London]: n.p., 1778), 8; see also *The Humble Petition of the British Subjects Residing in the Provinces of Bengal, Behar and Orissa, and Their Several Dependancies* ([London?]: n.p., 1779), 5, 62–64.

13. President and Council of Fort William to EIC Court of Directors (January 6, 1773), IOR/E/4/31, 227, BL.
14. See, e.g., Warren Hastings to Laurence Sulivan (February 1, 1770), Add MS 29126, 10, 13, BL.
15. *The Present State of the British Interest in India: With a Plan for Establishing a Regular System of Government in That Country* (London: J. Almon, 1773), 47. In the 1790s, Philip Francis (a member of Parliament and former member of the council in Bengal) proposed that enslaved men be able to serve on juries (only in cases involving other enslaved people) as a way to prepare them for emancipation. Linda Colley, "Gendering the Globe: The Political and Imperial Thought of Philip Francis," *Past & Present* 209, no. 1 (2010): 130.
16. Marshall, "The British in Asia," 504; H. V. Bowen, *The Business of Empire: The East India Company and Imperial Britain, 1756–1833* (Cambridge: Cambridge University Press, 2006), 3, 235.
17. George K. McGilvary, *Guardian of the East India Company: The Life of Laurence Sulivan* (London: Tauris Academic Studies, 2006), 68–69, 81–82.
18. Regulations Proposed for the Government of Bengal, Composed by Mr. Hastings ([c. 1765]), MSS Eur Orme OV 41, 23, BL.
19. Aldermen of Calcutta Mayor's Court to EIC Court of Directors (March 1, 1754), reprinted in *Bengal: Past & Present* 8 (1914): 33–36.
20. John Phillip Reid, *Constitutional History of the American Revolution* (Madison: University of Wisconsin Press, 1986), 1:178.
21. David Hartley, *The Right of Appeal to Juries, in Causes of Excise, Asserted* (London: J. Towers, 1763), 3.
22. [Alexander Dalrymple], *Considerations on a Pamphlet Entitled "Thoughts on Our Acquisitions in the East-Indies, Particularly Respecting Bengal"* (London: J. Nourse, P. Elmsly, Brotherton & Sewell, and J. Robson, 1772), 57–58; Morshedabad Council to Governor General and Council (March 23, 1775), TS 18/595, folder 2/C, 107–10, TNA; Dalrymple, *The Anarchy*, 219–20.
23. Extract of Fort William Revenue Consultations (March 8, 1776), IOR/H/127, 183, 188, BL (minute of Mr. Monson).
24. See Neil Sen, "Warren Hastings and British Sovereign Authority in Bengal, 1774–80," *Journal of Imperial and Commonwealth History* 25, no. 1 (1997): 75–77.
25. Copy of Lord Clive's Letter to the Select Committee at Fort William (January 7, 1767), MSS Eur E12, 38, BL.
26. Vaughn, *Politics of Empire*, 159–64; Clive to Harry Verelst (June 6, 1766), MSS Eur E231, 93, BL; Clive to Verelst (June 9, 1766), MSS Eur E231, 29, BL; [Clive], Hints of a Political System for the Government of India ([1772]), MSS Eur E12, 37, BL; EIC Court of Directors to President and Council of Fort William (March 4, 1767), in *FWIHC* 5:5; John Walsh to Clive (May 16, 1766), MSS Eur G37/40/2, 17, BL; Copy of Lord Clive's Letter to the Select Committee at Fort William (January 7, 1767), MSS Eur E12, 38, BL; Francis Sykes to [Clive?] (January 6, 1766), MSS Eur G37/38/1, 21, BL.

27. P. J. Marshall, *Bengal: The British Bridgehead: Eastern India 1740–1828* (Cambridge: Cambridge University Press, 1988), 94, 116.
28. Lord Clive ([1765?]), Shelburne Papers, vol. 99, 45, WLCL.
29. See Dalrymple, *The Anarchy*, 139–40; Vaughn, *Politics of Empire*, 131–32, 136–37, 161–63; Nicholas Hoover Wilson, "The Fixation of (Moral) Belief: Making Imperial Administration Modern," *European Journal of Sociology* 59, no. 1 (2018): 13–38.
30. Lord Clive, [Paper . . . Drawn Up in the Intention of Giving It in Evidence to the Select Committee of the House of Commons] (1773), MSS Eur E12, 57, BL; see also [A Defence of the Dual System of Government in Bengal in Clive's Hand, Offering Historical Precedents] ([after 1765]), MSS Eur G37/6/20, 1, BL.
31. EIC Court of Directors to President and Council of Fort William (May 17, 1766), in *FWIHC*, 4:185.
32. Lord Clive ([1765?]), Shelburne Papers, vol. 99, 45, WLCL; see also Clive (1773), MSS Eur E12, 57, BL (emphasizing the cost advantage of outsourcing tax collection).
33. See Ranajit Guha, *A Rule of Property for Bengal: An Essay on the Idea of Permanent Settlement* (Durham: Duke University Press, 1996), 27–28; Thomas R. Metcalf, *Ideologies of the Raj* (Cambridge: Cambridge University Press, 1995), 8–9.
34. Clive to Laurence Sulivan (December 30, 1758), in George Forrest, *The Life of Lord Clive* (London: Cassell, 1918), 2:119–20; Bryant, "Indigenous Mercenaries," 6 (quoting Clive, Miscellaneous Papers [1769–70], MSS Eur F128/4, 20, BL).
35. Bryant, "Indigenous Mercenaries," 24; P. J. Marshall, "Western Arms in Maritime Asia in the Early Phases of Expansion," *Modern Asian Studies* 14, no. 1 (1980): 26; see also Lord Cornwallis to Archibald Campbell (July 26, 1787), in *Correspondence of Charles, First Marquis Cornwallis*, ed. Charles Derek Ross (London: J. Murray, 1859), 1:266 ("[T]he native courts-martial have always been required to act according to the English martial law, and not according to the Mahommedan law."); Alexander Dow to Lord Shelburne (October 6, 1768), Shelburne Papers, vol. 99, 107, WLCL (describing sepoys as behaving "like all other men" when subjected to similar conditions).
36. Copy of General Orders Issued at Allahabad (January 17, 1768), in *House of Commons Sessional Papers of the Eighteenth Century*, ed. Sheila Lambert (Wilmington, Del.: Scholarly Resources, 1975), 63:136. Smith shared Clive's vision of Bengal as a militarized and extractive colony, although the two men did not get along personally. See Richard Smith to Robert Orme (August 15, 1767), MSS Eur Orme OV 37/18, 141–55, BL. In the 1780s, Smith would join with Burke and other moderates in attacking the Company's government of Bengal. Bourke, *Empire & Revolution*, 538–41; J. A. Cannon, "Smith, Richard," in *The History of Parliament: The House of Commons, 1754–1790*, ed. Lewis Namier and John Brooke (London: Published for the History of Parliament Trust by H.M.S.O., 1964), http://www.historyofparliamentonline.org/volume/1754-1790/member/smith-richard-1734-1803.
37. Richard Smith to Governor Verelst and Select Committee of Bengal (March 2, 1768), in *House of Commons Sessional Papers*, ed. Lambert, 63:137–40.
38. President and Council to Colonel Smith (March 18, 1768), in *House of Commons Sessional Papers*, ed. Lambert, 63:141–42.

39. President and Council to Colonel Smith (February 10, 1768), in *House of Commons Sessional Papers,* ed. Lambert, 63:136–37.
40. See also EIC Court of Directors to President and Council of Fort William (November 11, 1768), in *FWIHC,* 5:156 (criticizing the Select Committee for the public manner in which it criticized Smith, but declining to comment on "the merits of the Question").
41. Prasannan Parthasarathi, *The Transition to a Colonial Economy: Weavers, Merchants and Kings in South India, 1720–1800* (Cambridge: Cambridge University Press, 2001), 122–24, 147–48; Om Prakash, "From Market-Determined to Coercion-Based: Textile Manufacturing in Eighteenth-Century Bengal," in *How India Clothed the World: The World of South Asian Textiles, 1500–1850,* ed. Giorgio Riello and Tirthankar Roy (Leiden: Brill, 2009), 217; John Darwin, *After Tamerlane: The Global History of Empire since 1405* (New York: Bloomsbury Press, 2008), 193; Bishnupriya Gupta, "Competition and Control in the Market for Textiles: Indian Weavers and the English East India Company in the Eighteenth Century," in *How India Clothed the World,* ed. Riello and Roy, 281–308; Philip Francis to Welbore Ellis (January 13, 1777), MSS Eur E15, 467, BL.
42. See, e.g., Richard J. Ross, "The Commoning of the Common Law: The Renaissance Debate over Printing English Law, 1520–1640," *University of Pennsylvania Law Review* 146, no. 2 (1998): 378–79; Edmund Law, *Litigiousness Repugnant to the Laws of Christianity: A Sermon Preached at the Cathedral Church in Carlisle, at the Assizes Held There August 10, 1743* (Cambridge: Joseph Bentham, 1743).
43. Court of Cutcherry [Thos. Hewitt, John Bathoe, J. Holme Jr., and W. Maxwell] to President and Council of Fort William (March 7, 1768), IOR/P/1/43, 163v–164r, BL; Seventh Report from the Committee of Secrecy Appointed to Enquire into the State of the East India Company (May 6, 1773), in *House of Commons Sessional Papers,* ed. Lambert, 136:324–25; Brimnes, "Beyond Colonial Law," 519; see also Nandini Chatterjee, *Negotiating Mughal Law: A Family of Landlords across Three Indian Empires* (Cambridge: Cambridge University Press, 2020), 182 (describing varieties of arbitration in the Islamic world); cf. Bernard S. Cohn, "Some Notes on Law and Change in North India," in *An Anthropologist among the Historians and Other Essays* (Delhi: Oxford University Press, 1987), 570 (arguing that Indian dispute resolution encouraged compromise).
44. Court of Cutcherry to President and Council of Fort William (March 7, 1768), IOR/P/1/43, 163v; Court of Cutcherry to President and Council of Fort William (May 18, 1764), IOR/P/1/37, 189, 190, BL (lamenting a growing tendency to appeal even in cases in which the defendant had confessed a debt in court).
45. *India Tracts by Mr. Holwell and Friends,* 2d ed. (London: T. Becket and P. A. de Hondt, 1764), 120; Court of Cutcherry to President and Council of Fort William (January 25, 1765), IOR/P/1/38, 38, BL. On conciliation courts in nineteenth-century Europe and North America, see Kessler, *Inventing American Exceptionalism,* 200–262.
46. J. Z. Holwell to President and Council of Fort William (December 15, 1752), in *India Tracts by Mr. Holwell and Friends,* 137; see also Benton, *Law and Colonial Cultures,* 118; Fraas, "'They Have Travailed into a Wrong Latitude,'" 367.

47. Robert Orme, Account of the Jemmidarry of Calcutta Written . . . for Mr. Robbins at Fort St. George (May 19, 1751), MSS Eur Orme OV 12, 153, 165, BL.
48. James Murray, [Report of the State of the Government of Quebec in Canada] (June 5, 1762), Add MS 35913, 94, 103, BL; George Turnbull to Thomas Gage (July 25, 1767), Gage Papers, vol. AS 67, WLCL; Copy of Mr Secretary Whately's General Plan for an American Bill (December 7, 1764), Add MS 35910, 310r, 316r, BL.
49. See Burset, "Arbitrating the England Problem"; Justin duRivage and Claire Priest, "The Stamp Act and the Political Origins of American Legal and Economic Institutions," *Southern California Law Review* 88 (2015): 893.
50. James Jaffe, *Ironies of Colonial Governance* (Cambridge: Cambridge University Press, 2015), 58; cf. Marc Galanter and Jayanth K. Krishnan, "'Bread for the Poor': Access to Justice and the Rights of the Needy in India," *Hastings Law Journal* 55 (2004): 789 & n.1 (noting that twenty-first-century "India is among the lowest in the world in per capita use of civil courts"); Rohit De, *A People's Constitution: The Everyday Life of Law in the Indian Republic* (Princeton, N.J.: Princeton University Press, 2019), 10 (noting that suits between private parties "declined after independence," although "litigation against the state increased exponentially"); Tirthankar Roy and Anand V. Swamy, *Law and the Economy in Colonial India* (Chicago: University of Chicago Press, 2016), 176–77 (criticizing "litigation culture" in contemporary India).
51. H. V. Bowen, *Revenue and Reform: The Indian Problem in British Politics 1757–1773* (Cambridge: Cambridge University Press, 1991), 104, 118–32; Lucy Stuart Sutherland, *The East India Company in Eighteenth-Century Politics* (Oxford: Clarendon Press, 1952), 177–205; Jonsson, *Enlightenment's Frontier*, 136–38.
52. A Short View of the Administration of Justice by the Country Government, Collected from the Proceedings of the Council of Control, Established in September 1770 at Moorshedabad ([1771]), MSS Eur Orme India XVII, 4762, 4768, BL; see also President and Council, Fort William to EIC Court of Directors (November 3, 1772), IOR/E/4/31, 79, 91–92, BL; M. P. Jain, *Outlines of Indian Legal History*, 3d ed. (Bombay: N. M. Tripathi, 1972), 71–72.
53. EIC Court of Directors, General Letter to Select Committee at Bengal (March 16, 1768), quoted in Seventh Report from the Committee of Secrecy, 326; EIC Court of Directors to President & Council of Ft. William (June 30, 1769), in *FWIHC*, 5:208–15.
54. Warren Hastings, Regulations Proposed for the Government of Bengal (1772), in M. E. Monckton Jones, *Warren Hastings in Bengal, 1772–1774* (Oxford: Clarendon Press, 1918), 161.
55. A Short View of the Administration of Justice ([1771]), MSS Eur Orme India XVII, 4765. For Becher, see Marshall, *Bengal*, 116. The cruelty of Mughal punishments had long troubled Company officials, although their own ideas of humanity could also be disturbing. See, e.g., Proceedings of the Court of Cutcherry (July 11, 1761), MSS Eur F218/2, 4v, BL ("The Court . . . being of opinion that the sentence passed upon Felons in Calcutta to suffer Death by the Chawbuck [i.e., being flogged to death] to be of too cruel a kind, agreed . . . that he shall suffer Death by being blown from a Gun."). Although the Council didn't say so, the problem of financially interested prosecution

had also become an issue in England. See Langbein, *The Origins of Adversary Criminal Trial*, 158–65.
56. A Short View of the Administration of Justice, 4766, 4768.
57. Extracts of Instructions to the Commissioners . . . Relating to the Presidency at Fort William in Bengal (September 15, 1769), in *FWIHC*, 5:240.
58. Cutcherry to President and Council of Fort William (September 25, 1770), IOR/P/1/46, 74v, BL; Consultation Minutes (January 4, 1770), IOR/P/1/46, 76, BL; William Barton to Charles Bentley (January 21, 1772), IOR/P/1/51, 407–8, BL; The Collector's Orders to Those That Have Been Proposed to Make the Collections . . . (October 1, 1767), IOR/P/1/41, 400, BL; President and Council, Fort William to James Alexander et al. (December 20, 1771), IOR/P/1/49, 400v, BL; EIC Court of Directors to Governor and Council (April 10, 1771), in *FWIHC*, 6:77; Consultation Proceedings (July 20, 1768), IOR/P/1/43, 259v, BL; Samuel Middleton and George Hurst to President and Council of Fort William (April 6, 1772), IOR/P/1/51, 338r–338v, BL; Translation of a Bengal Award (January 21, 1772), TS 18/595, folder 2/C, 24, TNA.
59. Quoted in Seventh Report from the Committee of Secrecy, 328.
60. Charles Stuart to Governor General and Council (April 26, 1772), IOR/P/2/1, 5v, BL.
61. William Barton to Charles Bentley (January 22, 1772), IOR/P/1/51, 409–10, BL.
62. President and Council, Fort William, Circular Letter to Subordinate Councils (February 26, 1772), IOR/P/1/51, 394, BL; George Vansittart, E. Stephenson, and Evan Law to President and Council of Fort William (March 19, 1772), IOR/P/1/51, 279, BL; cf. Jaffe, *Ironies of Colonial Governance* (describing the difficulty, in nineteenth-century India, of finding anyone willing to serve for free on panchayats, or village councils).
63. Public Letter to Court (March 9, 1772), in *FWIHC*, 6:369.
64. Charles Bentley to President and Council of Fort William (February 15, 1772), IOR/P/1/51, 388, 309–10, BL; see also Note of February 1767, IOR/P/1/43, 92, BL; Court of Cutcherry to President and Council of Fort William (September 3, 1770), IOR/P/1/47, 147v, BL; Consultation Proceedings (February 9, 1768), IOR/P/1/43, 86v, BL; Public Department Minutes (September 25, 1770), IOR/P/1/47, 148, BL.
65. William Barton to Charles Bentley (January 22, 1772), IOR/P/1/51, 411, BL.
66. Bentley to President and Council of Fort William (February 15, 1772), IOR/P/1/51, 388, 309–10, BL. The Board of Police, which governed Charleston, South Carolina, during the British occupation of that city in 1780–82, also experimented with fining unwilling arbitrators. Wilson, *Bonds of Empire*, 226.
67. Samuel Middleton and George Hurst to Governor General and Council (May 4, 1772), IOR/P/2/1, 28v, BL; see also J. Long, ed., *Selections from Unpublished Records of Government for the Years 1748–1767 Inclusive Relating Mainly to the Social Condition of Bengal* (Calcutta: Office of Superintendent of Government Printing, 1869), 277 (reporting a petition in 1762 from the "black inhabitants" of Calcutta, who complained about "being liable to fines for non-attendance" as arbitrators at the Company's "Court of Cutcherry").
68. Charles Purling (Collector of Rungpore) to Warren Hastings (December 16, 1772), IOR/P/68/54, BL.
69. Charles Bentley to Governor General and Council (April 25, 1772), IOR/P/2/1, 4v,

BL. Verelst had also suggested paying arbitrators in a "laborious and intricate" labor dispute. Unlike Bentley's informants, however, Verelst thought that paying arbitrators might "secure their integrity," rather than pave the way for venality. Harry Verelst to William Aldersey (May 18, 1769), IOR/P/1/44, 213v, 214v, BL.

70. E.g., Edward Baker to President and Council of Fort William (April 3, 1772), IOR/P/1/51, 345v, BL.
71. Middleton and Hurst to Governor General and Council (May 4, 1772), IOR/P/2/1, 29r–29v, BL. Middleton "had been in India since 1753 and was well regarded by Hastings." T. H. Bowyer, "Middleton, Nathaniel (1750–1807), East India Company servant," in *DNB*, https://doi.org/10.1093/ref:odnb/69059.
72. Naib Dewan ([April] 1772), IOR/P/1/51, 339r, BL.
73. Samuel Middleton and George Hurst to President and Council of Fort William (April 6, 1772), IOR/P/1/51, 336v, BL.
74. Naib Dewan ([April] 1772), IOR/P/1/51, 339r, BL.
75. EIC Court of Directors to President and Council of Fort William (April 7, 1773), in *FWIHC*, 7:9.
76. Sulivan to Pitt (July 26, 1761), Shelburne Papers, vol. 99, folder 1, WLCL.
77. See Bowen, *Revenue and Reform*, 18–19; Vaughn, *Politics of Empire*, 96–101; Henry Vansittart, *A Narrative of the Transactions in Bengal, from the Year 1760, to the Year 1764, during the Government of Mr. Henry Vansittart* (London: J. Newberry, J. Dodsley & J. Robson, 1766), 2:356; see also Robert Travers, "Ideology and British Expansion in Bengal, 1757–72," *Journal of Imperial and Commonwealth History* 33 (2005): 14; Monckton Jones, *Warren Hastings in Bengal*, 97–101.
78. Quoted in Fraas, "'They Have Travailed into a Wrong Latitude,'" 413. Clive was not a fan of Vansittart. See, e.g., Clive to Harry Verelst (March 9, 1768), MSS Eur E231, 105, 106, BL (describing him as "the greatest Hypocrite the greatest Jesuit & the meanest dirtiest Rascal that ever existed").
79. Sen, "Warren Hastings," 74.
80. Laurence Sulivan to Lord Shelburne ([1766–67]), Shelburne Papers, vol. 90, 79, WLCL.
81. Mr. Vansettart's Answer to Several Queries Relative to the Company's Affairs, Received from Mr Sullivan (1766), Shelburne Papers, vol. 90, 91, WLCL.
82. See Spencer A. Leonard, "'The Capital Object of the Public': The 1766–7 Parliamentary Inquiry into the East India Company," *English Historical Review* 132, no. 558 (2017): 1128–29; McGilvary, *Guardian of the East India Company*, 60, 114, 155–56; L. Stuart Sutherland, "Lord Shelburne and East India Company Politics, 1766–9," *English Historical Review* 49, no. 195 (1934): 469.
83. Mr. Vansettart's Answer, 89.
84. Robert Travers, *Ideology and Empire in Eighteenth-Century India: The British in Bengal* (New York: Cambridge University Press, 2007), 102.
85. Hastings to Laurence Sulivan (September 7, 1772), Add MS 29127, 38v, BL.
86. See Travers, *Ideology and Empire*, 139.
87. Warren Hastings to George Colebrooke (March 7, 1773), in G. R. Gleig, *Memoirs of the Life of the Right Hon. Warren Hastings, First Governor-General of Bengal* (London: R. Bentley, 1841), 1:288, 293.

88. Proposed Regulations (1772), in Monckton Jones, *Warren Hastings in Bengal*, 158.
89. See Travers, *Ideology and Empire*, 117–18.
90. Governor and Council at Fort William to EIC Directors (November 3, 1772), in *House of Commons Sessional Papers*, ed. Lambert, 136:345–46.
91. Committee of Circuit to the Council at Fort William (August 15, 1772), in *House of Commons Sessional Papers*, ed. Lambert, 136:346–51.
92. Plan for the Administration of Justice, Extracted from the Proceedings of the Committee of Circuit (August 15, 1772), reprinted in *Proceedings of the Governor and Council at Fort William*, 17–22.
93. Plan for the Administration of Justice. Hastings later modified this stance, allowing arbitrators to be fined "for affected delays." Warren Hastings, Dewanny Adawlut (after 1775), Add MS 29206, 335v, BL.
94. Burset, "Arbitrating the England Problem," 27 n.133.
95. See J. Duncan M. Derrett, "The Administration of Hindu Law by the British," *Comparative Studies in Society and History* 4, no. 1 (1961): 25–26.
96. Plan for the Administration of Justice, 21.
97. J. Duncan M. Derrett, *Religion, Law, and the State in India* (New York: Free Press, 1968), 232–34; Bernard S. Cohn, "Law and the Colonial State in India," in *History and Power in the Study of Law*, ed. June Starr and Jane Fishburne Collier (Ithaca, N.Y.: Cornell University Press, 1989), 141; Travers, *Ideology and Empire*, 119–22.
98. Warren Hastings (July 16, 1771), Add MS 29126, 74v, BL.
99. See Chapter 1.
100. Case for the Opinion of the Honble. Councillor Wedderburn His Majesties Solicitor General (May 23, 1772), MSS Eur G37/17/32, 2, BL.
101. Warren Hastings to Laurence Sulivan (December 4, 1774), in Gleig, *Memoirs*, 1:469.
102. Armitage, *Ideological Origins*, 173; see also Stern, *The Company-State*, 122.
103. See Marshall, *Making and Unmaking of Empires*, 160–61.
104. Memorandum from Chatham Papers [c. 1767?], PRO 30/8/99, 263, TNA.
105. Philip Francis to Lord North (March 23, 1775), MSS Eur E15, 69, 74, BL; see also Jonathan Eacott, *Selling Empire: India in the Making of Britain and America, 1600–1830* (Chapel Hill: Published for the Omohundro Institute of Early American History and Culture, Williamsburg, Va., by the University of North Carolina Press, 2016), 202–3; Leonard, "'The Capital Object of the Public,'" 1128–29; Vaughn, *Politics of Empire*, 198; cf. Fraas, "'They Have Travailed into a Wrong Latitude,'" 410 (noting that in the early 1750s, Captain Caroline Scott, an army officer and a veteran of Cumberland's campaign to pacify Scotland, had urged that Bengal be made a "province of England").
106. Commentators also thought that English law—especially juries—"would draw the inhabitants of the neighbouring countries to" the parts of India controlled by Britain. *Present State of the British Interest in India*, 150.
107. William Pulteney, Commons Debates (May 18, 1772), *PH*, 17:471–73.
108. Mr. Vansettart's Answer, 89.
109. Holwell to John Payne (October 27, 1759), MSS Eur Orme OV 21, 21, 34, BL.
110. P. J. Marshall, "The Whites of British India, 1780–1830: A Failed Colonial Society?,"

International History Review 12, no. 1 (1990): 28; see also P. J. Marshall, "British Immigration into India in the Nineteenth Century," *Itinerario* 14, no. 1 (1990): 25–44.

111. David Arnold, "White Colonization and Labour in Nineteenth-Century India," *Journal of Imperial and Commonwealth History* 11, no. 2 (1983): 135; Court of Directors to President and Council at Fort William (May 17, 1766), in *FWIHC*, 4:186. The immediate impetus for the decision was to prevent abuses arising from land speculation. But the policy was widely seen as tied to the broader question of European colonization. See, e.g., Extract from Proceedings of the Board of Revenue (May 9, 1775), in *Reports from Committees of the House of Commons*, vol. 6, *East Indies—1783* (London: Reprinted by order of the House of Commons, 1806), 844.

112. Smith, *Wealth of Nations*, 2:634–35.

113. The *Wealth of Nations* recommended the fiscal and political integration of "all the different provinces of the empire inhabited by people of either British or European extraction." Smith, *Wealth of Nations*, 2:933. Jennifer Pitts suggests that Smith's reference to "European extraction" implies a reluctance "to make the same claim for colonies inhabited by non-European populations." Jennifer Pitts, *A Turn to Empire: The Rise of Imperial Liberalism in Britain and France* (Princeton, N.J.: Princeton University Press, 2005), 55. It's possible, however, that that reluctance might have had more to do with his assessment of political reality than his views about ethnicity or race. Cf. ibid., 39–40, 55–56 (discussing Smith's universalism). It's also possible that Smith's emphasis on "European extraction" was aimed at the Quebec Act.

114. John Clark, *Observations on the Diseases in Long Voyages to Hot Countries: And Particularly on Those Which Prevail in the East Indies* (London: D. Wilson and G. Nicol, 1773), 346 (quoting Lind, *Essay on Diseases*, 146). Clark's and Lind's works were both influential. See A.-H. Maehle, "Clark, John (bap. 1744, d. 1805), physician," in *DNB*, https://doi.org/10.1093/ref:odnb/5466; Michael Bartholomew, "Lind, James (1716–1794), Naval Surgeon and Physician," in *DNB*, https://doi.org/10.1093/ref:odnb/16669.

115. Lind, *Essay on Diseases*, 220.

116. Erica Charters, *Disease, War, and the Imperial State: The Welfare of the British Armed Forces during the Seven Years' War* (Chicago: University of Chicago Press, 2014), 157–58; Harrison, *Climates and Constitutions*, 58–110; see also Jonsson, *Enlightenment's Frontier*, 86 (discussing the enthusiasm of Sir Joseph Banks [1743–1820] for "the possibility of ecological exchange and acclimatization"). According to Charters, optimism about European adaptability declined in the later eighteenth century, in part due to the mortality of European soldiers in India during the Seven Years' War. It's worth noting, however, that Clark and Lind both published their books after the war; and their views remained influential during the period when Britain decided not to colonize India. See also Harrison, *Climates and Constitutions*, 133–47.

117. Clive to Richard Clive (September 23, 1765), CR 3/1, 38–39, National Library of Wales, accessed via Microform Academic Publishers, *The East India Company*.

118. Jonsson, *Enlightenment's Frontier*, 49; see also Pitts, *Turn to Empire*, 22–58 (discussing Smith's universalism).

119. Smith, *Wealth of Nations*, 1:91.

120. John Campbell, *A Collection of Letters Relating to the East India Company, and to a*

Free Trade (London: W. Owen, 1754), 24–25; Campbell, *Political Survey of Britain*, 1:631–33, 2:633; see also Onur Ulas Ince, "Deprovincializing Racial Capitalism: John Crawfurd and Settler Colonialism in India," *American Political Science Review* 116, no. 1 (2022): 152 (describing a nineteenth-century plan for British settlement in India, which involved "replacing legal pluralism by a civil and criminal justice system based on English laws and a uniform tax system, applicable to British-born and Indian subjects without exception").

121. George Johnstone, *Thoughts on Our Acquisitions in the East Indies Particularly Respecting Bengal* (London: T. Becket and P. A. De Hondt, 1771), 23, 26–27.
122. "London. Continuation of the India Debate," *Gazetteer and New Daily Advertiser*, December 20, 1771.
123. Johnstone, *Thoughts on Our Acquisitions*, 42.
124. See Guha, *A Rule of Property for Bengal*, 21–42; Travers, *Ideology and Empire*, 62–65.
125. Alexander Dow, *The History of Hindostan from the Death of Akbar, to the Complete Settlement of the Empire under Aurungzebe* (London: T. Becket and P. A. de Hondt, 1772), 3:cxxii, cxxxvi–cxxxvii.
126. Ibid., cxxii, cxli.
127. See Chapter 3. Laurence Sulivan had made a similar recommendation a year earlier. He urged Hastings to encourage "[d]istricts of the smallest possible size and value," so that "all confederacies among the opulent are broke up," and "competitions will be numerous as they must fall within the grasp of the middling people who will better attend to cultivation and improvement." Laurence Sulivan to Warren Hastings (April 10, 1771), Add MS 29132, 422, BL.
128. Dow, *History of Hindostan*, 3:cxli.
129. Ibid., 3:cli, cliii.
130. Ibid., 3:cxx–cxxi, cxxxviii–cxxxix; cf. Dow to Shelburne (October 6, 1768), Shelburne Papers, vol. 99, 107, 108–10, WLCL.
131. Dow, *History of Hindostan*, 3:cxlvii; see also ibid., cxlix ("Let our justice to our own subjects . . . entice foreigners with their wealth to settle among us.").
132. Ibid., cxli.
133. See, e.g., Richard Barwell to Ralph Leycester (November 15, 1772), MSS Eur D535/2, 77, BL.
134. William Bolts, *Considerations on India Affairs, Particularly Respecting the Present State of Bengal and Its Dependencies*, 2d ed. (London: J. Almon, P. Elmsly, and Brotherton & Sewell, 1772), iv, 11, 32, 75, 90; see also ibid., 4 ("In speaking of British subjects, we would be understood to mean his Majesty's newly-acquired Asiatic subjects, as well as the British emigrants residing and established in India."). The claim that Mughal sovereignty had been destroyed was a common theme among critics of Clive's program. See, e.g., Thomas Pownall, *The Right, Interest, and Duty, of the State, as Concerned in the Affairs of the East Indies* (London: S. Bladon, 1773), 39–40.
135. For the influence of Dow and Bolts, see Warren Hastings to Laurence Sulivan (November 11, 1772), Add MS 29127, 43, BL; Warren Hastings to Robert Palk (November 11, 1772), Add MS 29127, 49, BL; and Alexander Wedderburn to David Wedderburn (April 1, 1772), GD164/1700, Rosslyn Papers, NRS.

136. East India Judicature Bill (1772), in *House of Commons Sessional Papers,* ed. Lambert, 22:389–404; Bowen, *Revenue and Reform,* 93–100. Drafts of the bill are archived at IOR/A/2/8, BL.
137. Commons Debates (March 30, 1772), *PH,* 17:377–78.
138. Dow, *History of Hindostan,* 3:cxliii–cxlv.
139. William Bolts, *Considerations on India Affairs: Part II* (J. Almon, 1775), 179–82.
140. [Timothy] Brecknock, "To the Printer," *Gazetteer and New Daily Advertiser,* May 20, 1767, 1. This and other letters from Brecknock were sometimes reprinted in the colonies. See, e.g., *New-York Gazette,* August 3–10, 1767, 2. Although the *Gazetteer* sometimes published pseudonymous letters, Timothy Brecknock was a well-known contributor to that publication. See, e.g., D. G. C. Allan, "The Contest for the Secretaryship, 1769–70," pt. 3, *Journal of the Royal Society of Arts* 113 (December 1964): 35 (describing him as "a regular contributor to the *Gazetteer* on questions of legal history," who "may have been given favoured treatment by the editors"); "Anecdotes of the Late Timothy Brecknock," *European Magazine and London Review,* June 1786, 392 (describing him as "the *Attorney-General to the Gazetteer*").
141. Brecknock to Duke of Richmond (July 8, 1766), SP 37/5, 142–43, TNA. For Brecknock's views of conquest, see Brecknock, "To the Printer," *Gazetteer and New Daily Advertiser,* June 25, 1767, 1; and Timothy Brecknock, *A Treatise upon Perennial Ways and Means: With Other Political Tracts, Inscribed, to the King* (London: T. Becket, 1762), viii–ix.
142. Brecknock, "To the Printer," *Gazetteer and New Daily Advertiser,* May 20, 1767, 1.
143. Brecknock's proposal drew a response from "Massaniello," *Gazetteer and New Daily Advertiser,* June 2, 1767, 1.
144. Although he at one time supported the Duke of Newcastle, Brecknock wrote a pamphlet in 1764 that was so ultra-monarchist that Parliament ordered it to be publicly burned. Brecknock, *Ways and Means*; Joanna Innes, "Jonathan Clark, Social History and England's 'Ancien Regime,'" *Past & Present,* no. 115 (1987): 166 n.3; Sack, *From Jacobite to Conservative,* 118–19. Starting in the late 1760s, however, he sided with the populists. See, e.g., "To the Printer," *Gazetteer and New Daily Advertiser,* July 6, 1770, 1 (defending American colonists' resistance to taxation); "To the Printer," *Gazetteer and New Daily Advertiser,* November 22, 1768, 2 (announcing Brecknock's intention to publish a weekly series of "Anti-Grenvillian Letters"); "To the Printer," *Gazetteer and New Daily Advertiser,* April 29, 1767, 1 (arguing that the revenues of Bengal are the "property of the Crown"). His political evolution concluded in 1786, when he was hanged in Ireland for conspiracy to commit murder. Innes, "Jonathan Clark," 166 n.3.
145. [Morgann], *Plan for the Abolition of Slavery,* 16–17. Nor were such schemes limited to the colonies. See, e.g., Lord Morton to Horatio Walpole (October 12, 1754), WLP 17/1/19, NRO (hoping to educate in England "a young Lad of about twelve years of age who is head of one of the largest Clans in the Highlands," so that "English birch may drive out Highland Chiefship and proper Company make him a Loyall and affectionate subject of King George").

CHAPTER 5. DESPOTIC HUMANITARIANISM AND THE NEW IMPERIAL COMMON LAW

1. Jonathan Allen Fowler, "Adventures of an 'Itinerant Institutor': The Life and Philanthropy of Thomas Bernard" (PhD diss., University of Tennessee, Knoxville, 2003), vi; Michael J. D. Roberts, "Head versus Heart? Voluntary Associations and Charity Organization in England, c. 1700–1850," in *Charity, Philanthropy and Reform: From the 1690s to 1850*, ed. Hugh Cunningham and Joanna Innes (London: Palgrave Macmillan, 1998), 77.
2. [Bernard], *Appeal to the Public*, 35–36.
3. See Karen Halttunen, "Humanitarianism and the Pornography of Pain in Anglo-American Culture," *American Historical Review* 100, no. 2 (1995): 303–10; Catherine Arnold, "Affairs of Humanity: Sovereignty, Sentiment, and the Origins of Humanitarian Intervention in Britain and Europe" (PhD diss., Yale University, 2017), 400–402; Norman S. Fiering, "Irresistible Compassion: An Aspect of Eighteenth-Century Sympathy and Humanitarianism," *Journal of the History of Ideas* 37, no. 2 (1976): 195 & n.2; Lynn Hunt, *Inventing Human Rights: A History* (New York: W. W. Norton, 2007), 70–112; Samuel Moyn, "Theses on Humanitarianism and Human Rights," *Humanity Journal Blog* (September 23, 2016), https://perma.cc/89BH-NNP9.
4. Lisa Ford, "Anti-Slavery and the Reconstitution of Empire," *Australian Historical Studies* 45, no. 1 (2014): 71–86; Rob Skinner and Alan Lester, "Humanitarianism and Empire: New Research Agendas," *Journal of Imperial and Commonwealth History* 40, no. 5 (2012): 729–47; Penelope Edmonds and Anna Johnston, "Empire, Humanitarianism and Violence in the Colonies," *Journal of Colonialism and Colonial History* 17, no. 1 (2016): http://doi.org/10.1353/cch.2016.0013; Benton and Ford, *Rage for Order*; cf. Halliday, *Habeas Corpus* (linking habeas corpus to executive power); Karen M. Tani, "Welfare and Rights before the Movement: Rights as a Language of the State," *Yale Law Journal* 122, no. 2 (2012): 314 (discussing rights as instruments of state power).
5. See, e.g., Hunt, *Inventing Human Rights*, 119–22; Amanda B. Moniz, *From Empire to Humanity: The American Revolution and the Origins of Humanitarianism* (Oxford: Oxford University Press, 2016); cf. Brown, *Moral Capital*, 27 (arguing that the imperial crisis of the 1760s and 1770s "directed unprecedented attention to the moral character of colonial institutions and imperial practices").
6. Travers, *Ideology and Empire*; Christian R. Burset, "Redefining the Rule of Law: An Eighteenth-Century Case Study," *American Journal of Comparative Law* 70, no. 4 (forthcoming), https://ssrn.com/abstract=3803975.
7. Warren Hastings to Lord Mansfield (March 21, 1774), in Gleig, *Memoirs*, 1:399, 400, 403.
8. Warren Hastings to Lord Mansfield (January 20, 1776), in Gleig, *Memoirs*, 2:20–21.
9. Lord Mansfield to Warren Hastings ([1775]), Add MS 39871, 2r, BL.
10. 98 Eng. Rep. 1045, 1047–49; 1 Cowp. 204, 209–12 (K.B.).
11. Lord Mansfield to George Grenville (December 24, 1764), in *Grenville Papers*, ed. Smith, 2:476–77.

12. Mansfield to Hastings ([1775]), 2r (punctuation modernized). For Mansfield's use of natural law, see Lieberman, *Province of Legislation Determined*, 95–97.
13. Verelst, *A View of the Rise*, 145.
14. Alexander Wedderburn, Speech in House of Commons (June 13, 1774), in *Proceedings and Debates*, 5:226.
15. Edward Thurlow, Speech in House of Commons (May 26, 1774), in *Proceedings and Debates*, 4:453–56; see also Guy Carleton to Lord Shelburne (December 24, 1767), in *Constitutional History*, ed. Shortt and Doughty, 1:288–89 (describing the imposition of English law in Quebec as a "Sort of Severity, if I remember right, never before practiced by any Conqueror").
16. Catherine S. Arnold, "Affairs of Humanity: Arguments for Humanitarian Intervention in England and Europe, 1698–1715," *English Historical Review* 133, no. 563 (2018): 835–65; Arnold, "Origins of Humanitarian Intervention," 5–6, 29–30, 401–2.
17. Arnold, "Origins of Humanitarian Intervention," 22, 348–96; Hunt, *Inventing Human Rights*, 70–112; Thomas W. Laqueur, "Bodies, Details, and the Humanitarian Narrative," in *The New Cultural History*, ed. Lynn Hunt (Berkeley: University of California Press, 1989), 176–205; see also Philip Hamburger, "More Is Less," *Virginia Law Review* 90, no. 3 (2004): 873 (describing the eighteenth-century American context); Jud Campbell, "Republicanism and Natural Rights at the Founding," *Constitutional Commentary* 32 (2017): 92 & n.34; [Allan Ramsay], *An Essay on the Constitution of England*, 2d ed. (London: T. Becket and P. A. DeHondt, 1766), xvii ("The Romans had, surely, as good a right to give their laws to Britain as either the Saxons or Normans.").
18. See, e.g., Adam Smith, *The Theory of Moral Sentiments*, ed. D. D. Raphael and A. L. Macfie (Indianapolis: Liberty Fund, 1982) (1759) ("A disappointment in love, or ambition, will, upon this account, call forth more sympathy than the greatest bodily evil.").
19. "To the Printer," *Public Advertiser*, June 22, 1774.
20. [Bernard], *Appeal to the Public*, 35–36. These arguments came just as Protestant dissenters in Britain increasingly invoked natural rights in their appeals for toleration. Miller, *Defining the Common Good*, 324–25.
21. Lord Clare, Commons Debates (June 7, 1774), in *Proceedings and Debates*, 5:119; see also Alexander Wedderburn, Commons Debates (June 10, 1774), in *Proceedings and Debates*, 5:198 ("[T]hat form of administration of justice is best which the people over whom justice is to be exercised think best."). Clare came from an Irish Catholic family, and although he became a Protestant, he reconverted before his death. John Brooke, "Nugent, Robert," in *History of Parliament*, ed. Namier and Brooke, http://www.historyofparliamentonline.org/volume/1754-1790/member/nugent-robert-1709-88.
22. Meredith, *Letter to the Earl of Chatham*, 19–20.
23. "To the Printer," *Public Advertiser*, June 22, 1774.
24. Lind, Future Government of British Settlements in India, 193; see also *A Review of the Principles and Conduct of the Judges of His Majesty's Supreme Court of Judicature in Bengal* ([London]: n.p., 1782), 30–31.
25. *PH*, 17:1361.

26. Hastings to Mansfield (March 21, 1774), in Gleig, *Memoirs*, 1:400; see also George Rous, Opinion Wrote on the Draft of the Proposed New Charter of Justice for Fort Saint George and Bombay (August 4, 1794), IOR/H/414, 217, BL ("Either therefore the whole Body of English Laws must be instantly adopted which were an extravagant Act of Tyranny or some intermediate Government must be exercised.").
27. *Humble Petition of the British Subjects*, 66.
28. Edmund Burke, Commons Debates (May 31, 1774), in *Proceedings and Debates*, 4:491.
29. Burke, Speech on Quebec Bill (June 10, 1774), in *Writings and Speeches*, ed. McLoughlin and Boulton, 2:472–73; see also Isaac Barré, Commons Debates (May 26, 1774), in *Proceedings and Debates*, 4:460 ("I never yet knew it was found a grievance to any nation to give them the English laws, the English constitution.").
30. Isaac Barré, Commons Debates (May 8, 1770), in *Proceedings and Debates*, 3:279.
31. George Johnstone, Commons Debates (June 7, 1774), in *Proceedings and Debates*, 5:319.
32. See Neatby, *Quebec*, 127–41; Christie, *Formal and Informal Politics*, 70.
33. Quoted in Neatby, *Quebec*, 99.
34. Guy Carleton to Secretary of State (August 7, 1769), CO 43/12, 232, TNA; see also Guy Carleton to Lord Shelburne (January 20, 1768), in *Constitutional History*, ed. Shortt and Doughty, 1:201–2.
35. William Hey to George Germaine (1775), quoted in Christie, *Formal and Informal Politics*, 70.
36. Francis Russell, Amendments Proposed in Matters of Judicature by the Government of Madras (1793), IOR/H/416, 74–75, BL (summarizing The Opinion of Mr Solicitor [Stephen] Popham [February 1784], IOR/H/427, 111–14, BL).
37. "Calcutta," *Hickey's Bengal Gazette, or Calcutta General Advertiser* (July 29–August 5, 1780), 1.
38. See Chatterjee, *Negotiating Mughal Law*, 39–40, 179; Nandini Chatterjee, "Reflections on Religious Difference and Permissive Inclusion in Mughal Law," *Journal of Law and Religion* 29, no. 3 (2014): 413–14; Farhat Hasan, "Law as Contested Communication: Literacy, Performativity and the Legal Order in the Mughal Empire," *Oxford Journal of Law and Religion* 8, no. 2 (2019): 410–11.
39. For Hastings's claims to preserve Mughal law, see Benton, *Law and Colonial Cultures*, 133–34; and Travers, *Ideology and Empire*, 123.
40. Lauren Benton, "Historical Perspectives on Legal Pluralism," in *Legal Pluralism and Development: Scholars and Practitioners in Dialogue*, ed. Brian Z. Tamanaha, Caroline Sage, and Michael Woolcock (Cambridge: Cambridge University Press, 2012), 25; Sally Engle Merry, "Colonial Law and Its Uncertainties," *Law and History Review* 28, no. 4 (2010): 1068; Fraas, "Making Claims"; Fyson, "The Conquered and the Conqueror," 205; Daniel Blouin and William Clajon, Recueil de Pièces traduites de l'Anglais . . . (July 8, 1771), Gage Papers, vol. AS 138, folder 17, WLCL; Proposals of Inhabitants of Detroit, about Erecting Courts of Justice There [1766 or 1767], Gage Papers, vol. AS 60, WLCL; Maseres, *Account of the Proceedings*, 132. For later demands for English law by litigants and lawyers in India, see Abhinav Chandrachud, *An Independent, Colonial*

Judiciary: A History of the Bombay High Court during the British Raj, 1862–1947 (New Delhi: Oxford University Press, 2015); Jaffe, *Ironies of Colonial Governance*, 75–76, 128–54; and Sharafi, *Law and Identity in Colonial South Asia*, 202–4.

41. William Hey to Lord Chancellor Bathurst (August 28, 1775), in *Constitutional History*, ed. Shortt and Doughty, 2:670.
42. Francis Maseres, Testimony to the House of Commons (June 2, 1774), in *Proceedings and Debates* 5:18.
43. Poser, *Lord Mansfield*, 349–55; Duke of Newcastle to Mansfield (February 5, 1767), Add MS 32980, 48, BL.
44. Memorandum from Mansfield to Lord Henderland (1787), in John Campbell, *The Lives of the Chief Justices of England*, 3d ed. (London: J. Murray, 1874), 2:553–54.
45. Vallejo v. Wheeler (1774) 98 Eng. Rep. 1012, 1017; 1 Cowp. 143, 153 (K.B.); see also Buller v. Harrison (1777) 98 Eng. Rep. 1243, 1244; 2 Cowp. 565, 567 (K.B.) (Mansfield, C. J.).
46. See Burset, "Redefining the Rule of Law."
47. Fitz-Gerald v. Pole (1754) 2 Eng. Rep. 297, 304; 4 Brown 439, 448 (H.L.) (argument of counsel).
48. See Emily Kadens, "Justice Blackstone's Common Law Orthodoxy," *Northwestern University Law Review* 103 (2009): 1598. Michael Lobban has aptly summarized eighteenth-century views of precedent as a "competition of conveniences." Lobban, *The Common Law*, 86.
49. John Glynn, Commons Debates (May 26, 1774), in *Proceedings and Debates*, 4:464 (emphasis added).
50. See Chapter 1. Relatedly, during negotiations for the Treaty of Paris, he had warned that it was "most dangerous" to give too much freedom to French clergy in Quebec. Lord Mansfield (January 13, 1763), PRO 30/47/6, TNA.
51. Alexander Wedderburn, Report 11 ([1772]), R2903-0-4-E, Edmund Burke Fonds, National Archives of Canada; Alexander Wedderburn, Commons Debates (May 26, 1774), in *Proceedings and Debates* 4:468.
52. Board's Minute (May 21, 1773), IOR/P/2/3, 275v, BL.
53. [Warren Hastings], Regulations Proposed for the Government of Bengal ([1772]), in Monckton Jones, *Warren Hastings in Bengal*, 157; see also President and Council of Fort William to EIC Court of Directors (January 6, 1773), IOR/E/4/31, 227, 230, BL (stating that the Company could modify Mughal-era arrangements if "any Inconvenience should be found to arise from" them).
54. John Day, EIC Advocate General, Memorandum (December 27, 1782), IOR/H/423, 389, 391, BL; Francis Russell, Solicitor to the Board of Control, Heads of Defects in Matters of Law and Judicature in India (March 20, 1794), IOR/H/414, BL.
55. Governor General and Council to EIC Court of Directors (February 29, 1780), MSS Eur E36, 637, 655, BL.
56. A[rchibald] Macdonald, Observations on the Subject of English Judicature in India (December 31, 1782), IOR/H/411, 91, 92, BL; see also Francis Lind, Future Government of British Settlements in India ([1776–81?]), IOR/H/339, 192, BL ("That with respect to criminal trials, nothing can be more cruel, than to introduce our Ideas &

our measures of Right & Wrong among a people whose manners, customs & Religion have given them Ideas of Right & Wrong so very repugnant" to those of England.).

57. See, e.g., Blackstone, *Commentaries*, 4:344; Hume, *History of England*, 2:72; Kames, *Historical Law-Tracts*, 73–74; William Robertson, *The History of the Reign of the Emperor Charles V* (London: W. & W. Strahan, 1769), 1:51.

58. William Tennant, *Thoughts on the Effects of the British Government of the State of India: Accompanied with Hints Concerning the Means of Conveying Civil and Religious Instruction to the Natives of That Country* (London: Longman, Hurst, Rees, and Orme, 1807), 147.

59. Joseph Priestley, *A Comparison of the Institutions of Moses with Those of the Hindoos and Other Ancient Nations* (Northumberland, Pa.: A. Kennedy, 1799), 242. On Priestley, see Philip Hamburger, *Separation of Church and State* (Cambridge, Mass.: Harvard University Press, 2002), 74–75; Wendell Bird, "New Light on the Sedition Act of 1798: The Missing Half of the Prosecutions," *Law and History Review* 34, no. 3 (2016): 599–600; and R. B. Rose, "The Priestley Riots of 1791," *Past & Present* 18 (1960): 68–88.

60. James Forbes, *Oriental Memoirs: Selected and Abridged from a Series of Familiar Letters Written during Seventeen Years Residence in India*, 2d ed. (London: Richard Bentley, 1834), 2:23. Nathaniel Brassey Halhed, who translated the first English version of a Hindu "code," attempted to domesticate Hindu ordeals by comparing them to "a certain water ordeal" prescribed in the Book of Numbers. Nathaniel Brassey Halhed, *A Code of Gentoo Laws, or, Ordinations of the Pundits: From a Persian Translation, Made from the Original, Written in the Shanscrit Language* (1776; repr., Holmes Beach, Fla.: Gaunt, 2001), lviii.

61. Nandini Chatterjee, "Hindu City and Just Empire: Banaras and India in Ali Ibrahim Khan's Legal Imagination," *Journal of Colonialism and Colonial History* 15, no. 1 (2014); Ali Ibrahim Khan, "On the Trial by Ordeal, among the Hindus," ed. Warren Hastings, *Asiatick Researches* 1 (1799): 389–404.

62. [James Forbes], A Series of Letters ([1765–84]), Osborn d155, 198–205, BRBML (describing an ordeal in the Madras presidency); cf. James Forbes (February 10, 1772), MSS 66, vol. 5, 97–103, Yale Center for British Art. On ordeals in India, see Bernard S. Cohn, "From Indian Status to British Contract," in *An Anthropologist among the Historians*, 465; Richard W. Lariviere, "Introduction," in *The Divyatattva of Raghunandana Bhaṭṭācārya: Ordeals in Classical Hindu Law* (New Delhi: Manohar, 1981), 43–48; David Skuy, "Macaulay and the Indian Penal Code of 1862: The Myth of the Inherent Superiority and Modernity of the English Legal System Compared to India's Legal System in the Nineteenth Century," *Modern Asian Studies* 32, no. 3 (1998): 523 n.33.

63. Naib Dewan, Answer to the 2d Paragraph of the Councils Letter (May 1772), IOR/P/2/1, 32, BL.

64. Travers, *Ideology and Empire*, 125.

65. *History of Parliament*, ed. Namier and Brooke, 191; Ian R. Christie, *Wars and Revolutions: Britain 1760–1815* (Cambridge, Mass.: Harvard University Press, 1982), 30–33. In 1767, the Duke of Newcastle identified fifty-four MPs as allies of Bedford or Grenville and ninety-one as old-school Tories. Parliamentary Lists (March 2, 1767), Add MS

33001, BL. A few months earlier, the Marquess of Rockingham had identified thirty-five MPs who followed Bedford, seventy-one who followed Bute, and eighty-three old-school Tories. [Analysis of House of Commons] (December 20, 1766), WWM/R/86, Rockingham Papers, SA. Even if every member of all of these groups could be counted on to support a particular paternalist measure, that amounted to no more than a third of the House of Commons. Another group of ninety-four MPs—denigrated as "Swiss" by Rockingham, after the famous mercenaries—could be counted on to back any measure supported by the government (thanks to its control of patronage). Since the paternalists were in power during the 1770s, they could generally count on "Swiss" support. But even so, that gave them a bare majority at best. The election of 1768 changed these proportions, but the North Administration still had to depend on independent MPs who could withdraw their support at any time—and who did, on several occasions.

66. Lawson, *Imperial Challenge*, 134–38.
67. Colin Haydon, *Anti-Catholicism in Eighteenth-Century England, c. 1714–80: A Political and Social Study* (Manchester: Manchester University Press, 1993), 189–92; Faulkner, "Burke's First Encounter with Richard Price," 103–4.
68. Alexander Hamilton, "A Full Vindication of the Measures of the Congress, &c." ([December 15,] 1774), in *Hamilton Papers*, ed. Syrett and Cooke, 1:45–78.
69. Samuel Sherwood, "The Church's Flight into the Wilderness: An Address on the Times (1776)," in *Political Sermons of the American Founding Era, 1730–1805*, ed. Ellis Sandoz, vol. 1 (Indianapolis: Liberty Fund, 1991), 493–529; Paul Revere, "The Mitred Minuet," *Royal American Magazine*, 1774 (reproducing an anonymous English print in which bishops dance around the Quebec Act, while the devil flies above); see also "To the Members of the House of Commons," *Public Ledger*, May 31, 1774 (linking civil law to the St. Bartholomew's Day Massacre); "The Thistle Reel," *London Magazine*, 1775 (print showing the devil overlooking Mansfield, who holds the Quebec Act); Ebenezer Baldwin, "Appendix," in Samuel Sherwood, *A Sermon, Containing Scriptural Instructions to Civil Rulers, and All Free-Born Subjects* . . . (New Haven, Conn.: T. and S. Green, 1774), 66; cf. Memorandum to the Board of Trade, Some Thoughts on the Settlement and Government of Our Colonies in North America (March 10, 1763), Shelburne Papers, vol. 48, folder 44, 523, WLCL (urging policymakers to "introduce the Protestant Religion into Canada & if possible to give it the superiority over the Popish").
70. *Proceedings and Debates*, 5:230.
71. See, e.g., Charles James Fox, Commons Debates (May 26, 1774), in *Proceedings and Debates*, 4:471; see also Bourke, "Edmund Burke and the Politics of Conquest," 410; Faulkner, "Burke's First Encounter with Richard Price," 102–5; Francis Maseres to Fowler Walker (July 17, 1767), in *Maseres Letters*, ed. Wallace, 47–53.
72. "To the Printer," *Public Advertiser*, November 16, 1774, 1; R. H. Helmholz, "Use of the Civil Law in Post-Revolutionary American Jurisprudence," *Tulane Law Review* 66 (1992): 1656; David Thomas Konig, "Legal Fictions and the Rule(s) of Law: The Jeffersonian Critique of Common-Law Adjudication," in *The Many Legalities of Early America*, ed. Tomlins and Mann, 97–117.

73. John Dalrymple, *The Address of the People of Great-Britain to the Inhabitants of America* (London: T. Cadell, 1775), 53. For Dalrymple's biography, see Donovan, "The Military Origins of the Roman Catholic Relief Programme of 1778," 92–93; and Sher, *Church and University,* 108 n.75.
74. Horace Walpole to Duke of Richmond (October 27, 1775), in W. S. Lewis, ed., *The Yale Edition of Horace Walpole's Correspondence* (New Haven, Conn.: Yale University Press, 1937), 41:312.
75. Lawson, *Imperial Challenge,* 128–29; see also J. C. D. Clark, "The Decline of Party, 1740–1760," *English Historical Review* 93 (1978): 504 (describing the political implications of low attendance).
76. *Observations and Reflections on an Act, Passed in the Year, 1774,* i.
77. "Address to the Inhabitants of Quebec," October 26, 1774, in *Journals of the Continental Congress,* ed. Ford, 1:105–13.
78. Alexander Wedderburn to David Wedderburn (April 1, 1772), GD164/1700, Rosslyn Papers, NRS.
79. Hastings to Laurence Sulivan (November 11, 1772), Add MS 29127, 43, BL; see also Hastings to Palk (November 11, 1772) ("I am sorry the House of C[ommo]ns should think of establishing Laws for this Country, ignorant as they are of the Laws in being, of the manner and Customs of the Inhabitant, or of the form of Government. I hope the Act will not take place, for should it, everything we have done will be destroyed, and my labour will prove like the Toil of Sisyphus.").
80. Walpole to Horace Mann (April 9, 1772), in *Walpole Correspondence,* ed. Lewis, 23:400.
81. See Vaughn, *Politics of Empire,* 103–4.
82. See Kinkel, *Disciplining the Empire;* Eliga H. Gould, *The Persistence of Empire: British Political Culture in the Age of the American Revolution* (Chapel Hill: Published for the Omohundro Institute of Early American History and Culture, Williamsburg, Va., by the University of North Carolina Press, 2000), 75–97.
83. Campbell, *Collection of Letters,* 18–19.
84. Malcolm, *Life of Clive,* 2:126; see Vaughn, *Politics of Empire,* 107.
85. See du Rivage, *Revolution against Empire,* 47–49, 149–50; Vaughn, *Politics of Empire,* 113–14.
86. P. D. G. Thomas, "Charles Townshend and American Taxation in 1767," *English Historical Review* 83, no. 326 (1968): 42–44; see also du Rivage, *Revolution against Empire,* 12–13 ("Between 1765 and 1774, the Stamp Act and the Townshend Duties raised a total of about £36,000 from the North American colonies").
87. Chatham to Duke of Grafton (c. December 7, 1766), in *Autobiography and Political Correspondence of Augustus Henry, Third Duke of Grafton, K.G.,* ed. Sir William R. Anson (London: John Murray, 1898), 110.
88. Rockingham to Burke (October 24, 1772), in *Burke Correspondence,* ed. Copeland, 2:346.
89. Quoted in Bowen, *Revenue and Reform,* 51; see also George Sackville Germain to John Irwin (March 2, 1767), George Sackville Germain Papers, vol. 3, WLCL.
90. See Daniel J. Hulsebosch, "The American Revolution (II): The Origin and Nature of Colonial Grievances," in *British North America in the Seventeenth and Eighteenth Cen-*

turies, ed. Stephen Foster (Oxford: Oxford University Press, 2013), 289–317; Alison Gilbert Olson, *Making the Empire Work: London and American Interest Groups, 1690–1790* (Cambridge, Mass.: Harvard University Press, 1992).

91. In the 1780s, many moderates, most notably Burke, would also find themselves alarmed at the scale of extractions from India. See, e.g., Edmund Burke, Speech on Almas Ali Khan (July 30, 1784), in *Writings and Speeches*, ed. McLoughlin and Boulton, 5:465.

92. Richard B. Sheridan, "Beckford, William," in *DNB*, https://doi.org/10.1093/ref:odnb/1903; Chatham to Lord Shelburne (May 24, 1773), in *Correspondence of William Pitt*, ed. William Stanhope Taylor and John Henry Pringle (London: John Murray, 1838–1840), 264–65; Jonathan Shipley, *A Speech: Intended to Have Been Spoken on the Bill for Altering the Charters of the Colony of Massachusett's Bay* (London: T. Cadell, 1774), 4; Thomas Paine, "Reflections on the Life and Death of Lord Clive" (March 1775), in *The Complete Writings of Thomas Paine*, ed. Foner, 2:22–27; du Rivage, *Revolution against Empire*, 153–55; Memorandum to Lord Shelburne, A Paper Containing Thoughts on the Present State of the East India Company &c. (November 24, 1766), Shelburne Papers, vol. 90, 237–48, WLCL; Bowen, *Revenue and Reform*, 20–23.

93. Duke of Newcastle to Lord Rockingham (September 12, 1768), WWM/R/1/1096, Rockingham Papers, SA; Duke of Richmond to Lord Rockingham (June 12, 1767), WWM/R/1/797, Rockingham Papers, SA; William Dowdeswell to Lord Rockingham (August 12, 1768), Dowdeswell Papers, folder 12, WLCL; cf. [Benjamin Franklin], "'Benevolus': On the Propriety of Taxing America," [April 11, 1767], in *The Papers of Benjamin Franklin*, ed. Labaree et al., 14:110–16 (stating that the East India Company and the American colonies were "in exactly *similar* circumstances").

94. A Paper Relating to the Claim of the East India Company to Have the Dominion & Revenues from Their Acquisitions in India . . . ([1766 or 1767]), Shelburne Papers, vol. 90, 536–39, WLCL.

95. Charles Pratt and Charles Yorke, Legal Opinion (December 24, 1757), in *House of Commons Sessional Papers*, ed. Lambert, 26:6–8; see also George Hay, Charles Pratt, and Charles Yorke, Report to William Pitt (August 16, 1757), in *House of Commons Sessional Papers*, ed. Lambert, 26:1–2 ("[A]ll such Places, as may be newly conquered in this Expedition, accrue to the Sovereign, and are vested in His Majesty, by Right of Conquest."). For background on the opinion, see Bowen, *Revenue and Reform*, 53–54. The Company's focus on booty is unsurprising; acquiring property was a primary purpose of eighteenth-century European warfare, even when the conqueror was not a profit-seeking corporation. See James Q. Whitman, *The Verdict of Battle: The Law of Victory and the Making of Modern War* (Cambridge, Mass.: Harvard University Press, 2012), 18–21, 223.

The Pratt-Yorke opinion later took on new meaning in colonial North America, where it was misread to suggest that grants from American "Indians" were valid despite the Proclamation of 1763's prohibition against the unauthorized transfer of Native American lands. Jack M. Sosin, "The Yorke-Camden Opinion and American Land Speculators," *Pennsylvania Magazine of History & Biography* 85, no. 1 (1961): 38–49; Banner, *How the Indians Lost Their Land*, 102–3. Not everyone accepted the Pratt-Yorke framework. See George Johnstone, Commons Debates (March 30, 1772), *PH*, 17:377 ("I deny that conquest by a subject lawfully made vests the property in the state, though I maintain it conveys the sovereignty.").

96. Edmund Burke to Charles O'Hara (March 31, 1767), in *Burke Correspondence*, ed. Copeland, 1:302; see also PRO 30/8/99, vol. 3, 263, TNA; Bourke, *Empire & Revolution*, 344.
97. Rockingham to Edmund Burke (October 24, 1772), in *Burke Correspondence*, ed. Copeland, 2:344–45; Edmund Burke to Committee of Correspondence of the General Assembly of New York (January 5, 1774), in *Burke Correspondence*, ed. Copeland, 2:503; Bourke, *Empire & Revolution*, 361.
98. Griffin, *The Townshend Moment*, 135–38; Leonard, "'The Capital Object of the Public,'" 1140–44; Bowen, *Revenue and Reform*, 101–2.
99. 13 Geo. 3, c. 63; see Willem G. J. Kuiters, "Reactions to Change: European Society in Bengal under the East India Company Flag, 1756–1773," *Itinerario* 23, no. 3–4 (1999): 63; Travers, *Ideology and Empire*, 144; Vaughn, *Politics of Empire*, 216.
100. Regulating Act, §§ 14, 16.
101. James Grant to [James Wemyss] (June 11, 1773), Rosslyn Papers, box 1, folder 11, WLCL; see also *Review of the Principles and Conduct*, 21 & n.*(suggesting, based on the text, that the "judicial and political parts of . . . the *Regulating Act*, were drawn by different hands").
102. Lord Bathurst to Sir John Eardley Wilmot (November 1773), OSB MSS File 919, BRBML; Edward Thurlow to Lord Suffolk (January 20, 1774), TS 18/594, TNA; Thomas M. Curley, *Sir Robert Chambers: Law, Literature, and Empire in the Age of Johnson* (Madison: University of Wisconsin Press, 1998), 186, 451; B. N. Pandey, *The Introduction of English Law into India: The Career of Elijah Impey in Bengal, 1774–1783* (Bombay: Asia Publishing House, 1967), 38 & n.3.
103. See Benton, *Law and Colonial Cultures*, 136–49; Muller, *Subjects and Sovereign*, 166–208; Travers, *Ideology and Empire*, 181–206.
104. Elijah Impey, *The Speech of Sir Elijah Impey . . . Delivered by Him at the Bar of the House of Commons, on the Fourth Day of February, 1788* (London: John Stockdale, 1788), 33–34, 118–19; see Halliday, *Habeas Corpus*, 281–90. It's possible that Impey's theories of Indian law and political economy were influenced by his connection to prominent populist politicians. When he left for India, he took two portraits with him: one of his friend, the populist barrister John Dunning; and the other of Lord Shelburne, populists' leader in Parliament. Elijah Barwell Impey, *Memoirs of Sir Elijah Impey* (London: Simpkin, Marshall, 1846), 11 & n.†; John Brooke, "Dunning, John," in *History of Parliament*, ed. Namier and Brooke, http://www.historyofparliament online.org/volume/1754-1790/member/dunning-john-1731-83.
105. East India Company Act 1781, 21 Geo. 3, c. 70, §§ 8, 17–19.
106. Burke to Alexander Wedderburn, Baron Loughborough (February 2, 1781), in F. P. Lock, "Unpublished Burke Letters (III), 1763–96," *English Historical Review* 118, no. 478 (2003): 955; Burke, Speech on Bengal Judicature Bill (June 27, 1781), in *Writings and Speeches*, ed. McLoughlin and Boulton, 5:140; "News," *Lloyd's Evening Post*, June

18–20, 1781, 6; C. W. Boughton Rouse, Commons Debates (February 19, 1781), *PH*, 21:1199–1201, 1203.
107. Despite some scholars' statements to the contrary, decisions such as *Campbell v. Hall* (1774) didn't make legal pluralism inevitable. See Vernon Valentine Palmer, "A Descriptive and Comparative Approach," in *Mixed Jurisdictions Worldwide: The Third Legal Family*, ed. Vernon Valentine Palmer, 2d ed. (Cambridge: Cambridge University Press, 2012), 27–28 (summarizing and critiquing this view).
108. Campbell v. Hall (1774) 98 Eng. Rep. 1045, 1047–49; 1 Cowp. 204, 209–12 (K.B.).
109. Ibid., 98 Eng. Rep. at 1045; 1 Cowp. at 204. There had been earlier challenges to the tax in colonial courts and before the Privy Council, but *Campbell* was widely viewed as the crucial test case. See Marshall, *Edmund Burke and the British Empire in the West Indies*, 57–58; Quintanilla, "The World of Alexander Campbell," 242; Edward Stanley Edward to Grey Cooper (February 17, 1775), T 1/516/250–51, TNA.
110. *Campbell*, 98 Eng. Rep. at 861; Lofft at 677.
111. Ibid., 98 Eng. Rep. at 891, 892; Lofft at 733, 735.
112. An Opinion of Mr Levingstone on Some Transactions at the Ilinois (June 1, 1772), Gage Papers, vol. AS 111, WLCL. The author of the opinion, Philip Livingston (1740–1810), was a lawyer and a member of the prominent New York family of that name.
113. *Campbell*, 98 Eng. Rep. at 873, 875; Lofft at 698–99, 702.
114. Ibid., 98 Eng. Rep. at 1048; 1 Cowp. at 210. Cowper's report described the decision as unanimous. But a later reporter stated that "Mr. Baron [Francis] Maseres has told me" that Justice Willes had dissented from the holding that the Crown could legislate for a conquered colony until it renounced the right to do so. 20 Howell's State Trials at 1389.
115. 98 Eng. Rep. at 1048; 1 Cowp. at 210; see also Mansfield to George Grenville (December 24, 1764), in *Grenville Papers*, ed. Smith, 2:476 ("The fundamental maxims are, that a country conquered keeps her own laws, 'till the conqueror expressly gives new.").
116. Muller, *Subjects and Sovereign*, 29–30.
117. Fabrigas v. Mostyn (1773) 20 Howell's State Trials 181 (C.P.); see Willis, "The Standing of New Subjects," 15–16.
118. See James Johnston to [Lord Dartmouth] (January 12, 1774), CO 174/8, 49–50, TNA; Mostyn to [Dartmouth?], CO 174/8, 51–52, TNA (complaining about "the damnest cough that I ever had in my Life," which "shakes my Constitution almost as much as Lord Chief Justice de Grey's Opinion and Speach, does the Constitution of the Island of Minorca").
119. Mostyn v. Fabrigas (1775) 98 Eng. Rep. 1021; 1 Cowp. 161 (K.B.).
120. At least, that's how Francis Buller characterized the case when arguing *Mostyn*. 20 State Trials at 196–97. The earlier case, *Pons v. Johnston* (1765), is unreported, and Buller's opposing counsel doubted that "the question of jurisdiction" had really been "agitated" there. Ibid., 213; see also News, *Lloyd's Evening Post* (July 3–5, 1765) (reporting that "the Plaintiff was nonsuited" on non-jurisdictional grounds). But Buller's recollection was corroborated by the defendant, who remembered Pratt as declaring "that the Tribunals in Westminster Hall had nothing to do with what happen'd in

the Island of Minorca." Johnston to Lord Dartmouth (January 12, 1774), CO 174/8, 49, TNA.
121. Eugene C. Gerhart, "Chief Justice Vanderbilt and Teaching Procedure," *Syracuse Law Review* 4 (1953): 205.
122. Discussed in *Mostyn*, 98 Eng. Rep. at 1032; 1 Cowp. at 180.
123. See, e.g., Wall v. McNamara (1779) (unreported but quoted in Sutton v. Johnstone [1786] 99 Eng. Rep. 1215, 1239; 1 Term Rep. 493, 536–37); Hay v. Haldimand (1787), reported in *The British Register* (London: J. J. Tutot, 1787), 3:294–97; Rafael v. Verelst (1776) 96 Eng. Rep. 621, 622–23; 2 W. Blackstone 1055, 1059 (de Grey, C. J.).
124. The Governors of Plantations Act, 11 Will. 3, c. 12 (1698), provided that governors, deputy governors, and commanders in chief could be tried in King's Bench for any "Crime or Offence contrary to the Laws of this Realme or in force within their respective Governments," and that punishments would correspond to those "usually inflicted for Offences of like Nature committed here in England." In 1802, Parliament extended that statute to all public officials. Criminal Jurisdiction Act, 42 Geo. 3, c. 85.
125. See *Mostyn*, 98 Eng. Rep. at 1028; 1 Cowp. at 174; Burset, "Redefining the Rule of Law."
126. Francis Sykes to Warren Hastings (December 20, 1774), Add MS 29135, 392, BL.
127. See Willem G. J. Kuiters, "Law and Empire: The Armenians Contra Verelst, 1769–77," *Journal of Imperial and Commonwealth History* 28, no. 2 (2000): 1–22.
128. After Picton's conviction, the defense moved for a new trial, and the case remained pending when Picton became the highest-ranking casualty at Waterloo. Lauren Benton and Lisa Ford, "Island Despotism: Trinidad, the British Imperial Constitution and Global Legal Order," *Journal of Imperial and Commonwealth History* 46, no. 1 (2018): 34–37; James Epstein, "Politics of Colonial Sensation: The Trial of Thomas Picton and the Cause of Louisa Calderon," *American Historical Review* 112, no. 3 (2007): 712–41.
129. One newspaper described *Mostyn* as the most important case "[s]ince the case of ship-money" and praised it as securing "the lives, the properties of millions of his Majesty's subjects" overseas. "News," *Gazetteer & New Daily Advertiser*, February 3, 1775; see also "News," *Public Advertiser*, February 14, 1775 ("Fabrigas is an Example, that in England the Injured will ever find Redress.").
130. [Robert Clive], Paper dated 24th November 1772 Containing Proposals for the Government of the East India Company, Shelburne Papers, vol. 98, 148, WLCL. Jurisdiction in King's Bench had been secured by The East India Company Act (1770), 10 Geo. 3, c. 47, which was passed at the Company's urging. See Bowen, *Revenue and Reform*, 93–94.
131. Verelst, *A View of the Rise*, 5, 13; cf. "To the Printer," *Public Advertiser*, December 19, 1775 (citing *Mostyn* to condemn Governor Carleton's alleged abuse of Thomas Walker in Quebec, and warning that "Should the Tyrant and the Victim ever re visit this Country, an English Jury will judge of it."); "To the Printer," *Gazetteer and New Daily Advertiser*, July 10, 1766, 1.
132. Gregory, *Minorca, the Illusory Prize*, 85–86; Kuiters, "Law and Empire."

CONCLUSION

1. Declaration and Resolves of the First Continental Congress (October 14, 1774), in *Journals of the Continental Congress*, ed. Ford, 1:66–73; *Papers of John Adams*, ed. Taylor, 2:232 n.3.
2. Letter to the Inhabitants of the Province of Quebec (October 24, 1774), in *Journals of the Continental Congress*, ed. Ford, 1:104–13; see also Brad A. Jones, "A 'Fit Instrument': The Quebec Act and the Outbreak of Rebellion in Two British Atlantic Port Cities," in *Entangling the Quebec Act*, ed. Hubert and Furstenberg, 244–45.
3. The Declaration of Independence para. 15 (1776). Legal pluralism in Bengal also troubled Americans, although Quebec was more salient for obvious geographical reasons. See, e.g., "London," *Pennsylvania Gazette*, May 21, 1772, 1.
4. See, e.g., Thomas Jefferson to George Rogers Clark (December 25, 1780), in *The Papers of Thomas Jefferson*, vol. 4, ed. Julian P. Boyd (Princeton, N.J.: Princeton University Press, 1951), 237–38. On legal uniformity in the early Republic, see Christian R. Burset, "A Common Law? Legal Pluralism in the Eighteenth-Century British Empire" (PhD diss., Yale University, 2018), 380–84; and Rana, *The Two Faces of American Freedom*, 109.
5. *Writings and Speeches*, ed. McLoughlin and Boulton, 3:140, 153. On the legal peculiarities of Ireland, Wales, Durham, and Chester, see Baker, *Introduction to English Legal History*, 31; and Halliday, *Habeas Corpus*, 143–44.
6. James Duane's Notes of Debates (October 15, 1774), in *Letters of Delegates to Congress, 1774–1789*, ed. Paul H. Smith et al. (Washington, D.C.: Library of Congress, 1976–2000), 1:199; see also John Sullivan to John Langdon (October 6, 1774), in ibid., 151 (describing the Quebec Act as "the most dangerous to American Liberties among the whole train" of recent British legislation).
7. See Maya Jasanoff, *Liberty's Exiles: American Loyalists in the Revolutionary World* (New York: Alfred A. Knopf, 2011), 200; Taylor, *American Revolutions*, 329; Christie, *Formal and Informal Politics*, 149–50; David Milobar, "Conservative Ideology, Metropolitan Government, and the Reform of Quebec, 1782–1791," *International History Review* 12, no. 1 (1990): 45–64; cf. Lord Grenville to Lord Dorchester (October 1789), Add MS 59230, 235, BL.
8. See Neatby, *Quebec*, 260; see also *Thoughts on the Canada Bill Now Depending in Parliament* (London: J. Debrett, 1791), 9 (urging Parliament "to abate, or, if possible, to remove" the "prejudices" of Canadiens in favor of their own customs); [Maseres], *Review of the Government and Grievances of the Province of Quebec;* [James Monk], *State of the Present Form of Government of the Province of Quebec, with a Large Appendix* (London: J. Debrett, 1789).
9. Neatby, *Quebec*, 162–63; 31 Geo. 3, c. 31; Welland, *Political Economy and Imperial Governance in Eighteenth-Century Britain*, 161–63; Jasanoff, *Liberty's Exiles*, 206–7; Taylor, *American Revolutions*, 330–31.
10. [Maseres], *Review of the Government and Grievances of the Province of Quebec*, 44–45 (emphasis added).
11. Speech on Quebec Bill (May 11, 1791), in *Writings and Speeches*, ed. McLoughlin and Boulton, 4:352.

12. Halliday, *Habeas Corpus*, 289–90; Travers, *Ideology and Empire*, 185–200, 236; Derrett, *Religion, Law, and the State in India*, 316; Jain, *Outlines of Indian Legal History*, 121–35; Sutherland, *East India Company*, 366–414; Guha, *A Rule of Property for Bengal*, 17; Jon E. Wilson, *The Domination of Strangers: Modern Governance in Eastern India, 1780–1835* (Houndmills, U.K.: Palgrave Macmillan, 2008), 45–46.
13. Eric Stokes, *The English Utilitarians and India* (Delhi: Oxford University Press, 1989), 25–26; Jakob De Roover and S. N. Balagangadhara, "Liberty, Tyranny and the Will of God," *History of Political Thought* 30, no. 1 (2009): 118; Lord Cornwallis, Minute for Regulating the Courts of Criminal Justice (November 1790), Melville Papers, MS 3386, ff. 209–79, NRS; Nicholas Hoover Wilson, "From Reflection to Refraction: State Administration in British India, circa 1770–1855," *American Journal of Sociology* 116, no. 5 (2011): 1437; Wilson, *Domination of Strangers*, 188–90; Robert Travers, "Indian Petitioning and Colonial State-Formation in Eighteenth-Century Bengal," *Modern Asian Studies* 53, no. 1 (2019): 118–20; cf. Taisu Zhang, "Cultural Paradigms in Property Institutions," *Yale Journal of International Law* 41 (2016): 411 (noting that large-scale legal transplants often involve a substantial expansion of state power).
14. William Jones, "The Best Practicable System of Judicature for India" (1784), in *The Collected Works of Sir William Jones*, ed. Garland Cannon (New York: New York University Press, 1993), 1:cxxxiii; cf. William Jones, Charge to the Grand Jury, at Calcutta (December 4, 1783), in *The Collected Works of Sir William Jones*, ed. Cannon, 7:4. For Jones's politics, see Garland Cannon, Introduction, in *Collected Works of Sir William Jones*, ed. Cannon, 1:xlvii.
15. William Jones, *An Essay on the Law of Bailments* (London: J. Nichols, 1781), 114–16; see Chapters 3 and 4.
16. See also Jones to Thomas Law (September 28, 1785), in *The Letters of Sir William Jones*, ed. Garland Cannon (Oxford: Clarendon Press, 1970), 2:685–86 (comparing Hindu oath-taking to Quaker affirmation). For the contrast between Jones in England and Jones in India, see David Ibbetson, "Sir William Jones and the Nature of Law," in *Mapping the Law: Essays in Memory of Peter Birks*, ed. Andrew Burrows and Lord Rodger of Earlsferry (Oxford: Oxford University Press, 2006), 619–39; and David Ibbetson, "Sir William Jones as Comparative Lawyer," in *Sir William Jones 1746–1794: A Commemoration*, ed. Alexander Murray (Oxford: Oxford University Press, 1998), 26–27. For criminal juries, see Jones to John Shore (February 7, 1788), in *The Letters of Sir William Jones*, ed. Cannon, 2:787–89.
17. Quoted in Stokes, *The English Utilitarians and India*, 219–20; see also Julia Stephens, "An Uncertain Inheritance: The Imperial Travels of Legal Migrants, from British India to Ottoman Iraq," *Law and History Review* 32, no. 4 (2014): 758; Karuna Mantena, *Alibis of Empire: Henry Maine and the Ends of Liberal Imperialism* (Princeton, N.J.: Princeton University Press, 2010), 21–55; Pitts, *Turn to Empire*, 101–62.
18. James Mill, for example, pointed to Bentham's plan for a new French judiciary as a possible model for India. Stokes, *The English Utilitarians and India*, 60–70.
19. See Granville Sharp, *A Declaration of the People's Natural Right to a Share in the Legislature: Which Is the Fundamental Principle of the British Constitution of State* (London: B. White, 1774), 97 n.25; Brown, *Moral Capital*, 155–206; George Bernard Owers,

"Common Law Jurisprudence and Ancient Constitutionalism in the Radical Thought of John Cartwright, Granville Sharp, and Capel Lofft," *Historical Journal* 58, no. 1 (2015): 67.

20. Granville Sharp, *A General Plan for Laying Out Towns and Townships, on the New-Acquired Lands in the East Indies, America, or Elsewhere* ([London]: n.p., 1794), 19–20; see also Granville Sharp, *An Account of the Constitutional English Polity of Congregational Courts,* 2d ed. (London: B. White and C. Dilly, 1786).
21. Sharp to Benjamin Franklin (June 17, 1785), Granville Sharp Collection, New-York Historical Society, https://digitalcollections.nyhistory.org/islandora/object/islandora%3A153653.
22. Granville Sharp, *A Short Sketch of Temporary Regulations (until Better Shall Be Proposed) for the Intended Settlement on the Grain Coast of Africa, Near Sierra Leona,* 3d ed. (London: H. Baldwin, 1788), vii–xii; Sharp, *General Plan,* 19–24; Eacott, *Selling Empire,* 394; Peter Powers, *Tyranny and Toryism Exposed Being the Substance of Two Sermons, Preached at Newbury, Lord's Day, September 10th, 1780* (Westminster [Vt.]: Spooner & Green, 1781), 5.
23. Kathleen Wilson, "Rethinking the Colonial State: Family, Gender, and Governmentality in Eighteenth-Century British Frontiers," *American Historical Review* 116, no. 5 (2011): 1315–16; Newman, *A Dark Inheritance;* Harrison; Christie, *Formal and Informal Politics,* 289; Curtin, "The White Man's Grave," 102–4; cf. Pitts, *Boundaries of the International,* 9 ("An apparent recognition of the validity of non-European laws also served as the basis of one important justification of slavery before the nineteenth century."); Adom Getachew, *Worldmaking after Empire: The Rise and Fall of Self-Determination* (Princeton, N.J.: Princeton University Press, 2019), 20.
24. See, e.g., Wilson, *Bonds of Empire;* Greene, "Liberty, Slavery, and the Transformation of British Identity in the Eighteenth-Century West Indies," 310–12.
25. Cf. Sally Engle Merry, *Colonizing Hawai'i: The Cultural Power of Law* (Princeton, N.J.: Princeton University Press, 2000), 103 (surmising that the 1852 Hawaiian constitution applied American-style law to everyone because "racially separate courts violated [the] abolitionist convictions" of the constitution's Massachusetts-trained architect).
26. See also Brewer, "Slavery, Sovereignty, and 'Inheritable Blood,'" 1071.
27. George Rous, Legal Opinion (January 5, 1781), IOR/L/L/7/287, BL.
28. Cf. Pitts, *Boundaries of the International,* 9 (discussing the connections between slavery and legal pluralism in *Somerset's Case*).
29. Henry Brougham, Commons Debates (June 13, 1811), *Hansard Parliamentary Debates,* 1st series, 20:616; see also Burset, "Redefining the Rule of Law" (discussing Edmund Burke's similar, earlier skepticism of the common law in colonial contexts).
30. See Benton and Ford, *Rage for Order;* cf. Ford, *The King's Peace,* 143 ("By 1809 the question was not whether the imperial constitution could countenance legal divergence, but how much injustice could be done in defense of the colonial peace.").
31. The phrase (a reference to the Treaty of Paris) comes from Francis Parkman via Calloway, *The Scratch of a Pen.*
32. See, e.g., C. W. Boughton Rouse, Commons Debates (February 19, 1781), *PH,* 21:1202.
33. Hannah Weiss Muller, "'As May Consist with Their Allegiance to His Majesty': Re-

defining Loyal Subjects in 1774," in *Entangling the Quebec Act,* ed. Hubert and Furstenberg, 51.
34. Cf. E. P. Thompson, *Customs in Common* (London: Merlin Press, 1991); Hartog, "Pigs and Positivism."
35. See Dow, *History of Hindostan,* 3:cli, cliii; Bolts, *Considerations, Part II,* 179–82.
36. See also Ford, *The King's Peace,* 28–29.
37. See, e.g., Benton, "Historical Perspectives on Legal Pluralism," 25; Benton, *Law and Colonial Cultures;* Merry, "Colonial Law and Its Uncertainties," 1068; cf. Gregory Ablavsky, *Federal Ground: Governing Property and Violence in the First U.S. Territories* (New York: Oxford University Press, 2021), 12; Greer, *Property and Dispossession,* 297–98 (describing indigenous adoption of European conveyancing practices). For more recent examples of non-British populations voluntarily adopting a common-law system, see Mark Fathi Massoud, "How an Islamic State Rejected Islamic Law," *American Journal of Comparative Law* 66, no. 3 (2018): 579–602; and Carol Weisbrod, *Kites and the Sabbath: Legal Transplants and Pluralism in Hawai'i* (Lake Mary, Fla.: Vandeplas Publishing, 2014).
38. Lemmings, *Professors of the Law;* EIC Court of Directors to Governor General and Council (March 30, 1774), MSS Eur E27, 51, BL.
39. John P. Dawson, *A History of Lay Judges* (Cambridge, Mass.: Harvard University Press, 1960), 71; Dow, *History of Hindostan,* 3:cxlvi.
40. See, e.g., Marc Galanter, "'To the Listed Field . . . ': The Myth of Litigious India," *Jindal Global Law Review* 1 (2009): 65; Marc Galanter, "The Aborted Restoration of 'Indigenous' Law in India," *Comparative Studies in Society and History* 14, no. 1 (1972): 53–70; Marc Galanter, "The Displacement of Traditional Law in Modern India," *Journal of Social Issues* 24, no. 4 (1968): 65–90.
41. Jane Burbank and Frederick Cooper, "Rules of Law, Politics of Empire," in *Legal Pluralism and Empires,* ed. Benton and Ross, 280.
42. Cf. Katharina Holzinger et al., "The Constitutionalization of Indigenous Group Rights, Traditional Political Institutions, and Customary Law," *Comparative Political Studies* 52, no. 12 (2019): 1775–1809 (noting that the constitutions of former British colonies are more likely than other former colonies to recognize customary law).
43. José Luis Alonso, "The Status of Peregrine Law in Egypt: 'Customary Law' and Legal Pluralism in the Roman Empire," *Journal of Juristic Papyrology* 43 (2013): 351–404; Clifford Ando, *Law, Language, and Empire in the Roman Tradition* (Philadelphia: University of Pennsylvania Press, 2011), 1–36; Kimberley Czajkowski, "The Limits of Legal Pluralism in the Roman Empire," *Journal of Legal History* 40, no. 2 (2019): 110–29; Dolganov, "Reichsrecht and Volksrecht in Theory and Practice"; K. Tuori, "Legal Pluralism and the Roman Empires," in *Beyond Dogmatics: Law and Society in the Roman World,* ed. John W. Cairns and Paul J. du Plessis (Edinburgh: Edinburgh University Press, 2007), 44–45.
44. Chatterjee, *Negotiating Mughal Law,* 40, 189; see discussion in Chapter 5.
45. See Tamanaha, "The Promise and Conundrums of Pluralist Jurisprudence," 163–64; and the discussion in the introduction.
46. Clifford Ando, "Sovereignty, Territoriality and Universalism in the Aftermath of Car-

acalla," in *Citizenship and Empire in Europe 200–1900: The Antonine Constitution after 1800 Years,* ed. Clifford Ando (Stuttgart: Franz Steiner Verlag, 2016), 12.
47. Martijn van der Burg, "Cultural and Legal Transfer in Napoleonic Europe: Codification of Dutch Civil Law as a Cross-National Process," *Comparative Legal History* 3, no. 1 (2015): 98–99.
48. Quoted in Nelson, *The Middle Colonies and the Carolinas, 1660–1730,* 11.
49. Robert Cribb, "Legal Pluralism and Criminal Law in the Dutch Colonial Order," *Indonesia* 90 (2010): 48–50; John Ball, *Indonesian Legal History, 1602–1848* (Sydney: Oughtershaw Press, 1982), 28–76; Yahaya, *Fluid Jurisdictions,* 6–7.
50. Sanne Ravensbergen, "Anchors of Colonial Rule: Pluralistic Courts in Java, ca. 1803–1848," *Itinerario* 42, no. 2 (2018): 249; Benton, *Law and Colonial Cultures,* 170 n.6; Eduard Fagan, "Roman-Dutch Law in Its South African Historical Context," in *Southern Cross: Civil Law and Common Law in South Africa,* ed. Reinhard Zimmermann and Daniel Visser (Oxford: Oxford University Press, 1996), 38–41; Cribb, "Legal Pluralism and Criminal Law in the Dutch Colonial Order," 55. This analysis of Dutch legal pluralism is tentative; much of Dutch imperial legal history remains to be written. See Ravensbergen, "Anchors of Colonial Rule," 239; Lauren Benton and Devin Jacob, "Imperial Circuits of Law: Dutch East India Company Sovereignty," *Transnational Legal Theory* 2, no. 1 (2011): 124.
51. Quoted in C. Fasseur, "Colonial Dilemma: Van Vollenhoven and the Struggle between Adat Law and Western Law in Indonesia," in *European Expansion and Law: The Encounter of European and Indigenous Law in 19th- and 20th-Century Africa and Asia,* ed. W. J. Mommsen and J. A. de Moor (Oxford: Berg, 1992), 256.
52. Jeremy Adelman, *Sovereignty and Revolution in the Iberian Atlantic* (Princeton, N.J.: Princeton University Press, 2006), 28–50; du Rivage, *Revolution against Empire,* 20; Elliott, *Empires of the Atlantic World,* 301–10; Pincus, *Heart of the Declaration,* 68–73.
53. See, e.g., Woodrow Wilson Borah, *Justice by Insurance: The General Indian Court of Colonial Mexico and the Legal Aides of the Half-Real* (Berkeley: University of California Press, 1983), 2–5; Charles R. Cutter, *The Legal Culture of Northern New Spain, 1700–1810* (Albuquerque: University of New Mexico Press, 1995), 31–47; Elliott, *Empires of the Atlantic World,* 142; Henry Kamen, *Empire: How Spain Became a World Power, 1492–1763* (New York: Harper Collins, 2004), 10; Brian P. Owensby, *Empire of Law and Indian Justice in Colonial Mexico* (Stanford: Stanford University Press, 2008); Bianca Premo and Yanna Yannakakis, "A Court of Sticks and Branches: Indian Jurisdiction in Colonial Mexico and Beyond," *American Historical Review* 124, no. 1 (2019): 28–55; Richard J. Ross, "Legal Communications and Imperial Governance: British North America and Spanish America Compared," in *The Cambridge History of Law in America,* ed. Christopher L. Tomlins and Michael Grossberg, vol. 1 (Cambridge: Cambridge University Press, 2008), 104–43; Benton, *Law and Colonial Cultures,* 33–45, 81–102.
54. Quoted in J. H. Elliott, "A Europe of Composite Monarchies," *Past & Present,* no. 137 (1992): 63.
55. Borah, *Justice by Insurance,* 393; Christopher Peter Albi, "Derecho Indiano vs. the Bourbon Reforms: The Legal Philosophy of Francisco Xavier de Gamboa," in *Enlight-*

ened Reform in Southern Europe and Its Atlantic Colonies, c. 1750–1830, ed. Gabriel Paquette (Farnham, U.K.: Routledge, 2009), 237–38; Cutter, *Legal Culture of Northern New Spain*, 107; Gabriel B. Paquette, *Enlightenment, Governance, and Reform in Spain and Its Empire, 1759–1808* (New York: Palgrave Macmillan, 2008), 90; Bianca Premo, *The Enlightenment on Trial: Ordinary Litigants and Colonialism in the Spanish Empire* (Oxford: Oxford University Press, 2017), 90–91; Tamar Herzog, "Colonial Law: Early Modern Normativity in Spanish America," in *A Companion to Early Modern Spanish Imperial Political and Social Thought*, ed. Jörg Alejandro Tellkamp (Leiden: Brill, 2020), 119–20.

56. R. C. van Caenegem, *An Historical Introduction to Private Law*, trans. D. E. L. Johnson (Cambridge: Cambridge University Press, 1992), 122–24; Franz Wieacker, *A History of Private Law in Europe: With Particular Reference to Germany*, trans. Tony Weir (Oxford: Clarendon Press, 1995), 261–62; William W. Hagen, "The Partitions of Poland and the Crisis of the Old Regime in Prussia 1772–1806," *Central European History* 9, no. 2 (1976): 119.

57. For example, during the extended transition from British to Spanish sovereignty in East Florida (1783–85), the Spanish governor empowered British citizens to act as judge-arbitrators in cases involving British subjects. M. C. Mirow, "Judges for British Subjects in Spanish East Florida," *Washington University Journal of Law & Policy* 66 (2021): 1–41.

58. Matthew Mirow, "Spanish Law and Its Expansion," in *The Oxford Handbook of European Legal History*, ed. Heikki Pihlajamäki, Markus D. Dubber, and Mark Godfrey (Oxford: Oxford University Press, 2018), 792–93; Brian P. Owensby, "Between Justice and Economics: 'Indians' and Reformism in Eighteenth-Century Spanish Imperial Thought," in *Legal Pluralism and Empires*, ed. Benton and Ross, 143; Paquette, *Enlightenment, Governance, and Reform*, 91; see also Premo, *Enlightenment on Trial*, 159–90, 227 (describing struggles over the nature of indigenous custom and the extent of royal centralization).

59. Røge, *Economistes and the Reinvention of Empire*, 133. For local particularities in French colonial law, see Greer, *Property and Dispossession*, 176–77; and Carl J. Ekberg, *French Roots in the Illinois Country: The Mississippi Frontier in Colonial Times* (Urbana: University of Illinois Press, 2000).

60. Laurie M. Wood, *Archipelago of Justice: Law in France's Early Modern Empire* (New Haven, Conn.: Yale University Press, 2020), 11–13, 35–41, 174; Matthew Gerber, "Bastardy, Race, and Law in the Eighteenth-Century French Atlantic: The Evidence of Litigation," *French Historical Studies* 36, no. 4 (2013): 583; Francesca Trivellato, "'Amphibious Power': The Law of Wreck, Maritime Customs, and Sovereignty in Richelieu's France," *Law and History Review* 33, no. 4 (2015): 915–44; Silvia Marzagalli, "The French Atlantic," *Itinerario* 23, no. 2 (1999): 74. These conclusions are tentative, as the legal historiography of the eighteenth-century French Empire is comparatively sparse. See Laurie M. Wood, "Across Oceans and Revolutions: Law and Slavery in French Saint-Domingue and Beyond," *Law & Social Inquiry* 39, no. 3 (2014): 764, 773–75.

61. Quoted in Adelman, *Sovereignty and Revolution*, 26.

62. Røge, *Economistes and the Reinvention of Empire*, 249; see also Pernille Røge, "A Nat-

ural Order of Empire: The Physiocratic Vision of Colonial France after the Seven Years' War," in *The Political Economy of Empire in the Early Modern World*, ed. Sophus A. Reinert and Pernille Røge (Basingstoke: Palgrave Macmillan, 2013), 32–52; cf. Burg, "Cultural and Legal Transfer in Napoleonic Europe," 107 (noting Napoleon's unsuccessful attempt to achieve "uniform legislation for the whole of Europe").

63. Stuart Banner, *Legal Systems in Conflict: Property and Sovereignty in Missouri, 1750–1860* (Norman: University of Oklahoma Press, 2000), 36; Morris S. Arnold, *Unequal Laws unto a Savage Race: European Legal Traditions in Arkansas, 1686–1836* (Fayetteville: University of Arkansas Press, 1985), 45.

64. See, e.g., Ralf Michaels, "Comparative Law by Numbers? Legal Origins Thesis, Doing Business Reports, and the Silence of Traditional Comparative Law," *American Journal of Comparative Law* 57, no. 4 (2009): 788.

65. The inhabitants of Quebec and Bengal sometimes struggled to comprehend English law. But English lawyers also had trouble parsing French codes. See, e.g., Marriott, *Laws for the Province of Quebec*, 88; Neatby, *Quebec*, 105.

66. To be sure, civil-law systems had their own mechanisms for local adaptation, such as the Spanish formula of *obedezco pero no cumplo*, in which a local official symbolically submitted to a royal command without putting it into effect. See Mirow, "Spanish Law and Its Expansion," 792–93.

67. Edmund Burke, "Debates on Evidence" (April 30, 1794), in *Writings and Speeches*, ed. McLoughlin and Boulton, 7:168–69.

68. For civil law and political centralization, see the discussion below.

69. See, e.g., Daron Acemoglu, Simon Johnson, and James A. Robinson, "Reversal of Fortune: Geography and Institutions in the Making of the Modern World Income Distribution," *Quarterly Journal of Economics* 117, no. 4 (2002): 1279.

70. Dalrymple, *Feudal Property*, 2.

71. *Proceedings and Debates*, 5:612.

72. Bourke, *Empire & Revolution*, 483–87; see also Benton and Ford, *Rage for Order*, 150–51 (discussing competing views of empires as states or state systems); Alison L. LaCroix, *The Ideological Origins of American Federalism* (Cambridge, Mass.: Harvard University Press, 2010), 11–29 (describing early modern paradigms of federation).

73. Samuel Johnson, *A Dictionary of the English Language* (London: W. Strahan, 1755), s.v. "empire" (quoting William Temple, *An Essay upon the Original and Nature of Government* [1680]); see also Christopher Flanagan, "A Revolution for Empire: Ideas of Empire and the Making of the Constitution, 1787–8," *Journal of Early American History* 8, no. 2 (2018): 153–77 (describing different ideas of empire in the early United States).

74. Cf. Harland-Jacobs, "Incorporating the King's New Subjects," 203; Pincus, Bains, and Reichardt, "Thinking the Empire Whole," 617–18.

75. Burbank and Cooper, *Empires in World History*, 11–13; see also Mahmood Mamdani, *Define and Rule* (Cambridge, Mass.: Harvard University Press, 2012), 2; Benton and Ford, *Rage for Order*, 83; Daniel M. Klerman et al., "Legal Origin or Colonial History?," *Journal of Legal Analysis* 3 (2011): 379. For critiques of the idea that settler colonies were inexorably genocidal from the start, see Lisa Ford, *Settler Sovereignty: Jurisdiction and Indigenous People in America and Australia, 1788–1836* (Cambridge, Mass.:

Harvard University Press, 2010), 3; Greer, *Property and Dispossession*, 10–11; and Daniel K. Richter, "His Own, Their Own," in *The World of Colonial America: An Atlantic Handbook*, ed. Ignacio Gallup-Diaz (New York: Routledge, 2017), 209–34.

76. On the importance of institutions, see, e.g., Acemoglu and Robinson, *Why Nations Fail*; Douglass C. North, *Institutions, Institutional Change, and Economic Performance* (Cambridge: Cambridge University Press, 1990); and Douglass C. North and Barry R. Weingast, "Constitutions and Commitment: The Evolution of Institutions Governing Public Choice in Seventeenth-Century England," *Journal of Economic History* 49, no. 4 (1989): 803–32. Although scholars continue to debate institutions' *relative* importance, few disagree that institutions matter. See, e.g., Prasannan Parthasarathi, *Why Europe Grew Rich and Asia Did Not: Global Economic Divergence, 1600–1850* (Cambridge: Cambridge University Press, 2011), 84–85. For debates about which institutions matter, see, e.g., Bubb, "Evolution of Property Rights," 588–89; and Kevin E. Davis and Michael J. Trebilcock, "The Relationship between Law and Development: Optimists versus Skeptics," *American Journal of Comparative Law* 56, no. 4 (2008): 895–946.

77. See, e.g., Timur Kuran, *The Long Divergence: How Islamic Law Held Back the Middle East* (Princeton, N.J.: Princeton University Press, 2011); Zhang, "Cultural Paradigms in Property Institutions," 365–66; Sandra Fullerton Joireman, "Inherited Legal Systems and Effective Rule of Law: Africa and the Colonial Legacy," *Journal of Modern African Studies* 39, no. 4 (2001): 571–96; Paul G. Mahoney, "The Common Law and Economic Growth: Hayek Might Be Right," *Journal of Legal Studies* 30 (2001): 503–25; Roy and Swamy, *Law and the Economy in Colonial India*, 2–4; James Q. Whitman, *Hitler's American Model: The United States and the Making of Nazi Race Law* (Princeton, N.J.: Princeton University Press, 2017), 147–48.

78. See, e.g., Rafael La Porta, Florencio Lopez-de-Silanes, and Andrei Shleifer, "Law and Finance after a Decade of Research," in *Handbook of the Economics of Finance*, ed. George M. Constantinides, Milton Harris, and Rene M. Stulz, vol. 2A (Oxford: Elsevier, 2013), 427; Rafael La Porta, Florencio Lopez-de-Silanes, and Andrei Shleifer, "The Economic Consequences of Legal Origins," *Journal of Economic Literature* 46, no. 2 (2008): 285–332. For the theory's continuing importance, see, e.g., Daniel Berkowitz and Karen B. Clay, *The Evolution of a Nation: How Geography and Law Shaped the American States* (Princeton, N.J.: Princeton University Press, 2012), 16–59; Priest, *Credit Nation*, 155; Anu Bradford et al., "Do Legal Origins Predict Legal Substance?," *Journal of Law and Economics* 64, no. 2 (2021): 207–31; Holger Spamann, "Empirical Comparative Law," *Annual Review of Law and Social Science* 11, no. 1 (2015): 135–36. For the theory's real-world impact, see Michaels, "Comparative Law by Numbers?," 771–72.

79. See, e.g., Daniel Berkowitz, Katharina Pistor, and Jean-Francois Richard, "The Transplant Effect," *American Journal of Comparative Law* 51, no. 1 (2003): 163–203; Ronald J. Daniels, Michael J. Trebilcock, and Lindsey D. Carson, "The Legacy of Empire: The Common Law Inheritance and Commitments to Legality in Former British Colonies," *American Journal of Comparative Law* 59, no. 1 (2011): 111–78; Klerman et al., "Legal Origin or Colonial History?"; Holger Spamann, "Legal Origin, Civil Procedure,

and the Quality of Contract Enforcement," *Journal of Institutional and Theoretical Economics* 166 (2010): 149–65.

80. Acemoglu, Johnson, and Robinson, "Colonial Origins," 1370; Daron Acemoglu and Simon Johnson, "Unbundling Institutions," *Journal of Political Economy* 113 (2005): 949–95; see also Acemoglu, Johnson, and Robinson, "Reversal of Fortune"; Stanley L. Engerman and Kenneth L. Sokoloff, "Factor Endowments, Inequality, and Paths of Development Among New World Economies," *Economia* 3, no. 1 (2002): 41–109; William Easterly and Ross Levine, "The European Origins of Economic Development," *Journal of Economic Growth* 21, no. 3 (2016): 225–57; cf. Jack P. Greene, "Reformulating Englishness: Cultural Adaptation and Provinciality in the Construction of Corporate Identity in Colonial British America," in *Creating the British Atlantic: Essays on Transplantation, Adaptation, and Continuity* (Charlottesville: University of Virginia Press, 2013), 24 (suggesting that the degree of a colony's anglicization depended on the quantity of English immigration).

81. See Daniels, Trebilcock, and Carson, "The Legacy of Empire," 153; Daniel Oto-Peralías and Diego Romero-Ávila, "The Distribution of Legal Traditions around the World: A Contribution to the Legal-Origins Theory," *Journal of Law and Economics* 57, no. 3 (2014): 563–64.

82. See Acemoglu, Johnson, and Robinson, "Colonial Origins," 1370; Acemoglu and Robinson, *Why Nations Fail*, 433 ("North America followed a different institutional trajectory than Peru because it was sparsely settled before colonization."). AJR don't expressly address colonial legal pluralism, but other scholars have plausibly interpreted their work as explaining why European settlers transplanted their legal systems to some colonies but not others. See Adam S. Chilton and Eric A. Posner, "The Influence of History on States' Compliance with Human Rights Obligations," *Virginia Journal of International Law* 56 (2016): 230; Oto-Peralías and Romero-Ávila, "Distribution of Legal Traditions," 569.

83. See, e.g., F. A. Hayek, *Law, Legislation and Liberty: A New Statement of the Liberal Principles of Justice and Political Economy* (Chicago: University of Chicago Press, 1973), 1:116; Mariana Pargendler, "The Role of the State in Contract Law: The Common-Civil Law Divide," *Yale Journal of International Law* 43 (2018): 184–86; Mirjan R. Damaška, *The Faces of Justice and State Authority: A Comparative Approach to the Legal Process* (New Haven, Conn.: Yale University Press, 1986); John Henry Merryman, *The Civil Law Tradition: An Introduction to the Legal Systems of Western Europe and Latin America*, 2d ed. (Stanford: Stanford University Press, 1985), 18.

84. John Levett to Richard Oswald (January 10, 1775), OSB MSS, Letters to Richard Oswald, vol. 10, box 2, folder 130, BRBML; John Levett to Richard Oswald (March 25, 1775), OSB MSS, Letters to Richard Oswald, vol. 10, box 2, folder 134, BRBML. Early Hayek would have approved. See F. A. Hayek, *The Constitution of Liberty*, ed. Ronald Hamowy (1960; repr., Chicago: University of Chicago Press, 2011), 297 (suggesting that codification in general, and the Prussian civil code of 1751 in particular, advanced the rule of law "beyond the stage reached in the common-law countries"). On Levett and his circle, see David Hancock, *Citizens of the World: London Merchants*

and the Integration of the British Atlantic Community, 1735–1785 (Cambridge: Cambridge University Press, 1995), 121.
85. David Lieberman, "Property, Commerce, and the Common Law: Attitudes to Legal Change in the Eighteenth Century," in *Early Modern Conceptions of Property*, ed. John Brewer and Susan Staves (London: Routledge, 1995), 144–58; Lawrence M. Friedman, "Lawyers in Cross-Cultural Perspective," in *Lawyers in Society: Volume 3, Comparative Theories*, ed. Richard L. Abel and Philip S. C. Lewis (Berkeley: University of California Press, 1989), 16–18; Henry Horwitz and James Oldham, "John Locke, Lord Mansfield, and Arbitration During the Eighteenth Century," *Historical Journal* 36, no. 1 (1993): 143; Christian R. Burset, "Merchant Courts, Arbitration, and the Politics of Commercial Litigation in the Eighteenth-Century British Empire," *Law and History Review* 34, no. 3 (2016): 615–47.
86. Fowler Walker to Lord Dartmouth (October 16, 1765), Add MS 35914, 39–40, BL; see also Thomas Townshend Jr., Commons Debates (May 26, 1774), in *Proceedings and Debates*, 4:443 (discussing "those subjects that had been invited by the Proclamation that told them they were to have the law of England").
87. This is not to say that the legal-origins or endowments theories must be discarded. AJR acknowledge that initial endowments were "*not* the only, or even the main, cause of variation in institutions"; their empirical approach requires only that differences in initial demographic conditions were "*a source of* exogenous variation." Acemoglu, Johnson, and Robinson, "Colonial Origins," 1371 n.4. Nonetheless, settler mortality may be a weaker instrument than hitherto believed. Cf. Spamann, "Empirical Comparative Law," 142.
88. Katharina Pistor, *The Code of Capital: How the Law Creates Wealth and Inequality* (Princeton, N.J.: Princeton University Press, 2019), 8; see also "Exorbitant Privilege," *Economist*, May 10, 2014, https://www.economist.com/international/2014/05/10/exorbitant-privilege.
89. Comparative lawyers have questioned that claim, suggesting that civil- and common-law systems can provide functionally equivalent solutions to many problems that businesses might face. See Pargendler, "The Role of the State in Contract Law," 182; Stefan Voigt, "Are International Merchants Stupid? Their Choice of Law Sheds Doubt on the Legal Origin Theory," *Journal of Empirical Legal Studies* 5, no. 1 (2008): 15.
90. See, e.g., Matthew S. Erie, "The New Legal Hubs: The Emergent Landscape of International Commercial Dispute Resolution," *Virginia Journal of International Law* 60, no. 2 (2020): 225–97; Assaf Likhovski, "Argonauts of the Eastern Mediterranean: Legal Transplants and Signaling," *Theoretical Inquiries in Law* 10, no. 2 (2009): 619–51.
91. See Oto-Peralías and Romero-Ávila, "Distribution of Legal Traditions."

Index

Italicized page numbers indicate illustrations.

Acemoglu, Daron, 10, 165, 251n87
Acts of Union (1707), 31
Adams, John, 64–66, 134, 205n2; *Dissertation on the Canon and Feudal Law*, 63
Africa, colonialism by difference in, 13. *See also* Senegambia
Alam II (Mughal emperor), 91
alternative dispute resolution. *See* arbitration
American Revolution, 10, 151
Amherst, Jeffery, 39–40
Ando, Clifford, 160
Anglo-Mysore War (1767–69), 99
arbitration: in Bengal, 98–99, 101–3, 106–7, 225n67; in Florida, 247n57; in Quebec and Illinois Country, 53–58
Argyll, Duke of, 32
Armitage, David, 41, 109
Arnold, Catherine, 125
assimilation, 12–13, 35–38, 69, 75

Atkyns, John Tracy, 184n49
Australia, 13
authoritarian colonialism, 91, 137–38, 178n39

Bacon, Francis, 180n13, 211n75
bankruptcy law: colonial development and, 41, 45–48, 198n38; Debt Recovery Act and, 80; Quebec Act and, 79
Banks, Joseph, 228n116
Barbados: credit and bankruptcy law in Quebec and, 46; Grenada's legal framework and, 40
Barker, Hugh, 24–25
Barré, Isaac, 82, 127
Barrington, John, 194n3
Barrington, Lord, 55
Barton, William, 101
Becher, Richard, 100
Beckford, William, 104, 139–40, 141
Bedford, John Russell, fourth Duke of, 11, 17

INDEX

Bengal, 90–118; alternative proposals for legal pluralism in, 108–18; arbitration governance in, 98, 99, 101–3, 106–7, 225n67; Burke on legal pluralism in, 90–91, 141; civil law in, 91, 94, 97–99, 103, 106–8; as "conquered" vs. "ceded" colony, 140–41; corporal punishment in, 94–95; criminal law in, 91, 94, 100–101, 113–14; dismantling double government in, 99–103; double government in, 92–99; East India Company in, 1–2, 4; jurisdiction of courts in, 22–23, 115–16, 142–43; jury trials in, 90, 93, 94, 116, 154, 227n106; legal pluralism in, 4, 12, 103–8, 152–57; legal universalism in, 153–54; litigation suppression in, 98–99, 101, 106, 108; manufacturing industry in, 113; military discipline in, 96–98; paternalists and, 137–43; populists and, 12, 91, 104, 110, 137–40, 157–59; reforms of legal pluralism in, 152–57; taxation in, 12, 91–96, 103–6, 113, 131, 140
Bengal Judicature Act (1781), 143, 152
Bentham, Jeremy, 1–2, 6, 32–33, 154
Bentley, Charles, 101–2
Benton, Lauren, 5, 121, 158, 174n18, 176n29
Bernard, Francis, 70, 119
Bernard, Thomas, 119–20, 125
Bilder, Mary Sarah, 8, 43–44
Bin Wong, Roy, 8
Blackstone, William, 18, 44, 46; *Commentaries*, 78, 79
Bland, Humphrey, 34
Bolts, William, 114–16, 140, 148; *Considerations on Indian Affairs*, 115, 116
Brecknock, Timothy, 117, 230n140, 230n144
Breidenbach, Michael D., 205n2
Brewer, Holly, 38
Brougham, Henry, 156–57
Browne, John, 25–26, 28

Buller, Francis, 240n120
Burbank, Jane, 8, 159, 164
Burke, Edmund: on assimilation, 38; on common law vs. statutory law, 162; on definition of empire, 163; "An Essay towards an Abridgment of the English History," 193n128; on extractive colonialism, 238n91; on heterogeneity of English law, 16; on legal pluralism in Bengal, 90–91, 141; on legal pluralism in Quebec, 69, 73, 79, 126–27, 152; as moderate, 11; on paternalist approach, 52–53; on Quebec Act, 73; *Speech on Conciliation with the Colonies*, 149–50, 163; on Stamp Act, 57; on tax on absentee landowners in Ireland, 69

Calvin's Case (1608), 20, 21, 119, 144
Camden, Charles Pratt, first Earl, 62, 141, 146, 238n95
Campbell, Alexander, 144
Campbell, John, 112, 138
Campbell v. Hall (1774), 122–23, 144–45, 146, 167, 240n107
Canada. *See* Quebec and Quebec Act (1774)
Caracalla (Roman emperor), 159
Carleton, Guy: credit and bankruptcy laws in Quebec and, 46–48; on English law preferences in Quebec, 127; Quebec Act and, 68–70, 72, 74, 78, 80–83
Carlos III (king of Spain), 161
Catholics: British common law and, 40–45; Quebec Act and, 64–65, 133–36, 196n18, 210n64; religious liberty and, 37
Chambers, Robert, 18, 58–59
Charles II, 21, 31
Chatham, William Pitt, first Earl of, 10, 49, 50, 86, 103, 136, 138, 139–42
Chatterjee, Nandini, 160
Chatterjee, Partha, 8

civil law: in Bengal, 91, 94, 97–99, 103, 106–8; compulsory process for, 185n55; economic development and, 251n89; Islamic law and, 143; in Quebec, 4, 151–52; in Spanish colonies, 248n66
Clare, Lord, 126
Clark, George Rogers, 58, 228n116
Clarke, John, 89
Clive, Robert: extractive colonialism and, 104–5; legal pluralism in Bengal and, 12, 92–93, 95–100, 103–5, 148; on living in Bengal, 112; paternalism in Bengal and, 138–39; tax collection and, 12
Cohn, Bernard, 107
Cojamaul, Gregore, 115–16
Coke, Edward, 18, 20, 180n13, 182n21, 211n75
Colley, Linda, 41
colonies of exploitation, 13
common law: Burke on, 162; Catholics and, 40–45; compulsory process for civil cases, 185n55; economic development and, 162–67, 251n89; exceptions to expansion of English law, 28–34, 145–48; expansion of English law and, 16–24; metropolitan courts and colonial law, 24–28; paternalists and, 143–48; strategic legal pluralism and, 9
Common Pleas (court), 16, 146–47
Company of Merchants Trading to Africa, 84–85
Constitutional Act (1791), 152
contract law, 79, 143
Conway, Henry Seymour, 204n105
Cooper, Frederick, 8, 159, 164
Cornwallis, Charles, 152–53
corporal punishment, 94–95
Coventry Act (1670), 196n19
Cover, Robert, 7
credit and debt, 45–48, 80, 198n36. *See also* bankruptcy law

criminal law: in Bengal, 91, 94, 100–101, 113–14; Islamic, 100–101, 113–14, 224n55; Mughal institutions and, 224n55; paternalists and, 215n104; populists and, 215n104; Quebec Act and, 4, 12, 65–66, 75–83
Cromwell, Oliver, 31, 34
cutcherry courts, 98

Dalrymple, Alexander, 94
Dalrymple, John, 33, 34, 136, 163
Dartmouth, Lord, 82–83
debt. *See* credit and debt
Debt Recovery Act (1732), 80, 214n99
de Grey, William, 43, 45, 61, 77, 82, 145–46, 204n104
Derrett, J. D. M., 107
Douglas, Thomas. *See* Selkirk, Thomas Douglas, fifth Earl of
Dow, Alexander, 113–14, 116, 159; *History of Hindostan*, 113
Dundas, Henry, 62–63
Dunning, John, 44, 77, 82, 104, 154, 197n28, 239n104

East India Company: Anglo-Mysore War (1767–69) and, 99; on English law preferences in Bengal, 128; expansion of English common law and, 1–2, 4, 21–24, 91; Mughal law and, 132–33. *See also* Bengal
East India Judicature Bill of 1772, 115
ecclesiastical courts, 107
economic development: arbitration's role in, 53–58; bankruptcy law and, 41, 45–48, 198n38; civil law and, 251n89; common law and, 162–67, 251n89; credit law and, 45–48, 80, 198n36; feudal law and, 58–62; paternalists and, 50–53; Quebec Act and, 72–75
Eden, William, 62
Egmont, John Perceval, second Earl of, 11, 34, *59*, 59–62, 203n101
Elizabeth I, 18

empathy: humanitarianism and, 119–20; natural rights and, 121–28
Enlightenment philosophy, 9, 32, 62, 161
Entick v. Carrington (1765), 71
Erving, John, 70
Exchequer, 16
extractive colonialism, 13–14, 93–95, 108–10, 140, 167, 222n36, 238n91

Fábrigas, Anthony, 148
family law: in Bengal, 107, 143; legal pluralism and, 210n71; Quebec Act and, 76
Felipe V (king of Spain), 161
Ferguson, Adam, 62–63
Ferguson, Niall, 8
feudal law, 32, 58–62, 80–81, 188n86, 188n88
Florida: arbitration in, 247n57; legal pluralism in, 11–12, 83–84; Proclamation of 1763 and, 40
Forbes, Duncan, 34
Forbes, James, 132
Ford, Lisa, 121
Fox, Charles James, 69
Fraas, Mitch, 22
France and French law: common-law courts, 167; legal pluralism in colonies, 160–61; Quebec and, 11–12, 40, 65–66, 69–70, 73, 79–80, 151–52; Seven Years' War (1754–63) and, 2, 10, 39, 50, 67, 139, 162, 172n4; taxation in French colonies, 160
Francis, Philip, 110, 221n15
Franklin, Benjamin, 67–68
frankpledge, 154–55

Gage, Thomas, *51*; arbitration governance and, 53, 55–57, 73; civil law in Illinois Country and, 53, 55–57, 73, 78; criminal law in Illinois Country and, 81; feudal law and, 11, 41, 58; as paternalist, 50; Quebec Act and, 66, 70, 78

George I, 49
George III, 39, 49, 145, 177n37
Gershon Levy and Company, 46–48
Gibbon, Edward, 76
Gibraltar, 28–30, 143
Gibson, Thomas, 187n78
Glenorchy, Lord, 33–34
Glynn, John, 71–72, 82, 130, 144, 145
Governors of Plantations Act (1698), 241n124
grand juries, 71, 207n31
Grange, Lord, 32
Grant, James, 84, 92
Great Fire of London (1666), 17
Grenada: Catholics in, 42–45; legal pluralism in, 83–84, 144–45; Proclamation of 1763 and, 40; taxation in, 45, 144–45
Grenville, George, 11, 50, 84–85, 92, 93
Grotius, 126
Guadeloupe, legal pluralism in, 194n3
Guha, Ranajit, 153

habeas corpus, 70, 76, 83, 119, 143, 178n39
Hale, Matthew, 16, 211n75
Halhed, Nathaniel Brassey, 235n60
Hall, William, 144
Halliday, Paul, 211n74
Hamilton, Alexander, 134
Hardwicke, Philip Yorke, first Earl of: heritable jurisdictions and, 31–32; oaths for non-Christian litigants and witnesses and, 25–26, 79, 186n67; "Scotch Reformation" of, 32, 34, 36, 58, 62, 105
Hartley, David, 94
Hastings, Warren, *123*; East India Company business model and, 94; on English law preferences in Bengal, 127; legal pluralism in Bengal and, 12, 95, 103–8; on natural rights and legal pluralism, 121–26; paternalism in Bengal and, 131, 137

Hay, Douglas, 81
Henry VIII, 17
heritable jurisdictions, 31–34, 60, 105, 188n88
Hey, William, 46, 77, 78, 129
Hillsborough, Lord: arbitration governance and, 53; bankruptcy law and, 48; manufacturing industry in Quebec and, 72, 158; Quebec Act and, 72, 80–81; Senegambia and, 86
Hindus: civil law and, 143; criminal law and, 113–14; double government in Bengal and, 92; legal pluralism in Bengal and, 91, 105–8, 131, 172–73n5; oaths for Hindu litigants and witnesses, 24–27; ordeal trials and, 131–32, 235n60; reforms of legal pluralism in Bengal and, 156
Hollis, Thomas, 134
Holwell, John Zephaniah, 111
humanitarianism, 13, 119–48; empathy and, 119–20, 121–28; imperial common law and, 143–48; natural rights and, 121–28; paternalist vision in Bengal and, 137–43; paternalist vision in Quebec and, 133–37; sincerity of paternalist arguments, 128–33. *See also* paternalists
Hume, David, 33, 36
Hurst, George, 102–3
Hutchinson, Thomas, 71

Illinois Country, 54; arbitration and governance in, 53–58; British empire expansion and, 2; civil law in, 4, 53, 55–57, 73, 78; criminal law in, 4, 81; legal pluralism in, 11–12; paternalists and, 11–12; Quebec Act and, 65. *See also* Quebec and Quebec Act (1774)
Impey, Elijah, 142–43, 239n104
India: expansion of English common law in, 21–24; oaths for non-Christian litigants and witnesses in, 24–28. *See also* Bengal

inheritance law: in Bengal, 107, 143; gavelkind custom and, 17; Quebec Act and, 81
Inns of Court, 19, 20, 181–82n20
Ireland: anglicization through law in, 69; credit and bankruptcy law in Quebec and, 46; legal pluralism in, 18, 149–50; Quebec's legal framework and, 40
Islamic law: arbitration and, 102; in Bengal, 91, 131; civil law, 143; criminal law, 100–101, 113–14, 224n55; legal framework in Bengal and, 173n5

Jacobites, 9, 16, 31, 42
Jamaica: English vs. Spanish law in, 20, 190n23; legal pluralism in, 156; racial hierarchy in, 36
James I (of England) and VI (of Scotland), 30
James II, 70
Jenkinson, Charles, 93
Johnson, Samuel, 36, 163–64
Johnson, Simon, 165, 251n87
Johnstone, George, 84, 112–13, 115–16, 127, 140
Jones, William, 153–54; *Essay on the Law of Bailments*, 153
Jonsson, Fredrik Albritton, 112
jurisdiction of courts: in Bengal, 22–23, 115–16, 142–43; expansion of English common law and, 16, 18, 146–47; financial incentive for judges to expand, 184n46; heritable jurisdictions, 31–34, 60, 105, 188n88; metropolitan courts and, 24; Regulating Act and, 142; in Spanish colonies, 161
jury trials: in Bengal, 90, 93, 94, 116, 154, 227n106; humanitarianism and, 125–26; in Quebec, 70–72, 207n31, 213n91

Kames, Lord, 33, 34
Kane, Richard, 30

Kazakhstan, common-law courts in, 167
King's Bench, 16, 19, 24, 146–47
Kinkel, Sarah, 50
Knox, William, 42, 74, 84

land: Debt Recovery Act and, 214n99; feudal law and, 188n86, 188n88; gavelkind custom and, 17; Quebec Act and, 214n101; speculation, 228n111
Langbein, John, 25
Lee, William, 26
legal-origins theory, 164–66, 251n87
Leisler's Rebellion (1691), 20
Lennox, George Henry, 148
Levett, John, 166
Levi, Isaac, 46
Lind, Francis, 126, 228n116
Lind, John, 77, 78
Lobban, Michael, 234n48
Locke, John: *Second Tract on Government*, 37; *Two Treatises of Government*, 37–38
Long, Edward, 36
Lyttelton, Lord, 68

Macaulay, Thomas Babington, 154
Macdonald, Archibald, 131
MacNamara, Matthias, 89
Maitland, F. W., 7, 78
Mansfield, James, 72
Mansfield, William Murray, first Earl of, 52, 122; arbitration governance and, 56; on bankruptcy laws, 46; *Campbell v. Hall* case and, 122–23, 144–46; East India Company and, 23, 28; Grenada and, 45; on legal pluralism, 129–30; on manufacturing in colonies, 52; *Mostyn v. Fabrigas* case and, 145–48; on natural rights and legal pluralism, 121–26; as paternalist, 11, 50, 178n39; Quebec Act and, 70; on Regulating Act (1773), 142; Senegambia and, 89; *Somerset's Case* and, 20; *Vaughan* case and, 43–44
manufacturing: in Bengal, 113; in Quebec, 72–73, 113, 158; Stamp Act and, 52; textiles, 86
Marriott, James, 68, 72
Marshall, P. J., 111
martial law, 17, 56, 97
Maryland, religious minorities in, 42
Maseres, Francis, 45–48, 67–68, 73, 75–78, 136, 152, 197n27
Melvill, Robert, 43
Meredith, William, 68, 77–78, 126, 195n13
metropolitan courts, 24–28
Middleton, Samuel, 102–3
Milles, Christopher, 88
Minorca, as exception to expansion of English common law, 28–30, 145–48
moderates: Bengal and, 91, 141; humanitarianism and, 127; Quebec Act and, 69, 76–77, 79, 82; strategic legal pluralism and, 10, 11; taxation and, 139
Montcalm, Marquis de, 39
Montesquieu, 51–52, 76, 97, 119; *The Spirit of Laws*, 9, 16, 32–34
More, Thomas, 15, 17
Morgann, Maurice, 35–36, 42, 62, 117, 156
Morse, Edward, 88
Mostyn, John, 145–46
Mostyn v. Fabrigas (1774), 145–48, 241n129
Mughal institutions and law: civil law and, 100; criminal law and, 100, 224n55; East India Company and, 105, 106, 115, 132–33; legal pluralism and, 96, 100, 115, 128, 160; reforms of legal pluralism in Bengal and, 153; sovereignty and, 229n134. *See also* Islamic law
Munro, Thomas, 153
Murray, James, 42, 98

INDEX

Murray, William. *See* Mansfield, William Murray, first Earl of
Muslims: civil law and, 143; double government in Bengal and, 92; interventionist legal pluralism and, 105–8; ordeal trials and, 132. *See also* Islamic law
Mutiny Act (1749), 138

Namier, Lewis, 5–6
Native Americans, 192n119
natural rights, 121–28
Navy Act (1749), 138
neo-Europes, 13–14, 163, 165
neogothic colonial law, 58–62
Newcastle, Thomas Pelham-Holles, first Duke of, 32, 49, 235n65
Newfoundland, as exception to expansion of English common law, 28–30
New Jersey, 112, 119
New York: anglicization through law in, 69; English vs. Dutch law in, 20–21
North, Lord, 69, 71, 141–42
Norton, Fletcher, 43, 54–55

oaths: in Bengal, 185n61; corporal oath, 25; on cows, 27–28; in Minorca, 30; for non-Christian litigants and witnesses, 25–28; Quaker Affirmation Act and, 185n53; Quebec Act and, 65
O'Hara, Charles, 86–89, 219n141. *See also* perjury; Quaker Affirmation Act (1696)
O'Hara, James. *See* Tyrawley, James O'Hara, second Baron
Omichund v. Barker (1736), 24–28, 37, 44, 79, 158, 162
ordeal trials, 131–32, 235n60
Orme, Robert, 51–52, 97, 98
Oswald, Richard, 166

Paine, Thomas, 205n2
Parker, Thomas, 26
Parthasarathi, Prasannan, 98

paternalists: alternative labels for, 178n39; arbitration, governing through, 53–58; authoritarianism of, 178n39; Bengal and, 92, 95, 137–43; Grenada and, 83–84; humanitarianism and, 119–48; Illinois Country and, 11–12; neogothic colonial law and, 58–62; political economy and, 131; Quebec Act and, 11–12, 68, 70, 72–73, 75, 81–82, 133–37, 152, 213n91; religious persecution and, 125–26; Senegambia and, 86; sincerity of arguments, 128–33; strategic legal pluralism and, 10–11, 12–13; taxation and, 139; vision of empire, 49–53. *See also* humanitarianism
Pelham, Henry, 49
Pelham-Holles, Thomas. *See* Newcastle, Thomas Pelham-Holles, first Duke of
Pennsylvania: property law in, 80; religious minorities in, 42
Perceval, John. *See* Egmont, John Perceval, second Earl of
perjury, 25. *See also* oaths
Petty, William. *See* Shelburne, William Petty, second Earl of
Picton, Thomas, 147–48, 241n128
Pistor, Katharina, 167
Pitt, William (the Elder). *See* Chatham, William Pitt, first Earl of
Pitt, William (the Younger), 215n104
Pitts, Jennifer, 35, 228n113
Pocock, J. G. A., 9
Pons v. Johnston (1765), 240n120
Pontiac's War (1763–65), 46, 55
populists: alternative labels for, 178n39; anti-Catholic rhetoric of, 136; Bengal and, 12, 91, 104, 110, 137–40, 157–59; humanitarianism and, 127; Quebec Act and, 65–66, 69, 75, 82, 136, 210n64; Senegambia and, 86; strategic legal pluralism and, 10; taxation and, 139

Postlethwayt, Malachy, 42, 86
Pownall, John, 41
Pratt, Charles. *See* Camden, Charles Pratt, first Earl
Priest, Claire, 214n99
Priestley, Joseph, 131–32
Privy Council, 19, 22, 24, 43, 44
Proclamation of 1763, 40, 47, 53, 55, 72, 74, 144, 212n77, 238n95
property law, 80–81, 214n101. *See also* land
Protestants: British common law and, 41–45; humanitarian interventions and, 124–25; Quebec Act and, 210n64; reforms of legal pluralism in Bengal and, 156; religious liberty and, 37
Pulteney, William, 110

Quaker Affirmation Act (1696), 185n53
Quebec and Quebec Act (1774), 64–89; British empire expansion and, 2; Catholics and, 42; civil vs. criminal law and, 4, 12, 65–66, 75–83; credit and bankruptcy law in, 45–48; economic dependence and, 72–75; isolation of Quebec as goal of, 67–69; legal pluralism and, 11–12; paternalists and, 133–37; reforms of legal pluralism, 151–52; subordination encouraged by, 69–72

racial hierarchy: geographical variances in, 191n118; imperialism and, 35–36; legal pluralism and, 156–57; Native Americans and, 192n119; in Senegambia, 88–89, 219n136
Rafael v. Verelst (1774–76), 147, 148
Raynal, Abbé, 161
Regulating Act (1773), 90, 142
religion: assimilation and, 36–37; humanitarianism and, 124–25. *See also* Catholics; Hindus; Muslims; Protestants

Revere, Paul, *134*, 136
Rex v. See name of opposing party
Reza Khan, Muhammed, 91, 102–3, 107–8, 132–33, 154
Robertson, William, 62–63
Robinson, James, 10, 165, 251n87
Rockingham, Lord, 11, 236n65
Rodney, George Brydges, 29
Røge, Pernille, 161–62
Roman Empire, 159–60, 193n128
Rosenthal, Jean-Laurent, 8
Roubaud, Pierre, 39
Royal African Company, 85
Royal Navy, 50
royal prerogative, 18–19
Russell, John. *See* Bedford, John Russell, fourth Duke of
Ryder, Dudley, 23, 26, 28

Savigny, Friedrich Carl von, 76
Savile, George, 136
Scotland: bankruptcy law in, 47; as exception to expansion of English common law, 30–34; feudal law in, 58, 62–63; Hardwicke's "Scotch Reformation" and, 32, 34, 36, 58, 62, 105
Scott v. Brebner (1771), 43–44
Seeley, J. R., 5
Selkirk, Thomas Douglas, fifth Earl of, 63
Senegambia: British colonialism in, 2, 11–12, 84–89, 163, 219n136; French colonialism in, 218n130; racial hierarchy in, 88–89, 219n136
settler colonies, 13, 110. *See also specific colonies*
Seven Years' War (1754–63), 2, 10, 39, 50, 67, 139, 162, 172n4
Sharp, Granville, 59, 154–56
Shebbeare, John, 42, 83–84
Shelburne, William Petty, second Earl of: Bentham and, 154; criminal law and, 215n104; Impey and, 239n104; legal pluralism in Bengal and, 114;

INDEX

legal pluralism in Quebec and, 35, 42; as populist, 10; Sulivan and, 104
Sherwood, Samuel, 136
slavery: legal pluralism and, 19–20, 156–57; racial hierarchy and, 35–36; Senegambia and, 86; in West Indies, 87–88, 156
Smith, Adam, 72, 73; *The Wealth of Nations*, 63, 80, 111–12, 228n113
Smith, Joseph H., 43
Smith, Richard, 97, 222n36
Solon, 126
Somerset's Case (1772), 20
South Asia: colonialism by difference in, 13; expansion of English common law in, 21–24. *See also* Bengal; East India Company
Spain: civil law in, 248n66; Jamaica and, 20, 190n23; legal pluralism in colonies of, 160–61, 248n66; Minorca and, 30
Spenser, Edmund, 18
Stamp Act (1765), 51, 57, 95, 99, 208n49
Sterling, Thomas, 56
Stern, Philip, 21
St. John's Island (now Prince Edward Island), 61, 63, 204n104
Stuart, Charles, 101
Stuart, Charles Edward ("Young Pretender"), 42
Sulivan, Laurence, 93, 95, 103–5, 108–10, 115, 137, 229n127
Supreme Court of Judicature (Calcutta), 108, *109*, 142–43

Tamanaha, Brian, 7, 8
taxation: of absentee landowners in Ireland, 69; in Bengal, 12, 91–96, 103–6, 113, 131, 140; extractive colonialism and, 99–100, 140; in French colonies, 160, 161; gavelkind and, 17; in Grenada, 45, 144–45; Seven Years' War and, 139
Tennant, William, 131

Tenures Abolition Act (1746), 188n88
testimony of witnesses, 25–28, 30, 65, 185n53, 185n61
textile manufacturing, 86
Thompson, E. P., 81
Thurlow, Edward, 70, 77, 124, 126, 142, 144
Tilly, Charles, 7, 175n19
tolerance: legal pluralism and, 8; paternalism and, 136; populists lacking, 10
Toleration Act (1689), 37
Tories, 11, 49. *See also* paternalists
tort law, 79
Townsend, James, 215n104
Townshend, Charles, 139
Townshend, Thomas, Jr., 75
Travers, Robert, 107, 121, 133
Treaty of Paris (1763), 40, 42, 48, 83, 137, 172n4, 234n50
Treaty of Utrecht (1713), 29, 30
Trinidad, legal pluralism in, 147–48
Turnbull, George, 98–99
Tyrawley, James O'Hara, second Baron, 187n81

United Arab Emirates, common-law courts in, 167
universalism, 153–54, 161–62

Vansittart, Henry, 103, 104, 105, 111
Vaughan, William, 74
Vaughan, Rex v. (1769), 43
Vaughn, James, 95
Verelst, Harry: arbitration governance and, 99, 226n69; Bolts and, 114–15; humanitarianism and, 124; legal pluralism in Bengal and, 92–93, 97, 99, 124; on martial law, 97; *Rafael v. Verelst* (1774–76) case and, 147, 148
Voltaire, 17, 97

Wake, William, 27, 187n78
Wales: anglicization through law in, 69;

Wales (*continued*)
  expansion of English common law and, 30–31; legal pluralism in, 149–50; Quebec's legal framework and, 40
Walker, Fowler, 79, 167, 214n101
Walker, Thomas, 196n19, 241n131
Wallace, James, 145
Walpole, Horace, 136, 138
Walpole, Robert, 49, 59
War of the Spanish Succession (1701–14), 124
Webb, Philip Carteret, 25, 184n49
Weber, Max, 7
Wedderburn, Alexander: career of, 199n55; on French criminal law, 130; on jury trials, 213n91; as legal adviser to Clive, 108, 197n28; legal pluralism in Bengal and, 108, 137; as paternalist, 50, 63, 137, 199n55; Quebec Act and, 74–75, 81, 124; *Scott v. Brebner* case and, 44
West Indies: slavery in, 87–88; strategic legal pluralism in, 11–12. *See also specific colonies*
Whately, Thomas, 86, 99
Whigs, 11, 49, 105
Wilkins, John, 57
Willes, John, 26, 28
Wilmot, John Eardley, 44–45, 197n27, 197n34
witness testimony, 25–28, 30, 65, 185n53, 185n61

Yorke, Charles: *Considerations on the Law of Forfeiture*, 33; credit and bankruptcy law in Quebec and, 46; feudal law and, 61, 204n104; legal pluralism in Bengal and, 23, 141, 238n95; legal pluralism in Grenada and, 45; Montesquieu's influence on, 33; Quebec Act and, 76–77
Yorke, Philip. *See* Hardwicke, Philip Yorke, first Earl of

Zenger, John Peter, 70